# Collins

# Cambridge International AS & A Level Digital Media & Design

## STUDENT'S BOOK

Philip Veal, Steven Forsyth, Richard Brennan, Mike Acosta, Lesley Ann Davis, Natalie Proctor and Mike Wyeld

William Collins' dream of knowledge for all began with the publication of his first book in 1819.

A self-educated mill worker, he not only enriched millions of lives, but also founded a flourishing publishing house. Today, staying true to this spirit, Collins books are packed with inspiration, innovation and practical expertise. They place you at the centre of a world of possibility and give you exactly what you need to explore it.

Collins. Freedom to teach.

Published by Collins
An imprint of HarperCollins*Publishers*
The News Building,
1 London Bridge Street,
London,
SE1 9GF, UK

HarperCollins*Publishers*
Macken House, 39/40 Mayor Street Upper,
Dublin 1, D01 C9W8, Ireland

**Browse the complete Collins catalogue at**
**www.collins.co.uk**

ISBN 978-0-00-864344-7

British Library Cataloguing-in-Publication Data
A catalogue record for this publication is available from the British Library.

Authors: Philip Veal, Steven Forsyth, Richard Brennan, Mike Acosta, Lesley Ann Davis, Natalie Proctor, Mike Wyeld
Publisher: Elaine Higgleton
Content editors: Emma MacDonald, Mollie Schofield
Commissioning editor: Rachael Harrison
Project manager: Audrey Cowan
In-house editor: Amy Wright
Development editors: James Tulloch, Elina Helenius, Sonya Newland
Copyeditor: Caroline Low
Proofreader: Karen Williams
Permissions researcher: Rachel Thorne
Image researcher: Sophie Hartley
Cover designers: Kevin Robbins and Gordon MacGilp
Cover illustrator: Ann Paganuzzi
Typesetter: Jouve India Ltd.
Production controller: Sarah Hovell
Printed and bound by: Ashford Colour Press Ltd, UK

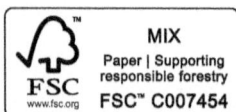

**MIX**
Paper | Supporting
responsible forestry
**FSC** www.fsc.org **FSC™ C007454**

This book contains FSC™ certified paper and other controlled sources to ensure responsible forest management.

For more information visit: www.harpercollins.co.uk/green

# CONTENTS

# Introduction

Welcome to the Collins *Cambridge International AS & A Level Digital Media & Design Student's Book*, which provides in-depth coverage of the Cambridge International AS & A Level Digital Media & Design syllabus (9481) for examination from 2026. It is a handbook for students (which can also be used by teachers) with the aim of presenting information, ideas and activities that will enable you to develop your digital media skills and broaden your understanding of the subject, while developing creativity, confidence and independence.

This Student's Book has been designed to support you on your course, whether you are studying digital photography, moving image, or games design and mobile and multimedia applications, and you will find a wide range of practical activities and critical-thinking tasks throughout.

The focus of the syllabus is the creative aspects of digital media and design, not the technical. This resource includes some content that explores these technical areas (such as mobile app development), but this is only as background information and you do not need to know this material for your exam. These sections have been clearly flagged as beyond the syllabus requirements.

The Student's Book promotes six key concepts that are identified in the syllabus as helping students to develop a deep understanding and to make links across the whole subject. The information in this section is taken from the Cambridge International Education syllabus. You should always refer to the appropriate syllabus document for the year of examination to confirm the details and for more information. The syllabus document is available on the website at www.cambridgeinternational.org.

- **Communication:** The essential purpose of any piece of digital design is to communicate. Designers need to understand that the relationship their work builds with the audience is influenced by many things, including their chosen media and methods. Effective communication is also essential for operating in today's design world, which demands collaboration and engagement with wider cultures and emerging technologies.
- **Creativity:** Creativity is at the heart of a designer's processes. It pushes designers to question, investigate, experiment and take risks to create solutions that are original and effective. Creative practitioners use curiosity, imagination and innovation to solve design problems in new ways.
- **Innovation:** Innovation means experimenting with processes, approaches and technologies. A willingness to innovate builds confidence and helps develop awareness of new ways of looking at things, which is fundamental to digital media and design. A skilled designer selects the techniques and processes that communicate their message in the most effective way.
- **Intention:** an intention is the starting point of any project, from which a designer starts to develop ideas. An intention or purpose can come from a brief, proposal or research, while at other times it might begin as an idea or feeling. Though an intention is the reason to start a project, it is important to understand that the intention can evolve as work develops.
- **Critical reflection:** Critical reflection and user feedback are the ongoing processes that help designers to learn what works and what does not. Designers need to evaluate how the media, techniques and processes they choose affect how their work communicates meaning. This process can help work become more relevant and coherent.
- **Research and context:** First-hand research helps designers to develop their ideas and refine their practice. Actively researching and responding to other practitioners, cultures and creative movements gives the designer a broader view. A designer can use this to improve their practice and understand how their work connects with its intended audience.

# How to use this book

This book is designed to help guide you throughout your course. It includes a number of features that will help you in your studies. The book is divided into three parts:

**Part 1: The digital media and design industry**

In this section, you will learn about the different tools and technologies in the digital media industry, and how the design world is constantly innovating.
*This forms a useful introduction to digital media and design but note that this is **beyond the requirements of the syllabus.***

**Part 2: Skills and methods**

There are skills and methods that are useful for you to know about regardless of your particular area of study. This section will introduce you to these, before you learn about them in more detail in each area of study. You will learn how to work in the digital media and design industry, and explore some of the basic creative skills you will need to be successful.

**Learning Aims**

Helpful lists that show you what you should have learned by the end of the chapter

**Comprehension**

Activities in Part 1 designed to check your understanding of the topic that you are studying

**Industry insight (beyond the syllabus requirements)**

Engaging insights into how the topic you are studying is used in real-world applications. You do **not** need to know these for your exams.

**Top Tips**

Practical hints on how to develop the skills referred to, or succeed in the Project work tasks

**Case studies**

Engaging examples of how the techniques and skills you are learning about are used in the real world, either in industry or by artists

## AREAS OF STUDY

**Part 3A: Digital photography**

**Part 3B: Moving image**

**Part 3C: Games design and mobile and multimedia applications**

Part 3 is divided into three sections, one dedicated to each area of study. Within each section you will find detail about the history and background of the subject, along with creative ideas for your study. Practical guidance is also provided, allowing you to develop the skills you need to produce creative and interesting pieces of digital media. Activities are designed to test your comprehension and to practice these skills. You will also have the chance to read case studies that demonstrate how the content you are reading can be used in the real world.

If we have referred to images in the text, where possible, we have included the relevant image in the book. However, where this has not been possible, we recommend that you view the image online.

**Skills Task**

Activities designed for you to put into practice a technical skill or working practice that you are studying

**Key terms** Definitions of technical language to ensure that you fully understand all the terms used. You can also find these in the Glossary at the back of the book.

**Project work**

Projects aimed at producing a design outcome, or part of one, to help you put into practice both the knowledge and skills you need

**Links**

Information about where the topic is covered elsewhere in the Student's Book

**Further references**

References to books, articles, images or other materials you might like to consult for more information on the topics studied

# The digital media and design industry

*Good to know: beyond the syllabus requirements*

# 1 The history of digital media (beyond the syllabus requirements)

By the end of this chapter you will be able to:
- Understand what digital media means
- Talk about the history and development of communication
- Appreciate the impact of the digital revolution
- Understand the developments and contemporary creative practice in the applications of digital media

## 1.1 WHAT IS DIGITAL MEDIA?

This section is designed to start you thinking about digital media and what aspects of it might interest you. A useful starting point is to think about the history of both the term and the industry. Digital media is an important part of the history of communication and information sharing in human society. The term 'digital media' now covers such a confusingly wide range of formats that most people are unclear about what it really means. To begin our examination of the development of the digital media industry, let's look first at how this term evolved, and what it has come to refer to today.

The word '**digital**' essentially describes a way of expressing data. Data means the quantities, characters or symbols that a computer uses to perform operations, so it is one of the fundamental building blocks of computing technology. The word 'digital' originally referred to the way that data is created and used in computing code, the basic language of computers. All data is constructed from variations of two numbers, 0 and 1. This is known as binary code.

### Top Tip

The opposite of digital is analogue, which refers to something that has been created or built using non-computer-based methods. An example of an analogue artefact would be a geographical map printed or hand-drawn on paper.

We now use analogue to refer to the way that certain types of information are presented as well. For example, a mechanical pendulum clock that has hands and a dial to show the time would be analogue, while an electronic alarm clock with a digital display showing the time in numbers would be digital.

### Comprehension: **Analogue and digital**

List five things in your home that are analogue and five that are digital.

Can you think of any others that combine the two technologies in some way (for example, a digital clock that also has an analogue dial for display)?

**Digital** data expressed as a series of 0s and 1s; also relating to the use of computer technology

**Analogue** something created or built using non-computer methods

The term 'media' has two principle meanings:

- In its most general sense 'media' means anything that we use as a vehicle to hold or present **content** (text, audio, video or images). In this sense it can refer to portable hardware, such as flash drives, CDs and DVDs, but also to paper and ink in the form of a newspaper or book, or even oil paints and canvas in the form of a painting.
- In the more specific context of communication, 'media' refers to any means of **mass communication**. It is often used as a general term to describe all the means – virtual and physical – that we use to communicate on a large scale, any vehicle in broadcasting, publishing or the internet. In fact the broad range of mass communication channels we use in the world today is often referred to as 'The Media'.

Although the origins of the term digital media are rooted in computing science, we use the term today in a more general sense to describe anything that relates to computer technology and the internet. Digital media, as opposed to **print media** (newspapers, magazines, journals, books) or **broadcast media** (TV and radio), essentially refers to any medium that creates content in a format that can be read by a machine. This allows the content to be easily edited, manipulated, distributed and viewed using a wide range of electronic devices. Examples of digital media in our lives today are:

**Fig 1.1** Printed media in the form of newspapers

- computer programs and software
- digital images and video
- computer games
- web pages and websites
- social media platforms
- audio MP3 files
- ebooks.

In general the simplest way to define what digital media means today would be to say it is anything that is computerised and that communicates with people.

**Content** a piece of information or a message
**Mass communication** the imparting or exchanging of information on a large scale to a wide range of people
**Print media** content that is still produced in a hard copy, such as in newspapers, journals or books
**Broadcast media** the distribution of audio or video content

**Top Tip**

It is easy to confuse *media* with *content*. Remember, the difference is that content is the actual information or message itself, while the medium is the vehicle that we use to store or display that information or message. For example, a digital photograph is visual content. If that photograph is then shown on a website, the website is the medium that stores and displays it.

# 1.2 THE HISTORY OF VISUAL COMMUNICATION

In order to understand the impact of digital media on human communication, we need to look at how communication developed over time and, in particular, at some of the key milestones in communication history that transformed how human society evolved. During your course you will need to think about how to communicate your **ideas** to other people. You might find this background information useful when thinking about the most effective way to communicate.

## EARLY EXAMPLES OF VISUAL COMMUNICATION

Human communication began with the origin of speech, approximately 500,000 years ago. Visual symbols weren't used until much later. The oldest known visual symbols created by humans for communicating are cave paintings. The oldest surviving examples of these were found on the island of Sulawesi in Indonesia and are thought to be at least 35,000 years old. Prehistoric cave paintings have been discovered in many countries around the world, dating from around this period. Animals are the most common subjects shown, as in the famous cave paintings discovered at Chauvet and Lascaux in southern France (believed to be about 32,000 years old). Natural pigments in shades of red, brown, yellow and black were used to paint these life-like images of bison, cattle, horses and deer on the rock walls of the caves. Some experts think that the images were used to communicate information about hunting and where these animals could be found, while others believe they had a religious significance.

The next important advance in communication came around 9000 BC, when **pictographs** first appeared. These are a form of very primitive proto-writing where visual symbols are used to represent an object or a place. Pictographs were usually carved on rocks and stones. A series of pictographs could be arranged in chronological order to tell a very simple story or record an important event. Systems of visual symbols such as these allowed humans to record and communicate information in a more reliable and permanent way than through speech, which relied on the individual's own memory and interpretation.

Humans have a highly developed visual sense and learn to associate symbols with objects very easily. Many symbols seem to have an almost universal meaning in different cultures right round the world.

**Pictograph** a pictorial symbol for a word or phrase

### Top Tip

Because pictographs are so easy to understand, they are still used today to communicate across languages and cultures. In particular they are often used on signs to indicate public places, such as train stations, airports, hotels and public toilets. They are also used to communicate information in statistical diagrams or instructions. A good example of this is the universal set of pictographs used as laundry symbols on clothing labels.

**Fig 1.2** One of the earliest examples of a pictograph painted on a cave wall, Lascaux, France

# 1.3 THE RISE OF THE WRITTEN WORD

As human society became more sophisticated and interaction between larger numbers of people became more frequent, the need to communicate more complex messages increased. In some cultures pictographs remained but developed over time to become the basis of the characters used in writing. Some of the **ideograms** still used in Chinese writing today are examples of this.

**Fig 1.3** An example of how an ideogram is created from a pictograph

Ideograms are visual symbols like pictograms. However, they represent not just an object or place but also more complex ideas or concepts associated with it. For example, the symbol of an eye with a stylised tear below it meant sadness in the ideograms used by Native Americans in North America, the Aztecs in South America, and in ancient China, whereas in ancient Egypt it was used to represent protection, royal power and good health. Many different cultures around the world developed similar ideograms independently.

Most experts agree that writing as we know it evolved independently in at least three ancient civilizations in different parts of the world: in ancient China around 5,000 BC, in Sumer (modern-day Iraq) around 3100 BC, and in Central America (modern-day Mexico) around 300 BC. The first Western writing systems developed from the Sumerian writing system, cuneiform. The Greek and Roman alphabets, the Islamic script and the Cyrillic script are thought to have developed from this writing system.

In the East, written characters evolved from early ideograms and were mainly recorded either by carving letters on stone, or by using ink to make marks on paper, a technique which later arrived in Europe from China. It wasn't until the invention of the **printing press** in the 14th century that multiple copies of different written documents could be produced and pamphlets and books first appeared. The development of the printing press had a massive impact on the communication of ideas, the rise of education and the spread of information.

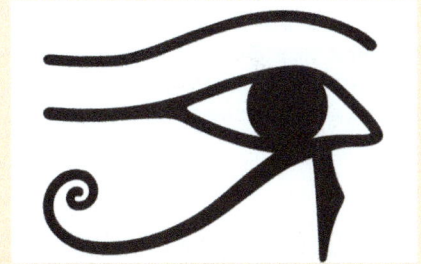

**Fig 1.4** The Eye of Horus is an ancient Egyptian symbol of protection, power and health

**Ideogram** a character showing the idea of something, without using the sounds you would use to say it
**Printing press** a machine for printing text or pictures from types or plates

## Comprehension: **Pictogram messages**

Try and create one of the simple messages below, or a message of your own, using pictograms.

**a.** It is going to rain next week.
**b.** My brother likes to play football.
**c.** My house is next to a river and a forest.

See if a friend can guess the meaning of your message.

How successful were you? How easy or difficult was it to communicate what you were trying to say using pictograms?

**Woodblock printing** a technique using wooden blocks to print text, images or patterns

**Line engraving** a technique in which a metal plate is engraved with lines of varying thickness

**Etching** a technique where a design is created by using strong acid to cut into the unprotected parts of a metal surface

**Lithography** a technique where an image is created by treating material with a greasy substance so that ink will stain some areas but not others

**Screenprinting** a printing technique where a mesh is used to transfer ink onto a substrate, except in areas made impermeable to the ink by a blocking stencil

**Fresco** a watercolour painting done quickly on wet plaster on a wall or ceiling, so that the colours penetrate the plaster and remain after it dries

**Mosaic** a picture or pattern produced by arranging together small pieces of stone, tile, glass or other material

# 1.4 THE VISUAL ARTS

Although the printing press with moveable type wasn't invented until the 1300s, techniques were available before this that meant visual images and simple texts could be mass-produced. These techniques can be seen as forerunners to modern photography.

## WOODBLOCK PRINTING AND ENGRAVING

**Woodblock printing** was used in China for centuries. A wooden carving of an image, or Chinese characters, was painted with coloured inks and pressed onto paper to reproduce the image many times.

Woodblock printing arrived in Europe from the East in the early-14th century. Later printing techniques, such as **line engraving**, **etching**, **lithography** and **screenprinting**, developed from this basic technology. Woodblock prints were often collected and bound into loose-paper books that were used to distribute information or ideas through visual images. An excellent example of early woodblock prints are those created by the Italian, Andreas Vesalius in the early 1500s, *On the Fabric of the Human Body*. These prints of incredibly detailed and accurate anatomical drawings remained the main teaching tool for medical students for centuries.

The woodblock printing technique was also widely used in Japan, where it eventually developed in the 1600s into a sophisticated art form in its own right, known as mokuhanga. In particular the prints of kabuki actors in the ancient Japanese capital of Edo, made by the printmaker Sharaku, have been hugely influential on artists in both the east and the west.

**Fig 1.5** A famous example of Japanese woodblock printing; *The Great Wave off the Coast of Kanagawa*, from the series 'Thirty-six Views of Mount Fuji' (c.1830–32) by Katsushika Hokusai, coloured wood block print, Library of Congress, Washington, D.C

# PAINTING AND COMMUNICATING A VISUAL MESSAGE

Before printed books were widely available, visual imagery was used in many cultures for religious purposes. **Frescoes**, **mosaics**, statues and paintings were the media most used to communicate the symbols, stories and ideas that were the basis of religious beliefs. Special techniques in colour, composition and symbolism developed to make these images as powerful and immediate as possible and to reinforce the religious teachings. People quickly learned how to read these visual images and associate their symbolism with the (often complex) ideas behind them. The **icons** used in churches from the early Byzantine (AD 330–1443) era are a good example of this, as are the Buddhist **thangka** in Tibetan monasteries.

Yet throughout history, people have also used visual images to communicate information in everyday contexts too. Signs showing an image of what a shop sells have been used since long before the invention of writing. Similarly, in many cultures, signposts located strategically along paths and roads show the distance between places and the direction of travel. Maps are two-dimensional representations of three-dimensional space and provide another fascinating example of how humans invented sophisticated systems of visual symbols to communicate information.

# THE INFLUENCE OF PHOTOGRAPHY AND FILM

The 19th century was an age of innovative inventions in many fields, including communication.

Photography developed through a series of experiments in the 1800s, to try and record visual images of the real world. Over time the photographic process, and the equipment needed for it, were refined and became simpler to use. As photographic images circulated more widely, people **realised** their immense potential as a vehicle for communication. Unlike painting or drawing, photographs were an objective representation of life. Painting an image successfully required a great deal of skill and often training, whereas using a camera was something most people could learn. Also, because photographs could be printed again and again, a wide **audience** could access them. In the century that followed, therefore, photography became an important vehicle for the communication of news, information, propaganda and advertising, as well as an exciting new creative medium for artists.

At the start of the 20th century, photographic technology using film had evolved to record moving images as well as static ones. Cinemas opened where the public could view moving images in the form of silent films, and soon became an extremely popular form of entertainment globally. At first, what a person would see in a cinema was very similar to what they would see in a theatre; however, as films became more sophisticated they developed their own visual language and cinema became a visual medium in its own right. Later, sound was added and different genres of films began to evolve, such as musicals and horror. At the same time film-makers recognised the vast potential of cinema not just to entertain but also as a vehicle for mass communication, and by the first half of the 20th century cinema had become an important medium for news and advertising too.

**Fig 1.6** An icon by Andrei Rublev, *The Trinity* (date unknown but c.1411 or 1425–27) Tempera, Tretyakov Gallery, Moscow

**Fig 1.7** A sign for a shoe shop or shoe repairer

**Fig 1.8** A pharmacy sign showing the caduceus symbol of a serpent coiled around a staff

## Link

See also Chapter 15, pages 140–142, for more detailed information on the history of photography.

**Icon** a religious image, generally of a holy figure; normally created on wood
**Thangkas** a Buddhist painting, usually on cotton or silk, of a deity

**Realise** produce work that successfully communicates or demonstrates ideas and intentions

**Audience** the group of people who read or watch your work

**Catch-up services** various services that allow viewers the opportunity to watch television shows and sport events after their initial airdate

**Online streaming** websites that allow users to watch content on the internet

**Fig 1.9** A still image from the film *The Cabinet of Dr Caligari* (1919)

## THE IMPACT OF TELEVISION

The idea of transmitting moving images together with sound using the wireless technology developed for radio, eventually led to the invention of the television. This development brought information and entertainment directly into people's own homes, meaning they were connected to the world as never before. The opportunity to present news and advertising visually that had developed in film could now be sent directly into people's homes. By the 1960s many people in the developed world were able to buy or rent television sets for their homes. The impact on society and the distribution of information and ideas was immense.

Television also transformed the entertainment industry, generating new genres, such as chat shows, quiz shows, talent shows and serialised genre shows. When commercial channels began to appear later, financed by advertisements during the commercial breaks between programmes, this also opened up opportunities for companies to promote their products.

Video recorders appeared in the 1970s and for the first time gave viewers some independence in their viewing habits. However, it wasn't until the start of the 21st century that advances in Wi-Fi (wireless) technology transformed television into a two-way communication medium. The development of **catch-up services** and **online streaming** via the internet, finally gave viewers the freedom to choose what, when and how to watch. It also gave them the ability to influence programme making by allowing them to respond to and comment on what they were watching. This change in how people watch entertainment and factual programming has had an impact on both how these new services create and offer their shows, as well as how traditional companies do so too.

The creation of video-sharing sites, such as YouTube® and Vine, has created new opportunities for the visual arts. Low-budget, short videos have opened up creative new avenues. For example, Vine's six-second videos provide a platform for a new, condensed style of storytelling.

### Comprehension: **Representing themes**

Choose one of the following themes:

1. motherhood
2. greed
3. nature.

Use the internet to find interesting examples of how that theme has been represented visually over the centuries in each of the visual media discussed:

- printing/etching
- painting/sculpture
- photography
- moving image.

# 1.5 COMPUTERS AND COMPUTER NETWORKS

Computers have had such a huge influence on society in the last fifty years that it is not an exaggeration to say they have shaped the course of history. When J. Presper Eckert and John Mauchly built the first massive, clunky computer – the ENIAC – at the University of Pennsylvania in the 1940s, it occupied about 170 square metres and weighed just over 27 tonnes. Less than 80 years later we now use its portable, fast and super-efficient successors to create, process and communicate information in every field, from education, to shopping, to medicine and music.

## HOW IT ALL WORKS

A **computer network** is a telecommunications network that allows a group of digital devices to share resources across multiple locations using a data link and either cable technology or wireless technology. Computer networks support an enormous number of applications and services, such as internet access, audio and video, shared servers and printers, email and instant messaging applications, and many others. The best-known and most widely-used computer network is the internet.

The internet is the biggest network of computers that exists. It links devices in all parts of the world and lets them communicate with each other using the Internet Protocol (IP), sometimes called Transmission Control Protocol (TCP); the method by which data is sent from one computer to another. Each computer (known as a host) on the internet has at least one IP address that uniquely identifies it from all other computers on the internet.

When you send or receive data (for example, an email or a web page), the message gets divided into little chunks called packets. These packets are sent around the internet from computer to computer (known as gateways) until one computer recognises the address belongs to a computer within its domain and sends it directly on. At the super-speeds available now this complex process takes only a few seconds. Any computer linked to the internet can send and receive data from any other computer, allowing two-way communication.

**Fig 1.10** ENIAC was the world's first programmable electronic digital computer, built between 1943 and 1946

### Industry insight (beyond the syllabus requirements)

Before the technology existed to actually build the internet, scientists had been working on the idea of worldwide networks of information as early as the 1900s. However, it wasn't until the 1960s that the first workable **prototype** was developed at the Massachusetts Institute of Technology (MIT) in the USA.

**Computer network** a group of computer systems and other computing hardware systems that are linked together
**Prototype** an early sample, model, or release of a product built to test a concept or process

### Comprehension: **Media timeline**

Look at the timeline for the development of communications media from the 19th century to the present day. What do you think will be the most important new developments in communications technology in the 21st century?

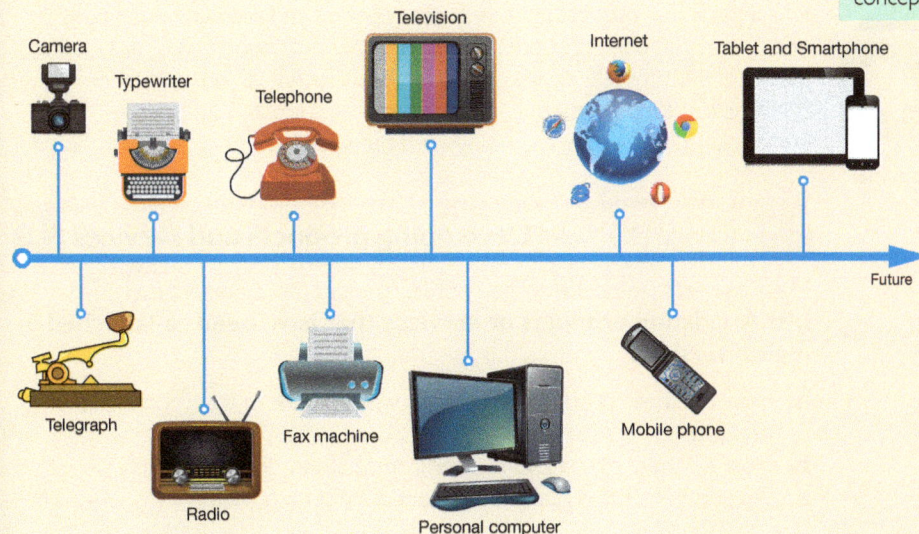

**Fig 1.11** A timeline of the development of digital technology

The rise of the internet as a mass communication computer network has had a revolutionary impact and has enabled other ground-breaking communications technologies, such as email, instant messaging, blogs, forums, websites and video conferencing.

**Digital Revolution** advances in technology that started in the 1980s, with the move from analogue electronic and mechanical devices to digital technology used today

**Information Age** period starting in the 1970s characterised by growth in use of personal computers and changes in how quickly and widely information is shared

# 1.6 THE DIGITAL REVOLUTION

Combined with the internet, the rise of the use of digital media in every field has caused such widespread and rapid transformation in our society that the phenomenon is often referred to as the **Digital Revolution**. Historians believe it has initiated a new and radical era in history – the **Information Age** – in which power lies in the creation, control and distribution of information using computer technology.

## INNOVATION IN OUR DAILY LIVES

The Digital Revolution has vastly increased the number of tasks that can be completed automatically. We can now manage our finances online, do our grocery shopping, adjust the controls of our central heating, book a holiday or find our way to our destination as we drive. It has also radically altered our ways of working and how organisations do business – we can work from home, meet virtually with colleagues in other locations, and send and receive our work by email. It has also changed the type of jobs we do.

By automating so much of our work, computers have allowed us to become more efficient and productive than ever before. By radically changing the way that we all access information, the internet has empowered people and promoted communication between individuals, nations and cultures. All of this has led to an incredible boom in the number of new products and services being created, as advances in technology continue to open up exciting new possibilities and expand our horizons.

## THE DEVELOPMENT OF APPS

The Digital Revolution has allowed for the creation of an enormous number of new applications (innovative uses of technology designed to fulfil a particular purpose) in a very short period and over an enormously wide range of fields. Apps are now used to perform hundreds of daily tasks, particularly on mobile devices. However, the concept of the 'application' is not new; it simply means a new product that is created through a combination of available technology and human need.

**Fig 1.12** A selection of application icons as they appear on-screen

Comprehension: **Developing products and services**

Make two lists (see below). Then answer the questions about them.
**List A: existing products or services that have been re-launched in digital versions**

a. How did these products or services work before, in their non-digital versions?
b. How do the digital versions differ from the non-digital versions?
c. Do you think the digital products and services are better? Why/why not?

**List B: new products or services that have been developed as a direct result of internet-related technology**

**a.** What new human needs do these products satisfy?
**b.** Could any of these products or services exist without the internet? What form would they take?

## TRANSFORMING COMMUNICATION

Some of the most biggest changes generated by the Digital Revolution have been in the field of communication. Advances in hardware have produced smaller, more portable devices, such as personal computers, smartphones and tablets, which, when loaded with new software apps, offer the same degree of interactivity and efficiency as desktop computers. At the same time, applications developed to enable access to 4G networks and Wi-Fi allow almost all of the human population around the world to be constantly connected, wherever they are, 24 hours a day, whether accessing information, working on the move, or communicating with friends, family and colleagues. In particular, social media platforms, such as Facebook, Twitter and Instagram, made possible by this increased connectivity, have revolutionised the way we receive news, exchange ideas and opinions and communicate with one another. These sophisticated apps use two-way communication to enable users not only to view content but also to create it (personal profiles) and interact with it (via posts, messages and chat). As these platforms have grown in popularity, producers have also realised their massive advertising potential, which has led to the exponential growth of online marketing.

Advances in video technology have made two-way **video calls** and **video conferencing** possible. The new generation of smartphone video apps, such as FaceTime®, allow groups of people to communicate face-to-face through web-enabled cameras on both mobile and desktop devices, and this is fast replacing the voice call as the most popular medium for everyday personal communication. Video conferencing, using apps such as Hangouts™ or Skype, allow a number of participants in different locations to connect and communicate by video link and is changing the way companies do business.

## TRANSFORMING ENTERTAINMENT

Advances in **video streaming** technology have quickly led to the emergence of **video sharing platforms** such as YouTube and Vimeo®. These applications enable users to create and publish video content, as well as to broadcast live video. Users can use live video streaming on their devices to watch a play being performed by actors in a theatre in a different city, a football match being played live in another country, or a vlogger painting her bedroom in real time. Online video companies, such as Netflix and Amazon Prime, use versions of the same technology to stream television programmes and films directly to subscribers' devices, a technology which is fast replacing traditional television as the most popular form of home entertainment.

The music industry is another good example of an existing field that has been completely revolutionised by digital technology. Following on from the early days of vinyl records in the 1960s, to cassette tapes in the 1980s, musicians can now create and record music digitally using simple apps accessible to all, without ever entering a recording studio, or necessarily having a contract with a record company. Their music can then be stored as

---

**Top Tip**

In 2015 it was reported that 24 per cent of teenagers in the United States go online 'almost constantly'. They are able to do this thanks to the availability and convenience of mobile devices, with 90 per cent of teenagers going online from a mobile device daily. Facebook was the most popular social media site in 2015, with 71 per cent of teenagers using this. However, the popularity of online sites can change quickly. In 2015, Vine was used by 24 per cent of teenagers, but in October 2016 new uploads to the site were disabled.

---

**Video call** visual communication via computers that allows the people participating in the call to see each other as they talk

**Video conferencing** a telecommunication technique that allows people in different locations to speak to and see each other using software

**Video streaming** multimedia that is constantly received by and presented to the end user

**Video sharing platforms** services that are able to host multimedia content

**Fig 1.13** A vinyl record player

**Fig 1.14** Cassette tapes

digital audio files and later uploaded, shared and distributed using any number of online platforms. Similarly, digital music service apps such as Spotify and iTunes®* have transformed the way we buy music. Users can select, listen to, buy and download their favourite songs direct to their smartphones and computers, without even leaving their homes.

In terms of the new industries that digital technology has given birth to, the most notable in the entertainment field is gaming. Video games have evolved enormously from the clunky, pixelated games of the 1980s, such as Space Invaders™ and Pacman™, to the incredible fully immersive experiences that are now possible using sophisticated audio and video technologies. Thanks to incredible advances in both hardware and software, players can now interact with each other from remote locations in incredibly realistic virtual environments that create a full-on sensory experience in real time. A whole industry has grown up around competitive gaming in e-sports leagues and international championships, and corporate sponsorship for these events is now almost as big as it is for traditional mass-spectator sports such as baseball and basketball.

The popularity of gaming with children and its ability to engage their curiosity has even led to changes in education. Online components now form an important part of teaching methodologies in most subjects and the traditional model of the classroom in schools is being revolutionised by remote learning, virtual teachers and learning management systems. Interactive exhibits are routinely used to enhance the visitor experience in museums, galleries and historical sites, enabling people to see, hear and feel other times and places virtually.

## Comprehension: **Apps for entertainment**

Think about the categories of entertainment listed below.

- Music
- Television programmes
- Films
- Video tutorials
- Sports/action games
- Multiplayer games
- Role-playing games
- Puzzles

Give examples of apps or programmes that you have used for each type of entertainment. Which are you favourites? Why?

---

* iTunes® is a trademark of Apple Inc., registered in the U.S. and other countries.

# 2 Design in our world
## (beyond the syllabus requirements)

## 2.1 WHY DO WE NEED DESIGN?

In the 1980s, the adjective 'designer' was often used rather ironically to describe objects or clothes that were stylish and exclusive but often expensive and impractical, as in 'designer handbag'. Today we know that design must be about more than just appearance. As Steve Jobs, the co-founder of Apple® pointed out, design is not just about what something looks like, but also about its usability, and great design is the successful marriage of the two. If the iPhone had been stylish to look at but had not worked effectively as a communications device, millions of people around the world would not have queued for hours outside Apple stores to buy it! The product's enormous success was due to its ground-breaking combination of style, **functionality** and **usability**. Understanding what design really is and why we need it will give you the necessary grounding to set off on your own creative journey, exploring contemporary practices that will contribute to the develop of your own ideas.

**Functionality** how something works
**Usability** how easy or complicated the process of using something is

**Fig 2.1** A billboard advertisement for Apple's iPhone X

15

'Design' is a term that has many connotations but essentially it means the thinking that informs the creative process needed to produce something new, or the ideas and planning necessary to visualise how the finished thing will look and work. In our fast-paced digital age, companies want their products and services realised quickly, efficiently and on budget, but overall they want them to perform effectively. Good design meets this need by considering carefully how and why something will be used, then planning the best way to realise it within the means the company has available to do this. Importantly the design phase of any project also provides the opportunity to test and evaluate its ideas and assumptions before going ahead and making the final product. This is critically important because it often prevents a company from making expensive mistakes in the production process.

## THE DIFFERENCES BETWEEN ART AND DESIGN

The argument over what is Art and what is Design has been raging for decades! Although both artists and designers create **artefacts**, the critical difference lies in their reasons for doing so. For example, a graphic artist might create a print to be displayed in an art gallery, while a graphic designer would be more likely to create a poster to advertise a particular product on a billboard. In both cases the artist and designer use a common visual language – they both make use of colour, shape and space in order to express their ideas and communicate with the viewer, and the end result is something to be seen and experienced visually. However, the **motivation** of the artist and the designer is fundamentally different.

**Artefacts** objects and artworks
**Motivation** reason for doing something

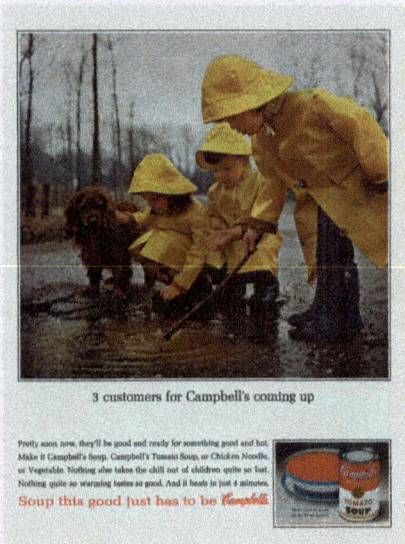

Fig 2.2 An advertisement for Campbell's soup, 1964

**Fig 2.3** *Campbell's Soup Cans* (1962) by Andy Warhol, synthetic polymer paint on thirty-two canvases, Museum of Modern Art (MoMA), New York

An artist often starts with nothing but a blank canvas or an empty screen. Works of art are developed from a view, opinion or idea that originates with the artist. The piece of art is created as a vehicle to share that idea with other people and invite them to relate to it in some way, to learn from it or be inspired by it. The most successful works of art are usually those that establish an emotional bond between the artist and his audience.

On the other hand, when a graphic designer sets out to create a new piece, there is usually a starting point (a brief) that informs the work. This could be a message that needs to be conveyed to the audience (for example, the fact that a new, improved toothpaste is now available) or an action that needs to be realised (for example, a new package for a toothpaste needs to be produced so that the toothpaste can be stored on supermarket shelves). In either case the designer's role is not to create something new to express his own opinion or idea, but to communicate something that already exists in an effective way for a specific purpose. That purpose is usually either to motivate the viewer/user to carry out an action (anything from buying a new toothpaste to following a road sign) or to help them learn a new piece of information. The most successful designs are those that communicate their message the most effectively.

## Comprehension: **Images of soup**

Look at the two images of Campbell's® soup (Figures 2.2 and 2.3) and answer the questions.

1. What idea do you think Andy Warhol was trying to convey through his artwork showing the identical cans of soup?
2. What message do you think the graphic designer was trying to convey through his advertisement for soup?
3. Which piece of work do you think is most effective? Give reasons for your answer.

# DESIGN AND PRODUCT DEVELOPMENT

Design is also important in the process of improving and adapting existing products or services to update them, or make them work better. When the design process is incorporated properly into the production workflow, the product can be tested, evaluated and refined to meet the needs of the user more closely. In short, good design allows the producers to really get their product right before it goes to market.

Some products and services, particularly digital ones, are designed to be regularly evaluated and updated in this way. The different versions of the product are known as **iterations**. An example could be a software company that wants to regularly update an app it sells to marathon runners. The **iterative design process** will regularly evaluate direct feedback from users on the current version of the product, then analyse their experience of using it. This will help to make sure that the next iteration of the app will not only include all the functionality that the users already like and use, but also new features based on its users evolving training needs that are designed to meet them effectively. This could give the software company a **competitive advantage** over other app producers and make their app more successful in the marketplace.

> **Iterations**  versions of a digital product
> **Iterative design process**  practice of constantly updating and improving versions of a digital product
> **Competitive advantage**  something a company's product has that makes it more attractive than its competitors' products

## Comprehension: **Evolving product functionality**

Think of an example of a product you often use that has been adapted over time with new versions being launched regularly. Answer the questions.

1. How exactly has this product evolved over time? What new features or functionality does it have now that is didn't have initially?
2. Why do you think the new features were developed?
3. Can you think of any other features/functionality that you would recommend it should have in future iterations?

# 2.2 HUMAN PERCEPTION AND VISUAL DESIGN

## HOW HUMANS SEE

Visual perception is the ability to interpret the surrounding environment using light reflected by the objects in it. The scientist Hermann von Helmholtz was one of the first people to study human visual perception. He examined the human eye in detail and concluded that the poor-quality information gathered via our eyes was not actually enough to explain how our complex visual sense worked! Helmholtz realised that vision also involves a large amount of processing of stored information on the part of the brain. Basically to make sense of the world our brains have to organise sensory stimuli into a meaningful whole. In the case of vision the brain uses assumptions and conclusions based on previous experience to interpret the sensory information it receives from the eyes. In short, human vision depends largely on inference and based on prior experience of the world.

Understanding how vision works helps explains the 'trick' it plays on us when we view images like the rabbit–duck optical illusion below. The image as a whole seems to switch back and forth from representing a duck to representing a rabbit as our eyes focus on different parts of it and our brain makes assumptions based on experience about what the image could be.

**Fig 2.4** The rabbit–duck optical illusion was first used by the American psychologist Joseph Jastrow in 1899

The Italian psychologist Gaetano Kanizsa designed an image to illustrate how the brain infers information based on its previous experience of visual data. The Kanizsa Triangle is actually just a series of lines and circles with pieces 'removed' from them, but what the eye sees when it processes these elements together is a white triangle at the centre. In reality this triangle doesn't exist!

## VISUAL PERCEPTION AND DESIGN RESPONSE

A thorough understanding of how the human visual sense works is essential to good visual design. Designers and artists can take advantage of the universal inferences that shape visual perception and manipulate them to create specific effects or elicit particular responses when they are composing visual images.

**Fig 2.5** The Kanizsa Triangle contour illusion, created by the Italian psychologist Gaetano Kanizsa in 1955

These are a few of the most common assumptions that designers often play with in this way:

- light usually comes from above
- objects lit from the front produce a shadow behind them
- objects are not normally viewed from below
- faces are only easily recognised if they are the right way up
- closer objects can block the view of more distant objects, but not vice versa.

Comprehension: **Exploring visual perception**

Look at the two images in Figure 2.6, which both play with our brain's assumptions about visual perception in some way.

**1.** What is the optical illusion created in each case?
**2.** Which of the assumptions listed above do these images play with to create the illusion?

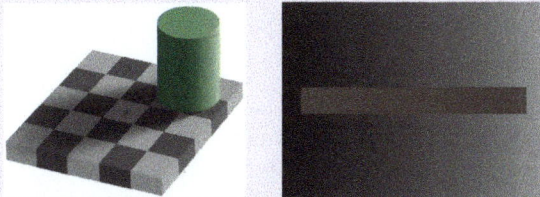

**Fig 2.6** Examples of optical illusions

# 2.3 KEY ELEMENTS OF VISUAL DESIGN

Any visual image, whether it is created using traditional media, such as paint and paper or complex digital software, uses four basic elements to create an impression of something the human eye can recognise:

- shape
- light and shade
- colour
- texture.

These elements work together to create the two-dimensional illusion of a three-dimensional object that the brain can interpret as something it has seen and processed before in the real world. In the example shown in Figure 20.7, the image has been broken down into these four constituent elements.

## SHAPE

This element relates to the basic physical outline and overall form of the object. Is it regular or irregular? Are the edges straight or curved? What does this shape suggest to the viewer? Can the brain associate it with something else that it knows? How does it relate to the background and space around it?

## LIGHT AND SHADE

How light falls on the object and where any shadows are created on it, is important for giving depth to an image and emphasising an object's three-dimensionality. Light and shade are also key elements in suggesting mood in an image.

Does the light highlight certain parts of the overall shape? Do the shadows hide some of it? What effect does this produce in the viewer's perception of the image? For example, the feeling evoked by a brightly lit image is quite different from the feeling evoked by the same image when it is shown half in shadow.

## TEXTURE

The way that the texture of an object is presented in a visual image is important for transmitting sensory information to the viewer. Texture is the way we represent the material that something is made of. It relies heavily on inference since to interpret it we can only use one of our senses (sight) to trigger associations in the brain related to our other four senses (touch, smell, taste, hearing). These associations then provide further information about the object's possible nature and characteristics. The eye notes the texture of the image and the brain associates this information with its knowledge of real world materials – how heavy it is, what it smells or tastes like, how it feels to the touch, whether it is likely to be cold or warm, wet or dry – to make assumptions about the object shown.

## COLOUR

The colour of an object is also important in helping us to understand an object in an image. A bright green colour used to depict a leaf tells us that that object is new, flexible, healthy, while an orange-brown colour used to depict the same leaf tells us the object is older, drier and beginning to decay. Like light and shadow, colour can also be used to create mood. Darker colours are usually associated with more sombre, quiet moods, while light,

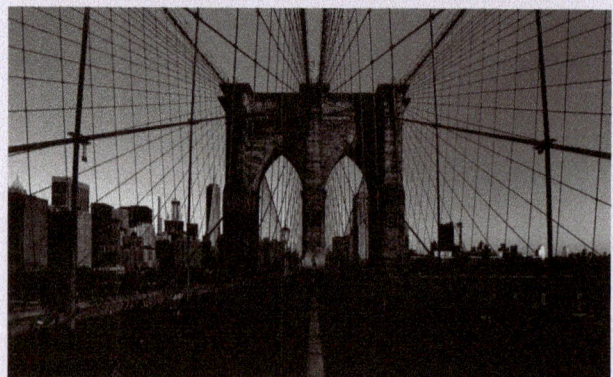

**Fig 2.7** The bridge images here show the different elements that make up the final version

bright colours are more cheerful and lively. By using unexpected or 'wrong' colours to represent a familiar object in an image, for example, portraying human teeth as black, a designer can play with viewers' expectations and produce strong reactions, such as astonishment or shock.

**Link**

See Chapter 11, pages 99–104, for more detailed information on the uses of colour in visual design.

## Top Tip

Humans respond to colour psychologically on different levels and associate meaning with it in various ways, from their experience of colours in nature, to links with their nation's history and culture, to their own personal experiences and emotions. However, some colour associations seem to be universal and cross-cultural in human society, for example, red means fire and green means nature. Designers can use these associations deliberately to convey visual messages more effectively.

## THE USE OF CONTRAST

Visual design theory also includes another important concept: contrast. This is concerned with how opposing elements work together to create powerful visual images. Contrast can be applied to any of the four elements previously discussed in this section by incorporating opposites within an image.

### Skills Task: **Analysing key elements in a digital image**

Examine Figure 2.8. This digital image was created as the prototype for a logo for a firm of architects specialising in kindergarten architecture. Answer the questions about it.

1. Which of the key elements described above have been used to create it? Consider the use of shape, light and shade, texture, colour and contrast.
2. What associations does the image have for you?
3. Do you think it would be effective as the company's logo? Why/why not?

**Fig 2.8** Prototype logo for an architecture firm

**Aesthetics** the look of an object
**Function** the job that something is designed to do
**Form** the shape and feel of an object
**Action** the job or task the user needs to perform

# 2.4 PRINCIPLES OF DESIGN

## AESTHETICS AND FUNCTION

*'Have nothing in your house that you do not know to be useful, or believe to be beautiful.'*

(William Morris)

This famous statement from the English Arts and Crafts designer William Morris in the 1880s perfectly describes what all designers are constantly aiming for in their work – the balance of **aesthetics** (how things look) and **function** (how they work) that lies at the heart of all good design. Designers in all fields must combine aesthetics and function to create effective designs. You will find that you have to make judgements about the aesthetics of your designs, versus the functionality.

## FORM FOLLOWS FUNCTION

*Whether it be the sweeping eagle in his flight, or the open apple-blossom, the toiling work-horse, the blithe swan, the branching oak, the winding stream at its base, the drifting clouds, over all the coursing sun, form ever follows function, and this is the law. Where function does not change, form does not change. The granite rocks, the ever-brooding hills, remain for ages; the lightning lives, comes into shape, and dies, in a twinkling.*
*It is the pervading law of all things organic and inorganic, of all things physical and metaphysical, of all things human and all things superhuman, of all true manifestations of the head, of the heart, of the soul, that the life is recognizable in its expression, that form ever follows function. This is the law.*

(Louis Sullivan)

This principle was first described by the American architect Louis Sullivan and is often used to evaluate design in the fields of Architecture, Product Design and Industrial Design. However, it is also relevant to digital design, particularly in relation to web products and games. The idea is that the design of any object should be defined above all by the job it has to do (its function). The shape and feel of the designed object (**form**) should grow naturally from this.

The 'form follows function' principle is easiest to apply where there is a clearly defined **action** that the user needs to be able to perform by using the object. For example, kitchen utensils are usually designed according to the 'form follows function' principle. The iconic kitchen products designed for the Alessi homeware company in the 1960s–80s were developed in this way, with their function as the starting point for intriguing, innovative and beautiful designs. In fact Alessi's kitchen utensils are now regarded as some of the most successful and iconic product designs of the 20th century.

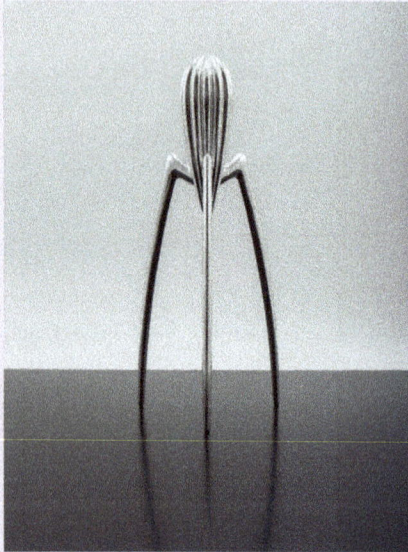

**Fig 2.9** Alessi's iconic lemon squeezer, by the designer Philippe Starck

**Fig 2.10** An Alessi kettle with bird whistle, designed by Michael Graves

## Comprehension: **Form follows function**

Find images on the internet of two digital and two non-digital products which you think are good examples of the design principle 'form follows function'. Explain why they are successful pieces of design in your opinion.

# 2.5 DIGITAL CONTEXTS – DESIGNING FOR RESPONSE AND ACTION

As the quantity of digital products continues to proliferate, what distinguishes one website, app or interactive exhibit from thousands of others is frequently the quality and effectiveness of its design. The role of the designer hasn't become less important with the arrival of digital media; if anything, it has become more important. Digital designers today are not only responsible for the way digital products looks (aesthetics) they are also largely responsible for the way they work for the user (function). The main aim for the designer, particularly when designing web-based products, is often to provoke a certain response in the user or get them to perform a task on-screen. However, the principle of 'form follows function' is essentially the same when working on website, app or games design as it is when working on product design or designing a building.

## DESIGN AND RESPONSE

In some types of digital design the aim is to make the user experience certain emotions or sensations. This is known as the **user response**. In games development, for example, the brief might be to create a virtual environment that makes the players feel afraid, apprehensive or wary as they navigate through it to play the game. One way designers do this is to apply key elements relating to colour and our perception of it. For example, particular combinations of colours, which simulate dark, gloomy and unsettling spaces, are frequently used to create combat game environments for this reason. Games designers may also use sound effects in combination with a particular colour palette to heighten the target response.

**User response** the emotions or sensations a user feels when using a product

Fig 2.11 Dark colours help to set the scene for the gameplay on this RPG Dark Souls 3 video game on PS4

In the field of product design, a graphic designer working on packaging for herbal tea, for example, might decide to use Eastern, mandala-inspired geometric patterns to evoke a sense of calm, meditation and well-being. Consumers will then associate these sensations with the product and buy it.

So how do designers know that they have created something that is meaningful and relevant to their users? In the case of digital design, many

Fig 2.12 This herbal tea packaging makes effective use of Eastern, mandala-inspired geometric patterns

**Grid system** the format used by graphic designers to compose pages
**Navigation bar** the bar across a screen with the menus and commands on it
**Drop-down menus** menus that appear in full on-screen when you click on an icon
**Text boxes** item of text set inside square frames on the page
**Banners** coloured strips running across the top of a page
**Intention** the user's aim in using a product/service
**Prototype** an early sample, model, or release of a product built to test a concept or process
**User experience** the user's feeling about interacting with a product/service
**User interaction** how a user uses a product/service

projects will go through a series of iterations or versions and gaining feedback from users is a vital part of this process. By involving users in this way designers are able to make judgements about their work to ensure that it meets with the target audience expectations.

## DESIGN AND ACTION

How elements are arranged within a space or frame is an important aspect of any visual design. Positioning is key, not just to highlighting parts of the design itself, but also to help users understand how to use a product, or to prompt them to perform a particular action as part of a process.

Graphic designers and web designers use a **grid system** to position the key elements of their design on the screen and give the page a strong visual structure and sense of order. The first thing they have to consider in making these decisions is how to help users achieve their goal easily. The grid system helps the user to use the content (function) while creating a strong visual structure for the product (aesthetic).

For example, a designer working on an app for mobile phones can use the grid system to position certain elements that will help the user navigate between screens, or recognise where they are at a given moment within a process. Features used to do this can be as simple as a breadcrumb trail showing the user where they are in the page structure, or more complex such as a **navigation bar** that allows them to see all the other parts of the site and select from layers of **drop-down menus**.

However, the principle also works for other products that can be designed to a grid system, such as printed books or interactive whiteboards. A graphic designer working on an instruction manual could use **text boxes**, **banner** headings, cross-referencing and footnotes to signal different types of information on the page and the fact that the user has to process, or react to them, differently – again, the page structure follows the function. Alternatively, in the case of a design for IWB software for primary schools, the designer could use the grid system to position colourful icons representing the key interactive functions down the side of the screen, so that children quickly learn how to use the touch technology and virtual tools to perform different actions.

## Link

See Chapter 6, pages 60–68, for more information on interaction design.

# 2.6 INTERACTION DESIGN

This is a specialist form of digital design that has evolved from software development strategies. Essentially it is the process digital designers use to create web products based on research into the behaviour and aims of the target users. Successful interactive design focuses on why users need a product, or what they want to achieve by using it, in the development of the design.

An interaction designer is the person in a product development team who creates the design strategy. They do this by:

- studying the user's **intention**
- identifying how the user could engage with the product
- creating **prototypes** to test their ideas and hypotheses
- making sure the final product works effectively in the hands of the user
- creating a positive **user experience**.

## Top Tip

Interaction Design and User Experience Design (UX) are often confused. A good way to remember the difference is that Interaction Design defines what a user needs to do, while User Experience Design improves how they do it. UX is also about designing the whole experience of using a product, not just the interactions that make up a process.

Designers describe **user interaction** as a series of basic steps that occur whenever a user engages with a digital product. Essentially 'engaging' can mean anything from simply clicking on a link to open a website to using a complex navigation and reward system in a computer game. However, all interactive products are based on three main elements of interaction that designers need to work round: purpose, goals and interface.

# 3 The digital landscape
## (beyond the syllabus requirements)

**Good to know:** beyond the syllabus requirements

This section forms a useful basis for your knowledge, but it is beyond the syllabus requirements and you do not need to know it for your exams.

By the end of this chapter you will be able to:
- Understand how innovation drives developments in digital technology
- Talk about the impact of digital technology on visual media
- Understand some of the issues around ethical manufacturing
- Understand the issues around data collection protection
- Define intellectual property, copyright and trademarks

## 3.1 THE PROCESS OF INNOVATION

The term 'innovation' is often confused with other terms, such as creativity or invention. In simple terms, innovation refers to doing things differently to make things better or to add value. This could relate to a website that helps users to find content in a new or interesting way, or a game that makes innovative use of a mobile device. However, it is important not to limit your creativity to existing **ideas** – always try to think of new approaches and bring original ideas to a design project. Remember, creativity and innovation are all around you, in every area of your life. Learn to recognise where new things are happening and try to understand how these innovations came about.

In Chapter 1, we looked at how digital technology now plays a significant role in everything we do, from how we work to how we access entertainment to how we find out information. Endless innovation seems to be characteristic of the digital revolution, and the **digital landscape** is constantly changing around us. In fact, technology is moving so fast that different versions of digital products and media are often operating at the same time on our televisions, computers and phones, and people often feel they cannot keep up with the evolution of the technologies they are using!

However, it is not only the products themselves that are evolving. As digital processes and **workflows** evolve, companies are developing new strategies for making their products and services, and creating new roles and job titles. Titles such as Interaction Designer or User Experience Designer are now quite usual in larger design studios, but they didn't exist fifteen years ago! Who knows what other roles will be available in ten years' time? At the same time the Digital Revolution is also generating a whole new range of ethical and employment issues for society to resolve, as our working practices and production methods move into previously uncharted territory. In this chapter we will look at some of the ways that digital technology is changing the working environment around us.

What is driving the seemingly endless innovation that characterises digital technology? In order to understand this, we first need to understand how innovation happens. There are two main schools of thought about what drives innovation in industry: the Technology Push and the Market Pull.

> **Top Tip**
>
> Innovation comes from a willingness to experiment with different ways of working and processes, and this will also help to build your confidence as a designer and to create the most effective forms of communication.

**Ideas** thoughts or concepts; plans or creative intentions; imagined images, experiences or memories
**Digital landscape** all the types of technology, applications and processes in the world around us influenced by digital technology
**Workflow** the sequence of processes through which a piece of work passes from initiation to completion

**Equilibrium**  balance
**Entrepreneur**  someone who starts
their own business, especially when this
involves identifying a new opportunity

# THE TECHNOLOGY PUSH MODEL

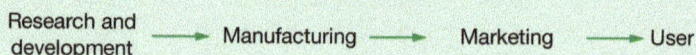

Some economists describe innovation as a series of steps called the
Technology Push model:

1. **Equilibrium:** This is a situation where everything works in a fairly
   efficient manner and all manufacturers producing the same thing are using
   the same method. This creates balance or equilibrium.
2. Innovation: An **entrepreneur** arrives and introduces a new way of
   working or of producing something (for example, creating a new machine
   to take over part of the production process).
3. Change: The entrepreneur can then generate a profit, either by using their
   machine to make their operation more efficient than their competitors' or
   by selling their idea to them so that they can adopt their innovation too.

**Technology push**

Research and development → Manufacturing → Marketing → User

# THE MARKET PULL MODEL

Other economists argue that innovation simply happens when people need
new products or services: the users of the product (the market) encourage
the innovation to happen by demanding new products. This is referred to as
the Market Pull model.

In the case of the Digital Revolution a combination of both of these
factors often feeds innovation. For example, a company might start making
a particular app using a new type of touchscreen technology (Technological
Push), but as the product starts to sell well and users' feedback is received
asking for more functions, the company could adapt the product to include
new features (Market Pull).

**Market pull**

Marketing → Research and development → Manufacturing → User

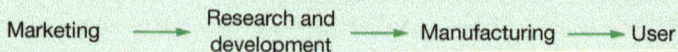

## Comprehension: **Innovation models**

Consider these two examples of products where a new technology replaced
a previous process that had been around for a long time. What do you know
about them?

* The introduction of the Kodak Brownie camera in 1900.
* The introduction of the first Apple iPhone in 2007.

Discuss the questions below:

1. What was the process/product used before the innovation?
2. Which aspects of the original process/product were improved by
   the innovation?
3. Which innovation model do you think caused the innovation:
   Technological Push, Market Pull, or both?

# 3.2 THE IMPACT OF DIGITAL TECHNOLOGY ON VISUAL MEDIA

Some of the most significant changes that the Digital Revolution has brought to society centre around the ways that content is now created. Thanks to digital technology, anyone can now take, edit and share photographs using a simple app on a smartphone. They can design their own websites using simple software packages and set up their business online. They can post videos directly on YouTube and extend their audience to millions of viewers instantly. The digital revolution has led to the **democratisation** of content creation, breaking down the barriers of specialist knowledge and skill, and allowing everyone access to easy-to-use tools. So, what now distinguishes one website, app or interactive exhibit from another is the quality and effectiveness of its design. The role of the designer hasn't become less important because of the Digital Revolution; instead it has become more important. In this section we'll look at some of the most significant and commonly used innovations that have transformed the way designers work.

**Democratisation** opening up to everyone regardless of ability

## RESEARCH AND PR

As well as transforming how design work is actually done, the internet has changed the way that designers look for inspiration and present their work. In the past they would have had to go to libraries, art galleries and museums to research ideas and look for influences, and were limited by the information they had access to locally. Now they can simply type a few key words into a search engine, such as Google or Firefox®, and instantly access thousands of inspirational images, subscribe to **photo libraries**, such as Getty's iStock or Alamy, and view the collections of artefacts in museums and galleries around the world on their websites. The latter allows you to research a whole variety of different designers and artists.

**Link**

See Chapter 17, pages 160–165, for more detailed information on selecting digital images.

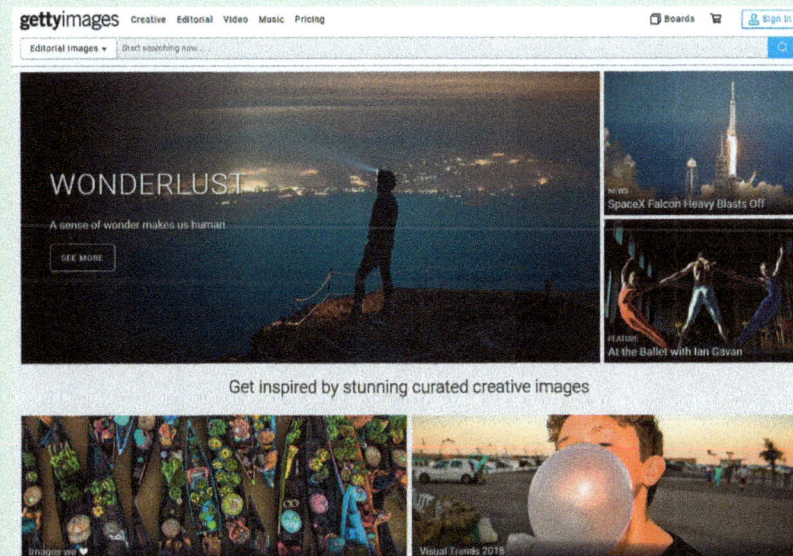

**Fig 3.1** The website of Getty Images

**Photo libraries** online archives of visual images with permission for reuse
**Showcase** to display to the public
**Creatives** people whose work involves being creative

Designers also use the internet for PR (public relations) to promote their work and attract new customers through their online presence, for example, via a Facebook page, a Twitter feed, a blog or a portfolio site where their work is **showcased**. The internet is a virtual shop window that allows **creatives** to display anything from simple animation work to complex interactive multimedia pieces, without limitations of size or quality, to a truly global audience.

## Skills Task: **Image research**

You have been asked to supply some visual references for a project based on the theme of 'borders'. Read the brief below then use the internet to research five visual images that you think could inspire this project. Explain your reasons for choosing each image.

- Explore what is meant by a boundary as the basis for developing a digital element to be included in an exhibition about migration. Focus on either one of these aspects:
  1. political boundaries – class, ethnicity, religion
  2. geographical boundaries – mountains, oceans, deserts, borders/ frontiers, walls, enclosures.

## CREATING AND EDITING DIGITAL IMAGES

### Link

See Chapter 18, pages 169–179, and Chapter 19, pages 180–189, for more detailed information on how to take digital photographs and how to edit them.

One of the most obvious examples of a process that has been revolutionised by digital technology is photography. Digital cameras, smartphones and tablets are now so common and easy to use that most of us cannot imagine life without them and we use then to document every aspect of our lives. Even amateur photographers are able to edit their own photographs easily using standard applications on their devices, such as iPhoto® or more specialised software, such as Adobe® Photoshop®, and achieve professional-looking results. Digital technology has made both the process of taking photos and that of displaying them, quicker, cheaper and easier to use for everyone.

**Fig 3.2** An example of before (left image) and after (right image) basic image editing on a mobile application

## Skills Task: **Using a camera app**

Look at the camera app on your laptop or tablet.

**1.** Can the app shoot both photos and videos?
**2.** Can you edit your photos with this app, or another one on your device?
**3.** What editing tools are available to:
   **a.** improve resolution?
   **b.** correct defects?
   **c.** size the final image?
**4.** Can you add any special effects to your images, such as converting them to black and white or adding a picture frame?

## FILM-MAKING AND ANIMATION

Digital technology has also transformed the process of creating and publishing moving images. It is now possible to shoot video using standard apps on most phones and tablets, and even professional film-makers often use these options in the research and development stages of projects to test out ideas.

In the field of animation, digital technology has vastly streamlined a process that used to be extremely painstaking and time consuming. Animation software is so easy to use by comparison that it has vastly extended the applications of the medium, and animation is now used to create TV commercials, films, cartoons, interactive websites, graphics and video games.

Classic animation techniques involved drawing the layers needed to make up individual frames by hand on paper. To make just one second of an animated sequence, 24 separate drawn frames were required. Most animators nowadays use a digital drawing tablet instead. This allows them to draw directly into an animation software program where they can then compose, edit and save their work. Toon Boom is an example of animation software frequently used to create 2D animation, or classical animation, in this way.

3D animation (also called CG or computer generated animation) is created solely using digital technology. All characters, lights, cameras and sets are modelled inside the computer software, animated and then displayed as a complete film. In 1995, Disney's *Toy Story* became the very first feature-length computer animated film to hit the big screen.

**Fig 3.3** Disney's *Toy Story* (1995), produced by Pixar Animation Studios, was the first feature-length computer-animated film

### Top Tip

The most commonly used animation software on the market is Autodesk™ Maya and 3ds Max. Autodesk Maya can be used for both 2D and 3D animation. 3ds Max is generally used for 3D animation in the gaming industry, although it does have other applications. The 1997 action film *Lost In Space* was completely created using 3ds Max.

### Link

See Chapter 22, pages 220–222, for more detailed information on animation software and its applications.

## MOBILE APPS AND GAMES

When Apple launched the App Store® in 2010 as a digital distribution platform for OS X® applications for its iPhones®, iPads® and iMacs®, it started the trend that saw app developers marketing their products directly to users online. This approach has led to massive changes in how digital applications are used and by whom, since most apps are now developed for mobile phones, the most widespread portable digital devices

Fig 3.4 Use of touchscreen on a mobile tablet device

**Immersive experience**  the perception of being physically present in a virtual world

**Virtual reality**  an artificially created environment that seems real to the senses

**Presence**  the sensations whereby a games user feels connected to the virtual world via digital technology

**Immersive art**  images and sounds that are projected or displayed in the space all around the viewer

**Formats without borders**  animated images, light and music projected onto points in the space around the viewer to create a 3D experience

in use globally. Fast forward to 2013 and there were already over 900,000 apps available, users had downloaded over 50 billion of them worldwide, and 800 apps were being installed onto mobile phones every second!

Innovations in app development, such as the introduction of touchscreen technology, together with improvements in internet access, connectivity and bandwidth, meant that interactive gaming was now possible on mobile devices. This phenomenon soon revolutionised the gaming industry and is a good example of the Technology Push theory of innovation dictating how new products develop (see above). Games designers have since been able to explore new areas of creativity in their designs, shaped by the functionality available through the new technology, and build fantastic immersive environments for cutting edge products.

## IMMERSIVE EXPERIENCES AND FORMATS WITHOUT BORDERS

Immersion is the perception of being physically present in a non-physical (artificial) world. In gaming the term **immersive experience** is used to describe a suspension of disbelief that allows the user to act, or react, to the stimuli they encounter in this virtual environment. Designers create this perception by surrounding the user with images, sound and other stimuli that generate a convincing virtual environment around the user, for example, via **virtual reality** glasses. This produces a form of spatial immersion called **presence**, a phenomenon that enables the user to interact with and feel connected to the world outside their physical bodies via digital technology.

Advances in audiovisual technology and data imaging have also opened up new areas of creative possibility for artists. They are now able to animate image sequences and project them onto buildings and landscapes with immense precision, effectively transforming the physical world around the viewer into a fully interactive 360-degree canvas. These techniques are often referred to collectively as '**immersive art**' or '**formats without borders**'. They allow the viewer to experience art in ways that push the boundaries of experience and involve the other senses as well as vision.

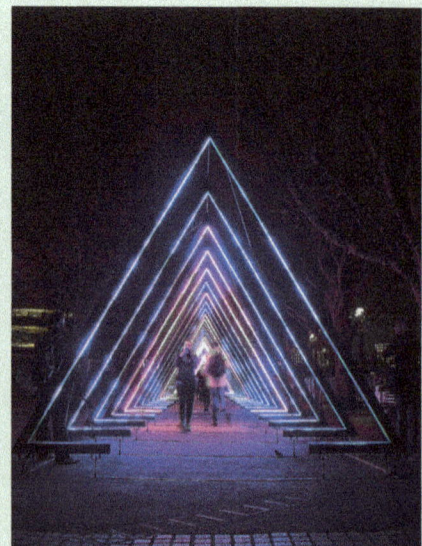

Fig 3.5 Examples of immersive art at the Lumiere London light festival, 2018

# 3.3 ETHICAL POLICY

New digital products have also generated a whole new range of ethical and employment issues, as working practices and production methods evolve. All manufacturing and commercial organisations in the developed world have to follow legislation and guidelines concerning the way they do business, to make sure that their production methods and working processes aren't damaging to employees, consumers or the environment. These regulations vary from country to country; however, their overall aim is to ensure that businesses comply with national and international agreements on environmental, economic and social issues. The commitments range from reducing carbon emissions to promoting equality among employees in the workplace.

Many organisations now publish their **code of ethics** online, to demonstrate their commitment to them. This can reassure potential clients and customers that the company is serious, responsible and reliable. Often when a new project is **put out to tender** a client will ask the participating companies to demonstrate their ethical credentials before considering them for the contract, so ethics are becoming an increasingly important part of any company's public profile.

## ETHICAL MANUFACTURING

Customers are now much more aware of and interested in the **ethics of manufacturing** and will often check out a company's ethical credentials before buying their goods or services. They may consider:

- Do the producers manufacture their goods using environmentally friendly production methods?
- Are they committed to using renewable energy and recycling materials in their processes to reduce their **carbon footprint**?
- Do they manufacture in parts of the world where workers have no employment legislation to protect them?
- Do they use children in their chain of production?

These considerations can seriously affect a company's reputation in the market place, so establishing an approved code of ethics is essential is today's digital landscape.

## SUSTAINABILITY

Many companies, large and small, have already made commitments to policies around **sustainability**, designed to reduce the impact of their business on the environment. For example, most businesses have now transitioned to a largely digital or paperless office. The digital revolution has made it possible to create, save and share data digitally, without having to print it out on paper, which is

**Link**

See Chapter 5, pages 48–59, for more information on tendering for a design project.

**Fig 3.6** Logos for use on a website's ethics policy page

**Fig 3.7** WFTO is a membership organisation and sets Fair Trade Standard for its member organisations so their businesses are compliant with the 10 principles of Fair Trade.

**Code of ethics** a company's official practice on ethical issues
**Put out to tender** invite proposals and quotes for a job
**Ethics of manufacturing** producing goods/services without damaging the environment or exploiting workers
**Carbon footprint** the total amount of carbon emissions a person generates through their use of fossil fuels each year (for example, by using airplanes to travel)
**Sustainability** the careful use of resources at a rate that ensures they will not run out but will be available for future generations to use

**Fig 3.8** The Edge in Amsterdam; considered to be the most sustainable office building in the world

an immense benefit for the sustainability of our forests. Similarly, recycling of paper, plastic and other materials (printer cartridges, DVDs, and so on) is now standard practice in most companies, which helps reduce waste in landfills.

Other policies that a business may decide to adopt around sustainability include operating a stricter travel policy, for example, by using video conferencing facilities for meetings involving staff in different locations instead of making them travel to meet physically. This reduces their employees' carbon footprint as well as travel costs. A business may also choose to work from specially constructed **low-energy buildings**, which are more effective at conserving energy for heating and power.

## EQUAL OPPORTUNITIES

Most countries also now have **equal opportunities** legislation in place that means companies have a legal duty to avoid discrimination by ethnicity, gender, religion or age when they recruit new employees. There are also guidelines and quotas about the employment of disabled workers. Many companies publish their **recruitment** policy on their website to demonstrate their commitment to equality in the workforce.

---

Comprehension: **Company code of ethics**

Access a design studio's website then find and read their code of ethics.

1. How many of the areas mentioned above does it cover?
2. Are there any areas you think are missing from its code of ethics?
3. Are its sustainability policies likely to be effective? Why/why not?
4. Thinking about this company's policies on recruitment and treatment of staff, would you like to work for this company? Why/why not?

---

# 3.4 DATA COLLECTION AND PROTECTION

Many products are designed with a specific **lifespan** in mind; some are even designed to stop working after a certain length of time so that consumers are forced to buy a replacement. This is known as **built-in obsolescence**. For physical products, such as cars and household appliances, it is important to consider from an environmental point of view what happens to the product when it becomes obsolete. For example, can an old microwave oven simply be thrown away, or does it need to be disposed of in a specific way, in a specific place, so that it doesn't damage the environment? Are there any parts that could be usefully recycled?

In the context of digital technology, as well as considering what happens to the hardware, we also need to think carefully about what is inside it – our data. This provides a comprehensive profile of the user often referred to as the **digital footprint** and it can remain on the internet for years and still be traced back to us, even when we think we have deleted it by changing our hardware.

When designers are developing digital applications or projects they need to be aware of issues such as lifespan, obsolescence, digital footprint and data protection, and ask themselves relevant questions in the planning stages so that they can build in the necessary **safeguards** for their users.

**Low-energy building** buildings constructed to save energy through better insulation, use of renewable energy sources, and so on
**Equal opportunities** giving everyone the same employment possibilities and legal rights in the workplace
**Recruitment** the process of advertising jobs and finding new employees
**Lifespan** the length of time a product is considered useful
**Built-in obsolescence** artificially limiting the lifespan to a certain length of time
**Digital footprint** the total amount of data stored about a person online
**Safeguards** security measures

# CONTENT MODERATING AND DATA COLLECTION

In our complex digital world, many online applications involve communication between users, whether person-to-person mobile messaging, or online blogs where multiple users reply to posts, or full social media platforms where thousands of users interact with content of all types as well as with one another. How can the owners of these platforms effectively monitor and **moderate content** if it is not posted by the company itself? Cases frequently appear in the news about users who post abusive or offensive content on social media, yet opinion remains divided over who is ultimately responsible for controlling this – should it be the platform owners, the government or an international, cross-borders regulatory body? This leads into a larger debate about whether the internet should be **censored** or whether to do so would mean interfering with an individual's right to free speech.

Over the last decade, internet giants, such as Facebook and Google, have increasingly been criticised for failing to tackle this issue. As a result they are finally establishing policies to regulate the content allowed on their platforms.

# CONSUMERS AND DATA PROTECTION

Before being granted full access to many online shopping websites, users are asked to register and create a profile, or even in some cases to supply their bank details. The issue here is one of data protection and online security: what happens to that data? How can users be sure that the data they have supplied is being held securely by the website owner, and that no one else has access to it?

Browsing data is often used by website owners to track users' activity in the form of cookies. How is this information managed and protected? Can it be sold to third parties? If it is stored, then for how long can it be kept? To avoid complex legal problems around the issues of ownership of data, most websites now ask users to sign a **disclaimer** giving them permission to store or use the data they collect. However, **data protection** and **data mining** are extremely controversial areas in online business and many countries do not have any legislation to regulate them.

---

## Comprehension: **Protecting customer data**

Go to the home page of a website you often use. Find the information posted on the site about customer data protection. Can you find the answers to these questions?

1. What type of user data will be stored on the site?
2. What can it be used for?
3. What can it not be used for?
4. What safeguards has the site put in place against the misuse or loss of users' data?
5. What will happen to the data if the website closes down?

**Moderate content** to check and censor content published online
**Censorship** to remove certain types of offensive contents
**Disclaimer** written declaration that someone is not legally responsible for something
**Data protection** procedures to keep users' data safe online
**Data mining** analysing databases to generate profiles on users' habits

# 3.5 INTELLECTUAL PROPERTY

Intellectual property (often simply referred to as IP) is an area of ethics that concerns the ownership of 'creations of the mind', such as inventions, literary and artistic works, designs, symbols or logos, and names and images used in business. It doesn't cover ideas, although sometimes the definition can be extended to include the development of ideas (designs, plans, and so on). IP legislation allows the originators or creators of content to protect their work and ensure that they are recognised for creating it or to make money from its use. It can apply to content of various types (written/printed content, visual images, moving images, music and so on) produced using a wide variety of traditional and digital media. One of the greatest challenges brought about by the digital revolution has been protecting content that is now accessible to very large audiences through an enormous range of channels, most of which are not regulated. This has had far-reaching implications for how IP legislation has developed.

The concept of 'intellectual property' is protected in most countries through the use of **copyright**, **patents** and **trademarks**. By striking the right balance between the interests of innovators and creators and the wider public interest, IP legislation aims to create an environment where innovation can flourish and benefit everyone.

**Copyright** official ownership of intellectual property
**Patent** a licence to protect the use and applications of someone's invention
**Trademark** a visual sign that distinguishes goods/services of one company from others so they cannot be copied
**Royalty** money paid to the copyright holder each time their content is used
**Permission** approval for someone to use content from the copyright holder

## COPYRIGHT AND PERMISSIONS

Copyright is a legal term used to describe the rights that creators have over their literary and artistic works. The type of works covered by copyright range from books, music, paintings, sculpture and films to computer programs, databases, advertisements, maps and technical drawings. Copyright legislation protects a piece of content so that when anyone wants to access it or use it (whether downloading a piece of music to listen to it or reproducing a photograph in an online article, for instance) they have to pay its creator a fee, often called a **royalty**. When copyrighted content is reused it appears with the copyright symbol © next to it, showing to whom it officially belongs. When content has been officially copyrighted in this way, accessing it or using it without **permission** is breaking the law and you can be prosecuted for it.

### Comprehension: **Website copyright**

Imagine you are creating a website for the tourism agency in your town.

1. List some of the potential assets you would need for the project (visual images, moving images, sounds, music, logos, and so on).
2. Which of the assets from your list would you have to check for IP issues?
3. What type of issues would they be – copyright, patents or trademarks?
4. How do you think you could resolve them?

# PATENTS

A patent is an exclusive right granted for an invention. It provides the patent owner with the right to decide how, or whether, the invention can be used by others. In exchange for this right, the patent owner makes technical information about the invention publicly available in the published patent document. Usually, if someone else wants to use the invention they must pay a fee to the patent owner.

# TRADEMARKS

A trademark is a sign that distinguishes the goods or services of one company from those of other companies. Trademarks date back to ancient times when craftsmen used to put their signature or 'mark' on their products. Trademarks help to protect the authenticity of a product or service so that it cannot be copied and ensures that standards of quality are maintained. For example, Parma ham from the area around Parma in Italy is trademarked so that other types of ham from other producers and areas, which have not been produced in line with Parma's quality standards, cannot be sold under the same name.

**Fig 3.9** Patent mark on a patented object

**Fig 3.10** British wool trademark on a woollen garment

# 4 Tools and technologies
## (beyond the syllabus requirements)

By the end of this chapter you will be able to:
* Understand advances in technology and their impact on contemporary creative practices
* Understand commonly used image-sourcing and editing tools and what they do
* Talk about contemporary practices in animation and gaming software and what these do
* Understand contemporary web design software and what it does
* Describe how digital tools are incorporated into a workflow

**Fig 4.1** A sketch of a project workflow

**Product website** the manufacturer's website that explains the software's features and how to use them

## 4.1 DIGITAL TOOLS AND DESIGN WORKFLOW

As we have seen in previous chapters, the impact of the Digital Revolution on the creative industries in recent years has been immense. Advances in the functionality of the available design tools have enabled designers to explore new and exciting areas of creativity in a wide range of media, from 3D animation to website design, to interactive art and formats without borders. New applications and updates continue to alter design practice all the time such that it is often difficult to keep up with the pace of the evolving technology.

One of the most important things to grasp when working in digital design is the concept of workflow. Essentially this refers to how the different stages in the whole design process relate to one another and are combined to create the final product. Many of the digital tools and technologies discussed in this chapter can be used in different ways at different points in the workflow to complete various jobs – not all design teams will use them in the same way. When working on a project you may have access to other similar tools, not those mentioned here specifically. The best way for students to prepare for this constant learning curve is to study the commonalties between the most widely used tools, understand how they function and become adept at using them. This will mean that you have a sound knowledge base from which you can build on in the future when experimenting with other tools. You will then be able to ensure you always choose appropriate tools for particular stages in the workflow.

Each software product has its own particular strengths and weaknesses and this chapter only gives an overview of what they are generally used for. If you would like to find out more about a product's features and capabilities, check the information on the **product website**. Yet the best way to learn about any digital tool and what it can do is still through old-fashioned, hands-on experimentation – just start playing with it!

### Skills Task: **Experimenting with software**

Experiment with two design software programmes that you have access to. Examine their features and try them out. Print out the logo of each programme. On the back of each logo write a list of about 10 things you can use that particular software for. Which of the following steps in a typical design workflow do you think each programme would be suitable for? Explain your ideas.

- Brainstorming and generating ideas
- User experience and research
- Product development
- Producing a prototype
- Investigation and feedback
- Presenting your **proposal**

# 4.2 IMAGE EDITING TOOLS

## ADOBE PHOTOSHOP

The most widely used editing programme for visual images in the world is Adobe Photoshop. The software is now so familiar to everyone that it has even become a verb in English: to photoshop a photo means to re-touch and alter it so that its flaws cannot be detected, as in, 'this photo has been photoshopped so the celebrity looks much younger'.

A photography enthusiast called Thomas Knoll and his engineer brother John, developed the initial version of Photoshop. In the 1980s they became interested in combining photographic imagery with the digital technology of Apple Macintosh® computers. The early Macs weren't able to display the greyscale images contained in digitised photographs, so Knoll wrote an app to solve this problem. He then developed this further into an application called Image-Pro, which Adobe agreed to license from him. Finally, in 1990, Photoshop 1 was launched. Since then the software has become so popular and widely used that it is now the industry standard in graphics editing.

The functionality of Photoshop is based on techniques from the **darkroom** used to develop photos in analogue photography. Essentially it functions as a sort of digital darkroom for carrying out similar editing jobs on digital images. You can see this in the names of some of the digital tools available in the Photoshop menus even now, for example, the Burn and Dodge tools and the Red quick mask option.

Early versions of Photoshop were mainly used for re-touching photographic images. This was because the software was expensive so there weren't many designers who were experienced in using it. Layers were not introduced into the programme until version 3.0, but when they were they greatly increased the possible uses of the programme. The multiple layer blending modes and **painting tools** associated with later versions of Photoshop have since generated an entire visual style that is now commonly used in design.

### What is Adobe Photoshop used for?

The great strength of Photoshop as an editing tool is that it is very versatile and can be used for a wide range of design tasks. Photographers can use it to edit their photos, graphic designers can use it to build pages, and illustrators can use it to create backgrounds for games, and so on.

### How does it work?

Photoshop is used mainly for editing **raster graphics**. A raster graphics image is essentially a rectangular grid of dots of colour called **pixels** that can be displayed via a screen or printed on paper. The basic principle is that pixels are the basis for everything that you can do in Photoshop.

**Link**

See Chapter 18, pages 169–179, for more detailed information on the analogue photographic process.

**Proposal** an act of putting forward or stating something for consideration; design ideas of what a final outcome might look like
**Darkroom** the room used to develop photographic film in analogue photography (it must be closed to any light)
**Painting tools** software features used for drawing, shading and colouring
**Raster graphics** a digital image comprised of pixels
**Pixels** dots of colour that form a digital image on-screen

**Fig 4.2** Photoshop layered image that combines vintage-style images of New York's city symbols

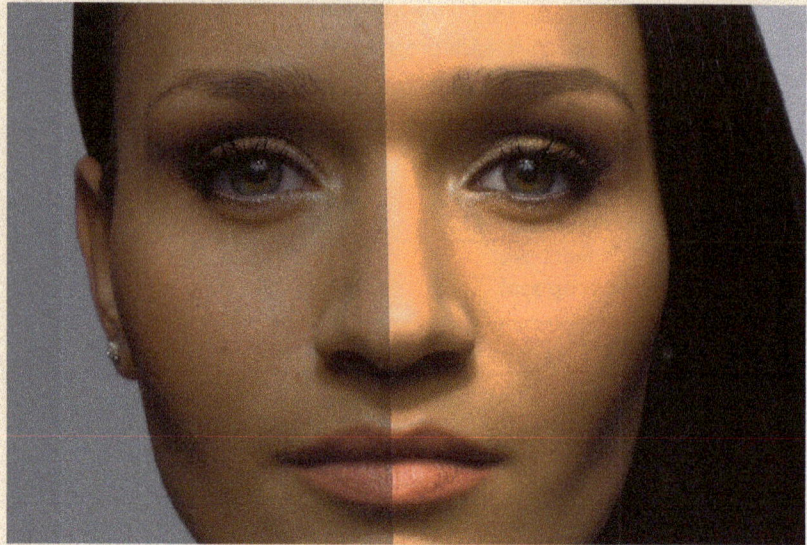

**Fig 4.3** An example of a standard image (left) and a photoshopped version of it (right)

**Link**

See Chapter 11, pages 104–106, for more information on colour models.

**Link**

See Chapter 17, pages 165–167, for more detailed information on image resolution.

**Render** to draw, make or represent artistically
**Image resolution** the number of pixels that form an image
**Art boards** screen format based on a sheet of paper on a physical desk, shown to clients to express ideas
**Vectors** lines forming 3D geometric shapes that are used to form digital images on-screen

The different ways a designer manipulates these pixels enables them to create, edit, control and display visual images. Photoshop is a raster-based software package that has the ability to create images in multiple layers and supports several colour models, including RGB, CMYK and duotone. It also has limited ability to edit or **render** text, vector graphics, 3D graphics and video.

The number of pixels that form an image is called the **image resolution**. The more pixels there are in the image, the higher the resolution and the better the image quality and sharpness.

**Skills Task: Identifying image resolution**

Select a photograph from a website. Use 'View command' on your device's menu bar to zoom in on it as far as you can. Can you see the pixels that make up the image as it gets larger?

## ADOBE'S® ILLUSTRATOR®

Adobe has also created other widely used creative industry applications, and one of the most popular is Adobe® Illustrator®. This programme was initially produced in the 1990s as a graphic design and illustration application and shares a lot of its functionality with Photoshop.

### What is Adobe Illustrator used for?

Illustrator was created to mimic many of the physical tools used by artists and illustrators when drawing graphic elements. As a result it uses **art boards** as the format of its screen space and incorporates many tools with names based on techniques in drawing and painting. Due to its ability to create flowing shapes and curving lines, Illustrator is often associated with **vector** art as a visual style.

## How does it work?

The fundamental difference between Illustrator and Photoshop is that Illustrator uses **vector graphics** as opposed to raster graphics. Vector graphics are based on geometrical vectors that connect locations called nodes on the screen creating polygons. These polygons are used instead of dots to create the images in Illustrator. Importantly this means that the images created are **resolution independent**, which means they maintain the same resolution and sharpness even when the image is enlarged.

Fig 4.4 An example of a vector graphic image

### Top Tip

An important consideration when using digital design tools is to understand the difference between **native file types** and **export file types**. Photoshop has its own native file type called .psd, but this is not readable by any other software programmes. In order to reuse an image created in Photoshop you have to export it in a different format such as .jpeg, which is readable by other programmes at other stages in the workflow.

### Link

See Chapter 17, pages 165–167, for more information on file formats for visual images.

### Skills Task: **Organising file types**

1. Produce a list of software programs you have access to. Print out their logos. Check on their product websites which native file types and/or export file types each one uses. Write them on the back of each logo (for example, Photoshop file types would include JPEG, GIF, PNG, TIFF, and so on).
2. Place the logos on a large piece of paper and draw connecting lines from each one to the others that make use of the same file format. This will help you to understand how file compatibility works.

**Vector graphics** a digital image comprised of vectors
**Resolution independent** when the quality of the image doesn't change when it is enlarged
**Native file types** file types used to create and store files within a programme
**Export file types** file types used to transfer files from one programme to another where they can be worked on

# ADOBE'S® INDESIGN®

Indesign is a desktop publishing and graphic design software application produced by Adobe. It is mainly used within the graphic design and print industry and was initially created as a competitor to QuarkXPress. InDesign was designed for laying out pages for the print industry, not for digital applications on the web.

## How does it work?

InDesign uses a grid system to manipulate and position elements such as text, banners and images on a page so that they can be presented in a structured, visually appealing way. For this reason it is very effective for creating products like posters, flyers, brochures, magazines, newspapers and books. However, it can also be used to publish content suitable for tablet devices when used together with the Adobe Digital Publishing Suite programme.

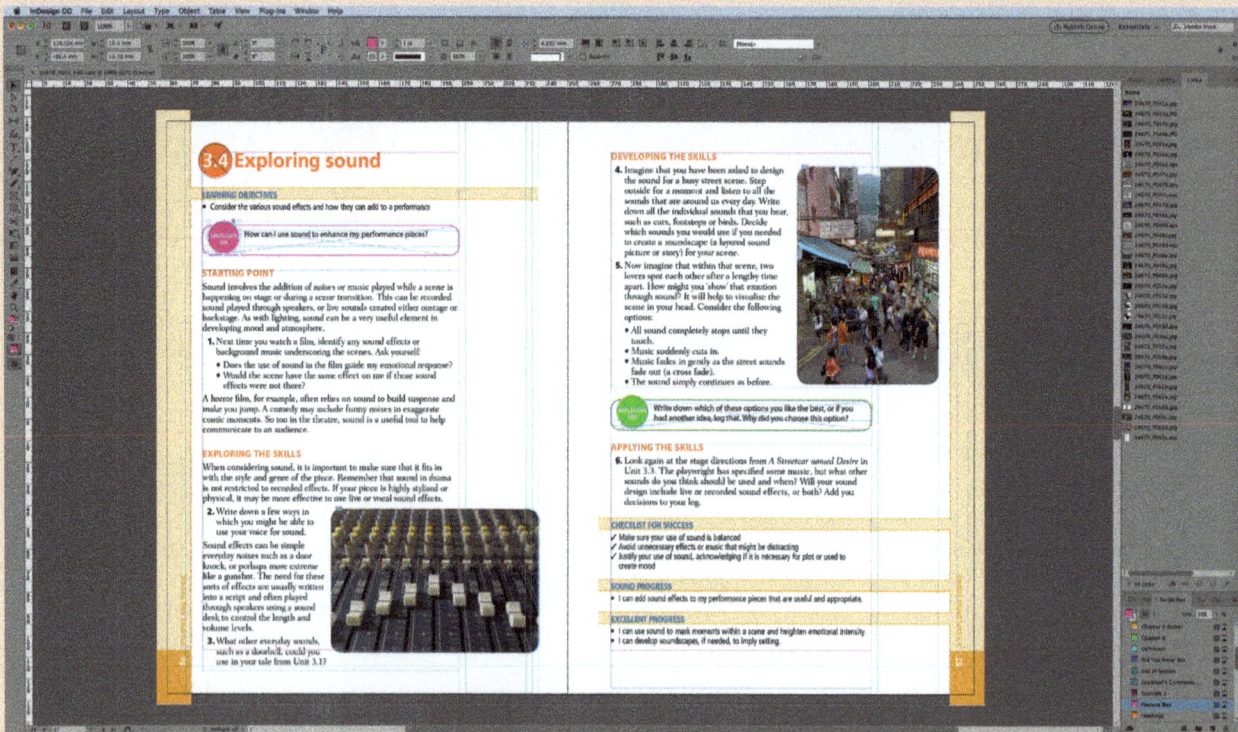

**Fig 4.5** How the grid system in the InDesign interface looks to a designer

## Skills Task: **Comparing image editing software**

Produce one document in InDesign and another in Photoshop to compare and contrast. Import a selection of images into both of the documents. Add some copy to a text box/boxes and experiment with positioning and sizing these elements within the page.

1.  What options does each programme give you for editing the images?
2.  What options are you presented with for typography and text manipulation?
3.  Which programme do you find easier to use? Why?
4.  Which do you think is better for creating a document containing images and text? Why?

# 4.3 GAMING AND ANIMATION SOFTWARE

## ANIMATE®

The precursor of Animate® was Adobe® Flash®, initially created as a 2D animation application for web publications. Later versions included the ability to add sound and greater levels of interaction. As a result Flash became widely used for creating online games, web animation and for video/audio playback. Between 2000 and 2010 it was used to enhance a lot of high-profile websites with animation and sound, through the addition of the Flash Player, a piece of software that the user could download and install in their browser.

### What is Adobe Animate used for?

Recent advances in software and hardware have made Flash largely redundant as an authoring tool; however, it is still a widely used creation tool in 2D animation. The most recent application that uses it is Adobe Animate. This programme combines fully interactive animation with powerful drawing and painting tools. In addition it can push out animated products to a wide variety of **platforms** including broadcast TV, the web and Flash.

> **Platforms** different types of digital delivery format, for example, mobile devices, desktop computers, DVDs

## AUTODESK 3DS MAX®

Autodesk 3ds Max® was first launched in 1990 and since then has gone on to become the accepted standard for 3D imaging all over the world. The strength of the programme lies in its ability to create an object then manipulate it in three-dimensional space, removing the restrictions imposed by working in only two dimensions.

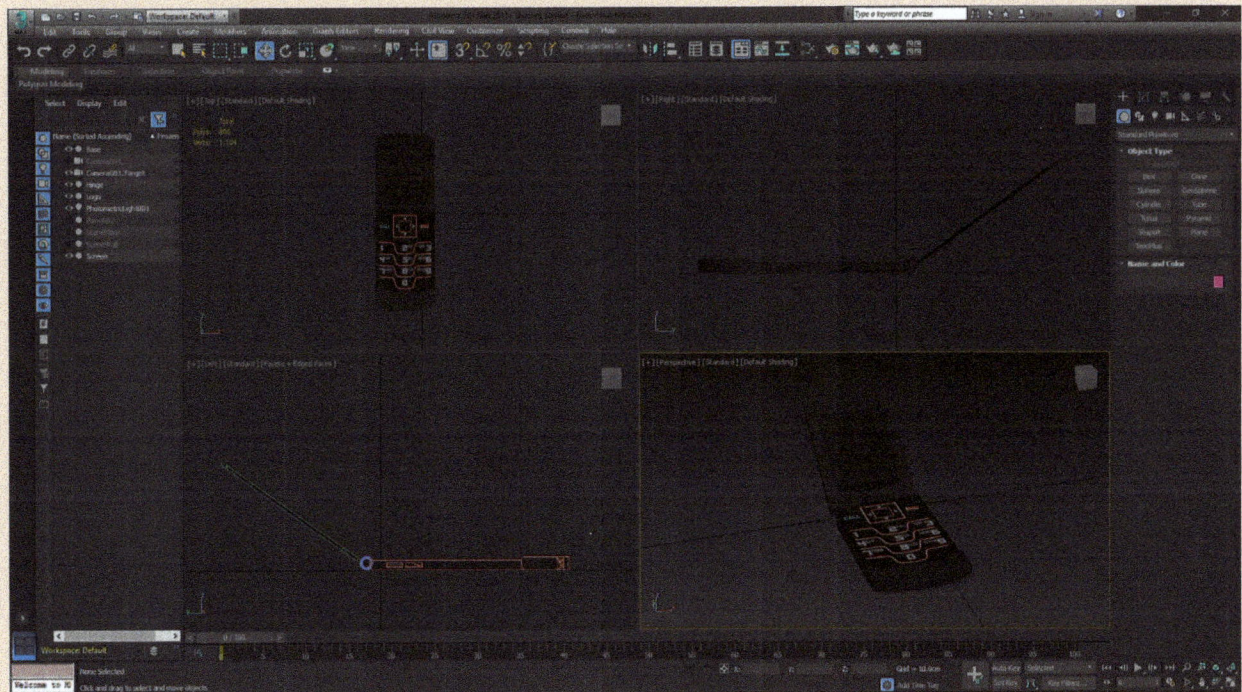

**Fig 4.6** How the 3D studio interface looks to a designer

### What is 3D Studio Max used for?

3D imaging technology now covers everything from very simple animations that form part of mobile applications and websites, to complex cinematic character animation and immersive gaming.

3D Studio is renowned for its powerful modelling capability, yet designers also like it because it can be easily incorporated into the development workflow for a wide variety of products across many delivery formats. For example, it could be used to produce a mobile app that requires a short sequence with an animated character, but it would be an equally appropriate tool for developing a complex environment in a console game that contains many props and sound effects.

## AUTODESK MAYA™

In addition to 3D Studio Max, Auto Desk also makes the Maya software.

Maya is a computer animation and visual effects application used predominantly in the gaming and film industry. Animation studios often use it to create models and visual effects in conjunction with 3D Studio, since it has more features for developing animation and **motion graphics**.

## OPEN SOURCE GAMING APPLICATIONS

In addition to the Autodesk products there are a number of open source (free) products available on the internet that can be used to achieve similar effects. For example:

- SketchUp is a free application that enables users to create 3D models and also access a library of existing example models.
- The Blender® project is a continually evolving, open source 3D modelling application that has been created by a community of designers, games developers and artists. Blender enables users to create models, animate images, and even create their own games and it is free!

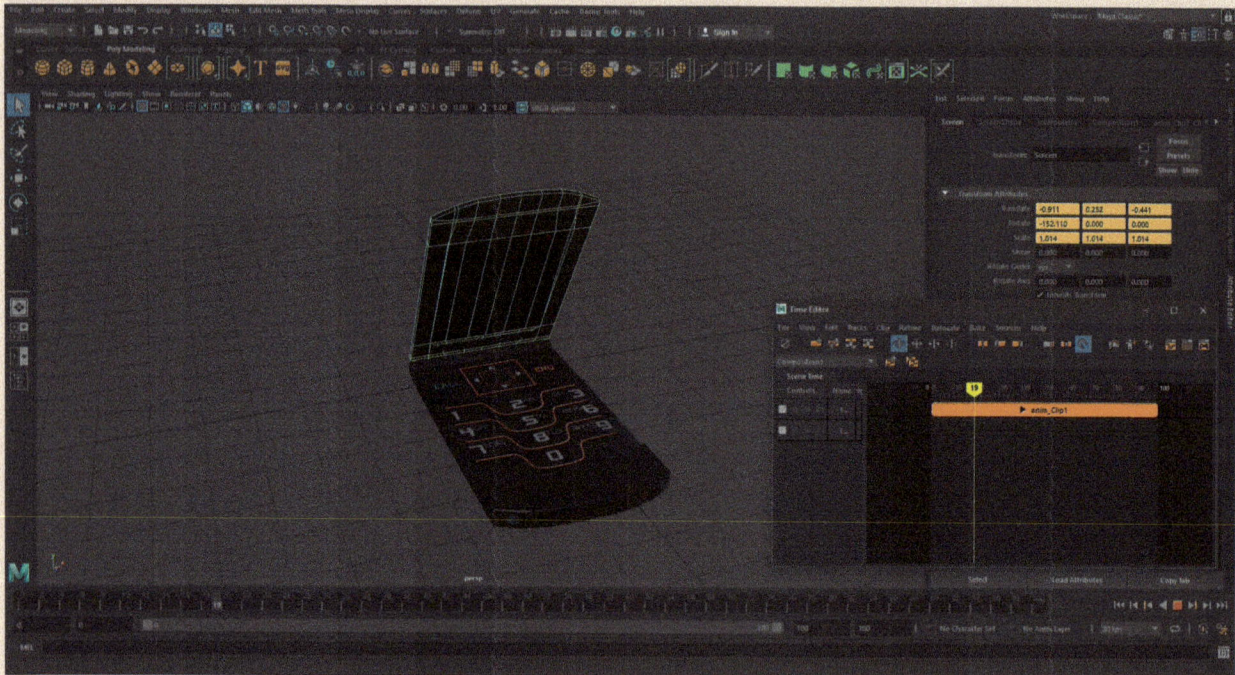

**Fig 4.7** How the Maya interface looks to a designer when animating

## OTHER PROGRAMMES USED IN ANIMATION AND GAMING

While the applications discussed above are used to create **game assets**, they are not used for the creation of the games themselves. This function comes at a different stage in the development process and requires a different type of application called a **gaming engine**. Unity is one of the most widely used applications for this task because it allows games developers to create interactive games and then export them to a variety of platforms. Creating multiple versions of the same game in different delivery formats can be time consuming and expensive, so using Unity helps developers avoid these costs.

**Fig 4.8** Logo for SketchUp 3D modelling software

For example, if a games development team is creating a driving game app for use on mobile devices but are then also asked to make it available online, Unity can be used. The programme will compile the various assets, such as the sound and graphics from the app, and then use them to re-create the same **game world** in the online platform that the user experiences in the mobile version.

Almost all websites and apps now make use of sound in one way or another – whether interactive sound to denote a button being pressed, a bell to signal an alert, or a musical soundtrack that plays over an animation sequence. In many products sound is an important part of the whole user experience; as a result sound production is an element that needs to be carefully considered by the designer.

In order for sound to be used as an asset for a multimedia product it needs to first be captured or recorded, then edited, and finally exported using the appropriate file type. Audacity® is an open source programme that lets you record live audio through either a microphone or a **mixing console**. With some operating systems Audacity can also be used to capture audio from live streaming. Other examples of similar software products for audio are Audition® and SOUND FORGE.

> **Game world** the virtual environment created for a particular game
>
> **Mixing console** electronic device for combining and changing volume level, timbre and/or dynamics of many different audio signals, for example, microphones being used by singers, acoustic instruments
>
> **Intuitive** easy to use for non-specialists
>
> **Asset library** storage area for assets used to build websites

### Skills Task: **Choosing tools for an app**

Which of the programmes you have read about in this section do you think could be used to design a game for mobile phones and tablets to help primary school children with their reading skills? Make a list and explain your choices.

# 4.4 WEB DESIGN SOFTWARE

When working in web design there are numerous aspects that you need to consider. Think of the websites that you visit day-to-day; they incorporate graphics, images and text, and potentially even animations, videos and sound. To create each of these elements requires different types of software, which are outlined in this section.

## ADOBE® DREAMWEAVER®*

The most widely used programme for web design is Dreamweaver, also from Adobe. It is an **intuitive** production tool that enables web designers to create and develop complex websites incorporating many digital elements. Basically Dreamweaver combines website code generation with extended **asset libraries** to make website production simple and effective. It was also one of the first applications to incorporate a WYSIWYG interface, ('What you see is what you get'). This acronym refers to the fact that the software features a browser that can display a visual representation of how the actual web page will look to the end user, rather than just showing lines of code (as website creation programmes did previously). The WYSIWYG interface is extremely useful for visual designers in evaluating and adapting their work.

---

* Adobe and Adobe InDesign are either registered trademarks or trademarks of Adobe Systems Incorporated in the United States and/or other countries.

## Link

See Chapter 28, pages 298–304, for more information on how website code works.

**Website code**  computer language used to build websites
**Website host**  browser where a website is located on the internet

## What is Adobe Dreamweaver used for?

Dreamweaver is essentially the engine room of website generation. It enables the designer to manipulate all the assets needed to build a website – texts, photos, graphics, moving images, sound – through the creation of **website code**. The programme is only used for the creation of the website framework, not to create the elements within that; visual images and other assets have to be created outside Dreamweaver and then imported into its library, before the designer can use them. The programme then pulls everything together using code. Dreamweaver can also connect with the **website host** via FTP (file transfer protocol), either to push pages live to a published website on the internet or to remove them from public view.

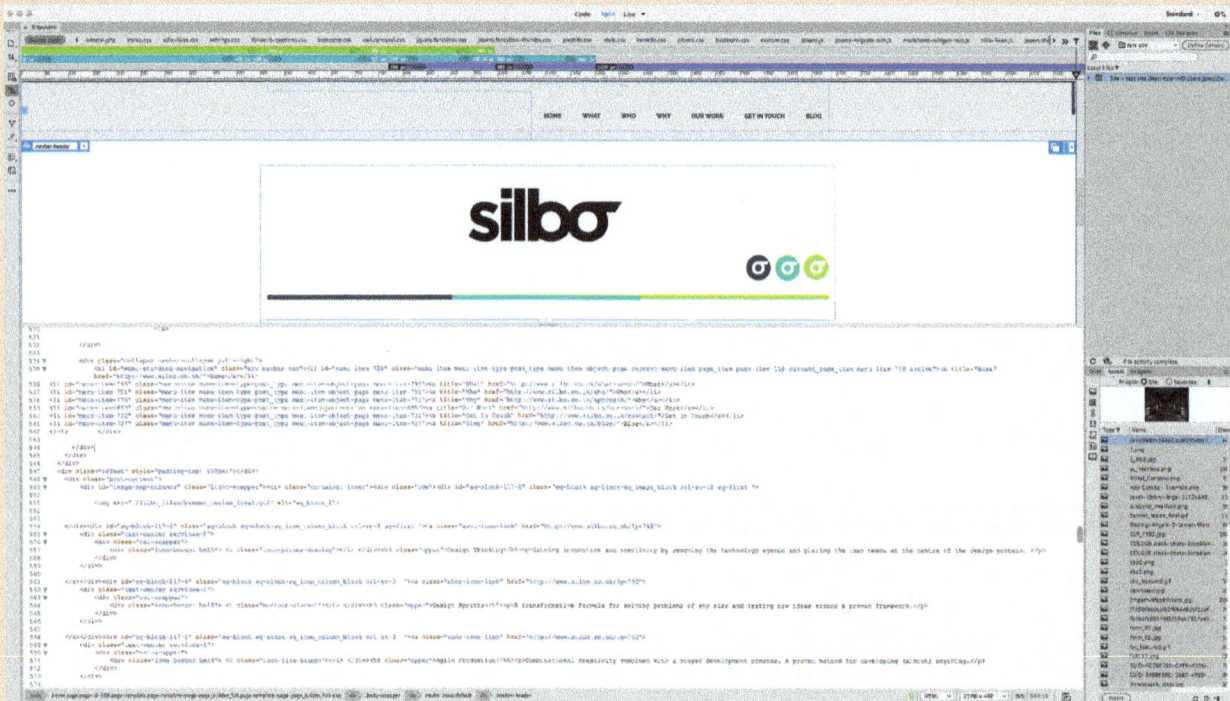

**Fig 4.9** The Dreamweaver interface showing an example website

## CONTENT MANAGEMENT SYSTEMS

Website designers and developers often create complex web projects that then have to be handed over to clients with little or no coding experience. So how can these clients then update their own websites? Content management systems (or CMS) are usually used to so this. To update a website without using CMS a client would have to be able to locate the right file within the site, download it from the live server, update the copy, save the file and then upload it again to the server. A content management system automates this process by storing all the files centrally and presenting the user with a simple interface to access them. Once the user had made the necessary changes in the original file and clicks on the 'save' option, the CMS makes all the changes to the live server automatically, so minimising the risk of errors.

Some developers choose to create their own custom-built content management systems, however, there are also a number of reliable and robust open source examples available, such as WordPress, Drupal™ and Joomla! All of these allow developers to either download templates to use as a basis for their design or create their own versions.

**Fig 4.10** Logos for WordPress, Drupal™ and Joomla!

# Skills and methods

# 5 The design pipeline

## 5.1 THE CLIENT BRIEF

### WHAT IS A CLIENT BRIEF?

Any creative project starts with a conversation and a request from the client. This may take the form of a formal tender issued by a large corporation or just a written request from an individual. In each case an extremely important aspect of the project is the **client brief**. This is a document created either by the client or by the client and the designer in collaboration that defines the project in enough detail to enable the designer to react creatively but also to deliver specific elements, such as **functionality**. In many cases the client brief will include other elements, such as timescales for completion, the criteria by which the success of the project will be measured, costs, background information relating to the bigger picture – which is the project's social or commercial purpose – and many other elements that help define the project. The client and the designer use a **pro forma brief** (or brief template) as the interaction tool to capture as much information as possible relating to the project before any work is started.

So why is this stage in the process so important? A brief is a starting point for the interaction between the designer and the client. Discussions can take place and emails can be exchanged, but until there is a clearly defined brief, there is no clear way forward. Failing to develop a client brief can cause big problems, from running over-budget or omitting a vital design element to simply not getting paid. In many ways the brief exists to take the risk out of the project by giving everyone involved absolute clarity.

> **Client brief** a document that describes a project in detail
> **Functionality** the exact functions a digital project needs to deliver
> **Pro forma brief** brief template

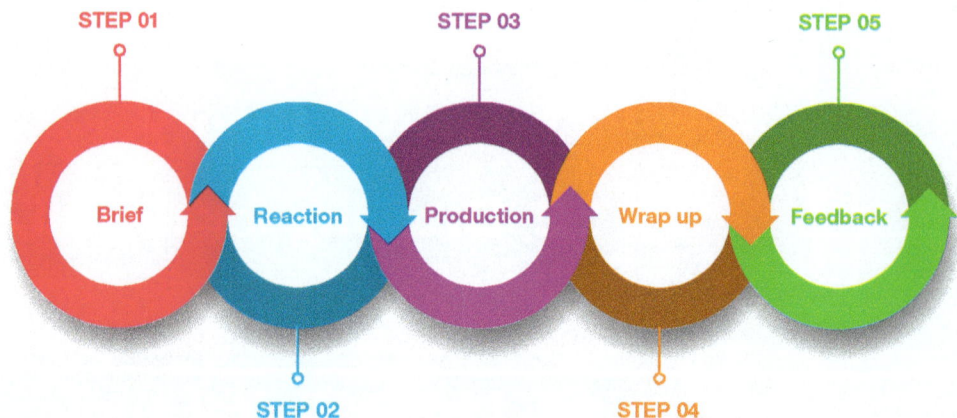

STEP 01     STEP 03     STEP 05

Brief    Reaction    Production    Wrap up    Feedback

STEP 02     STEP 04

**Fig 5.1** The design process shown in steps

## Skills Task: **Client brief**

Practise your skills by recording all the elements that could make up a client brief for a simple website. Consider:

- Is there a specific target audience?
- Is there a specific launch date, and so a deadline for your work?
- What are the sections and headings?
- Who will provide the copy and content?
- What is the budget?

### Who creates the brief?

Often the client will supply a brief, for example, an agency requiring an illustration may describe in detail what it requires along with costs and timescales; in this instance, the designer's job is simply to respond. In other cases a client may make a request and ask the designer to help define the brief. For example, a client may say, 'We need a website'; in this case the designer will need to work with the client in order to define everything in more detail before starting work.

**Top Tip**

At the start of a project it is useful to brainstorm the many ways the project could go wrong and make a list of all the pitfalls (for example, the lines of communication, who makes final decisions, scheduling and timescales). Once you feel you have everything covered you should have the core elements of your brief template.

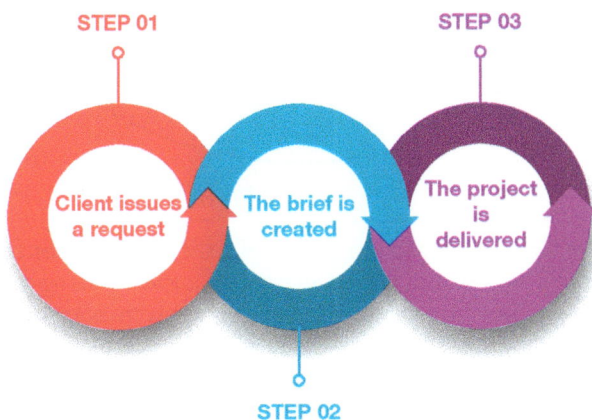

STEP 01 — Client issues a request

STEP 02 — The brief is created

STEP 03 — The project is delivered

**Fig 5.2** The steps for briefing a client

Once there is a clear understanding about what your project needs to achieve in terms of functionality, you can consider the emotional aspects: how does your client want its target market to feel and respond? This aspect of digital design is very important, so a shared vision between designer and client is essential.

One way to achieve this clarity is to use a **three-ring target approach**. This involves discussing with your client as many aspects of the project as possible, noting down the key phrases that they use then writing these words down onto sticky notes and placing them onto your target. The three-ring target is organised like this:

- the central ring has the most often quoted words
- the second ring has less frequently quoted words
- the third ring has the least quoted words.

This organisation can be done either in collaboration with the client or after a meeting. Once completed the target can be presented to the client for approval. If they disagree with anything then words can be moved (this is why you use sticky notes) or removed completely.

**Three-ring target approach**
method for brainstorming ideas

49

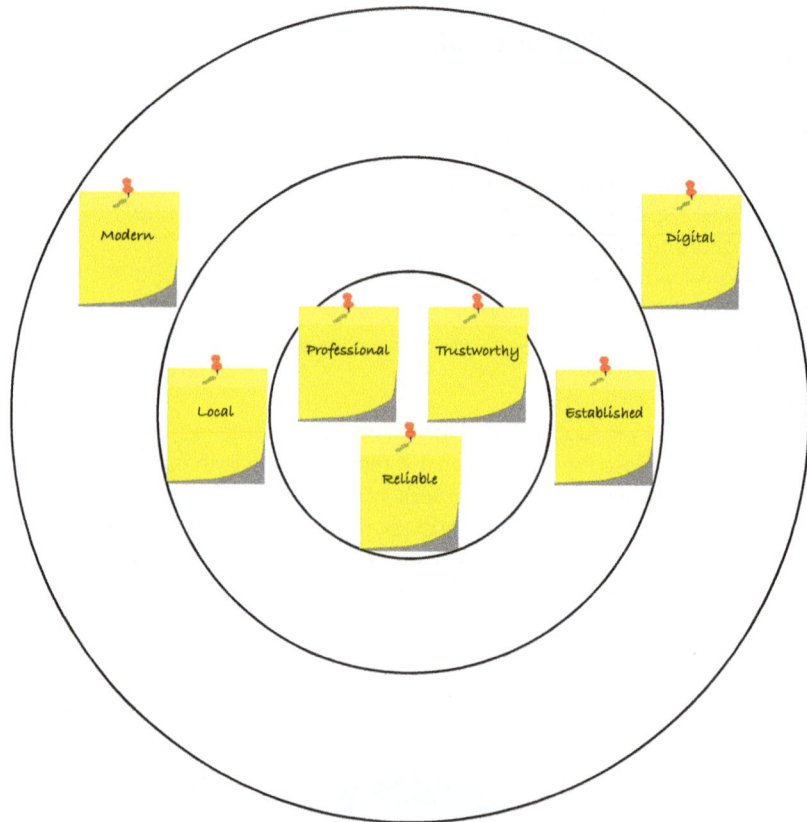

**Fig 5.3** The three-ring target approach is an effective method for brainstorming ideas

**High concept approach** method of explaining complex ideas simply by using existing examples

Another approach to developing a clear brief is the **high concept approach**, a technique used in the film industry. It involves using metaphors to describe new ideas by using them in combination with existing ideas and distilling them into a single sentence. For example:

- 'Flickr for Video' (YouTube)
- 'We network networks' (Cisco)
- 'Jaws in space' (*Alien*).

This approach works well, as it enables people to understand potentially complex ideas using simple language. It also makes things easy to remember.

In summary, the client brief is a critical aspect of any creative process. A good brief helps the relationship between designer and client by establishing strong channels of communication and clear project aims and, more importantly, building trust.

**Skills Task: Role play using the three-ring target approach**

In groups of four or more, aim to re-create a situation with a client and a project. Spend about 30 minutes exploring the project using the three-ring target method (as previously outlined). Once you have completed your target, record your ideas and present them to the class.

# 5.2 PRE-PRODUCTION PHASES

Many projects go through a three-stage process, which is broken down as follows:

- **pre-production** involves planning and research
- production is the actual creation of the **project asset**
- post-production is the final stage when everything is wrapped up.

Once you have your client brief and are ready to start your project, where do you begin? An important aspect of any creative project is to define the areas of the project where the designer can explore and experiment with ideas, and the areas where the client has more specific requirements. This involves a series of steps and processes starting with research.

> **Pre-production** project research carried out before production starts
> **Project assets** the fundamental building blocks to be used in the project

## PHASE 1: PLANNING AND RESEARCH

Ideally a client brief will define the project aims as well as some background information on the client or product. For example, a website brief may include something along the lines of: 'Company A is a manufacturer of product B. Through the design and implementation of a website, Company A intends to reach a global audience and achieve a significant increase in sales.' This information provides the designer with a starting point for further research, such as:

- Who are the target customers? Is there a specific demographic or sector?
- What elements make up the Company A brand?
- What is the product and how does it differentiate itself?
- What are the competitor products and brands?
- What other companies work in a similar way?

Many designers start by researching work by other artists that they feel has a connection in some way to the project they are working on. This could be anything from television advertisements that use interesting colours to Modern Art exhibitions that challenge the way that we look at the world. Personal experiences can also come into play when designers start to create. For example, one famous designer often cited 'The City of New York' as one of the most prominent influences on his work.

Once the designer has completed this research they should have a clearer picture of where they can be creative and where they need to follow client guidelines. This is especially important, as failing to fully understand this can waste time and lead to stressful situations with clients!

> **Top Tip**
>
> When planning how you will approach each phase, you always need to consider the timeframe and what deadline you are working towards.

### Skills Task: **Understanding a brand**

Research your favourite brand and find out the following:

- How does the brand use its logo and what are its main elements?
- What colours does the brand use and how are they used?
- Can you identify the fonts the brand uses and the typography?
- Does the brand have a 'personality'? If so, try to describe it.
- Does the brand speak with a particular 'tone of voice'? If so, try to describe it.

Develop your understanding by trying to identify other brands that work in a similar way.

> **Top Tip**
>
> Learn to understand your client's brand as much as possible. Many large corporations have very strict guidelines and failing to adhere to them can cause problems. For example, one large company does not allow the exclamation mark in any printed or online material.

## PHASE 2: IDEAS

Once you have an initial concept of what you need to do, how do you get the ideas flowing? There are a number of ways that designers and artists achieve this, yet it is important to understand that what works for one person doesn't necessarily work for another. Some methods for exploring ideas are outlined below.

### Brainstorming

**Brainstorming** involves collaborating with people to come up with and write down as many ideas as possible within a specific timeframe. Encourage people to be as creative as possible when brainstorming. Once you have written down your ideas, try combining them to make new concepts.

**Brainstorm** technique for generating multiple ideas and making sense of ideas generated
**Target session** method of recording ideas using a target model
**Brand values** what an organisation represents and how it wishes to be seen
**Creative jolt** a way of looking at things differently in order to generate ideas

### Top Tip

The ideas stage should involve a lot of sketching, notes and printouts. Some ideas you will discard but others can be used for other projects, so be careful not to throw everything out!

**Fig 5.4** A brainstorming session in progress

### Target session

This is a way of recording ideas using a target model.

### Skills Task: **Target session – linking the core concepts**

- On a large piece of paper or wall space, write down some of the core ideas that relate to your project.
- Then underneath and some distance away, write the core **brand values** of your client (these could be from your three-ring target exercise or from the client's own branding guidelines). Brand values are how the client wishes to be seen rather than what they do, so, for example, words such as 'trusted' and 'ethical' are values.
- Consider the connections – draw lines linking the ideas and values, and explore the relationship between the two. For example, how could 'website' and 'trustworthy' as a brand value be connected in an interesting way? If they can't, try other connections and see where the ideas take you.

### Creative jolt

Creative people often get stuck – writers call it 'writer's block'. This can be frustrating, especially when you have a deadline looming. One way to overcome this is to try a '**creative jolt**', which is a way of forcing yourself to see things differently, from another angle, in order to generate new ideas.

## Skills Task: **Creative jolt**

Try the following:

- Ask someone to show you something that they like and explain why they like it; this can help you to see things differently.
- If you are researching a client brief and feel stuck, look at something completely different for inspiration. Looking in unusual places can sometimes help by shifting your viewpoint.

Reflect on each of these exercises. How did they make you feel?

### Other ways to explore ideas

- Keep a sketchbook to record ideas as they come to you and when you are not at work.
- Use concept maps to note down all of the ideas that relate to your project then connect them with lines.
- Create a collage containing as many different aspects of your project as possible. Use type, colours and hand-drawn elements to create a strong visual impression that can help trigger new ideas.

## PHASE 3: CLIENT PRESENTATION

Once you have your ideas in the form of sketches and notes, how do you turn them into something to show the client?

Often the simplest way to show your work to a client is in the form of a **pitch/presentation**. You can do this either digitally using presentation software, such as Microsoft® PowerPoint®, or by printing out examples on paper and using **art boards**. The exact content of the presentation will be defined in the briefing document and **project plan**.

> **Link**
>
> See Chapter 8, pages 78–84, for more information on generating and developing ideas.

> **Art boards** visuals shown to a client to express ideas
> **Pitch/presentation** conveys information from a speaker to an audience; they are typically demonstrations of an idea or product
> **Project plan** plan to show how a project will be completed

**Fig 5.5** An example of a client presentation template

The main aim of the presentation is to demonstrate to the client that you are pursuing the agreed aims of the brief and making progress as outlined in the brief. The presentation is also a way of gaining feedback from the client and ensuring they are happy with how things are progressing. While it may be acceptable to simply show the client a set of visuals, there are other methods you can use, for example:

Top Tip

## Top Tip

Try not to take any form of criticism from the client personally. The important thing is to listen and to reflect on their thoughts, even if you do not agree!

- **Storyboarding** involves creating a series of images to represent screens and interactions. This would be used if the project involved a creation where the user had to follow a series of steps to achieve a specific goal; for example, in mobile apps, games, videos or websites with interactive elements.
- **Animatics** follow a similar approach to storyboarding, but use animated screens and images to convey how a user might progress through a series of steps or processes. This approach can also make use of sound effects, such as a voiceover and music, to enhance the presentation. This is especially useful for highly visual digital products that use animation and very complex websites.
- **Prototyping** involves creating a version of the final project that a user can interact with. For example, a mobile application prototype could be created and installed in a mobile device, to enable the client to fully experience the interactions in real time.

A critical aspect of any presentation is to gain feedback from the client; this can be done informally by taking notes or by asking the client to update a document.

## Skills Task: **Storyboarding and presenting**

Design a basic storyboard in groups of four. This needs to be a series of images that show a progression of some sort, so you need to think about what you need to show and then show it clearly; it is best to base it on something you are familiar with. Your storyboard could be an animated sequence from a game or a series of steps within a mobile app, and it can be either hand-drawn or created digitally.

Once you have created your storyboard, present it to your class, as if you were in a working scenario. Aspects of your presentation you need to consider include:

- What will you talk about? Do you need a script or just an outline?
- How will you show your storyboard – as pictures on a wall? On a screen?
- What questions do you expect to be asked? Have your answers ready.
- How will you gain feedback from the audience?

Encourage everyone to ask questions and to share their thoughts. Review any feedback you get from the class. What did you do well? How could you improve your storyboarding and presentation skills next time?

## Project work: **Defining a client brief**

Start with a group of between four and seven people. Two people will act as the client and choose what the project is; it should be something that already exists but could be anything from a mobile app to a complex website or even a TV commercial.

Role-play in groups to create a working brief for the project. Start with a basic idea and use the process to clarify your thoughts; this will enable you to establish an overall **creative direction**. Write down as much as possible, especially anything that is mentioned more than once, as this will act as a good indicator as to what the client is aiming for. Speak to the client to consider their organisation from as many different angles as possible, including how they see themselves and how they would like to be portrayed.

**Storyboarding** method of showing a process as a series of images
**Animatics** method of showing a process as a series of images using animation
**Prototyping** method of creating an early sample, model, or release of a product
**Creative direction** the overall approach to be taken in terms of visuals

Do not be afraid to ask what may be seen as quite unusual questions in order to get the information you need (you may need to explain your approach here to the client).

If possible, discuss with the client a list of similar examples that you have researched; this should help you establish the kind of creative approach that the client likes and where you can possibly draw some influence. The types of question you should be asking are:

- How does the client see themselves?
- Are they approachable or elitist?
- Are they positioned as a high quality or reasonable price brand? If not, establish what the main focus is.
- Is there a specific aspect that overrides everything that the organisation does? For example, 'reliability' or 'trusted'?
- Do they consider themselves to have a history or heritage?
- Is there a specific market that they cater for as well as a customer type?

Record everything in the three-ring target discussed earlier, placing the core words in the centre and the secondary/tertiary words in the outer rings.

The above approach will help you (and the client) establish what they want from the project in terms of creative direction and functionality. The next stages should help the designer turn these initial guiding ideas and principles into something substantial and usable that can be presented to the client.

This exercise is often just as useful for the client as it is for the designer, as it forces the client to consider aspects of their organisation they may not be fully aware of. Likewise, playing the part of the client is a useful exercise in thinking in a way that you may be unfamiliar with. Try to have fun!

# 5.3 PRODUCTION PHASES

While creativity remains at the heart of a designer's process, the next challenge is to turn ideas, imagery and prototypes into actual working examples, so you can hand everything over to the client and complete the project. For designers working in a digital environment, planning and **workflow** also become important parts of the process to ensure that the **digital outcome** matches the outline of the brief. First, you need to understand that the project will be made up from a series of assets that you will combine.

> **Workflow** the sequence of processes through which a piece of work passes from initiation to completion
> **Digital outcome** a work or product which is hosted in a digital environment

## ORGANISING ASSETS

A digital asset is digitally stored content. It could be an extensive library of images, videos, text files, code for a website or a simple illustration. The important thing to remember is that when you move beyond the pre-production stage, all your assets have to fit into a bigger picture and be used by the production team and/or the client. For example, the process for a graphic design or print project is quite simple: the client just needs to like the work and the correct file format needs to be handed over. However, the creation of a game asset within a large development team is very different and much more complex, due to the stakeholders and participants in the larger team structure.

## PUTTING TOGETHER A TEAM

Moving into the production phase of a project usually involves working within a team. Teams can be made up of two to three people, or in some cases many more. For example, in the game company example we discussed earlier, this type of team would be made up from:

- developers: people tasked with generating the fundamental game code
- designers/artists: people tasked with creating artwork and visual assets to be used throughout the game
- production/project managers: people tasked with managing the top-level production process as well as smaller processes within the larger development
- product owners: people tasked with **agile**-specific aspects of the project.

**Agile** project management term to describe a repetitive approach to planning and guiding project processes

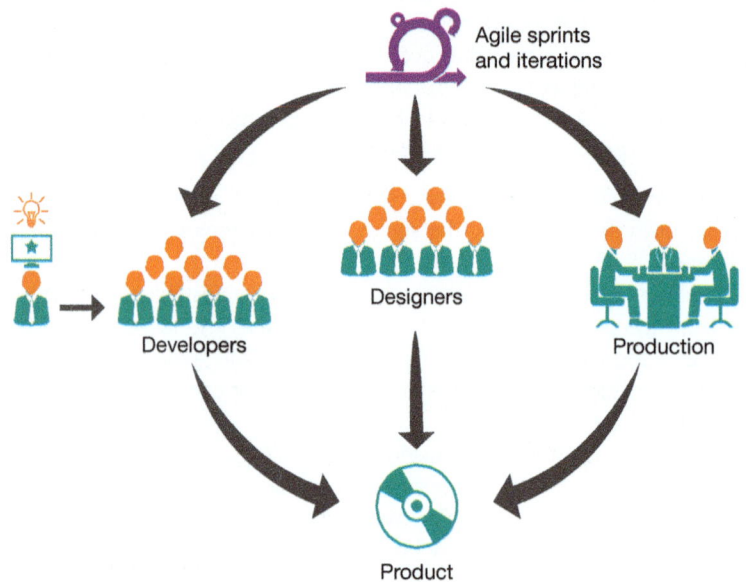

**Fig 5.6** How an agile project is organised

## Skills Task: **Understanding assets**

Pick a digital product of some sort that you feel familiar with and try to list all the assets that are used to make up the final product.

How many assets are there? Are there assets that are combined to make bigger assets? For example, smaller images within an interface (for example, buttons that the user clicks on to navigate around the site). Consider all the elements, for example, server hardware is still an asset.

Once you feel you have everything in place, write down all the assets on sticky notes and group them together on a large wall space according to type. For example, which are coding elements and which are visual elements? Finally, group some assets that contain others.

Refine your asset structure by assigning specific software to each asset. For example, for a website you would assign Photoshop to images and Dreamweaver to coding assets.

This approach can be useful when trying to define your team structure as well as the software that you need to complete the project. As with the client brief, this process helps to provide a big picture.

**Top Tip**

Understanding assets can become very complex if you are analysing a complex game. If you get lost, try something simpler and progress from there. As with everything, try to have fun doing it!

Now that you have a clear picture of what assets you need to create, what they need to look like, who you need in your team and what tools they need to use, you need to create a plan for your project.

# PROJECT PLANNING

Any project needs a project plan in order to meet the client's requirements and expectations. As well as keeping everything on track, the project plan also helps the development team stay focused on what they need to deliver by when. This process is called **project management**. Many organisations use **Gantt charts**, like the one below, for project planning. These provide a simple visual calendar model that works well in many different scenarios.

Many digital products will have a deadline that is imposed by the client. For example, a website project may have to correspond to a product launch or other media activity; a mobile application may have to be completed by a certain date in order to fulfil a contractual obligation. In each case, the deadline represents a clear instruction from the client that stipulates when something must be completed and this deadline must form part of any project plan. Failing to adhere to a deadline issued by a client can lead to disputes and, in some cases, a refusal to provide payment for your work.

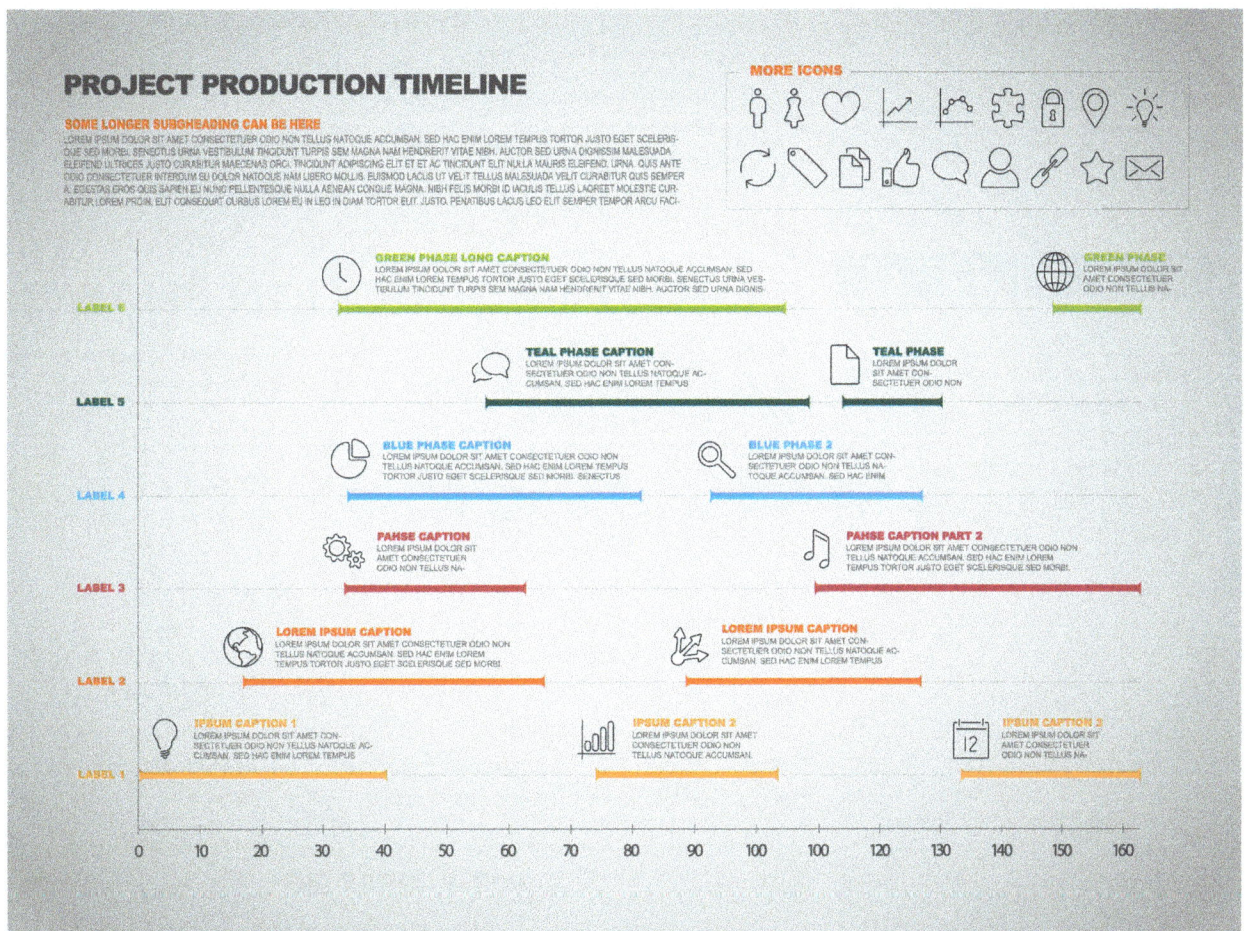

**Fig 5.7** A Gantt chart for a complex project

The elements that make up a project plan include:

- Start date – project start
- Tasks – specific pieces of work relating to the project (for example, interface design)
- Task timescales – when specific tasks are started and completed

**Project plan** plan to show how a project will be completed
**Sign-off** the final part of a project

- **Sign-off** date – when the task needs to be signed off (approved) by the client
- Live date – when everything goes live and is handed over to the client
- Resource – how many people are needed to complete the task
- Internal costs – what the internal costs to the company are
- External costs – what the external costs to the client are
- End date – project completion

Breaking down the project as detailed above, ensures that the project manager can keep track of resources and costs, as well as timescales.

### Project work: **Produce a simple project plan**

Start with an idea for a simple project – this could be something that is part of a bigger project, for example, an interface design for an application. Then create a simple project plan to deliver your project. Start with the list of project plan elements and incorporate everything into your plan. To do this you could use a basic online calendar or even a paper version. Also consider:

- Deadlines: are there specific dates that need to be incorporated? Does the client have specific dates in mind?
- People: who do you need and for how long?
- Software: what do you need access to?
- Hardware: are there any specific devices that you need access to?

# 5.4 POST-PRODUCTION PHASES

The post-production phases starts when the main part of the project has been completed. The final product must now be tested before everything is handed over to the client.

A testing phase is usually part of the initial brief and defined at the very start of the project. While some testing can be carried out during development, final testing usually happens before final handover. In industry, testing is usually split into two phases:

- Alpha testing refers to how a product is tested internally by the development team.
- Beta testing refers to a phase where a product is released to the public while still under development. This is a way of getting end users to test a product.

The principle aim of investigation and feedback is to ensure that whatever has been created is fit for purpose when it reaches the audience.

### Skills Task: **Compile a testing plan**

Design a testing plan for a very simple mobile game. In this scenario all the production is complete so there is no more development to do – the only thing left is to test the game and then handover to the client. Consider the following:

- What hardware is the game compatible with?
- What operating systems is the game compatible with?
- Have you played the game all the way through?
- Does it need a user to sign in? If so, does it all work as planned?

# PROJECT EDITS

As well as testing, the client may request minor edits before final handover. These could include things such as minor text changes to a website or colour changes in a mobile game. In each case it is important to define which phase the project is in to ensure clarity and to make sure the project runs smoothly. For example, during the production phase any changes would form part of the development process, but any changes afterwards would be part of post-production, as the main part of the project has been completed. Discussion with the client and project manager can help to clarify this.

## Top Tip

It is important to remember that even minor changes to a product can cause a project to go over budget if left unchecked! So make sure all changes to be made and the costs of those are clarified as early on as possible.

## Case study: Creating a proposal and client brief for a travel company

Pete works as a consultant for a development agency who has a large international travel company as a client.

The opportunity arose for the company to pitch for the redesign of the travel company's website, a potentially massive contract that involved a huge amount of work combining complex development and visual design. Pete's job was to help the development company secure the contract by creating a proposal and a client brief to convince the travel company to award the contact.

Initially the team thought that would just produce some visuals around what they could do, but then they decided to spend more time on the brief and set out some ground rules around how they could work together rather than simply saying what Pete's team would do.

Fig 5.8 Team analysis of how working practices could best meet the client brief helped Pete's agency to secure the contract

So they started to think about page design and how different areas of the pages could be assigned to different functions and interactions. For example, the screen was divided into areas corresponding to:

- Search
- Finding or accessing information using input boxes and menus
- Visualise
- Where the results of the search were displayed
- Complete
- The final act of completing the interaction, such as 'Buy Now'.

This meant that they could group the interactions and help the user to 'learn' where they were in the site and use it more effectively.

Pete's team combined this approach with some research into the brand and how they liked to be perceived. For example, the brand values revolved around being 'modern' and 'forward thinking', so the web presence had to show this. Their solution presented a radical departure from the way that travel websites look and thus reinforced the brand values.

Pete and the team created a set of rules around how everything should fit together rather than just a collection of ideas and visuals. The outcome was that it worked: the travel company awarded the contract and the feedback was that the rules created helped immensely with the website planning and made the workflow very effective.

# 6 Working with the brief

## 6.1 UNDERSTANDING A CLIENT AND PRODUCTION BRIEF

In the previous chapter you learned about how the client brief is created and by whom as well as the importance of the brief as a critical phase in the design process. The next stage is to interpret the brief in more detail. Think of this phase as building on what you already have. For example, if your initial brief was an idea for a story, this is where you will introduce your characters and plotlines. It is important not to alter the main aspects of the brief but to add detail to what is already there – so this stage is about interpretation rather than ideation.

Another critical aspect of this phase is the shift in focus from the client to the production team. If the brief is all about getting the client on side, then working with the brief is all about getting the team on side to deliver the project. This is the difference between a client brief and a production brief.

One way to ensure that everyone stays focused is to create a picture of your project that can be displayed in your workspace using the same three-ring target method from the previous chapter. At the centre, write the core focus of the project in a very succinct way. Try to wrap everything up into a single sentence, such as: 'A mobile application that enables the user to record physical activity and shop for fitness products.' If your project is too complex, spend some time clarifying the overall aims and find a way to express what the project will do as simply as possible.

### PRODUCTION PLANNING

Once you have created a picture of your project, such as a three-ring target, the next stage is defining the various elements of the production plan.

Depending on who is in your team (or if you are working on your own) there are a lot of elements that could inform the next stages of your project. The author and designer Dan Saffer created the diagram in Figure 6.1 for his book *Creating Innovative Applications and Devices* (Saffer, 2009) to illustrate what needs to be considered when creating anything that a user will interact with – which can be anything from a mobile application to a kitchen device. As you can see, there are many different aspects that make up a user experience.

## Top Tip

If appropriate, use the high concept approach from the previous chapter. Feel free to use drawings as well as words. Once you have your core statement, share it with your client to ensure they are happy with it.

## Link

See Chapter 5, page 50, for more information on the high concept approach to developing a clear brief.

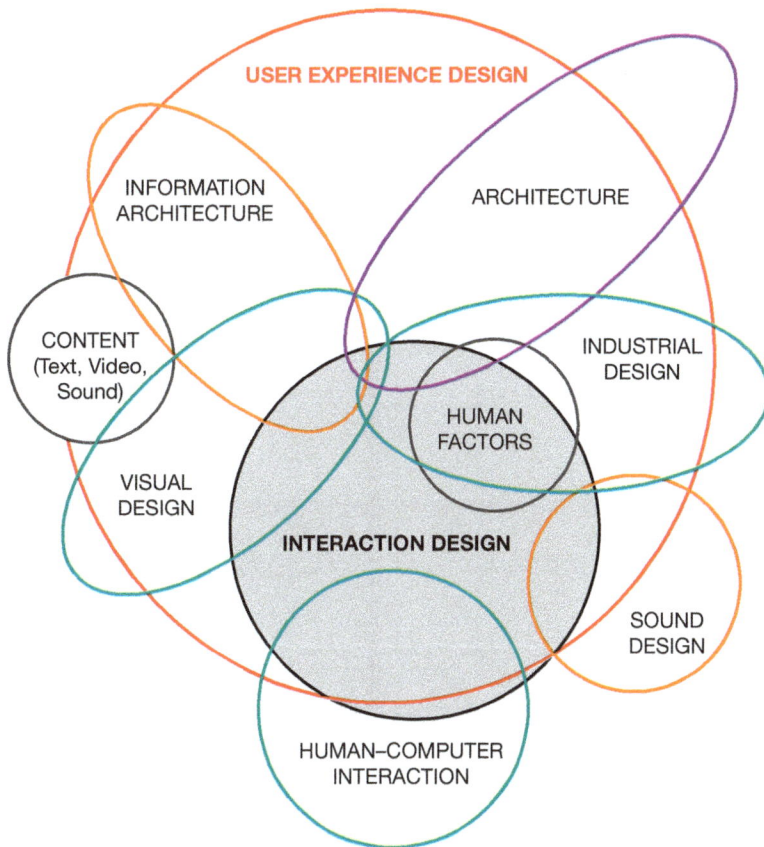

**Fig 6.1** The different aspects that make up a user experience – a model by Dan Saffer (2009)

**Architecture** where an application is used in physical space, for example, an interactive kiosk in a railway station

**Content** what is shown as part of the application, for example, website content

**Human–computer interaction** the way that users actually make use of a digital device

**Human factors** the user and what they are able to do

**Industrial design** the physical from that something takes, for example, a hand-held device

**Information architecture** how information is presented to the user, for example, menus and screens

**Sound design** how sound is used to communicate to the user, for example, a mobile phone alert

**Visual design** how something looks and its visual appeal

Your do not need to consider everything from this model when thinking about application design. However, it is useful to appreciate all the factors that make up Dan Sapper's model, even if your project only incorporates some of the elements.

## Sorting ideas

It is important to start adding detail to your picture/three-ring target – however, if you are working in a team, each team member will have a different viewpoint. For example, with a website, someone with a strong visual sense will think about how the display will look and what colours should be used, whereas someone with a development background may think about information architecture. Remember: both aspects of the project are equally important and you will need to get input from your team. You can do this by asking everyone to write ideas onto sticky notes and place them on your picture/three-ring target, according to how important they feel they are to the project. It is important to get as much input as possible from everyone.

### Top Tip

Once you have a picture/three-ring target covered with notes and ideas, it may look like a bit of a mess. Do not worry! The next stages are about clarification: sorting the ideas into specific areas that relate to your project in more detail. You can do this by creating headings such as 'Visual design', 'Content', 'Human factors', and so on.

## Skills Task: **App Development Canvas**

Develop your ideas using an existing model, such as the App Development Canvas. This model is great for planning complex applications that may need to incorporate other aspects, such as commercial models and technology platforms. The headings will be different depending on the type of project. A simple website may not need many headings but completing the process itself is important.

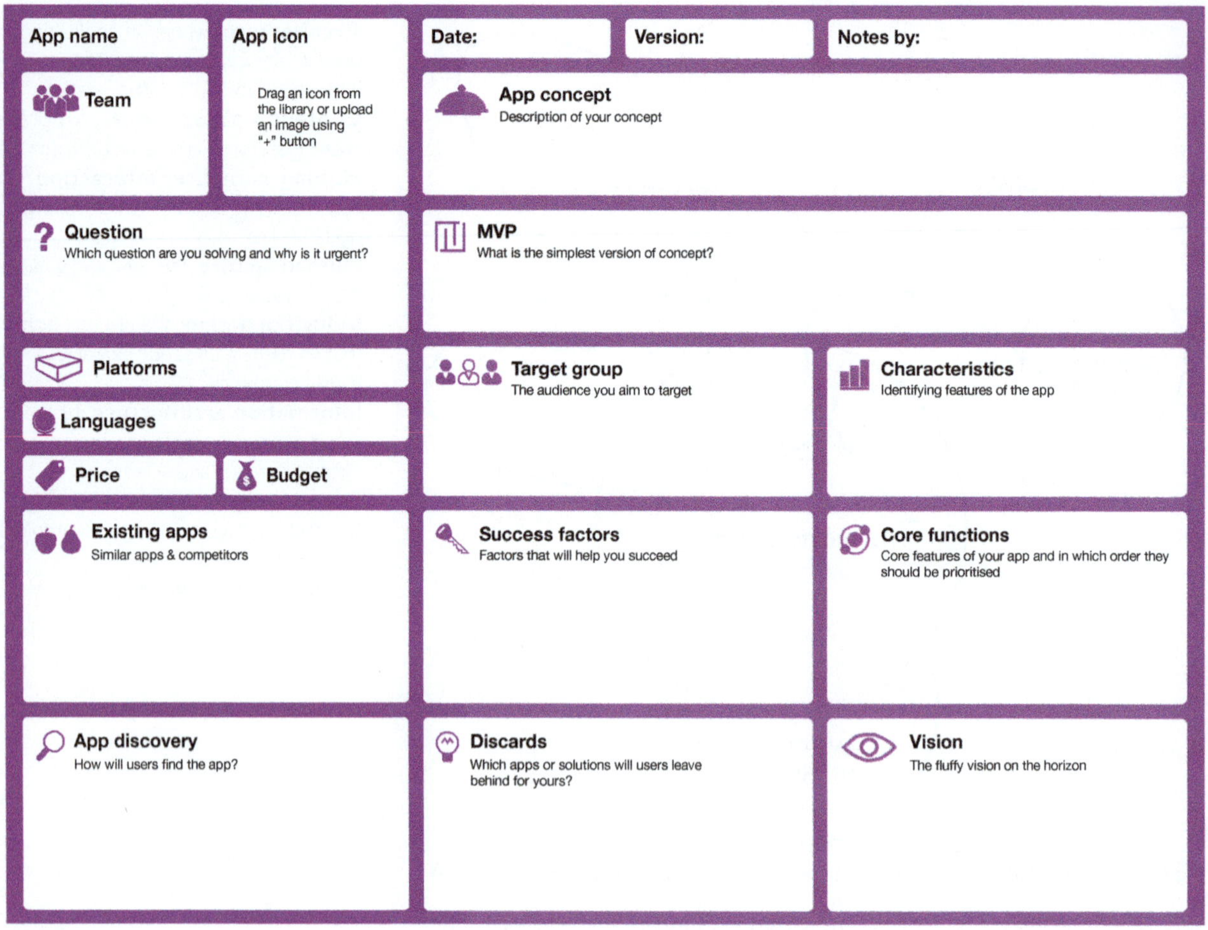

| App name | App icon | Date: | Version: | Notes by: |
|---|---|---|---|---|
| 👥 Team | Drag an icon from the library or upload an image using "+" button | 🍽 **App concept** Description of your concept | | |

? **Question**
Which question are you solving and why is it urgent?

▯ **MVP**
What is the simplest version of concept?

📦 Platforms

🌐 Languages

🏷 Price        💰 Budget

👤👥 **Target group**
The audience you aim to target

📊 **Characteristics**
Identifying features of the app

🍐 **Existing apps**
Similar apps & competitors

🔑 **Success factors**
Factors that will help you succeed

⚙ **Core functions**
Core features of your app and in which order they should be prioritised

🔍 **App discovery**
How will users find the app?

💡 **Discards**
Which apps or solutions will users leave behind for yours?

👁 **Vision**
The fluffy vision on the horizon

**Fig 6.2** The App Development Canvas

## CREATING A PRODUCTION PLAN

By now your project should be making more sense, as you have split everything down into smaller pieces and defined areas of activity. You can now turn what you have into a definite production plan.

### Chunking

**Chunking** is all about organisation. It is used when dealing with large amounts of written information. When writing a document, such as a production brief, chunking can help to envision the content into topics and subtopics. This avoids overly long paragraphs and enables the reader to access relevant information as quickly as possible. When chunking you can use things such as highlighting, bullet points and key words. The important thing is to create an organised format that is easy to understand.

### Narrative

A narrative (step-by-step) approach is used when developing production plans. For example, **user interaction** with an application/website is often described in terms of outcomes, such as: 'press this to go forward to the next page'. If you use a narrative approach you can also relate the interaction to the bigger aims of the website, for example: 'I have read the initial page content and now need to dig deeper. I still need to see where I am within

**Chunking** a method of organising a lot of written content
**User interaction** the way that a user interacts with an application or product

the page structure so I can navigate back to the start.' This approach tells the designer much more about the motivations behind the interaction, enabling the designer to respond to the brief more accurately.

You should now have an extensive interpretation of your client brief that includes a lot more detail and has defined areas and types of activity that you need to focus on.

**Top Tip**

When using a narrative approach, try to include what could go wrong as well as what could go right. What does the user NOT want to happen?

# 6.2 UNDERSTANDING THE TARGET AUDIENCE, USER EXPERIENCE AND USER INTERFACE

So far you have focused on the project aims and what you need to do to meet those aims, but what about the end user of the product? If you are going to create something relevant and useful then you need to consider end users and incorporate them into your project plan.

There are many ways to think about the end user, from survey research and questionnaires to website eye tracking and monitoring. The following sections outline some methods for understanding the **user experience** and user interface.

## PERSONAS

**Personas** are a type of virtual user model that enables a designer to predict how a user will act and think in a given scenario and why they will want to carry out a specific task. Personas are not actual people – they are fictional individuals whose characteristics and motivations are made up from a series of factors and elements. They are often produced as a result of some initial research.

A typical persona is made up from the following elements:

- **Demographic**: age, occupation, location, gender, any other aspects that make up 'who they are'.
- Goals: what they are trying to achieve; for example, 'wants to find good hotel deals'.
- **User behaviours**: what they do when they are in a similar situation; for example, 'multiple browser windows open, scans multiple websites with low attention span, has messaging software open at all times'.

**User experience** the experience of the user when using an application or product
**Persona** a method used to define a user
**Demographic** the social or age group that a persona belongs to
**User behaviour** what a user does when they interact

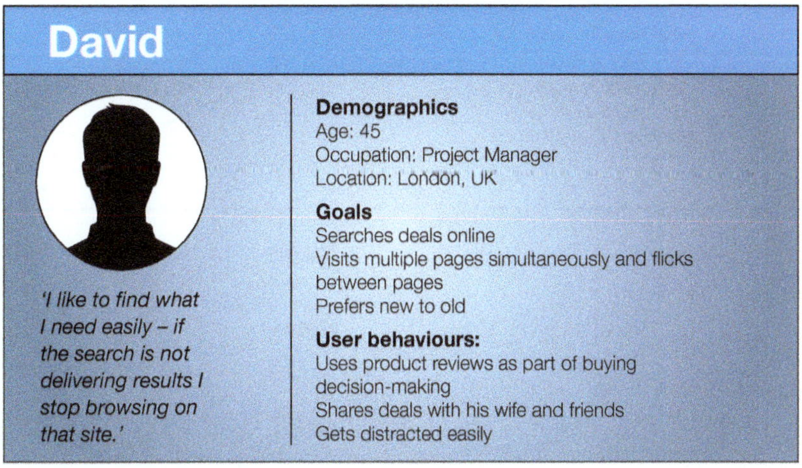
David
'I like to find what I need easily – if the search is not delivering results I stop browsing on that site.'
Demographics
Age: 45
Occupation: Project Manager
Location: London, UK
Goals
Searches deals online
Visits multiple pages simultaneously and flicks between pages
Prefers new to old
User behaviours:
Uses product reviews as part of buying decision-making
Shares deals with his wife and friends
Gets distracted easily

**Fig 6.3** An example of a business card describing a persona

## Top Tip

As with the other methods in this section, carry out empathy mapping as a team exercise whenever possible, using sticky notes to record ideas.

Sticky notes are useful because they can be moved easily without any crossing out. This is important, as you may put an idea in one place and then realise it belongs somewhere else. It is also a great way to generate new ideas by moving things around and seeing what happens.

## Skills Task: Research a persona

Identify a specific persona for a wearable fitness product website. Spend time considering in depth who this person is – do not just invent a name and occupation. Consider:

- What demographic do they belong to?
- Are there any specific traits that you can identify that would impact on them using a digital product?
- What are their main goals and objectives when using digital products?

Write a quote that they would use. Create a strong picture, and make sure you give them an age and a name!

### Empathy mapping

Empathy mapping involves digging deeper into the persona in order to try to understand what their motivations are and why they would use a digital application or service. It involves defining how the user is feeling, what they see, hear, and what they say and do in specific situations – as well as what they find difficult and what they want to achieve. An empathy map can be thought of as a simple customer profile that helps the designer to understand more so that they can deliver a better solution.

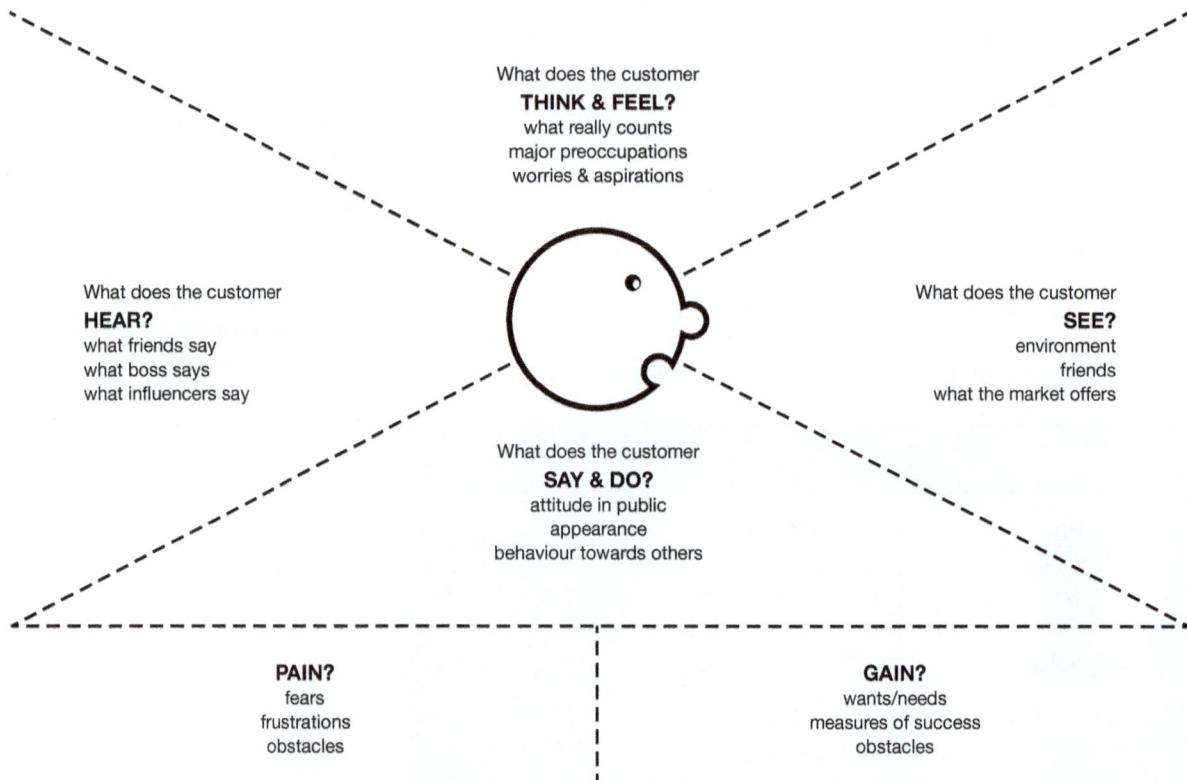

What does the customer
**THINK & FEEL?**
what really counts
major preoccupations
worries & aspirations

What does the customer
**HEAR?**
what friends say
what boss says
what influencers say

What does the customer
**SEE?**
environment
friends
what the market offers

What does the customer
**SAY & DO?**
attitude in public
appearance
behaviour towards others

**PAIN?**
fears
frustrations
obstacles

**GAIN?**
wants/needs
measures of success
obstacles

**Fig 6.4** An empathy map is one way of digging deeper into the persona

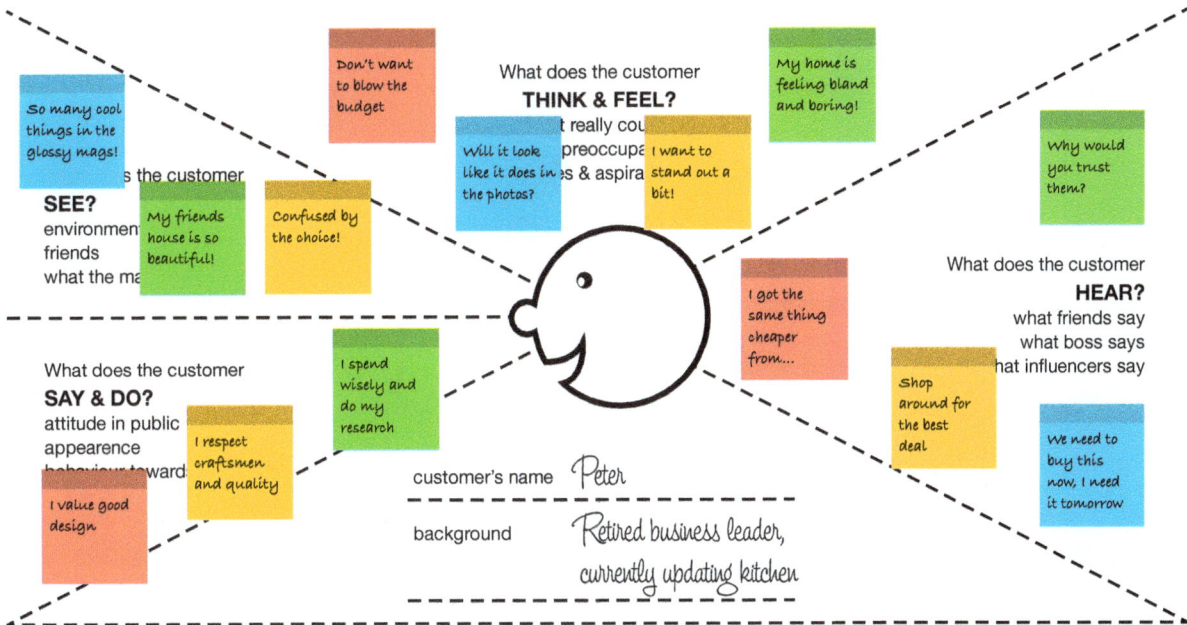

**So many cool things in the glossy mags!**

**What does the customer SEE?** environment friends what the ma...

**My friends house is so beautiful!**

**Confused by the choice!**

**Don't want to blow the budget**

**What does the customer THINK & FEEL?** t really cou... preoccupa... es & aspira...

**Will it look like it does in the photos?**

**I want to stand out a bit!**

**My home is feeling bland and boring!**

**Why would you trust them?**

**I got the same thing cheaper from...**

**What does the customer HEAR?** what friends say what boss says hat influencers say

**What does the customer SAY & DO?** attitude in public appearance behaviour toward...

**I spend wisely and do my research**

**I respect craftsmen and quality**

**I value good design**

**Shop around for the best deal**

**We need to buy this now, I need it tomorrow**

customer's name  *Peter*

background  *Retired business leader, currently updating kitchen*

**Fig 6.5** A completed empathy map

# DIVERGENT AND CONVERGENT THINKING MODELS

This is a method used for brainstorming sessions that allows you to fully explore ideas and reach conclusions.

- Divergent thinking explores endless possibilities and requires a willingness to keep an open mind.
- Convergent thinking focuses on refining ideas, clarifying goals and developing conclusions.
- Emergent thinking is the exploratory part in between the two.

**Link**

See Chapter 5, page 50, for more information on the high concept approach to developing a clear brief.

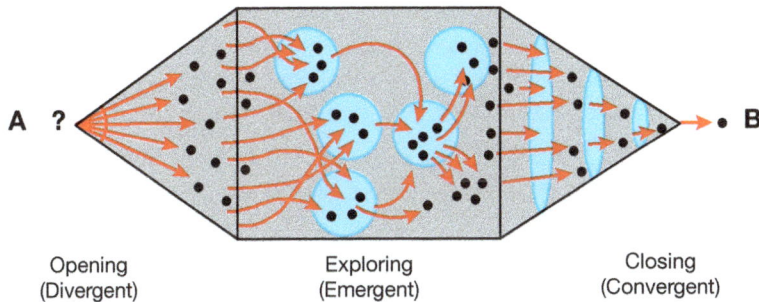

| A ? | | B |

Opening (Divergent)    Exploring (Emergent)    Closing (Convergent)

**Fig 6.6** Divergent, emergent and convergent thinking

**Top Tip**

Further examples of this approach include the use of 'gamestorming', where the divergent and convergent model is turned into a type of game that can be played with either clients or prospective customers.

# THE USER JOURNEY

Once you have a clear picture of your user, you can plan out the user journey. This is the series of steps that a user of a digital product follows in order to achieve their goals. In the case of a simple website, this would be a tree diagram showing pages. More complex applications will need specific steps to be defined in a **flow chart** diagram, such as 'Log in' or 'Set up account'.

**Flow chart** a method for showing how a user progresses through a process

**A.** Some UI Screen Ideas

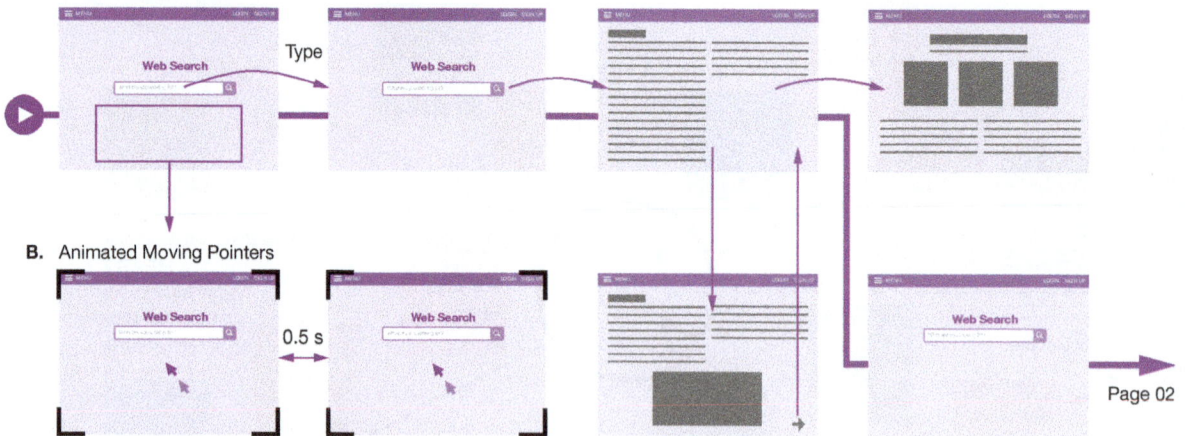

Type

**B.** Animated Moving Pointers

0.5 s

Page 02

**Fig 6.7** Flow chart to show a series of steps a website user might take when using a website

### Link

See Chapter 5, page 54, for more information on storyboarding.

**Characters** symbols that make up an alphabet or have particular meaning within a certain language

**Fig 6.8** A digital team working on a project

Once you have completed the flow chart – and agreed it with the client – you can start to show actual representations of each stage of the user journey instead of the flow chart elements. This process is the 'Storyboarding' process, as outlined previously.

## UNDERSTANDING THE TARGET AUDIENCE/USER

By now you should have a good understanding of who your users are and the journey they will take. There are other aspects of your digital world that could have an impact on your product. For example, will your product be used in more than one country? Will you need other language options? Here are some considerations:

- Language: Does your design work in all languages? What happens if you try to use different **characters** or language? Will the design still work?
- Culture: Have you used any culturally sensitive elements, such as colours, in your design? Can they be changed for new markets?
- Device specific issues: Have you designed something for one device only, for example, mobile phones? Is this device appropriate for other countries or target markets/users? Do you need to create more versions of your product for different devices?

Ask your client about this before you start – it may not be in the brief but it is always good to know!

## 6.3 WORKING AS A TEAM

By this point you should have plenty of ideas that relate directly to the brief, what your client wants and what will suit users of your design product. You now need to establish a team to complete the project.

As we mentioned in the last chapter, digital production teams can comprise anything from two to 100 people, depending on the size of the project. While roles within a team can vary, there is invariably a project manager who is responsible for managing the project schedule milestones and workflow. Project managers need to be excellent communicators but they also need to have a strong understanding of how teams work and what skills the other team members have.

Many digital teams now use the agile production method when working on large projects.

## THE AGILE METHOD

Agile came about when software development companies experienced problems when running large projects. Originally all software was created using a method called 'waterfall' whereby the client requested something, the developers made it and then handed it over – a very straightforward process. However, problems occurred when the client changed their mind and needed new features, which meant the developer had to go back to the starting board again.

The Agile method deals with this eventuality by arranging the project into several key elements:

- Agile epic – This is the 'big picture' of what your product is seeking to achieve; for example: 'The market leading health and fitness application.'
- Agile theme – A theme is smaller than the epic and contains more detail; for example: 'A leading health application to be used in conjunction with multiple mobile devices and other hardware.'
- Agile user story – This is the most basic element and describes a specific interaction; for example: 'User A logs into the application via their mobile device.' A user story should also contain the **failure point**, for example: 'If User A is not able to log in = feature failure.' All the user stories represent elements of your project that need to be created; this collection of stories is called the **product backlog**.

An epic can contain numerous themes and themes can contain many stories. You need to keep your epic, your themes and your user stories in one place called the **agile board**, which is a large wall space that is visible to everyone working on the project. Referring to the agile board, you then decide what to do and when.

---

### Project work: **Agile**

In small groups, create the epic, themes and up to five user stories for a digital media and design project. Present your ideas to the class. Ask for feedback. Develop the project in more detail by creating four more user stories with the help of your class.

---

### SCRUMs

A **SCRUM** is a process where a small group of developers decide how to create a solution to something raised in the user story. There are three main roles in the SCRUM:

- the **product owner** represents the voice of the customer and looks after the customer's needs
- the **SCRUM master** helps to organise the team and keeps everyone focused
- development team members are anyone working on the project as either a designer or developer.

**Failure point** part of a user story that describes when a feature is not satisfactory

**Product backlog** a list of outstanding features not yet developed

**Agile board** visual representation of the Agile process shown in a studio

**SCRUM** Agile process for problem solving

**Product owner** Agile team member who represents the client

**SCRUM master** Agile team member who organises and manages the team

### Sprints

Agile project management is organised into what are called 'sprints', which are specific periods of time marked out for the completion of tasks.

### Daily stand-up

**Daily stand-up** is a daily meeting when all team members report what they worked on yesterday, what they will be working on today and what is preventing them from making progress. It is carried out standing up (no sitting down) in order to keep the meeting short.

---

### Skills Task: **Daily stand-up role play**

In small groups, role play a daily stand-up based on the project idea from the preceding section. Use the SCRUM structure of SCRUM master, Product owner and Team member, and go through the three stages. Consider:

* What are the effects of standing up?
* What questions do the statements raise?

Contrast the roles – try the same meeting but swap roles. How does the meeting differ?

If you are unsure about how the roles are defined in an agile process, carry out some research online. This will return a lot of explanations and animations that explain Agile well.

---

**Daily stand-up** a daily meeting to discuss what the team is working on; team members are not allowed to sit down during the meeting, to keep it brief
**Burndown chart** a progress chart showing how a project is progressing

The Agile process enables teams to create a workflow that can incorporate new features as needed and involves constant feedback from the client in the form of the product owner. Do you need a new feature? Then write a new user story and add it to the backlog. Does the client need an update? Invite them to the daily stand-up. Does the client need to know when the project will be finished? Show them the **burndown chart**.

# 6.4 UNDERSTANDING ETHICAL AND LEGAL CONSIDERATIONS

You now have everything in place and your product is starting to look great, but what about the legal and ethical issues that may have an impact on your project? The following need to be considered:

### Accessibility

Is your project fully compliant with the relevant legislation regarding people with disabilities, such as visual or hearing impairment? Depending upon the scope of your project this may need to be a consideration. For example, if you are creating an e-commerce website, can the text be easily enlarged? If so, make sure that this is clearly stated.

### Terms and conditions

What are the terms and conditions of use in relation to your project? Are they clearly stated and visible? Ensure you consider all the ethical and legal issues when completing these.

For example, website Ts and Cs often include:

What is acceptable use of the website
What is prohibited use of the website
What the considerations are for registration, password and security
Are any other websites linked directly? If so, what considerations are there relating to third party content?

## Cookies

Does your project use things such as **cookies**? If so, is the cookies policy clearly stated for users of your website? It is now a legal requirement for websites to ask users for their consent (permission) before cookies can be used to store information about them. This is important to protecting users' online privacy. Consider where users will be using your website and how they will opt-in to the cookies policy.

## Data protection

Does your product hold any user data at all? If so, what measures have been taken to protect it? Anyone holding user data has to follow strict rules called 'data protection principles'. These rules vary between countries, so it is essential that you research these guidelines in full before starting a project. Failure to abide by data protection legislation can result in a large fine.

## Copyright

Copyright (official ownership of intellectual property) is used to protect your work and also the work of other artists or designers. This legal protection can also be provided by a **Creative Commons licence**, which allows authors, artists and designers to grant or waive specific rights in a simple and easy-to-understand way.

## Model release and permission

Your projects may well include photographs of people. If this is the case, it is essential that you obtain permission from the person in the photograph before you use the image, as the failure to do so could lead to you being fined.

Many of these considerations will fall under the remit of the client and not the designer or developer, but having an understanding can help save a lot of time and effort as the project progresses. For example, the initial brief should clearly define where the responsibilities lie for things such as copyright and data protection. If this is not clear, it should be raised as a concern and addressed. Failing to do this could result in a project that contains multiple (unintentional) issues that lead to expensive legal action.

## Cultural sensitivities

Does your project take into account any cultural sensitivities that may exist? It is important to always consider issues such as ethnicity, gender and religious beliefs to ensure that your designs will not cause offense.

**Cookies** small bits of information generated by a website and saved by your web browser that enables a website to remember your preferences, for example, your login username and password, web pages visited
**Creative Commons licence** copyright licence that allows authors, artists and designers to give people the right to share, use, and build upon work they have created

# 7 Research techniques

Research is an essential part of the planning and preparation process for any digital design. It ensures that your ideas are valid and likely to be accepted by your clients and potential audience or end user. Research helps you to:

- understand the target market/client brief
- assist with creative inspiration
- understand good practices/methods.

In this chapter you will learn about the **skills** and techniques required to undertake effective research that can contribute to the ideas and concepts used within your own production work.

# 7.1 PRIMARY AND SECONDARY SOURCES

There are two main types of research: primary research and secondary research. Many researchers will use a mixture of primary and secondary **sources** of information to meet their research goals.

## PRIMARY RESEARCH

Primary research involves the researcher gathering information for themselves, firsthand, from groups or individuals relevant to the design project. For example, a new YouTube video series released to a teenage audience will need to appeal to a range of teenagers, so a company may test the series concept with a **survey sample** of teenagers from different backgrounds, to see whether they are likely to watch it.

Primary research methods are often considered the most valid, as the researchers themselves gather the information. This allows the researcher to gauge the reaction of the subject and to ask them more in-depth questions if required.

### Gathering primary research

There are many different primary research methods. Your choice of method will depend on what you want to know and how much information you need to gather. Popular methods such as questionnaires and surveys allow the researcher to ask targeted questions that produce very specific information from their chosen audiences; we will look at how to construct these in more detail later in the chapter.

Sometimes it is better to speak directly to members of the target audience; this will allow the researcher to ask 'follow up' questions to gather more useful information. You can do this by setting up individual interviews with your chosen subjects or a **focus group** discussion with many subjects.

**Skills** abilities or accomplishments
**Sources** places to collect data, such as the internet, books or research participants
**Survey sample** selected people who are a representative of the target audience or society as a whole
**Focus group** gathering of a group of people to participate in a discussion about a product/service

# SECONDARY RESEARCH

Secondary research is quite different to primary research because you use information that has already been gathered and published by other people, for example, on the internet. You need to choose your secondary sources carefully and be focused in order to find useful information. Secondary research allows you to gather large amounts of information from a range of sources; however, it can be very time consuming.

**Fig 7.1** Libraries are an excellent place to find secondary research materials

## Gathering secondary research

Today, the most used secondary resource is the internet, because most people have access to it and it is a quick and easy method of accessing the work of others. Sources range from blogs, websites and vlogs to ebooks, e-magazines and scholarly articles published online. Using the internet to source information requires discipline and you must use **refined searches** to ensure that they target the right information. The table on page 72 lists some common refined search techniques you could use.

When carrying out secondary research using the internet, you can cut and paste the information into editable documents that you can easily annotate.

ChatGPT is an AI-powered platform that accesses existing internet content and then presents the results in a written format. While the uses of ChatGPT are still open to discussion, the platform can be used as an effective research tool or to generate ideas around a predefined subject.

Make sure you keep a **reference** of all secondary sources so that you can properly credit the original author(s); many works are subject to copyright, and incorrect referencing of sources is considered **plagiarism**. In addition, keeping a full bibliography of your sources allows you to return to your research throughout the design process, to ensure your ideas are still on track and verifiable against your research.

You can of course use traditional publications, such as books, magazines, trade and academic journals, or newspapers; again, you must credit the original authors and clearly reference all secondary information. (We will cover this in more detail later in the chapter.) There are different methods and styles used to reference resources, for example, the Vancouver or Harvard reference styles, and you will generally be told which format you should use.

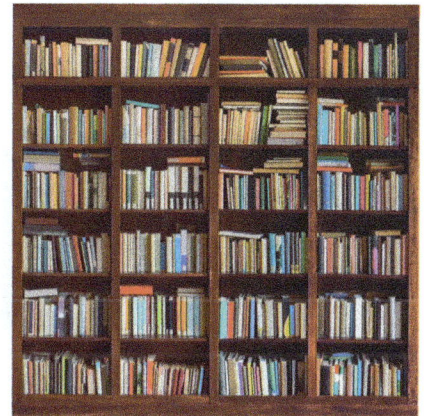

**Fig 7.2** Books can be a valuable source of secondary research

**Refined search** making a search more precise by using key words or definitions
**Reference** an author that is mentioned in a piece of research
**Plagiarism** copying someone else's ideas or work and using them as though they were your own

## Top Tip

Search engines, such as Google, track and adapt to your search history. You should also be aware that search results are manipulated by paid search, such as AdWords™. This is when companies pay for their adverts to appear within the sponsored listings on the search results. So, remember when searching that this can impact on the results you see – and the top results may not be the most useful, so be critical!

| Search requirement | Search technique |
| --- | --- |
| Search social media | Put @ in front of a word to search social media |
| Search for a price | Put $ in front of a number |
| Search hashtags | Put # in front of a word |
| Exclude words from your search | Put – (minus sign) in front of a word you want to leave out |
| Search for an exact match | Put a word or phrase inside 'quotation marks' |
| Search for wildcards or unknown words | Put * in your word or phrase where you are not sure what word you want to use |
| Search within a range of numbers | Put … between two numbers |
| Combine searches | Put OR between each search query |
| Search for a specific site | Put site: in front of a site or domain |
| Search for related sites | Put related: in front of a web address you already know |
| Get details about a site | Put info: in front of the site address |
| See Google's cached version of a site | Put cache: in front of the site address |

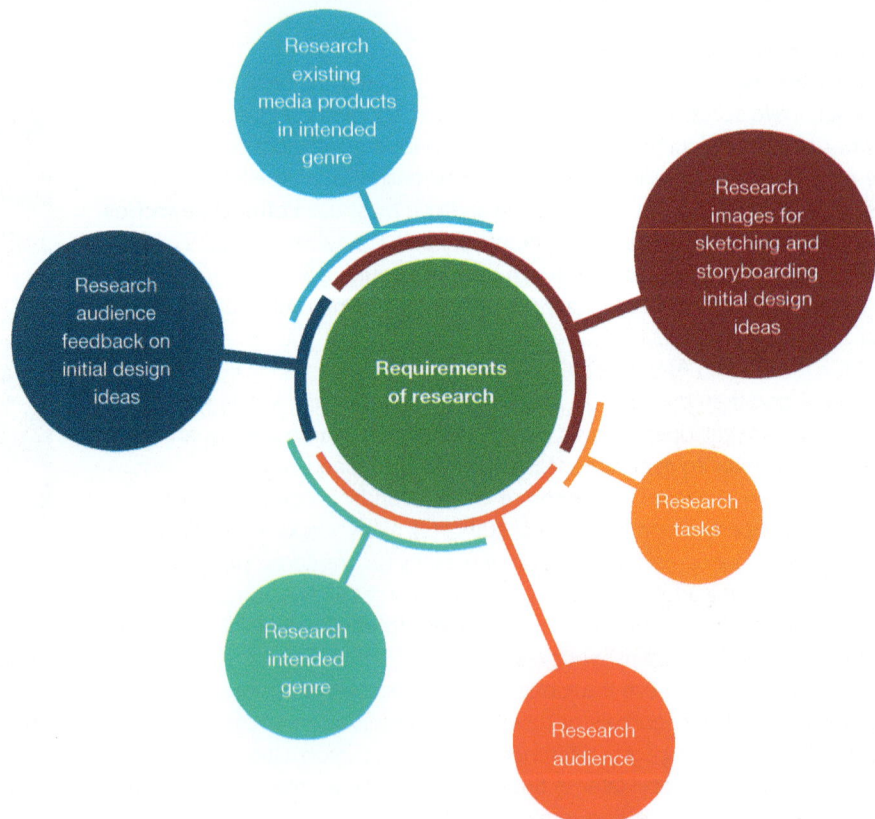

**Fig 7.3** The requirements of research

## Skills Task: **Choosing research methods**

You are beginning a project for a client that requires you to find images for the homepage of a website. The client is a local gym and they want to encourage more women to join and take part in exercise classes. Work in small groups.

**1.** Discuss how you could find out what images would attract the target market.
**2.** What primary research methods could you use?
**3.** What secondary research would help you find the right images?

After answering these questions, present your research plan to the class.

### Top Tip

When conducting your own research, start by writing down all the things you want to find out. This will help you to focus your activities and choose the best methods. You might find it useful to make a bulleted list or a mind map, like the one on page 82.

# 7.2 MARKET, USER AND VISUAL RESEARCH TECHNIQUES

In order to conduct research successfully, it is important to know who your **target audience** is and what they want. The target audience for a digital design, product or service is probably one of the most important factors for success. These are the people the researcher/designer must define and understand in order to satisfy them.

Client briefs will often provide information about the target audience for a product or service, but from this you would need to build up a picture of what that audience looks like. In particular, you need to find out about your target audience's needs and interests. If you are creating a project from scratch, without a brief, then you will need to decide on your target audience.

Market research techniques will help you investigate your target audience. They are also useful for looking at what competitors are doing or studying trends within the market.

For example, if you were planning on creating a mobile application that allowed people to order taxis straightaway, you would want to know that there was a likelihood of people needing taxis in the area. If there is already a well-established taxi company, or worse, well-established taxi applications, then the chances are that the application will not be successful as the customer already has enough services to choose from. If, however, all the current applications on the market only allow you to pre-book taxis then you may have found a 'gap in the market', in which case creating your application would be more likely to result in success.

**Target audience** the audience at which a product/service is aimed
**Closed questions** used to elicit research data; they limit the possible responses and include yes/no or male/female questions
**Open questions** used to elicit research data; they allow the respondent to give longer, more complex answers

## QUESTIONNAIRES AND SURVEYS

Questionnaires and surveys gather primary data in written formats. Questionnaires tend to require subjects to respond to a set of written or oral questions, while surveys can use a wider range of data sets including observation.

To effectively gather information you need to ask a range of questions using two different question types: **closed questions** and **open questions**.

• Closed questions can usually be answered with one-word responses such as 'yes' or 'no', or 'male' or 'female'. These questions allow you to gather important information quickly and efficiently.

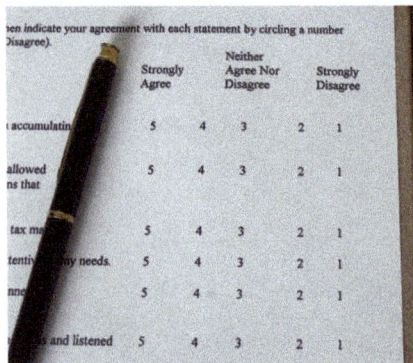

**Fig 7.4** Questionnaires can provide valuable quantitative data

**Fig 7.5** Online surveys can be a great way to reach a wide range of people

**Quantitative research** information that can easily be mathematically analysed or 'quantified' and often comes from secondary sources, such as large data sets

**Qualitative research** complex or nuanced information that requires interpretation and often comes from primary sources, such as focus groups

**Structured interview** clearly defined questions in a set order that are asked in exactly the same way to each interviewee

**Interview schedule** a set of prepared questions designed to be asked as worded

**Semi-structured interview** interview that contains a set of open questions that will prompt discussion and allow for follow-up questions to explore particular responses further

- Open questions require the respondent to provide more information, for instance an explanation of their experience or opinion.

You should consider using both question types within surveys and questionnaires, depending on what you want to achieve. For example, do you just want answers to who/what/when/where questions, which is **quantitative research**? Quantitative research is primarily statistical, and so produces data that can be measured mathematically. Or do you also want insights into 'how' and 'why' questions, known as **qualitative research**? Qualitative research is exploratory, and provides an understanding of opinions and motivations.

### Top Tip

A good way to understand question types is to take part in some online questionnaires and surveys and look at the different questions being asked. Consider: what question types are used more often, closed or open? Why is this?

## INTERVIEWS AND FOCUS GROUPS

Face-to-face discussions and interactions with the target audience are invaluable and allow the researcher to gain a greater insight into the audience's wants and needs. Interviews can be over the phone or face-to-face; focus group discussions tend to be face-to-face. During the interview make notes and record the responses using a digital recording device, to make sure you have captured everything. You can carry out either a **structured interview**, in which you only ask the pre-prepared questions you have written down in your **interview schedule** and do not deviate from them, or a **semi-structured interview**, which allows the respondent the opportunity to talk around your questions and provide you with greater detail and potentially more insights.

A focus group will allow the researcher to gather a number of people together and ask them questions or observe their discussions, record these sessions (audio or audiovisual) and play them back for review.

### Industry insight (beyond the syllabus requirements)

Web analytics is a form of research methodology that allows for data relating to the number of visitors to a website and the number of page views to be recorded and analysed. This enables the website owner to understand popularity and usage of their website and use this information to optimise their output.

Google Analytics™ service is one of these analytical tools. Data is gathered through a small piece of tracking code that sits in the HTML part of the website. Looking at the data gathered by an analytics programme helps website owners to see how many people visit the site, what they are searching for, where they live, and what pages are most popular. For businesses, this information helps to build a picture of their target audience and identify what is important to them.

# USER RESEARCH TECHNIQUES

These allow the researcher to study the users' behaviour and their wants and needs by observing them or asking them to perform tasks and analysing the data. This form of research is often used when there is an end product that the user has to interact with, such as an app or game.

A **user story** is often used in software development and helps create a simplified description of a user's requirements by allowing the developer to describe the type of user, what they want and why. In order to write a user story you need to know exactly who your end user will be. You can determine this by interviewing and observing your ideal end user, to understand their wants and needs. Creating a user story can help you refine all the information you have gathered about your target audience.

> **User story** describes the type of user, what they want and why

## User experience (UX)

The user experience relates to all aspects of an individual's interaction with a particular design, product or service. These aspects may include several fields of user experience, such as how information is organised (information architecture), visual and sound design as well as direct user interaction. This experience will define whether or not the user returns or remains loyal to a particular product or service.

Many companies ask their target audience what they thought of their products and services, or those provided by others, and use that information to improve what they have to offer. You may have been sent a survey after using a website to place an order. This will often ask you specifically about how easy or difficult you found the website to use. Companies use that feedback to design and implement changes to the website, in order to create a better user experience.

**Fig 7.6** Visual research can aid the aesthetics of the end product

## Visual research techniques

This is a qualitative research method that uses visual images to explore the subject's responses, behaviours or experiences. People's responses to different visual stimuli demonstrate their understanding of the world and their choices. This type of technique involves laying out visual stimuli, such as photographs or sketches, and then, in many instances, asking critical questions such as: What stories do the images tell? What use do you think the images are intended for? What is your emotional reaction to these images? You should make a note of these answers in a journal or logbook.

Images can be shown individually or in groups. To gain different perspectives, you might want to group images in different ways with the same or different people. This type of technique could be useful if you were designing a homepage for a website and wanted to get a sense of what will attract different audiences, or if you were planning a commercial or short film and wanted to gauge the emotional impact of different images.

## Shared inspiration bookmarking

The use of bookmarking is now common practice among web users, and shared inspiration bookmarking allows users to tag pages, which are then stored on the web and can be accessed from any computer. These often include social media pages and can be personalised. This is a good method of storing ideas, inspiration and information that can be recalled and reviewed again and again. It can also be used as a research technique, as bookmarking sites, such as Pinterest and del.i.cious, allow users to look at what other users have bookmarked, and so see lots of shared links and articles for inspiration.

# 7.3 SELECTING AND ORGANISING INFORMATION

When conducting research, you must sort and collate a large amount of information to make sense of it and ensure that it is relevant. This means discarding some work, so you need to be thoughtful and selective.

## SORTING

Sorting data is perhaps the most important part of the process, as it requires you to work through large amounts of materials and make decisions about what to include and what to discard. You can do this by ordering and categorising information according to meaning, relevance and usefulness.

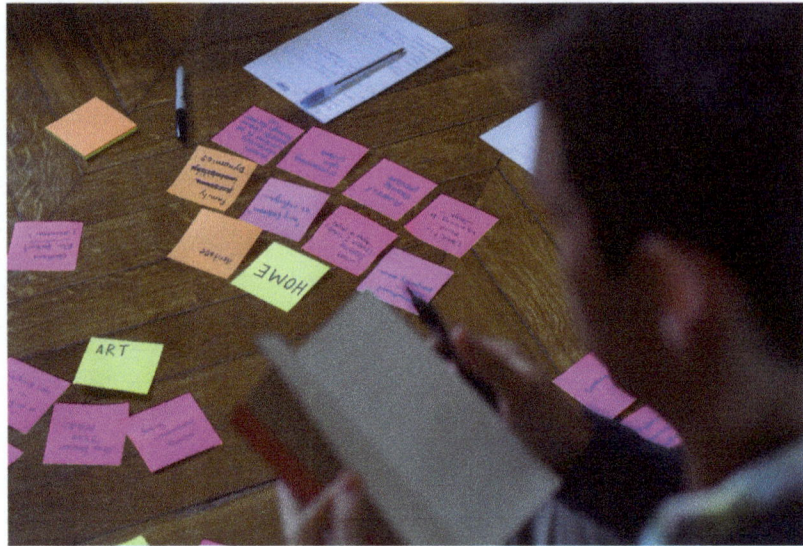

**Fig 7.7** Sorting data will give structure to your findings

### Cluster analysis

One way to sort your data is by using **cluster analysis**. This method connects different data objects according to their similarities, forming groups or clusters. For example, you could group images you have sourced based on what they represent, such as colour, size or content (for example, pictures of puppies). This is a very common technique used in statistical data analysis and allows the researcher to sort and structure their findings. In this way a researcher is able to connect their data and ensure it is relevant.

When conducting your own research you will gather a lot of information; the cluster analysis method will allow you to structure the information you have found and link it together.

## COLLATING AND STORING DATA

All information you gather must be collated and properly referenced and indexed; by doing this you can make sure that all of your information is in a logical order and can be easily referred to when required. Always take care to label all of your data so that it can be easily found. You can do this digitally using folders and file names. Alternatively, if you have hard copies of your research data, you will need a portfolio using file separators with an index at the front that outlines what is inside. You must also remember to keep a reference of where information has been found.

There are many ways that data can be stored. Many researchers prefer electronic formats such as file names and folders stored on a hard drive; if you use this method, be sure to keep backup copies. Paper copies are sometimes easier to work with, but whichever method you use, always keep a backup copy!

---

## Skills Task: **Selecting the right data**

Gather a large amount of information from the internet using different sources on the following topic: 'Do people prefer cats or dogs?'

1. Sort your findings into relevant data sets.
2. Use the cluster analysis method described above.
3. Collate the data, store your findings and back them up.

---

## Project work: **Research for ideas development**

You will be filming a documentary about the services offered by your local community centre. The centre wants you to research what it can do to better support the local community.

Produce a research plan for your topic, using the following headings

- Target audience
- Outcomes of the research
- Research methods and techniques to be used
- Questions for surveys/interviews
- How findings will be recorded

# 8.1 THE CREATIVE PROCESS

The process by which ideas are produced and expressed takes many forms and can vary depending on the medium. Yet whatever the means or method, the creative process will always begin with a concept or idea to be developed. Certain mediums, such as photography or games design, will dictate certain working practices, because there are accepted ways of working and specific types of documentation, such as mood boards and storyboards, that are necessary to complete production work. You will need to be aware of these requirements before you start the creative process, as they may impact on the feasibility of your ideas.

## INSPIRATION

Inspiration is the process of mental stimulation that drives you to do something creative. It is generally the start of the creative process and may come through a sudden, novel thought or idea, or develop from existing ideas, designs or products. For example, many films are based on books or true-life events. With today's creative technologies, the internet and multimedia landscape, inspiration can come from almost anywhere – many films today are also inspired by video games!

In the context of digital media design, inspiration will generally develop from the ideas, concepts and design goals expressed in the client brief. Designers will take these instructions and research around the ideas and concepts until they have an idea. Personal inspiration will still play a role, however, and designers will often build upon the ideas in the brief, using their own sources of inspiration and personal experiences to come up with the final idea.

Designers will often take inspiration from those that have come before them, meaning that they will research other artists and designers to see how they have approached similar ideas. You should always be careful with plagiarism when doing this type of research; you should approach it as a source of inspiration and use your own creativity to build from there. When responding to a brief you may also use research into other artists and designers to show how a successful idea has been approached previously, and so use this research as supporting material for your idea. Other genres and design movements may also provide you with sources of inspiration.

## IMMERSION AND EXPLORATION

Whether you have been given a client brief or are choosing to begin a project of your own, using **immersion** and exploration are both effective ways to ignite inspiration.

Immersion is a process by which you deeply involve yourself in a certain atmosphere or environment relevant to the design project you are working on. For example, if you are working for a local maritime museum that has commissioned you to design a website, you may want to spend a day or

**Immersion** placing yourself within the real-world environment that directly relates to or reflects your idea, concept or design process

**Link**

See Chapter 7, pages 76–77, more information on methods of storing data.

so within that environment, as immersion is one way of gaining a **critical understanding** of the product or service that your client provides. From a creative perspective, you may wish to immerse yourself in a type of design movement to get an understanding and appreciation of their approach.

This process of regularly providing specific stimuli allows your ideas to begin reflecting the environments and inputs you have been exposed to. You can then collect these ideas in either a physical portfolio or as electronic data stored in individual folders, as explained in the previous chapter.

**Creative exploration** and critical understanding will both stimulate inspiration. Searching for resources and information allows you to explore a wide range of ideas, practices and techniques from different sources, such as the internet, libraries or even talking to peers. You need not have a definite idea when you start your explorations, although it is likely you will be working from a client brief as a starting point and so will already have a rough outline of what the outcome needs to consist of.

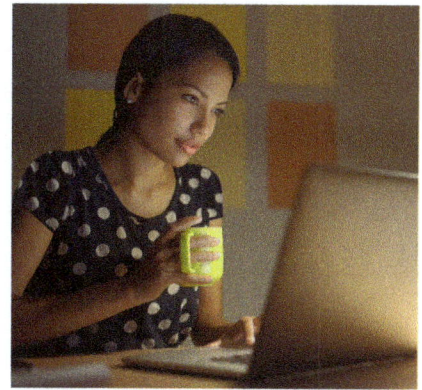

**Fig 8.1** Isolation can allow the creative spark to ignite

## ISOLATION

While not always suitable for everyone, many creative people work alone in order to be creative without interruptions or external influences. Spending time alone can allow your ideas to develop or spark inspiration, which you can then share with others to continue the creative process, so allowing others to provide you with an insight into whether your ideas are practical or workable. Alternatively, you may want to brainstorm with colleagues and then distil your ideas in **isolation**.

## ITERATION

As discussed in Chapter 2, many digital media products are developed through multiple versions or 'iterations'. **Iterative design** is a cyclical creative process whereby design prototypes are tested, analysed and refined, based on the results of the testing.

Iterative design is often used in web and games design. When it comes to developing ideas, a number of prototypes are created, all of which are developed and refined over time, based on analysis of the suitability or functionality of each iteration. For example, if you were working on a game, you might build prototype environments that can then be developed and adapted based on testing. In this example, it is important to continue to be aware of technological advancements in case there is something that should be implemented in your design after the initial planning phase.

Iterative idea creation is an on-going process that should hopefully result in improvements in the quality and/or functionality of a design concept. It also allows for changes to be made in the early stages of the creative process when costs are lower.

**Critical understanding** active engagement in analytical and independent thought. An ability to express an informed response

**Creative exploration** exploring different ideas and concepts within a design context

**Isolation** working alone, away from outside influences

**Iterative design** making many different prototypes of the same concept in order to develop it further

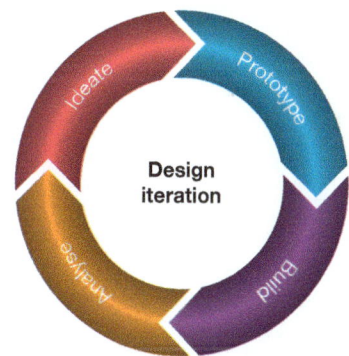

**Fig 8.2** Iterative design is a cyclical creative process

## Skills Task: **The creative process**

In groups, produce a short client brief from an online publishing company that wants to launch a new website about either home interior designs, motor racing or fashion and photography. Different groups should create different briefs. Then exchange your briefs and in your groups discuss and report on how you would generate ideas through:

**1.** Immersion          **2.** Exploration          **3.** Iteration.

Consider where/how you would immerse yourself, where/how you would explore for ideas and how you would iterate.

### Top Tip

The creative process is a very personal choice – so remember, what works best for one person may not work for somebody else. Experiment with different processes to discover what is best for you.

# 8.2 TECHNIQUES FOR GENERATING AND DEVELOPING IDEAS

There are many practical techniques you can use to develop and record ideas, such as creating mood boards, scripts and storyboards.

The methods you choose to record ideas will in part depend on the medium in which you are working. For example, if you are working in the **moving image** sector, you will have to follow set processes, such as following health and safety procedures and producing planning documents for the cast and crew to use. For this you will be required to produce standardised documentation, such as scripts and storyboards, and you may also need to provide a risk assessment and a call sheet that lets everyone know where they need to be at certain times. Producing this kind of documentation will help you refine your ideas into what is practical and feasible for the project.

Some mediums often require solitary work and so generating ideas can take more personalised formats. A photographer, for example, may have an idea for a project and can create a mood board that reflects their ideas and outlines design elements.

Whatever medium you are working in, you need to make sure that you keep the client and the end user in mind at all times.

> **Moving image** an area of creative practice which includes video, animation and documentary filmmaking

## INDIVIDUAL VS. GROUP WORKING

The type of project and the team of people you are working with will dictate working patterns and processes. There are times when developing ideas in isolation will be necessary, as certain aspects of the project cannot be worked on by many people at once. Working alone means that you can work without interference, although it can place extra pressure on the creative process because you are solely responsible for the outcome. At other times the creative process will require working with others. You may find that working individually allows you more freedom to draw upon your own personal experiences and cultural connections, that you may not feel comfortable sharing in a group.

Sometimes individuals are selected to work on certain parts of a project based on their skillset. For example, a graphic artist may be required to work

**Fig 8.3** Many different skills can be required as part of a production process

on images while a writer produces a narrative. Often individual work will be informed by the overall group process or dynamic, so it is important that you are able to follow instructions and understand the intentions of others.

Working in groups has the benefit of the support of others and the opportunity to discuss ideas, although sometimes too many ideas and too much input can become confusing and cause people to lose focus. Different projects will require different approaches. Some will require working alone taking photographs, others may involve a large crew including camera operators, set designers and sound technicians. It is best to decide in advance how a project will be tackled and how roles and responsibilities should be defined and allocated.

## BRAINSTORMING

Brainstorming is a way of generating ideas for a product. It can be a collaborative process that lets individuals share ideas and allows ideas to be discussed. There are many methods of brainstorming that can be used, such as word or visual association, or role playing.

A commonly used brainstorming process is SCAMPER, which is an acronym containing a number of action verbs, designed to prompt creative responses:

**S**ubstitute – remove and replace part of the current idea or content
**C**ombine – join or force together two parts of your ideas or content
**A**dapt – change part of your original idea or concept so it works better
**M**odify – arbitrarily change attributes (for example, size, colour) of the idea or content you are working on
**P**ut to another use – challenge the original idea or intention of your content
**E**liminate – remove any parts of your idea or design; reduce it to its core functionality
**R**everse – modify the order in which your ideas or content is arranged

### Skills Task: **Brainstorming**

You have been asked to design an application that allows you to draw text and images on photographs then share them with friends. To start, you need to think about what the interface will look like.

In small groups, brainstorm ideas. For each idea you think of, run through the SCAMPER process. Some of the actions will not be relevant, but challenge yourselves to use as many as you can for as many ideas as you can.

## DRAWING AND SKETCHING

Physical design techniques, such as drawing and sketching allow for the visualisation of a project before work begins. Beginning with sketches is the best way to start visualising an idea or concept, as these are rough drafts that can be changed and adapted over time. Once the sketches are moving in the right direction, you can start to draw your ideas in more detail. This will allow anyone working with your designs to visualise your work appropriately.

Sketchbooks are a visual means of storing your inspiration, drawings and experimentation and can be adapted and improved based on research findings, such as potential user reviews or feedback from peers.

## MIND MAPS

Mind maps are used in many creative industries and are a means of recording a range of creative ideas in one place. The centre of the mind map often contains a key word or concept. From that central concept you draw lines and add other key words or concepts to aid creative thought and expand a creative concept. You will rarely use all of these key words or concepts, but the process can often help to spark ideas and discussions.

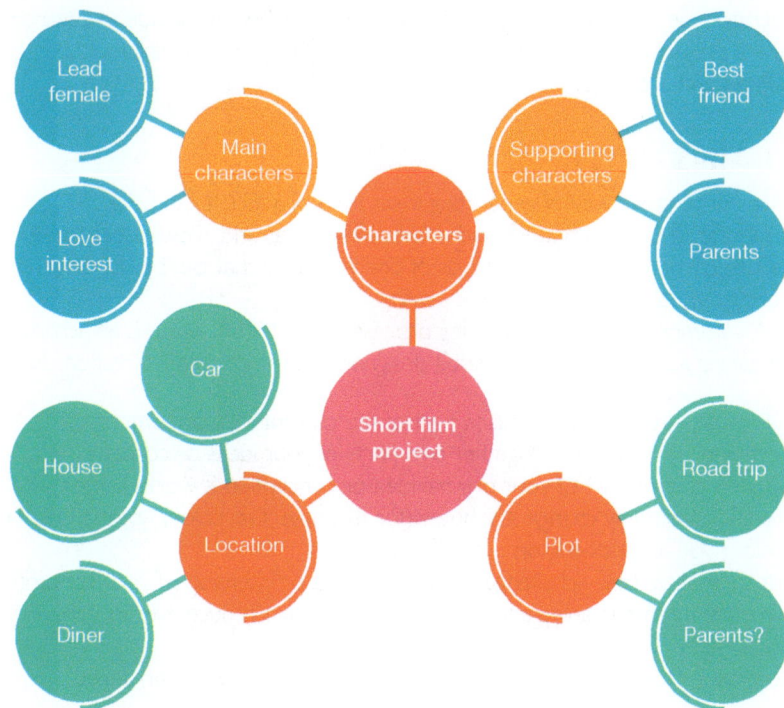

**Fig 8.4** Mind map for a short film project

## MOOD BOARDS

**Fig 8.5** An example of a mood board

Mood boards gather materials, either physical or digital, on content, style, colour, typography and other creative elements in a collage of images relating to the chosen idea or concept. You can source these from the internet or cuttings from magazines – wherever you find inspiration. A mood board gives people a feel for the project, generates a 'mood' or atmosphere, thereby helping others to understand your thought processes.

Mood boards are traditionally created by literally cutting and pasting clippings from print media such as magazines. There are now many online sites that allow you to store these digitally, such as Canva, Roomstyler and Milanote. Mood boards are commonly used in the creative arts and increasingly in disciplines such as photography and interactive media.

### Top Tip

Practical design techniques and outcomes vary for different projects, as do ways of working. Before you start a project, look at what is needed and what your required outcome is. What will you need to produce? How many people will you need to get involved? How will you allocate roles within the group?

# 8.3 SORTING AND ORGANISING IDEAS

The creative process generates many materials. This means you must be organised and regularly sort through them for relevance, discarding those that are not useful or are leading you in the wrong direction. It is easy to become overwhelmed, so a disciplined approach will always serve you well. You may want to use cloud storage and document sharing that would enable iterative ideation and allow you to share your ideas with others. You could also use Google Docs™, Dropbox, Slack, Evernote or Pinterest.

Once you have sorted your ideas they can be moved forward to the next stage of the project, and you can start developing appropriate documentation and prototypes.

## STORYBOARDS AND ANIMATICS

This is the stage after idea generation and development. **Storyboards** are used within certain mediums, such as moving image production and games design, to visually represent the concept or narrative. They are also used by camera operators, directors or designers when creating the product.

Creating a storyboard can be a long process as it contains both artwork/images and text, such as camera movements, edits and shot duration. Often professional companies use trained storyboard artists, as this is quite a creative discipline; however, amateurs will often produce their own.

It is important to draft storyboards in detail and clearly in order for them to be used as valid working documents. Working in pencil will make drafting and amendments easier and will save time by avoiding starting again from scratch. There are templates available for different disciplines, all of which allow space for relevant information and images to be added.

Many storyboards are created in black and white, as they are mainly required to provide a pictorial representation of the action taking place and do not dictate colour, background or set design. You may wish to produce colour copies of these if working on other mediums, but it is not always required.

An **animatic** is a digital, interactive storyboard format that allows you to produce your ideas in a more dynamic way. To create animatics, typically storyboards will be brought into an editing program, such as PowerProduction or SceneWriter Pro, and then 'cut' together with the timings and pace of the production added in. They can also include some basic sound effects and other sounds, such as dialogue recordings or soundtracks. As with traditional storyboards they can be black and white or colour, depending on what is required.

## CREATING PROTOTYPES

Creating **prototypes** is often an important part of the development process of digital media products. These are part of the iterative design process and allow for changes, as you can see what is and what is not working. Prototypes are not as well developed as the finished product, but should still contain some functionality and interactivity to allow end users to test them.

When you create a prototype you need to integrate your design ideas and concepts and make use of the skills and techniques required for end product construction. In essence, you will be creating a prototype in the same way that you would a finished product. However, be careful not to rely too heavily on a prototype, as you may need to discard it if it does not work well or if your client decides on a new or better concept.

**Storyboard** a graphic organiser that consists of illustrations or images displayed in sequence for the purpose of pre-visualising a motion picture, animation, motion graphic or interactive media sequence

**Animatic** a preliminary version of a moving image production, produced by filming or animating successive sections of a storyboard and adding sound and/or effects

**Prototype** an early sample, model, or release of a product built to test a concept or process

**Sitemap** diagram or model of a website's content that shows how the content is organised and how different content elements relate to one another
**Wireframe** an image or collection of images developed from the sitemap which show elements of a website or web page

# SITEMAPS AND WIREFRAMES

**Sitemaps** and **wireframes** are used to visualise the content of a website; they are produced after ideas generation but before you create the site.

- A sitemap shows how the web pages will flow from one to another; this is a sort of categorisation of pages showing which page relates to which.
- A wireframe is a visual representation of the content and layout of a particular web page on a website. It is more of a design element than the sitemap and will allow you to structure your ideas into a logical order.

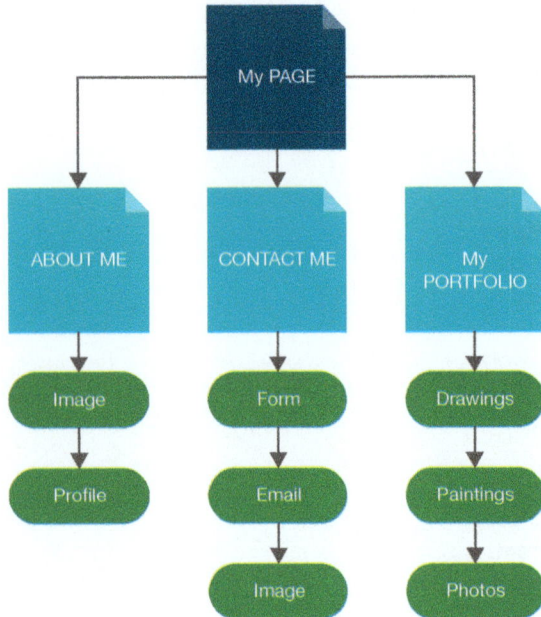

Fig 8.6 Sitemaps are used to visualise the content of a website before you create the site

Fig 8.7 Drafting your layout saves time and avoids potential mistakes

## Skills Task: **Developing ideas documents**

Choose **one** of the following tasks to complete, depending on your preferred medium.

1. Produce a storyboard and (if possible) an animatic for a moving image production.
2. Produce a mood board for a photography project on a subject of your choice.
3. Produce a sitemap and wireframes for a new website.

## Further references

- *Breakthrough Thinking: A Guide to Creative Thinking and Idea Generation* (Thomas Vogel, 2014)
- *Where Good Ideas Come From: The Natural History of Innovation* (Steven Johnson, 2010)

## Project work: **Ideas development**

Working in small groups, produce a new animated series for teenagers and young adults to be shown on YouTube as a series of 5-minute shorts.

1. Generate ideas using brainstorming, mind maps, mood boards and any other techniques you have learned.
2. Develop these ideas by creating storyboards for each 5-minute film in your series. Present them to the class and discuss their strengths and weaknesses.
3. Refine your storyboards based on the feedback from the class and, if possible, create animatics for your storyboards and show them to the class.

# 9 Evaluating and testing ideas

## Learning Aims

By the end of this chapter you will be able to:

- Understand different types of evaluation and feedback
- Understand how to apply feedback to ideas
- Refine ideas and designs in response to feedback
- Undertake appropriate testing in response to feedback

# 9.1 TYPES AND PURPOSES OF EVALUATION AND FEEDBACK

There are many ways in which to gather feedback, which can in turn be used to inform your evaluation process. The purpose of evaluation is to explore the ideas you have generated and the work you have produced, so you can identify areas that have worked well (strengths) and areas that could be improved upon (weaknesses). Many individuals and organisations like to do a **SWOT analysis** on their work, looking at the Strengths, Weaknesses, Opportunities and Threats to their ideas or products; this allows them to reflect on what is going well and what can be improved. This technique can also be applied to skills that you have gained while studying, allowing you to consider how well you are managing to apply these skills to your work and whether you may need to improve on them.

The purpose of gaining feedback is to help you to make judgements about the design decisions you have made, it is a process of reflection and evaluation that will help you further develop your ideas or make necessary changes to your plans.

It is important to remember that the evaluative process is supposed to be a positive one and should assist you in improving. Try not to take any feedback you receive too personally and instead apply what you have been told to making things better. You should also ensure that any feedback you give is constructive and objective, so as to assist the person you are feeding back to.

## DISCUSSIONS

Discussions are an effective way of gathering feedback from either an individual or a group of people. It is important that you are prepared to record the outcome of discussions, so either make notes on what is said or record the discussion in an audio or audiovisual format that you can then review later and make notes on. Questioning can be more or less structured, as with any research interview, with open or closed and follow-up questions.

If you are leading or chairing a meeting, it is important to ensure that you keep control of the environment at all times and make sure that the discussion moves forward in a constructive manner. To do this, first set a **meeting agenda** that lists the desired outcomes for the discussion and then record the conclusions reached, the **action points** agreed and who will implement those actions. Depending on the situation, you can then make a more formal written record of the meeting – this is known as **meeting minutes**.

**SWOT analysis** method of evaluating a design or product by focusing on its Strengths (S), Weaknesses (W), Opportunities (O) and Threats (T)

**Meeting agenda** document showing the key topics for discussion and desired outcomes of a meeting

**Action points** actions to be implemented, often agreed in a meeting

**Meeting minutes** a formal written record of what occurred in a meeting and the outcomes, decisions or action points

**Digital photography** photography where images are captured, digitised and stored as a computer file

You will need a stimulus or focus for the discussion, such as materials for the members of the discussion group to review and talk about. These could include a storyboard if working on a moving image project, some rough shots for **digital photography** or the wireframe/sitemap for a website or interactive media project. You must also ensure that the discussion remains focused; if it seems to be going off topic, try and draw things back to the main focus and use questioning to draw out responses from others. You could do this by setting (time) limits for discussion on a particular topic and introducing a new one from your agenda, or passing a question over to another person in the group who has not had much input.

**Fig 9.1** Discussions are an essential means of sharing ideas

## Link

See Chapter 7, for more information on focus groups and surveys.

## FOCUS GROUPS AND SURVEYS

Focus groups and surveys are a means of conducting research into an original idea or concept and assist with development. They can also be very useful when reviewing ideas or a design, and provide insights into how well your work engages the target audience and fulfils the client brief.

Focus groups, in particular, are commonly used within the digital media industry. Many film, television and game production companies hold 'test screenings' with a selected audience, who they ask to provide feedback on a rough edit of the product. The results can have huge effects on the final edit and film endings have been changed dramatically as a result of focus group feedback. For example, the ending of the original *Bladerunner* movie was changed to a more upbeat version after the first version of the film got negative reviews from test audiences in the USA.

Surveys can be used effectively with larger groups of potential users of your digital media design and can provide you with valuable feedback on your ideas and your work. These can be printed surveys posted or digital versions emailed out to people, often using online survey tools, such as SurveyGizmo or SurveyMonkey. Remember to make sure that the questions within your survey are focused on what it is you want to know and that the results will provide you with valuable information that you can apply to improve your design. You should use a range of open and closed questions within your survey, but remember that when you give someone time and space to offer comments they may lose focus. Try to maintain that focus within the wording of your questions – it will help not to make the survey too long, as people will lose interest. You should think about what you want to know then ask people targeted questions based on that requirement.

## USER TESTING

User testing is commonly used by the gaming and interactive media sectors to gain valuable feedback from a representative sample of potential users of the product.

There are different ways that user testing can be carried out, either remotely or under observation. During an observed test, participants interact with the design while observers watch, listen and take notes. **Remote testing** requires testers to complete a questionnaire or report that will provide the media producer with feedback. **Screen capture software** can be used so that you can effectively record the user's experience on-screen. This is a very effective tool for reviewing how a user moves through a website or interprets the instructions to a game. You may find that something you considered intuitive is not so for the user, and you may find that different users have different interpretations of your design. All of this is useful for refining your ideas.

As with other testing methods, you will need to ensure that you have a clear idea of what the outcome of the testing needs to be. However, be careful that you do not introduce bias into the testing procedure by influencing or 'leading' users through their experience of your design, whether through your verbal instructions and responses to participants or non-verbal reactions (such as wincing if a participant makes a mistake). In all that you say and do, you must remain neutral and objective.

## EVALUATING FEEDBACK

When evaluating feedback it can be difficult to be objective about what has been said about your designs. Here are some key questions to ask:

- What were your purposes when gathering the feedback?
- Have you asked the right questions?
- Is what people are saying valid and useful? (Relate their responses back to your design goals/client brief/ purposes of gathering feedback.)
- Are the changes suggested reasonable and workable? For example, are they affordable? (Relate responses back to the technical or functional limitations of the design/client brief.)

Use careful **selection**/**de-selection** techniques, such as sorting and sifting, to decide what feedback to act upon. Then make changes based on the majority view of your feedback sample – remember: it is not feasible to make all suggested changes.

By carefully reviewing feedback against criteria such as those above, you can ensure that any changes you implement are likely to be the best for your design. It may make sense to rank feedback, or assign it points based on how many people suggested something. This can be a useful tool when selecting what to implement. Although it is always important to consider feedback constructively, you should make sure you implement changes that suit the design, your budget, your client and your end user.

**Remote testing** testing a product when the participant and the tester are in different locations

**Screen capture software** software that enables remote testing through recording (capturing) what the participant does on their computer

**Selection/de-selection** the process of choosing what to include and leave out of your research or feedback findings

## Top Tip

When evaluating feedback, make a chart or checklist to record your findings. Prioritise the information that is useful and leave out information that is not relevant.

Choose a website for a local retailer or service provider that provides products or services to both adults and children. Research how well this website works. Then, working in groups:

1. Create a survey for potential customers to complete, telling you what they think about the website. Use a variety of question types.
2. Conduct observations of classmates using the site and record your findings.
3. Choose an appropriate method to record any other customer feedback.
4. Report your findings to the class.

Likes

Criticisms

Questions

Ideas

**Fig 9.2** Feedback capture grid

# 9.2 APPLYING FEEDBACK

## MAKING DECISIONS ABOUT FEEDBACK

Once you have gathered and evaluated feedback, you need to decide whether to apply that feedback to your work. Your decisions should be based on the following factors:

- the frequency and consistency of the feedback
- the feasibility of applying suggested changes
- analysis of cost vs. benefit – whether the work/effort/expense is worth it when considering what you will get in return.

If users point out some major faults or omissions that would undermine your design's success then you may have no choice but to apply their feedback. If the feedback you received does not seem relevant to your particular product then you may choose not to act upon it. If the suggested changes are rather minor and can be achieved relatively easily then you should probably apply those changes.

For example, if 25 per cent of people surveyed indicated you should change the colour of one of the buttons on your website to make it more prominent, you would likely implement this, even if the other 75 per cent of people did not mention the colour at all. However, if the same 25 per cent then requested the button be moved, which may be a much harder change to implement, you may evaluate further to see if the change is really needed.

## REFINING IDEAS AND DESIGNS

If consumer feedback is sought early enough, you can apply it to your initial ideas and designs. By gaining feedback at a very early stage, designers can save valuable time and money during the development process. Refining ideas is easier than reworking an almost completed product. Designs or storyboards can be redeveloped to bring them more in line with the requirements of the target audience. For example, an animated character could be tested with test audiences prior to any work being completed. If audiences do not like something about the character then this change could be implemented in future designs and storyboards. As with all feedback, whatever changes you apply, they must be done as a result of careful and considered evaluation of the comments.

## TESTING IN INTERACTIVE DESIGN

When working with interactive designs, such as websites and games, it is often best to create a prototype of your chosen product for potential consumers to interact with in order to gain feedback. Prototypes are less time consuming to produce than moving straight to making the final product and they can be easily changed and adapted. To get appropriate critical feedback it may be beneficial to produce a number of different prototypes with different elements, in this way allowing users to compare and contrast ideas and decide which is best.

You can give your participants, or 'test subjects', a number of prompts to work from that will allow them to express themselves. For example, ask them what they like, what they would add if they had unlimited choice, or allow them to make a 'wish list' of all the things they would ideally like to see. You could do this by providing them with flashcards to fill in or by holding focus groups or discussions.

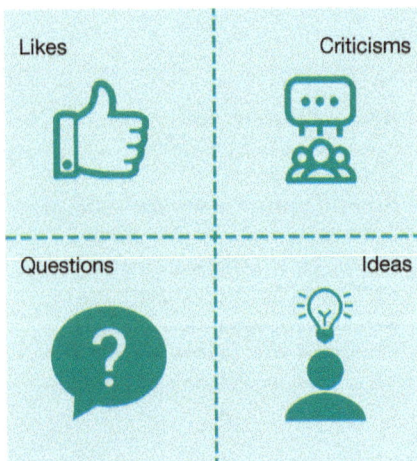

You will need to be systematic about your choices of test subjects and ensure that the people you ask to test your product fit the profile of your ideal user. If you are making a design for children, for example, there is no point testing it on retired people.

Finally, make sure you are asking the right questions so that the responses you receive will be appropriate. Take a neutral approach to what is said; a critical response is not a criticism of you, rather an opportunity to make your product better. Below is an example of a simple document you could use to capture feedback.

## DOCUMENTING EVALUATION AND TESTING PHASES

When gathering feedback, whether face-to-face or remotely, it is critical that you keep detailed, organised records of your findings. You will need to go through a number of stages:

- Stage 1: Design feedback documents for your test subjects to use – these could be surveys or simply a list of questions.
- Stage 2: Find a method of recording your findings, in order of usefulness and relevance.
- Stage 3: Finally, consider how you will implement any changes that you have decided are suitable or relevant. This could be in the form of a chart or graph, a 'to do' list or even a pictorial representation of what it is you want to achieve once you have implemented changes.

### Top Tip

The most important thing to do when undertaking any type of feedback process is to ensure that you are not offended by what people have to say about your work. It is hard not to feel strongly about something that you have worked hard on designing and making, but taking an objective view on any feedback is a critical part of the design process.

### Project work: **Implementing changes following feedback**

You have received the following feedback on the design of your website's homepage.

'The colours of the buttons are boring.'

'The navigation menu is too difficult to find.'

'The main image is too big and distracting.'

'The font isn't very exciting; I'd like it to be in Comic Sans.'

'When I view on a mobile browser I can't see the images.'

'The colour of the buttons blends into the background, a bright colour would be better.'

'I have to scroll for ages to find the menu.'

'The font size is too small.'

1. Review the feedback and decide which elements to implement using the techniques discussed in this chapter.
2. Map out how you will implement your planned changes.
3. Keep a record of the changes you have made and why you have made them.

## Case study: **CBS Television City Research Center**

Television shows, like any other product, are rigorously tested with audiences to ensure that the people who will be viewing them like what they see. You may have heard of the term 'pilot' in relation to television shows. This is a first attempt at a television show that will then be tested with audiences. Sometimes this is the first episode of the show that will be broadcast on television; however, many pilots are not broadcast. This is because a lot can change from a pilot – actors might be replaced while storylines and characters can radically alter, so the original first attempt would be a terrible introduction to the show. Some pilots that were not broadcast can be found on YouTube.

CBS, an American television channel, tests their programmes in a unique way – by making use of tourists in Las Vegas. At the CBS Television City Research Center, people have the opportunity to view pilot shows from CBS, MTV, Nickelodeon and other networks. They also test commercials, websites and technology-based products, such as the Nintendo Wii™, Microsoft Xbox 360™, Apple iPhone and Dell notebook computers.

CBS is doing a form of user testing; viewers are provided with a test pad that allows them to track their emotions and engagement while watching the show. If they do not like a certain character, they can register their displeasure while that character is on the screen. By taking 'real-time' readings the network can see exactly what is and is not working on a pilot show and then implement changes as they see fit. If everyone in an audience dislikes one character, CBS could decide to remove the character entirely, although that might be a short-sighted decision if it is not the character everyone dislikes but the actor. To fully evaluate what feedback should be implemented, CBS also uses a 15-minute survey after the show has finished. This is also on the touch pad, but offers more qualitative data as to why the user responded in a certain way; for example, why did they dislike the actor? By using a combination of different techniques to gather feedback, CBS can be confident that they are evaluating the feedback correctly and implementing changes as needed.

**Fig 9.3** CBS carry out user testing during pilot episodes of their series to implement changes and improvements for subsequent episodes.

# 10 Design theories

## Learning Aims

By the end of this chapter you will be able to:
- Understand semiotics and semantics
- Understand aesthetics, unity harmony and balance
- Understand form and function

# 10.1 SEMIOTICS AND SEMANTICS

Any designed object has to communicate with its users and audience on a number of levels. This includes everything from a printer button on a website to a compass in a complex game world. In each case the core principle of 'user communication' is the same: users have to know what to do and the designer has to help them do it. To ensure this understanding, the designer uses 'signs' to indicate meaning and a number of tools and methods. The core principles behind how signs and these tools work are called **semiotics** and **semantics**. In other instances, users are passive observers, for example, of a film or visual image. In these instances, the creators of these will still have used semiotics and semantics to convey meaning, whether that is emotion or user instructions.

## SEMIOTICS

Semiotics is the study of signs, **symbols**, their use and interpretation. This covers all aspects of communication and language from symbols such as signs and colours, to gestures and facial expressions. The word derives from the Greek *sēmeiotikos*, meaning 'of signs'. Understanding these signs underlies all aspects of communication, from reading road signs to reading body language.

## SEMANTICS

Semantics is the study of meaning. When a dictionary defines a word by what it actually means, that is a semantic explanation. Semantics is considered a subset of semiotics and often forms part of a **semiotic system**.

There are two main types of semantics:

- Logical semantics relate to meaning defined by logic, for example, what a word means in the dictionary definition. Logical semantics in digital design, for example, could relate to the words used to guide users through a website using basic navigation such as 'Click here'.
- Lexical semantics relate to how word meanings are interpreted and the relationships between them. For example, the word 'crash' might initially bring to mind a car accident, but it could also mean the sound of cymbals hitting each other.

In summary, semiotics and semantics are how we make sense of the world and how ideas and thoughts are communicated. This in turn impacts on how we make decisions and choices.

> **Top Tip**
>
> Always be careful that a sign you are using in one market is valid in another market. For example, the 'thumbs up' symbol means something good in many Western countries, but is offensive in other parts of the world.

> **Semiotics** the study of signs and symbols and their use and interpretation
> **Semantics** a subset of semiotics that refers to language
> **Symbol** a sign that does not resemble anything but conveys an idea
> **Semiotic system** a system of sign and symbols that work together

## SYMBOLISM AND ASSOCIATION

To see how semiotics and semantics apply to digital design, we need to understand symbolism and **association**:

- Symbolism refers to the way we use signs to represent ideas or qualities.
- Association is what we associate signs with.

Charles Sanders Peirce was an American philosopher and mathematician who also contributed much to modern semiotics theory. Peirce classified signs into three categories: Icon, Index and Symbol.

### Icons

A graphical **icon** is a sign created to resemble something. An icon could be illustrative, meaning it shows something very literally, for example, a printer icon showing an actual printer. Alternatively, an icon could be **diagrammatic**, meaning it shows a representation or diagram of something, for example, a Wi-Fi icon in a mobile application.

### Index

An **index** is a sign that has a direct link with the object it is related to. An index often relates to a sensory feature or something that will happen.

### Symbols

A symbol has no logical link to what it represents but manages to convey an idea clearly. Many digital symbols operate in this way and help users navigate through complex procedures.

Fig 10.1 Symbols for a printer and speaker volume

Fig 10.2 Examples of digital symbols

> ### Skills Task: **Signs in your local environment**
>
> Spend some time walking around your local environment – this could be your school, your home or both. Make a list of things that 'communicate' with you. This could be as simple as an exit sign or as complex as a control panel on a device. Classify the objects into semantic and semiotic signs.

## ASSOCIATION

As well as using signs and symbols to convey ideas we often use association. For example, we see icons and symbols that may already exist in the real world, or those that form part of a culture reference, for example, colour associations often work in this way.

Other teachers of semiotics, such as Ferdinand de Saussure, define a sign in a much simpler way, namely that a sign is a combination of:

1. a **signifier**, meaning the form which the sign takes
2. the **signified**, meaning the concept that the sign seeks to represent.

The printer icon from earlier in this section is a good example of this: the signifier is the icon on a computer screen or web page and the signified is the actual printer.

These ideas and concepts are important because any digital product or experience will be full of signs. These may be colour schemes for branding, navigational aids, buttons and, simply, written words that help to explain and guide the user. Understanding these signs is the key to creating a strong experience for your user and making sure they can achieve what they want to achieve.

**Association** a way of interpreting a sign through making links with other known objects or information
**Icon** a graphical sign that resembles the thing it represents
**Diagrammatic** a graphical icon that shows a diagram or representation of something
**Index** a sign that has a direct link to the object it represents and often has a sensory aspect
**Signifier** the form that the sign takes
**Signified** the concept that the sign seeks to represent

In this section you have explored signs and how they communicate meaning and guide understanding. In the next section you will explore the fundamentals of visual design.

# 10.2 AESTHETICS, UNITY, HARMONY AND BALANCE

## THE GOLDEN SECTION RATIO

Throughout history designers and artists have used a simple method called the golden section ratio to create things that are visually appealing and 'look right'. This involves the use of a rectangle with the ratio of 1:1.618.

Scholars have found evidence that this method dates as far back as the 5th century BC. Renaissance artists, such as Leonardo Da Vinci used this method to create paintings and sculptures such as *The Last Supper*. German psychologist Gustav Flechner found that people from different cultures tended to prefer a '**golden ratio**' rectangle to other rectangles.

The golden section ratio can also be found in the natural world, such as human proportions and the growth patterns of plants and animals; for example, the spiral shapes of shells show a system of growth that expands in golden section ratio.

**Aesthetics** principles relating to beauty
**Golden ratio** a visual method for dividing space

**Fig 10.3** The golden section ratio shown as a nautilus shell

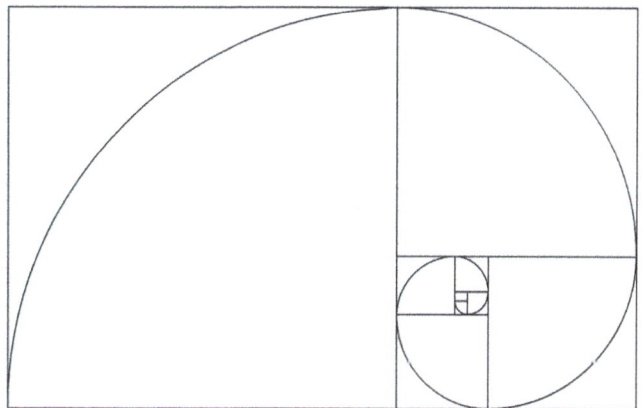

The human body also has golden section proportions, and this may explain why we prefer this ratio. The Greek scholar Marcus Vitruvius advised that temples and buildings should be built using human proportions, as they were inherently 'correct'. This approach became known as the Vitruvius Canon and was used widely by artists such as

Leonardo da Vinci, who drew a famous image of the human body with the golden spiral superimposed over the top. Architects also interpreted the Vitruvian Canon to build Notre Dame Cathedral in the 12th century and modernist buildings in the 1930s.

## Skills Task: **Construct a golden section rectangle**

1. Begin with a square.
2. Divide the square down the middle.
3. Divide the right-hand section by drawing a line from the exact centre of the square to the top right corner.
4. Using this diagonal as a radius, use a compass to draw a curved line outside the initial square until you reach the bottom right corner.
5. Connect the bottom edge of the square with your curved line.
6. Once you have completed this, try to apply the rectangle to a favourite photograph or artwork to see if the golden section applies in any way. You may be surprised!

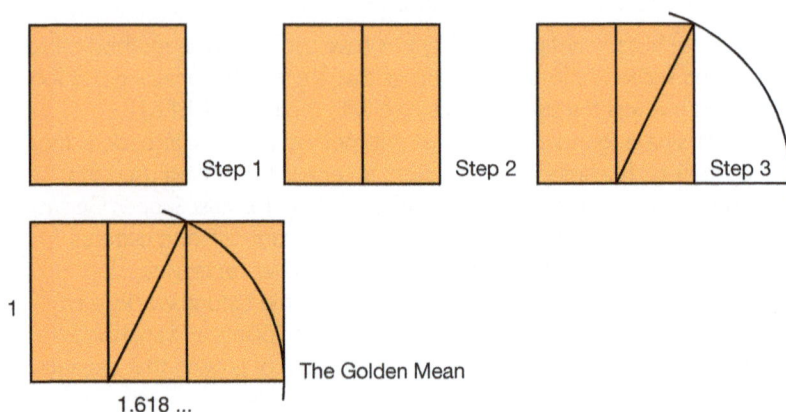

Step 1    Step 2    Step 3

1

1.618 ...

The Golden Mean

**Fig 10.4** Constructing a golden section rectangle

**Balance** the way that elements appear in a visual design
**Harmony** how a visual design appears to 'work'
**Symmetrical balance** the way symmetry is used in a visual design; also known as static balance

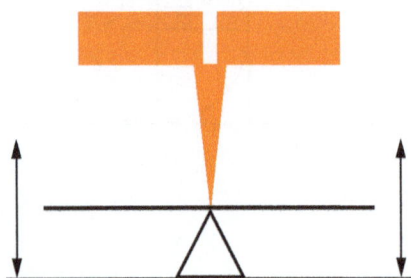

**Fig 10.5** Symmetrical (or static) balance

## BALANCE AND HARMONY

**Balance** refers to the resolution of tension caused by opposing visual forces or elements, for example, graphic designers balance these forces to provide a sense of **harmony** in layout designs. Balance is essential to make a design harmonious and visually appealing. This is because one of the most fundamental principles of visual perception is the need to balance one visual force with another. Alternatively, if a graphic design project is intended to create a sense of chaos, the graphic designer would deliberately disrupt the balance to create a disorganised appeal.

There are two main types of balance: symmetrical and dynamic.

### Symmetrical balance
**Symmetrical (or static) balance** occurs when visual designers place the key elements of a design around a central point. All the other elements are then equally arranged around the central point and a sense of balance is achieved.

## Dynamic balance

Dynamic balance involves designers creating tensions between visual elements in order to create a sense of movement of energy. In this example the elements are placed to the left, creating a tension in the visual design.

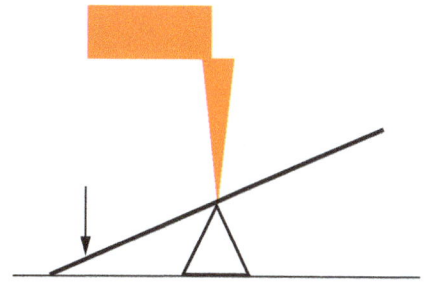

**Fig 10.6** Dynamic balance

---

## Skills Task: **Exploring balance in an image**

Select a painting, photograph or graphic design. Identify where the balance of the image lies: is it symmetrical or dynamic? If the balance is symmetrical, mask parts of the image by placing pieces of paper over the edges. Consider:

- What happens to the image?
- Does it start to feel uncomfortable? Is your eye is trying to 'correct' the tension?

---

## Dynamic tension

As well as balance, designers may use other techniques when creating visual compositions. **Dynamic tension** is a method where designers use elements within a composition as 'visual signposts' that guide the eye around an image. Photographers often use this technique in order to add interest to static images or to draw the viewer's eye to a specific area.

**Dynamic tension** a method of leading the viewer around a visual design

**Fig 10.7** Dynamic tension can be used to add interest – notice how your eye is 'guided' around the main elements of the image

## Top Tip

People will often describe the balance or harmony of visual compositions by describing physical associations. For example, a viewer of a website may say that everything seems to be 'falling off the bottom of the page' or that it looks 'crowded'. This is because we often describe visual elements according to how we would feel if we were part of the composition. Understanding this can help you understand why certain designs do or do not work.

**Form** how a digital product look and feels to the user
**Function** what a digital product does for the user

## Skills Task: **Researching balance and harmony in images**

Identify some images that have used the methods discussed in this section. A good way to do this is to use transparent paper and place it over the image so you can draw directly onto it. Can you identify a golden section? Are there dynamic tensions at work? Once you have identified the methods, find a similar image that uses the same methods.

## FORM AND FUNCTION

The term **form** refers to the visual aspect of an object while the term **function** refers to what it does. For example, if we take a software product:

- the form relates to the colours, interface and any graphic elements that are incorporated into the design
- the function relates to what the software achieves from the user's perspective.

### Form follows function

Form follows function is a useful principle for digital media product design. It states that the design of any object should be defined or guided above all by its function. Form and all other aspects such as aesthetics are secondary. This approach is commonly used in design projects where the end user completes actions or tasks associated with the product. For example, designers use this method for mobile application development and interface design.

### Form and function working together

It is often said that function needs form in order to ensure design goals are reached. A functional element with no clearly defined form will not engage with a user and as a result they will not interact in the right way. On the other hand, form without function is just a graphic element with no specific use. The role of the designer is to carefully balance both form and function in a way that engages and also informs.

## Skills Task: **Exploring function and form**

Using an application that you are familiar with, examine the interface from the perspective of both form and function. If possible, create some wall space and use sticky notes to display the app functions and the form elements that support the functions.

# 11 Colour theory

# 11.1 COLOUR MEANING AND PSYCHOLOGY

Colour is principally used to add value and meaning to any visual communication. It can be used to harmonise and organise graphic elements and information. When used effectively, colour intensifies a visual message making it much more immediate and identifiable. The considered and appropriate use of colour can increase the speed of comprehension of the image or product, establish emotional themes, and produce instantaneous and memorable associations in the mind of the viewer.

However, colour is not always easy to understand; it is very subjective, as everyone has a favourite! Yet if you can grasp the basics and appreciate the importance of influencing factors, such as culture, environment and association in people's response to colour, you will succeed in using it to enhance your digital projects.

## HOW WE PERCEIVE COLOUR

We perceive colour when our eyes receive signals from the outside world in the form of visible light. Light travels in waves and the distance between the crests of two waves of light is called a **wavelength**. The technical term for a colour is a **hue**. Different wavelengths create different hues within the **visible spectrum** of light. For example, blues have shorter wavelengths than reds.

The eye processes light via a series of receptor cells called **rods** and **cones**, which are located at the back of the eyeball. These send signals to the brain via the **optic nerve**. Rods allow us to distinguish forms in dim light but only in black and white while cones allow us to perceive colour hues. There are three types of cones, which separately perceive red, green and blue light. These cells together allow us to identify millions of colours and to differentiate between them. Some animals can see parts of the light spectrum humans cannot, for example, bees and butterflies see **ultraviolet light**.

## THE PSYCHOLOGICAL EFFECTS OF COLOUR

Colours provoke powerful emotions. The way that people react to colour goes beyond the purely physical response and the psychological aspect of their reaction is often much stronger. For example, the colour lavender is, in sensory terms, simply a light purple. However, if it suggests to you a feeling of nostalgia, then there is a psychological element involved in your response, too.

**Wavelength** the distance between waves of light that determines colour
**Hue** the technical term for a colour
**Visible spectrum** the range of light that humans can see
**Rods** nerve cells in the eyeball that perceive black and white
**Cones** nerve cells in the eyeball that perceive red, blue and green
**Optic nerve** nerve that transmits light signals from the eyeball to the brain
**Ultraviolet (UV) light** an electromagnetic radiation wave

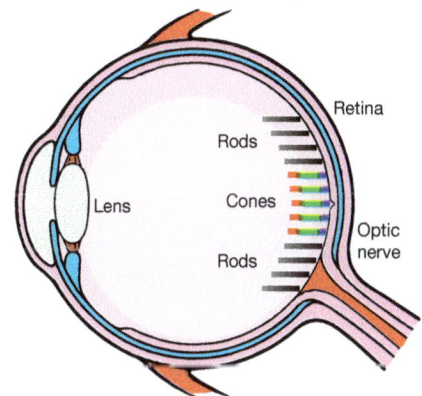

**Fig 11.1** Cross-section of an eyeball showing rods and cones

Humans respond to colour psychologically on various levels and derive meaning from it in various ways; from its associations with nature to links with society's history and culture, and to individual experiences and emotions. Experts agree that universal, cross-cultural perceptions of colour exist, for example, orange means 'warm' and green means 'nature' for almost everyone in the world. However, there are more culturally specific associations, for example, black may represent death in Western societies, but in China white is associated with death.

## COLOURS IN CULTURE

Word association studies using colour samples have demonstrated that most people from the same cultural background will associate given colours with the same ideas, objects and feelings. Show most people in the West a strong red and they will associate it with fire, passion, excitement, blood and danger. They will perceive the temperature of the colour as hot. Show them a sample of a light, bright blue and they will almost certainly associate it with the word 'sky'. Other shades of blue will evoke further typical associations, such as 'sea', 'water', 'clean' and 'calm', and the temperature will usually be perceived as cool. However, research shows that in many eastern countries these associations are not quite the same. Bright blue is also associated with fire, because a very hot flame (a gas flame, for example) can also be this shade of blue. In these cultures only dark blue would be associated with the sea.

Designers therefore need to be aware of the cultural associations of their target users and take these into consideration when making decisions about colour usage. David McCandless has researched how different cultures associate different meanings to colours and created the 'Colours in culture' diagram that you can see online.

### Skills Task: **Associating colours**

Show five friends or family members a selection of different colours and ask them to write down words that they associate with the colours. (If you have friends from a variety of cultural backgrounds, this will make this activity more interesting.) Consider:

1. Do they all use the same words, or are there noticeable differences?
2. Can you identify any cultural differences in the interpretations?
3. Do some interpretations relate to things that are personal to the viewer? For example, sports team colours?

Contrast your results to David McCandless's **colour wheel** from his 'Colours in culture' diagram. Do you see any differences or do your results correspond with his research?

**Colour wheel** a diagram showing the primary, secondary and tertiary colours and their relations to each other

## PERSONAL RESPONSES TO COLOUR

An individual's response to colours may be influenced by a number of factors. How people see colours varies, for example, what one person perceives as turquoise, another person may see as green. Some people also have difficulty distinguishing between red and green (red–green colour blindness).

How people describe colours is also subjective and depends on their personal vocabulary. For example, Person A may describe a hue as 'dark pink' while Person B might say it is 'fuchsia'. Similarly, how people interpret different colours is complex and subjective, so Person A and Person B are unlikely to respond in the same way.

The effect of using a particular colour is never certain, so it is important for designers to have a sound understanding of colour theory so they can use it effectively to elicit the desired response in the majority of viewers/users.

## EMOTIONAL RESPONSES TO COLOUR

Many artists use colour to communicate emotions. A good example is the contrast between Picasso's 'blue period' paintings – considered to convey sadness and melancholy – and his 'rose period' paintings, which are generally associated with happiness. While this is an important aspect of visual communication, it is also important to understand how much of a dominant colour is used in a particular image and where. For example, try to imagine how different the image of the guitar player (Figure 11.2) would be if Picasso had painted the guitar a bright yellow colour, or if the background wall was brilliant white. What would happen if the dominant **colour palette** in the rose period painting (Figure 11.3) was changed to blue? Would the boy appear sadder, or would he seem the same?

> **Top Tip**
>
> When thinking about colours and how they are used in a work or product, try to remember your initial response to the piece – your 'gut feeling'. Usually this first automatic response is the one the majority of viewers will have and is the main one the designer was trying to evoke.

> **Skills Task: Describing colours**

Show five friends or family members a selection of different coloured objects, or pictures of objects, and ask them to describe the colours used and why those colours were used.

1. Do they agree, or are there noticeable differences of opinion?
2. What cultural references do they use to describe the colours?
3. What subjective interpretations do people use when talking about the colours?

# 11.2 CREATING COLOURS AND COMBINATIONS

## PRIMARY COLOURS

The traditional model of colour, known as the 'artist's model', is based on the three primary colours from which all other colours can be created – red, yellow and blue (RYB). However, designers use colour systems with different primary colours when using digital software, for example, the RGB (red, green, blue) colour system.

The colour wheel in Figure 11.4 shows how combinations of the RYB primary colours can be mixed to produce all the other colours. The secondary colours (orange, purple and green) are created by mixing two primary colours together in equal measure, and the tertiary colours (for example, yellow-orange, red-purple, blue-green) are created by mixing a primary colour with a secondary one in equal measure.

**Colour palette** a combination of colours adopted by a client

**Fig 11.2** *The Old Guitarist*, 1903; a painting from Picasso's blue period, oil on panel, The Art Institute of Chicago

**Fig 11.3** *Boy wearing a Collar*, 1905; an example from Picasso's rose period, gouache on board, Private Collection

> **Link**
>
> See later in this chapter, on pages 104–105, for more information on the RGB colour system.

In design, colour is described in three ways:

- by its name
- by how pure it is
- by its value or lightness.

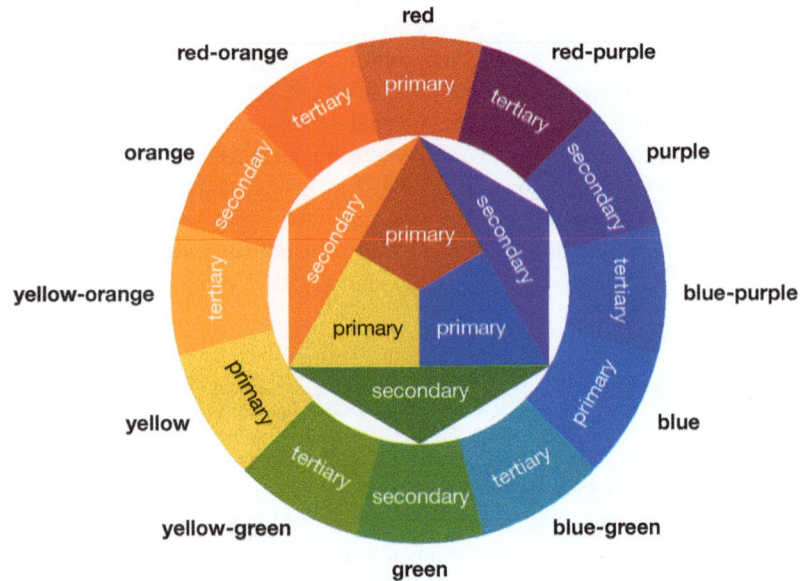

**Fig 11.4** The colour wheel showing the 'artist's model'

**Chroma**  the purity of a hue in relation to grey
**Saturation**  the amount of pure colour in a specific hue
**Intensity**  the brightness or dullness of a hue
**Luminance**  the amount of light
**Shade**  a hue produced by adding black
**Tint**  a hue produced by adding white

The technical term designers use for a colour is 'hue'. For example, although red, pink and terracotta are all reds, they are all different hues distinguished by their **chroma**, **saturation**, **intensity** and **luminance**:

- chroma is the purity of a hue in relation to grey
- saturation is the amount of pure colour in a specific hue
- intensity refers to the brightness or dullness of a hue
- luminance is the amount of light reflected from a hue.

We also talk about **shades** and **tints** when describing colour:

- a shade is a hue produced by adding black
- a tint is a hue produced produced by adding white.

The following colour chart (Figure 11.5) shows the variations of a single, highly saturated hue – the intense yellow colour to the far left (1). The next box along (centre left) shows a tint created by adding white (2); the next box along (centre right) shows a shade created by adding black (3); the far right box shows the same hue but with more chroma (grey) added (4). Notice how different these variations look and how the fourth variation doesn't seem yellow at all.

**Fig 11.5** Colour chart showing variations of a single, highly saturated hue

## COMBINING COLOURS

The colour wheel in Figure 11.6 shows how the primary and secondary colours relate, how tertiary colours fit into the model, and how they relate to each other. For example: blue-reds are cooler than yellow-reds, red-purples appear hotter than blue-purples. The colour schemes most often used in design practice are detailed below.

**Fig 11.6** Colour wheel showing warm and cool colours

| Type of colour scheme | Description | Visual example |
|---|---|---|
| Monochromatic schemes | Created by taking a single hue and adding black or white to create shades or tints. Monochromatic schemes are harmonious and easy on the eye, but are weaker at highlighting areas of interest in a design. |  |
| Analogous schemes | These colours are adjacent to each other in the colour wheel. Analogous schemes are harmonious, like monochromatic schemes, but have the added advantage of being effective in highlighting areas of interest. |  |
| Complementary schemes | These use pairs of colours that lie opposite each other in the colour wheel. They are good for highlighting and work best when one colour is more dominant than the other. The less dominant colour is used to accent certain features of the overall design. |  |
| Split complementary schemes | These are made up of three colours. For example, if the base colour is green, the other two in the scheme would be orange and purple, the colours on either side of red. These schemes create a lot of impact but are often difficult to balance. |  |
| Triadic schemes | These use three colours that are equidistant from each other on the colour wheel, for example, orange, green and purple. This creates vibrant colour harmonies, even with pale or unsaturated hues. To use a triadic harmony successfully, the colours should be carefully balanced. Ideally one colour would be dominant with the other for accent. |  |

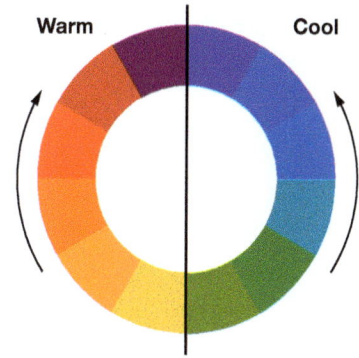

## CREATING COLOUR SWATCHES

A group of colours selected to work together on a particular project is called a **colour swatch**. Creating a colour swatch is an important part of the design process, as it will influence many areas of the final product and how it is perceived.

One way to create colour swatches is to use Johannes Itten's Colour Star, which uses the colour wheel and star-shaped templates to create colour combinations. To do this one of the templates is placed over the colour wheel; the template highlights colour combinations that work well together based on where they are on the wheel. To change the actual colours, simply move the template to generate new combinations.

Another approach is to base the swatch on an existing image that makes good use of colour. Using one of the numerous online resources for creating colour swatches, you can create a colour combination automatically. The colour swatch below was created in this way using Adobe Photoshop.

### Top Tip

Inspiration is often found in unusual places. The most obvious colour references will come from your favourite brands and images, but interesting colour combinations can appear anywhere in the natural and human-made world, so keep looking all around you!

**Fig 11.7** A colour swatch created from a landscape image

# COLOUR STRIKES

Figure 11.8 shows the British Airways colour palette. (Source: British Airways brand management.) As well as representing the flag of the United Kingdom, the blue colour is traditionally used to represent authority; when combined with the white and red, the effect creates a feeling of confidence and authority, which is very important for an airline. However, when the colours are shown side by side, the strong luminance in the dark blue and the strong red (both primary colours) make a vivid combination, while the purple-blue works against the strong red because it is taken from between the cool and warm colours on the colour wheel. The borders of the blocks of colour seem to vibrate slightly, caused by the cones in your eye reacting to the juxtaposition of the strong colours. This is called a **colour strike**.

In Figure 11.9, if we take the colours above and separate them by a thin white line to cancel out the colour striking effect, you will notice that the light grey-lilac colour has far less of an effect on the dark blue than the red does, because they are shades of the same hue. The effect of this combination is far more harmonious than the first.

**Fig 11.8** The British Airways colour palette, showing colour strike

**Fig 11.9** Separating colours to cancel out colour strike

**Colour strike** a combination of strong colours that creates an optical illusion

## Skills Task: **Create a colour strike**

Open a document in Photoshop (or a similar programme) and place two strong complementary colours on shapes of equal size directly next to each other. Record what happens when you do any of the following:

- Insert a thin white line between the colours.
- Reduce the size of one of the colours.
- Introduce a third colour next to the first two.
- Alter the colour values of the main colours.

## Project work: **Making a colour swatch**

Choose an image that you think uses colour effectively and follow the steps below to make your swatch.

- Import your image into the software programme (for example, Photoshop).
- Use the colour selector to select the dominant colours from the image. To do this, use the eyedropper tool to click on an area of the image that has the colour you want. Your selected colour becomes the foreground colour.
- Save the colour in the colour palette. To do this, click on the foreground colour and select 'Add to swatches' from the dialogue box.
- Repeat the steps above for each colour.
- Create some abstract shapes and colour them using the colours from your palette.
- Finally, ask your family and friends to comment on the colour combinations and shapes you have created, for example: what thoughts or feelings do they bring up when they look at them? Record their responses and evaluate.
- Present your findings to the class.

Now answer these questions:

**1.** What happens when you change the size of one shape compared to the others?

### Top Tip

A simple way to experiment with the effect of colours on one another is to paint different hues onto pieces of card of the same size and then place them next to each other. Stand back and look at them, then swap the positions of the cards. What happens to your perception of the colours?

2. What happens when you swap the colours of the different shapes?
3. Do some colours work better with some shapes than with others and if so why?
4. Which of these changes alter your emotional response to the colour combinations?

Ask your family and friends to comment on your ideas and record the answers. When you have some responses, refer back to your initial image – you may be surprised at how different the responses were!

# 11.3 DIGITAL COLOUR MODELS

Digital designers use two main colour models to create colours. These are called CMYK and RGB.

## THE CMYK COLOUR MODEL

CMYK is the model used for colour printing. The letters CMYK refer to the base colours used – cyan (blue), magenta (hot pink), yellow and key (black). It involves printing tiny dots of each colour in different proportions so that they are visually 'mixed' in the eye of the viewer to create the colours required. CMYK is known as the **subtractive colour model** because the more colour that is mixed, the darker the final colour appears. Black is needed because cyan, magenta and yellow cannot be mixed to produce a true black. CMYK also works on the assumption that the colours will be printed on a white background, usually paper.

## THE RGB COLOUR MODEL

RGB (red, green, blue) is the standard model for screen-based colour usage. It combines red, green and blue light to produce different colours on-screen. It works on the principle that the computer monitor or tablet screen is a light source, and each pixel on it is made up of three components: red, green and blue light. Adjusting the relative brightness of each of these three primary colours (different from the traditional red, yellow and blue primary colours) in each pixel creates a range of colours. RGB is known as the **additive colour model** because the more colour added, the lighter and brighter the final colour will become, until white is produced. It is also the basis of the hexadecimal colour system used in web design.

## DIGITAL COLOUR MANIPULATION

Digital images are made up of coloured dots or pixels. Digital software, such as Adobe Photoshop, uses the **RGB** and **CMYK** colour models by assigning a colour **intensity value** to each pixel. The intensity values range from 0 to 255 for each of the RGB (red, green, blue) components in a colour image. For example, a bright red colour hue has an R value of 246, a G value of 20, and a B value of 50. When the values of all three components are equal, the result is a shade of neutral grey. When the values of all components are 255, the result is pure white, and when the values are 0, it is pure black.

Figure 11.11 shows the Photoshop Color Picker interface. At the bottom you can see the RGB intensity values for the hue selected. You can also see a vertical representation of the colour wheel to the right of the main colour panel. Grey colours (or chroma) ranging from white to black are shown at the top and bottom left area of the main colour box. This basic digital interface

**Fig 11.10** The CMYK colour model

**Subtractive colour model** colour model where adding colour makes the colour darker

**Additive colour model** colour model where adding colour makes the colour lighter

**RGB** standard colour model for screen-based colour based on mixing red, green and blue; an additive colour model

**CMYK** colour model used for printing based on mixing cyan (blue), magenta, yellow and key (black); a subtractive colour model

**Intensity value** number (between 0 and 255) showing the amount of colour used in a single pixel on a screen-based display

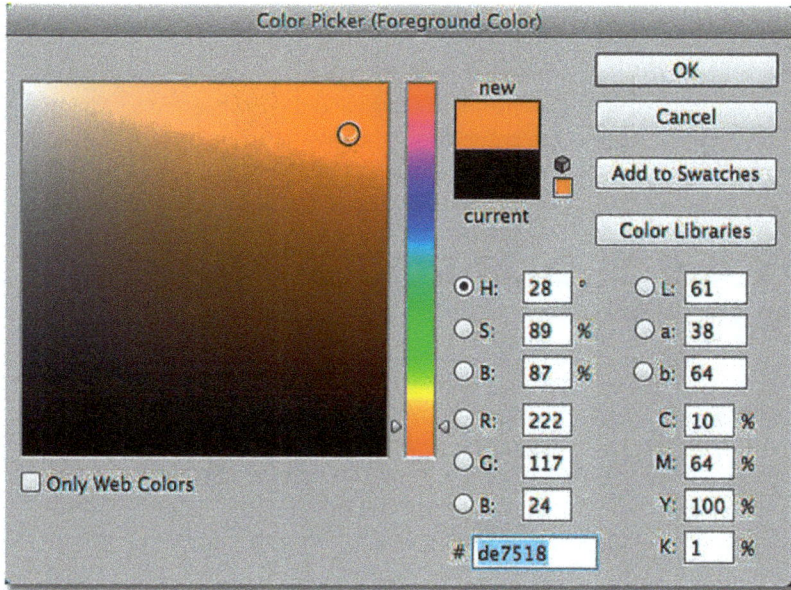
Fig 11.11 The Adobe Photoshop Color Picker interface

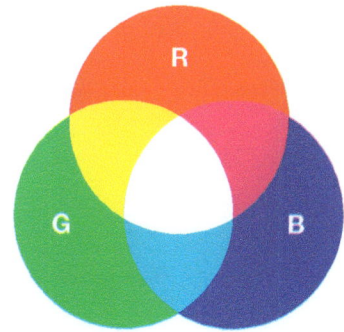
Fig 11.12 The RGB colour model

enables the designer to create multiple colour variations simply by moving a mouse and in this way changing the colour intensity.

## Indexed colour model

**Indexed colour** produces files with up to 256 colours in them. Although its palette of colours is limited, indexed colour can reduce file size while maintaining the visual quality so it is useful, especially if images are being supplied by a third party.

When converting to indexed colour from any of the other colour models, Photoshop builds a **colour look-up table (CLUT)**, which stores and indexes the colours in the image. If a colour in the original image does not appear in the table, the software program chooses the closest one, or simulates the colour using available colours.

The table below shows the main colour models and how they are used.

**Indexed colour** colour model of just 256 colours used to convert RGB or CMYK into smaller digital files while maintaining visual quality
**Colour look-up table (CLUT)** digital store of all colours used in an image used by the indexed colour model to match to one of 256 basic colours

| CMYK | RGB | Index |
|---|---|---|
| printed material, photography, brochures, books | TV, web, mobile applications, digital photography, presentations, multimedia applications | digital images when used for presentations and some web use |

## Skills Task: **Colour model research**

Which colour models could be used to produce the following products? Explain your answers.

- A mobile app for high school exams revision
- A sales brochure for a new car
- A short animated film about safety at work
- Packaging for a ready-to-go lunch box for kids

When you have decided on which colour mode you will need to use for each product, look into the processes and steps that you would need to take in order to create it. For example, the packaging product may need to be created using RGB in the initial stages and then converted to CMYK to be printed. Likewise, the images from the sales brochure may also need to be used on a website, so how would you do this?

# 11.4 COLOUR RULES AND EFFECTS

You need to think hard when choosing specific colours for a project, depending on the final message you want to convey. Does it need to portray vibrancy and energy, or is the intended effect more subtle? If a more subtle effect is required, you can reduce brightness or intensity. For example, instead of using a bright red-purple and vibrant yellow-green, you could substitute a deeper red-purple and a mid-toned khaki-green. Alternatively, if a softer approach is required, a red-lavender hue used against a misty green would be effective.

However, the main thing to remember when creating a colour swatch or palette is that the rules have to be rather elastic! As mentioned before, a specific hue is always greatly influenced by what is placed around it, so the following factors are also extremely important when planning your use of colour.

## CONTRAST

The green colour in the boxes in Figure 11.13 is identical in each case. However, the surrounding colours make the green appear different each time. That is because of the differences in the amount of light each hue reflects (**luminance**).

When producing a design, you must also consider the influence of adjacent colours. Colours of similar luminance generate a calm, non-invasive effect and create soft edges between them, while sharp changes in luminance create a more dramatic effect. Yellow and black is one of the most powerful colour contrasts. This works on both a visual level, with the bright yellow being registered first by the eye and striking against the negative almost non-colour of the black, and a psychological level as the combination instinctively reminds us of predatory animals, stinging insects and warning signs.

**Luminance** the amount of light each hue reflects

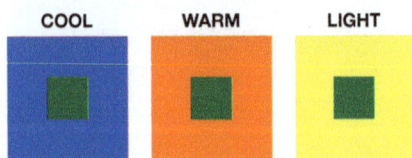

**Fig 11.13** Green box shown with cool, warm and light contrasting colours

## BACKGROUND TO FOREGROUND EFFECTS

Cooler colours from the visible spectrum 'recede' while warmer colours appear to 'advance'. A bright yellow is in most cases the most visible colour, as it the first to be registered by the eye. This is especially effective when a strong yellow is placed with an opposing cooler blue or green that will retreat in our field of vision.

## SATURATION

The purer a colour is the more saturated it becomes, and at full saturation the colour seems to represent boldness and clarity. The greyer a colour becomes (less saturated) the more it seems muted, subdued or toned down. Less saturated colours are usually used in conjunction with brighter tones because if they are used in isolation they can create an overly negative feeling.

Our emotional reaction to a hue is greatly influenced by its luminance or saturation level, so it is important to remember that basing an idea purely around a colour family is not the whole story. Colours are almost never used in isolation, so when you create a colour swatch you need to consider all the hues contained in it and their effects on one another. These combinations can often either make or break your intended message.

Saturation (0–100)

**Fig 11.14** Red on a scale from 0–100 saturation

## Project work: **Creating colour palettes**

Produce two new colour swatches, one for warmer colours and one for cooler colours, using the techniques from this chapter. Base your choices around things you are familiar with, for example, a sports team or a favourite product. Avoid anything that will create a colour strike – unless you want this effect.

Explain the colour choices to a friend or family member. How do they react?

- Do they understand what you were trying to achieve?
- Is their response the same as you intended? If not, how does it differ?
- If the responses do not match your intended effects, what happens if you alter your colour choices?

## Further references

- *Colour* (Zelanski and Fisher, 2009)
- *The Color Star* (Itten, 1987)
- *The Elements of Color* (Itten, 1970)
- *The Interaction of Colour* (Albers, 2006)

# 12 Drawing for digital design

## Learning Aims

By the end of this chapter you will be able to:
- Understand visual language and communicating ideas
- Explain formal elements of drawing for design
- Understand how to convey expression, meaning and narrative through drawing
- Understand how to apply digital drawing techniques to your work

In this chapter you will learn about drawing for digital design in order to create images ranging from a route map to a film poster. You will explore and experiment with **digital drawing** and painting tools to express your ideas with **visual communication** techniques. You will also reflect on your skills development and explore ways to best present your work. The work you create in this chapter could form part of a portfolio to help you progress to higher education or work experience. As discussed in earlier chapters, artists and designers usually start with a design brief from a client, which they first interpret by researching a subject or concept and then respond to by providing a solution using visual communication.

Digital drawing tools, such as **graphics tablets** (see Figure 12.1), digital styluses and specialist software can really bring your imagination to life on-screen. You can erase mistakes and make corrections much more easily than when using a pencil and paper. When using these digital drawing tools, you can easily move between drawing and painting by varying the dimensions of the lines and shapes you create. In this sense, digital drawing and digital painting can be interpreted as the same thing, and so in this chapter we will refer to both techniques as digital drawing.

**Digital drawing** using digital technology to draw or paint digital designs

**Visual communication** communicating through images, symbols or signals, for example, via an advertising billboard

**Graphics tablet** computing device for hand-drawing images, graphics and animations that uses a pen-like stylus

**Fig 12.1** A graphics tablet uses a pen-like stylus to create hand-drawn images and graphics

# 12.1 VISUAL LANGUAGE AND COMMUNICATING IDEAS

## VISUAL LANGUAGE

The term **visual language** describes how ideas and meaning are communicated through visual elements such as images and symbols (including words), and signals. Communication is frequently associated with verbal and written methods, but using visual language increases the impact and power of ideas and messages. Think about all the images you see on television, in the street and online, and how they are designed to influence how you think, feel and react. We may respond to visual language consciously or unconsciously, depending on our individual background, opinions or tastes.

Historically, signs and symbols were extremely important for those who had difficulty reading and writing. However, in a digital society we are surrounded by visual language everywhere we go, and words do not seem to be as important as they used to be. When you use your mobile phone, you probably do not need to click on an app icon to find out what it means – the symbol tells you all you need to know. For example, the image of an envelope in today's society instantly relates to sending an email.

> **Visual language** visual elements used to communicate ideas. For example, line, colour, shape, form, texture, scale, etc.
> **External factors** outside influences (for example, social, cultural, political) that impact the work of artists and designers

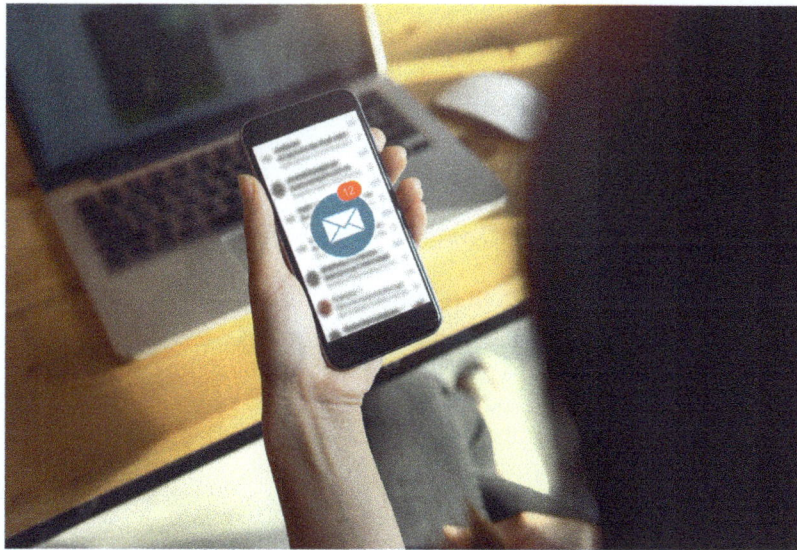

**Fig 12.2** An email icon on a mobile phone is an instantly recognisable symbol

When creating your digital designs, you must consider **external factors** that influence the visual language you use to communicate ideas and meaning. External factors that influence you may include:

- colour: the use of colour differs significantly across the world, as discussed previously; for example, red in India may represent celebration while in South Africa it might mean mourning, violence or struggle
- the different visual languages different platforms use, whether print media, online media, moving image media or social media
- social factors, such as religion, class or wealth, and societal norms that dictate what kind of imagery and symbolism is acceptable in a particular society or community
- cultural, historical and political factors; perhaps the most famous example is the different meanings of the swastika, an ancient religious icon in Asian societies that Western societies understand as the symbol of Nazi fascists

> **Link**
>
> See Chapter 11, page 98, for more information on the different messages conveyed by different colours in different cultural contexts.

- visual languages change; one of the key functions of art and design is to extend and expand our visual languages and to use those languages to communicate ideas more effectively or provocatively. (The next section will discuss examples in more detail.)

# 12.2 FORMAL ELEMENTS OF DRAWING FOR DESIGN

There are several elements you will need to consider when trying to communicate using visual language. These include:

- line
- tone
- form
- shape
- pictorial space
- composition
- colour theory
- semantics and semiotics
- harmony and balance.

It will also help to consider features such as texture, pattern, scale and volume.

Any visual design will be created from at least one of these elements and interpreted by using these formal elements to deconstruct its meaning. However, when we view an image we do not always interpret these elements separately but rather in combination. How you combine these elements will determine what meaning your work will convey.

You explored the use of semantics and semiotics and harmony and balance in sections 10.1 and 10.2 respectively, and investigated various aspects of colour theory in section 11. The other formal elements are outlined below.

## LINE

A line is a visible path between two points created by a pencil or in digital drawing a stylus drawing on a graphics tablet. A line is one-dimensional and can vary in width, direction and length. Lines can be horizontal, vertical or diagonal, straight or curved, thick or thin. They can be used to show different qualities, such as contours, expressions and movement.

In Figure 12.3, the artist has used line to show the folds and drape of the clothing worn.

## TONE

Tone is determined by the way light falls on to a 3D object and refers to the light or dark areas of the object. Where the light is strongest is called a **highlight** while darker areas are called **shadows**. There will then be a range of tones between the highlights and shadows. You can see this in Figure 12.4, where the designer has used tonal colours to create the illusion of a 3D sphere with a 2D drawing. You can do this using various software programmes by using a larger, soft edge brush tool around the edge of the sphere and darker shades of blue.

## FORM

A form has depth as well as width and height and is therefore a three-dimensional shape, for example, a cube, sphere or cone. Sculpture, product design and 3D design are all about creating forms. In 2D design, you can use tone and perspective to create an illusion of form (see next section).

**Fig 12.3** Yoshijiro Urushibara, *Kwannon or Kannon*, Buddhist divinity, drawing (1752) (Japanese school), Bibliothèque des Arts Décoratifs, Paris

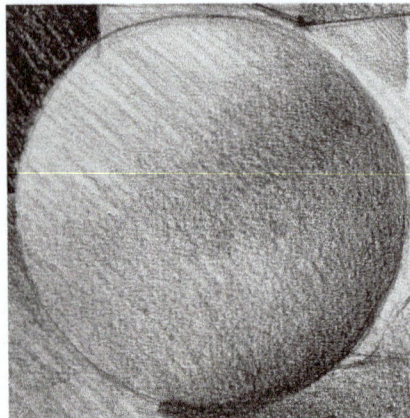

**Fig 12.4** Use of shading to create tone

**Highlights** lighter areas of an object that show tone and texture
**Shadows** darker areas of an object that show tone and texture

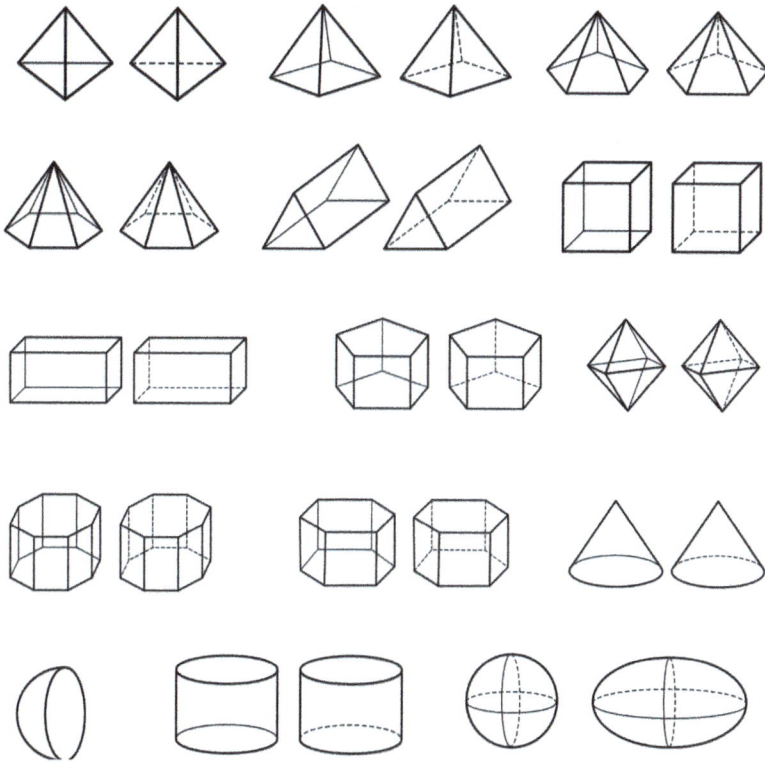

**Fig 12.5** Examples of 3D forms

## SHAPE

A shape has height and width and is an area usually enclosed by a line. A shape can be either geometric, like a circle, square or triangle, or irregular. When drawing shapes you must consider the size and position of each shape as well as the shape of the area around it. Areas created in the spaces between shapes are referred to as **negative space**. For example, in Figure 12.6 the designer has positioned layers of similar shapes vertically and reducing in size, to allow the negative space around the image to create an illusion of depth and distance.

## PICTORIAL SPACE

Pictorial space – positive and negative space – is closely related to composition. **Positive space** is the subject (main focus) of the image, and the space around it is the negative space. **Negative space** (for example, background) is used to support the positive space (for example, foreground) and is equally important; without negative space the positive space would have limited meaning. By understanding and creatively applying knowledge of the use of positive and negative space, artists and designers can greatly improve the overall visual compositions of a piece of design work.

## COMPOSITION

Composition is the purposeful organisation of elements within the work. Digital designers communicate and reinforce their messages through the interaction of colour, typography, imagery, layout and shapes. If your composition is not effective, then even the most impressive design will

**Negative space** empty areas surrounding drawings, which can be used to create particular visual effects
**Positive space** the subject of an image, or focus
**Negative space** the background of an image, which helps to draw attention to the positive space

**Fig 12.6** Triangles receding showing perspective/ negative space

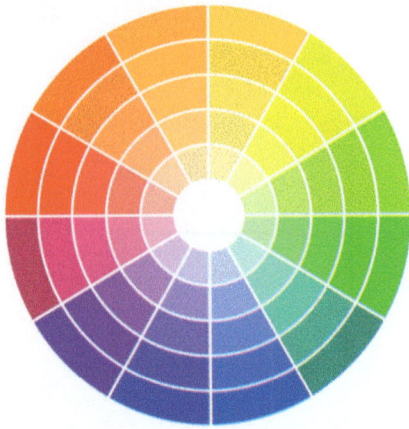

**Fig 12.7** A colour wheel showing harmonious and complementary colours

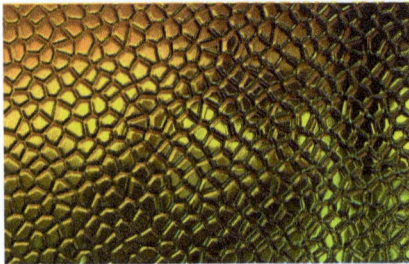

**Fig 12.8** Metallic texture giving a 3D appearance

> **Page layout** term often used to describe digital design compositions
> **3D filter** software tool that adds 3D properties, such as tone and texture, to 2D drawings
> **Motif** design used to create a pattern, often through duplication

not communicate your ideas. In most digital design professions composition is commonly referred to as **page layout**.

## COLOUR

The use of colour can dramatically change the meaning and feeling of your work, so consider the different messages conveyed by different colours in different cultural contexts. Even simple colour dichotomies such as black and white can be used in your drawing. Use the colour wheel in Figure 12.7 as a guide.

Remember:

- harmonious colours are next to each other on the colour wheel
- complementary colours are opposite each other on the colour wheel
- when complementary colours are used together these are known as contrasting colours
- limited colours are used to represent different tones and can create a very striking image.

## TEXTURE

Texture is the surface quality of something and can be how something feels or looks like it may feel. You can create texture in your design drawings by using techniques such as mark making to represent texture. You can also create visual texture by using different lines, shapes, colours or tones.

Figure 12.8 shows how the artist has used different digital image layers to create a realistic raised metallic texture. The artist could have created this by importing a photograph and selecting a part of that photograph to define as a paintbrush and then drawing sections of the image with the paintbrush to replicate that part. Alternatively, the artist may have created this by drawing a 2D image or using a photograph and then applying a digital **3D filter** to add tone and form.

## PATTERN

A pattern is a design created by repeating lines, shapes, tones or colours. A **motif** is the design used to create a pattern. A motif can be a very simple or complicated arrangement of shapes and other elements. Patterns can also be symmetrical, asymmetric, repeated or may have emphasis on a certain area of the design. For example, in Figure 12.9 the patterns have been generated by duplicating the motif. In digital software, this process can be very precise or quite randomly applied. The images below demonstrate repeated patterns.

## SCALE

Scale in art and design is defined by the size of one object compared to another. Scale is used in paintings, drawings, architecture sketches, and 2D and 3D mediums. In design the size of an object is often compared to the

**Fig 12.9** From right to left: textile design by English designer William Morris (1834–96); an abstract geometric Islamic pattern decorating the ceiling of the Aljaferia Palace in Zaragoza, Spain; a dragon pattern at the Gyeongbokgung Palace, Seoul, South Korea

human body (for example, life size, miniature, exceeding) to illustrate the scale and proportion. When referring to a piece of design work we use the phrase scale when explaining its size. Artists and designers create work to a scale to be able to show the relationship between objects correctly. For example, a designer may decide that one centimetre is equivalent to one metre; by working to this scale they can accurately represent how their designs would look in reality.

# VOLUME

Volume is the amount of space, mass or quantity (especially large amounts) that an object occupies. A shape that has three dimensions (length, width and depth) has volume and is measured in cubic units. However, volume can also be simulated in 2D. For example, when a 2D drawing of a 3D object is given the impression of volume through the use of colour, shading and lighting techniques. This element is closely related to shape and form.

## Skills Activity: **Drawing using formal elements**

Choose four of the formal elements of drawing for design discussed above and create several digital drawings that experiment with those four formal elements. Save each drawing as the title of the formal element. Share your work with the class/group and discuss.

- Many digital designers using software for drawing, first scan an image and use it as a background layer to guide their drawing. They then add a new layer and draw on that. They can then turn off the background layer or delete it before saving the final image.
- Many designers use templates for their page layout designs, as this keeps each page they create consistent. The template may include information, such as the colours used, type of font, font size and even a layout grid to show where all the different graphics will be placed.

Project work: **Design a route map**

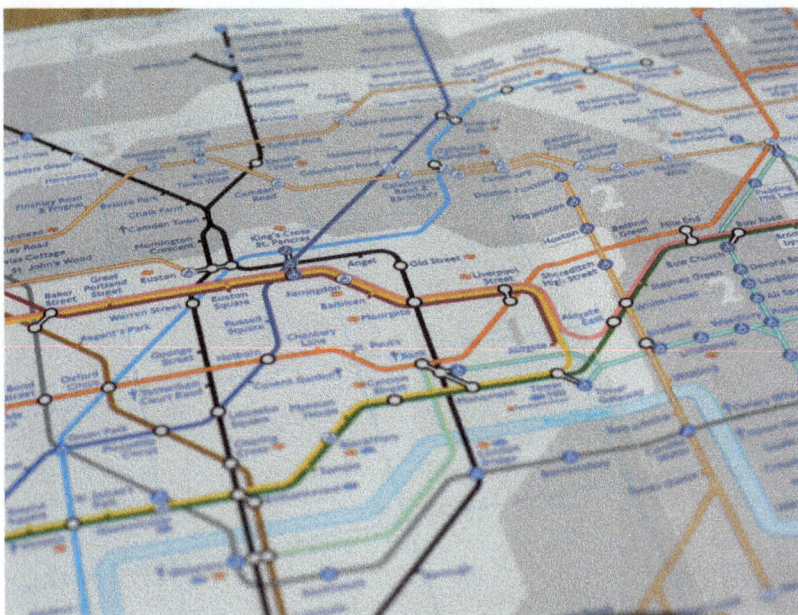

**Fig 12.10** Harry Beck's London Underground 'Tube Map' is a classic example of drawing for design

Research Harry Beck's work and identify why the Tube Map was so revolutionary and how it has influenced other designers. Then draw a map of your route (including any alternative routes) from home to school, or the route(s) your family members take from home to work. Try to emulate the Tube Map style or use your own style, thinking about the eight formal elements of drawing for design. Think about the distances travelled, important intersections or junctions, and any landmarks you want to show. Discuss how much your design reflects the reality of your route(s).

# 12.3 EXPRESSION, MEANING AND NARRATIVE

When you start to consider the expression, meaning and narrative in drawing for digital design, it is useful to think about some of the purposes that digital drawing design fulfils.

## EXPRESSING EMOTION

Drawings capture intense emotions, for example, by capturing facial expressions or a mood or ambience. This can be exaggerated or reduced with the use of formal elements. Figure 12.11 shows how the use of line, shape and tone, as well as star shapes, create a facial expression of happy surprise.

## MEANING

The meaning of a drawing can be very powerful or very subtle. The style of the artist and their chosen materials, techniques and processes determine whether the meaning is successful. A good example of this is poster art.

**Fig 12.11** Detail from a Japanese 'Manga' comic book (2008) – a character showing happy surprise

Figure 12.12, which advertises a classic murder mystery film, uses distorted typography to convey a feeling of disorientation and uncertainty, while the spiralling lines converging around a central 'hole' draw the viewer into the central figure and convey a feeling of falling that matches the film's subject and title, *Vertigo*.

## NARRATIVE

The narrative of an image can have various different meanings and the designer may devise ways to enhance them through drawing. Figure 12.13 shows examples from comic books that use just one word but which convey meaning very effectively through the drawing by using dramatic typography, shapes and colour combinations.

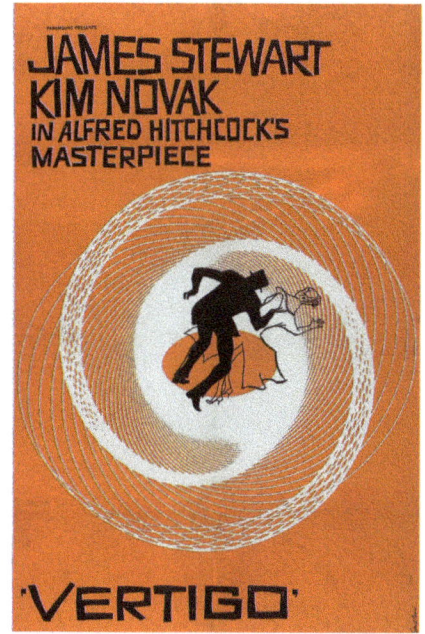

**Fig 12.12** A film poster for the 1958 film *Vertigo* by Alfred Hitchcock

**Fig 12.13** Examples of comic book expressions

---

Skills Task: **Using visual language and drawing**

Visit the illustrationweb website and choose an artist. Describe how they have used visual language and drawing to convey emotion, meaning or narrative using three key images. Also describe their style with reference to the formal elements of drawing for design.

---

Project work: **Designing a film poster**

Design an A4 film poster that communicates a genre of your choice. You must:

- include the film title
- use only three colours
- use at least three of the formal elements for drawing for design.

---

**Further references**

- *Digital Art: A Complete Guide to Making Your Own Computer Artworks* (Cousens, 2013)
- *Digital Painting for the Complete Beginner: Master the Tools and Techniques of this Exciting Art* (Beccia, 2012)

# 13 Using digital typography

## 13.1 THE FUNDAMENTALS OF TYPOGRAPHY

Language is based on words that are combinations of either letters or pictographs and characters. Type refers to the characters themselves; those that are printed or shown on-screen. Typography is the art of displaying these letters or characters so they have appeal, whether to make things easier to read, to communicate a message or just to make things look attractive.

Typography does not relate to the meaning of words. A good way to remember this is that typography relates to how words are written and not what is written.

Type and typography now form a huge part of how we communicate – from website newspaper and magazine content, to motion graphics for games, and titles for films and TV.

Typography can help to convey semantic meanings as well as simply making things look good. The following sections will explain the fundamentals of typography, such as typographic character, size, spacing and leading, and how they form an important part of the digital designer's toolkit.

### THE ANATOMY OF TYPE

Type is described using a number of different terms. How these elements come together to form a **typeface** is what gives typefaces their personality. Figure 13.1 shows the different elements of a typeface.

#### Typefaces and fonts

You may often find that the terms typeface and **font** are used to mean the same thing, but what is the actual difference?

> **Link**
>
> See Chapter 10, page 91, for more information on semantics.

> **Typeface** everything in a typeface family, for example, Bodini
> **Font** a subset of a typeface, for example, Bodini 10 pt Bold

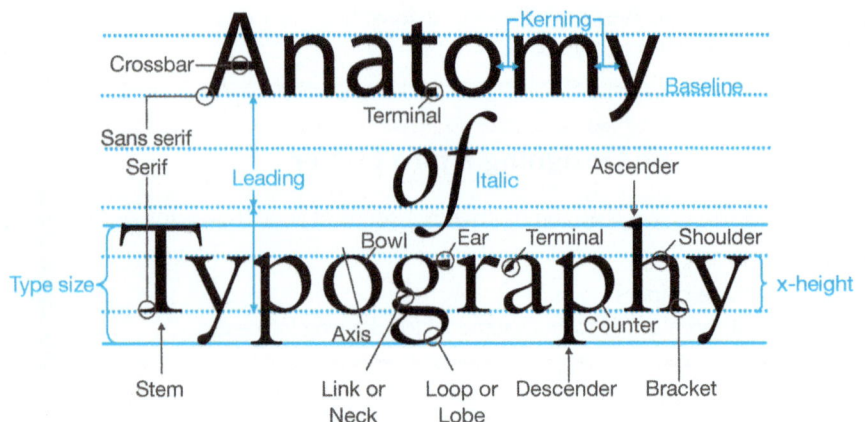

**Fig 13.1** Different aspects of typography

In traditional printing, every page was set out using metal letters. Printers needed thousands of metal blocks, each one corresponding to the individual letters needed. If you wanted to print using the Bodoni 'typeface', for example, you needed different blocks for every different size (10 point, 12 point, 14 point, and so on). In addition, you would also need the different variations in weight, such as bold, light and medium. In this case weight refers to how wide the main type elements are in relation to the overall proportion.

For example, the Bodoni typeface described all of the metal blocks created with the same basic visual design (in this case Bodoni). A font, meanwhile, described a subset of blocks in that Bodoni typeface where each font represented a particular size and weight of metal block. For example, bolded Bodoni in 12 point was a different font to normal Bodoni in 8 point.

### Measuring type size

Type size is traditionally measured using points (pt), where 72 points is equivalent to one inch (2.45 cm). For screen-based design, type is measured using pixels (px). Although a point is a fixed measurement, two different fonts can sometimes appear very different in size and proportion, even though they share the same point size. This is because some fonts have different x-heights and widths.

A font's size is measured from the lowest descender to just above the highest ascender. A font's x-height is measured from its baseline to the height of its lowercase x. As a result, fonts with short ascenders and descenders, or tall x-heights, will appear bigger. In addition, the width of certain types can also have an impact on how a font appears. A font size only refers to its height, so a very narrow font will always appear smaller than a font with wider characters, even if the actual font size is the same. Understanding the fundamental aspects of a font is key when you are creating visual designs that need to portray a certain visual feel.

## TYPEFACE CATEGORIES

There are four main styles of typeface: old style, transitional, modern and digital. The first three are visually identifiable while digital refers to digitally produced type that can include everything from experimental type to deliberately 'old-style' type.

### Old style

This refers to the calligraphic or hand-drawn heritage of type design. Practically all old style typefaces have **serifs**, which are the extra lines at the top and bottom of the letters; notice how the letter Y in Figure 13.2 is shown here both with and without a serif.

These visual styles are left over from traditional letter production methods whereby letters were physically carved into either wood or stone or hand-drawn using brushes and pens. Old-style typefaces convey an older look and may be used when trying to create a feeling of nostalgia.

The typeface shown in Figure 13.3 is Garamond. Note the serifs and the variation in the line thickness gives an impression of being almost hand-drawn.

### Transitional

This style also has serifs, but the main difference is in the thickness in the stroke used to create the type – the type is moving away from hand-drawn calligraphy towards a cleaner, more fabricated look, see Figure 13.4. These font styles became common in the mid-18th century and fall between the old and modern style, and therefore have the name 'transitional'.

**Top Tip**

You can create fonts using a specific font creation application or a combination of graphics packages, such as Adobe Photoshop or Adobe Illustrator. Each character in the font has to be created individually, including all of the other elements, such as punctuation marks and numbers, before everything is imported into a font making application. This turns the individual characters into the font file that can then be imported into a user's computer. The font is then available for use.

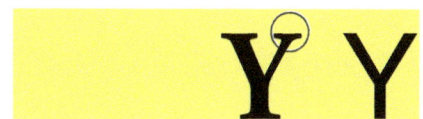

**Fig 13.2** Typeface with (left) and without (right) serifs

**Fig 13.3** Garamond is an old style typeface

**Fig 13.4** Transitional typefaces combine old and modern typeface styles

**Serif** the lines at the top and bottom of a letter

## Modern style

Fig **13.5** Helvetica is one example of a modern style typeface

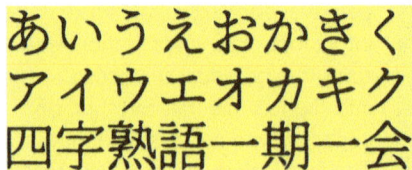

あいうえおかきく
アイウエオカキク
四字熟語一期一会

Fig **13.6** Minchō is one style of typeface used to display Japanese characters

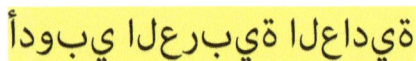

أبودي العربية العادية

Fig **13.7** An Arabic typeface

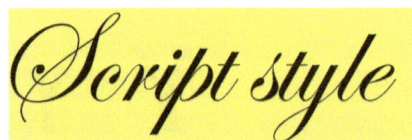

*Script style*

Fig **13.8** Edwardian Script is one example of a script typeface

■□□□□◆◆◆❖◆⊠⊠⌘
TOOLS

Fig **13.9** Symbol fonts are made up of icons rather than type or characters

The typeface shown in Figure 13.4 is Times New Roman. Note the more consistent line width and how the words now look a lot cleaner and consistent.

### Modern

This type style reflects the move towards the clean fabricated look with no serifs and no variation in stroke width. This style is reflected in the modernist art and design movements, such as the Bauhaus and the Swiss school of graphic design.

The typeface shown in Figure 13.5 is Helvetica. Note the complete lack of any serif and how 'clean' the type looks.

### Non-Latin style

Non-Latin is a term used to describe typefaces that are not based on Roman letters and characters. Typefaces that use Arabic, Chinese and Japanese characters fall into this category.

Ming or Song is a category of typefaces used to display Chinese and Japanese characters. Minchō Figure 13.6 is a good example of this type of font, as it maintains the character of earlier print examples while still being readable on-screen.

Meyro was one of the earliest Japanese fonts created for a computer screen and is incredibly versatile and readable at small sizes.

While Arabic typography does not follow the same rules as a Latin style, there are some good examples of Arabic typefaces that can be used in a digital environment. For example: Adobe Arabic Regular and Adobe Arabic Bold Italic can both be used to create professional and elegant effects and have a strong visual appeal.

### Digital style

This style is usually created by a font designer and seeks to capture a contemporary look or feel.

Some digitally created fonts and typefaces reproduce older styles. They fall outside the four main categories, as they are technically digital but visually may be transitional or modern.

### Script style

Script typefaces reproduce handwritten lettering. They are often used to express the personality of the writer or an era in which the style of lettering is associated.

The typeface shown in Figure 13.8 is Edwardian Script. Edwardian is a term used to describe the period between 1901 and 1910 in British history. This font has been designed to replicate the way that letters were written at that time and to evoke that period in history.

### Symbol style

Symbol fonts are made up of icons rather than type or characters. They can be used as decorative elements or to provide an alternative visual language for information graphics. An example of a symbol font is Wingdings (Figure 13.9).

**Top Tip**

Symbol fonts provide a wide range of resources with which to create designs. The font Picto People, for example, uses variations on human forms, while the font Tools uses illustrations of hand tools. These typefaces act as 'icon banks' that you can incorporate into design projects.

# TYPOGRAPHIC PERSONALITY

Typefaces also have personalities or characteristics that designers use to craft visual messages. For example:

- The typeface Goudy is often described as graceful and elegant due to its thin lines and elegant serifs.
- The typeface Bodoni demonstrates a stronger visual appeal due its squat, almost aggressive appearance that recalls old-style newspaper script. As a result it is often used for magazine headlines and fashion publications.

In order to create relevant messages for clients, designers must be aware of the inherent personalities and messages that a typeface conveys.

# COMBINING TYPEFACES

You may want to combine different typefaces to create an effect. One way is to use variations within a typeface, such as the bold or italic forms. If you want to mix completely different typefaces there are some simple rules.

- When adding new typography to your design, try to limit the variations. Consider changing the size, weight or font but not all three at once. This can make a design difficult to read.
- Old style typefaces often work well with a subcategory of modern faces called Grotesque typefaces, such as Franklyn Gothic, Gill Sans and Optima. This is because many Grotesque typefaces were designed using Old Style proportions. This allows the typefaces to work well together visually.
- Consider the reader at all times. Are you adding interest by using multiple fonts or just making things difficult to read? Find out which typefaces work well together and which combinations to avoid.

## Skills Task: **Typography**

Research a typeface you are familiar with. Analyse the history of the typeface – what kind of typeface it is and where it has been used. Then try to identify the message that the choice of typeface is conveying. Is the designer trying to convey a sense of history or something more modern? Try to do this exercise on a website, game and print publication. Are there any critical differences in the way that typefaces are used?

In addition to choosing typeface and font, there are many other ways in which you can use typography.

# MICRO AND MACRO TYPOGRAPHY

**Micro typography** refers to how you manipulate specific characters within a word to create an effect or to make something easier to read.

One example of this is known as the 'marbles theory': the strokes and shapes of individual letters can cause optical effects that make some letters seem closer or further apart than they really are. This can make some letter combinations appear ugly. Now imagine dropping marbles into the spaces between the letters, and then adjusting the individual letter spacing so the same number of marbles will fill the gaps. The example in Figure 13.12

# Goudy

# Bodoni

**Fig 13.10** It is important to consider the 'personality' of each typeface

# Garamond

# Gill Sans

**Fig 13.11** Old style (Garamond) and modern (Gill Sans) typefaces can work well together visually

**Micro typography** the way that letters are adjusted individually to create an effect

# marbles

# marbles

**Fig 13.12** Micro typography refers to how specific characters are manipulated within a word – note here the variation in the spacing of the letters in 'marbles'

> **Top Tip**
>
> Designers also deal with micro typography by looking at the type in a more abstract way; for example, by squinting or holding the paper upside down to identify the gaps between the letters.

shows the original version and the amended version. In the original example the a-r-b spaces appear too close together. The second version shows the letters spaced individually, to create a more harmonious effect.

**Macro typography** refers to how you arrange type on a page or screen. This enables you to use blocks of type to decorate or to draw attention to specific areas. Typography elements you might use in this way include:

- Column height and width: how much space a block of type takes up on a page
- Colour: the colours used to display the type and its background
- Font size: the actual size of the type used
- Leading: the horizontal space between lines of text (the term comes from when lines of lead were used to separate lines of text and more lead meant a bigger gap between lines)
- Alignment: how blocks of type are arranged. This includes:
  - Flush left: this is often the most comfortable option for Western audiences, as it enables the reader to read each line along the same vertical axis. The uneven side of the text block on the right (called the 'rag') allows the letter spacing to remain consistent throughout the paragraph.
  - Flush right: this setting is commonly used for languages that read right to left, such as Arabic and Hebrew. For Western languages flush right is appropriate for small amounts of type only (such as captions and call-outs) because the uneven starting point makes it harder to read.
  - Centered: for similar reasons to the flush right option, centered text is only appropriate for small sections of text.
  - **Justified**: this is type that is evenly aligned right and left with each line the same length, which makes this option ideal for newspapers, magazines and websites with limited space. The disadvantage is that letter spacing can be forced into uneven patterns.

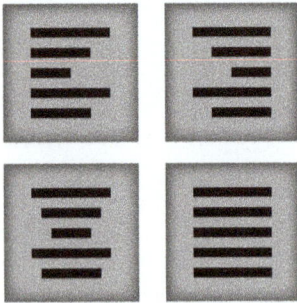

**Fig 13.13** Differences in alignment: flush left (top left); flush right (top right); centred (bottom left) and justified (bottom right)

> **Macro typography** the way that blocks of type are displayed on a page or screen
> **Justified** type that is aligned right and left in a block

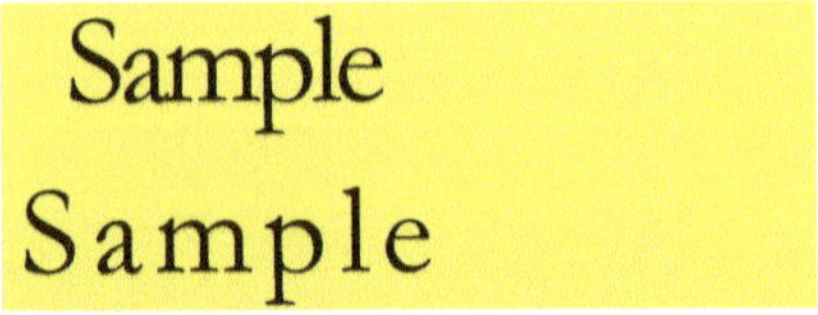


**Fig 13.14** Horizontal scale alters the horizontal width of the characters

## 13.2 SPACING AND ALIGNMENT

As well as the macro typography discussed earlier, many design applications enable the designer to manipulate the specific type characters and how they display.

### TRACKING AND KERNING

Tracking and kerning are options available in some graphic applications that enable the designer to alter the letter spacing. Tracking is an option that is applied to a series of letters and kerning is only applied to pairs of letters.

Vertical scale alters the vertical height of the characters.

Horizontal scale alters the horizontal width of the characters.

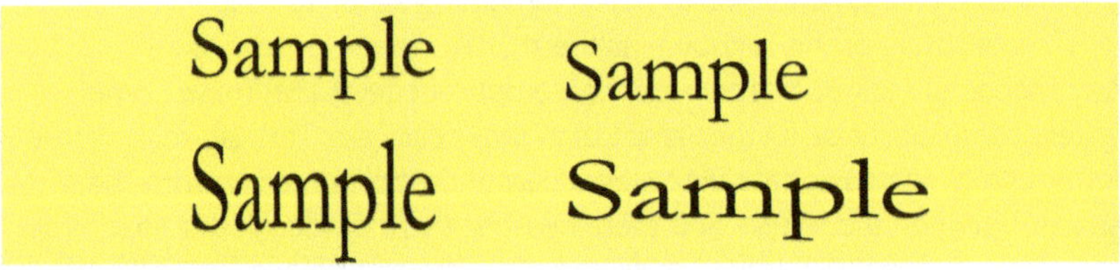


**Fig 13.15** Vertical scale alters the vertical height of the characters

> **Top Tip**
>
> While it can be tempting to be creative with typefaces in this way, be cautious: typefaces are designed specifically to show in proportion, so sometimes it may be better to find a typeface that works rather than altering one to fit.

# 13.3 HOW TYPE IS USED IN A DIGITAL ENVIRONMENT

Most graphics packages have a text or type manipulation function. In Adobe Photoshop, for example, you can add text by clicking the text tool and creating a text box. The interface then presents you with a list of fonts that you can use.

# 13.4 USING TYPE ON DIFFERENT FORMATS

## TYPE IN TV AND FILM

Type plays a very different role in the moving image format than online or print. The standard approach in the moving image is to use audio and video as the main formats for driving narrative. As a result, type is often used in a supportive role for titles, captions, subtitles and information graphics. While type performs a much smaller role, the same principles around typographic character still apply. Consider the use of on-screen graphics in the BBC's *Sherlock* television series, where the text on the screen is used to signify the inside of the lead character's mind. The use of different fonts here is another indicator of his state of mind, with scrawled text indicating a fraught mind.

## TYPOGRAPHIC ILLUSTRATION

Type and numbers are some of the most recognisable shapes in our semiotic system. As a result, designers often use type in an expressive way to convey messages.

The font example below (Figure 13.16) has been created to convey the idea of speed and motion. The use of blurred lines conveys a sense of movement, while the slant on the letters themselves creates the impression of that movement at speed.

By contrast, the font example shown in Figure 13.17 has been created to give a three-dimensional effect that uses angle to create an architectural feel. The arrangement of the letters brings to mind a set of buildings.

## MOTION GRAPHICS / MOTION TYPOGRAPHY

Type can also be animated and used to convey messages, either as complex 3D animation sequences or simple animated gifs used on websites. Consider the Google Doodle, which has made use of many of these techniques at various times. In each case the following guidelines relate to how you can animate type.

### The frame

The frame is the space that contains the animation and there are different ways of using the frame when animating type:

- Frame as container: here the type cannot extend past the boundaries imposed by the frame. The type can move around the frame but is always contained by it. Imagine the text here bouncing between the walls of the frame before resting in the central area shown.

---

**Skills Task: Exploring typography**

Work in pairs. Demonstrate your understanding of typography by choosing a phrase below and typing it out in three different fonts of your choosing.

- My name is [insert your name]
- I am so excited
- Today I am going to the beach

Print out your phrases and consider each phrase in its different font. Consider how different fonts convey different emotions. On your printouts, list the different words you associate with each phrase. What differences do you notice? What similarities do you find between the emotions associated with the different fonts?

**Fig 13.16** Font to convey the idea of speed and motion

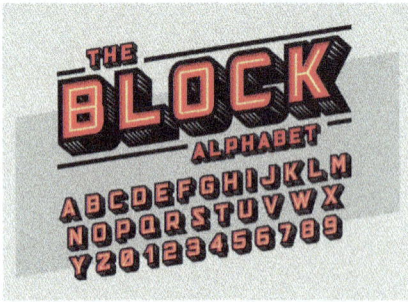

**Fig 13.17** Font to create a three-dimensional effect

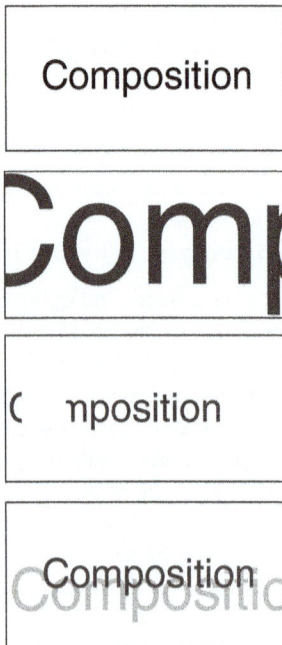

**Fig 13.18** Ways of using the frame when animating type: (from top to bottom) frame as container; frame as window; mask; depth

- Frame as window: this approach uses the frame as a window through which the type is viewed. This way the type can extend beyond the frame. Imagine the text zooming from very large to small, so giving the impression that the viewer was looking through the letter 'O'.
- Mask: this takes the window approach to another level by introducing a mask; this is an invisible element that 'hides' the type. Imagine the mask slowly revealing different parts of the text, forcing the reader to read the word a letter at a time before finally showing the complete word.
- Depth: the use of depth can be applied using a number of methods including colour, texture and movement. This approach also works well with the application of scale to emphasise certain elements. Imagine background images fading in and out and receding into the background to create the impression of depth.

### Type on smaller devices

Due to the advances in the mobile web, smartphone and tablet screen resolutions are now high enough to display small type with clarity. There are, however, some things you need to take into consideration when using type on smaller devices.

A website that has been designed to be viewed on a monitor can appear too small and virtually unreadable on a mobile device. Website designers use a production method called Cascading Style Sheets (CSS) to automatically resize type when it is viewed on a mobile browser, but long passages of copy can then become difficult to read on a small screen due to scrolling. When designing copy for websites to be viewed on mobile devices, creators have to consider things such as paragraph breaks and subheadings to improve readability for their users. This is an aspect of accessibility. Generally, sans serif fonts are considered easier to read on mobile devices. Font size is no longer such an issue for creators, as users can amend the size of text easily themselves.

Some high-resolution screens have issues with legibility and cause eye strain. Many ebook readers, on the other hand, use E-Ink technology and are not back lit, giving a very similar reading experience to paper. In each case you should consider the end user and how they will view the type.

# 14 Using digital audio

## 14.1 PHYSICAL PROPERTIES OF SOUND

Good sound is critical to any film, video game, installation or digital project. Adding sound to your projects can often seem like a mysterious process, but it is worth treating sound with as much creativity and style as the other parts of your project. Walter Murch, an American editor and film-maker who is often credited with creating the term '**sound design**', once said that 'sound is 52 per cent of your film'. Although sound designers and directors will debate this, what is certain is that good sound will distinguish your project. In addition, creating good sound is often a pleasurable part of the process.

### WHAT IS SOUND?

What we call 'sound' is a physical kinetic energy known as acoustic energy. Acoustic energy is ever changing waves of pressure in the air (or water or another medium). Our ears collect these **sound waves** into the auditory canal,

> **Sound design** the process of acquiring and generating audio for a project
> **Sound waves** pressure waves of acoustic energy generated by something vibrating

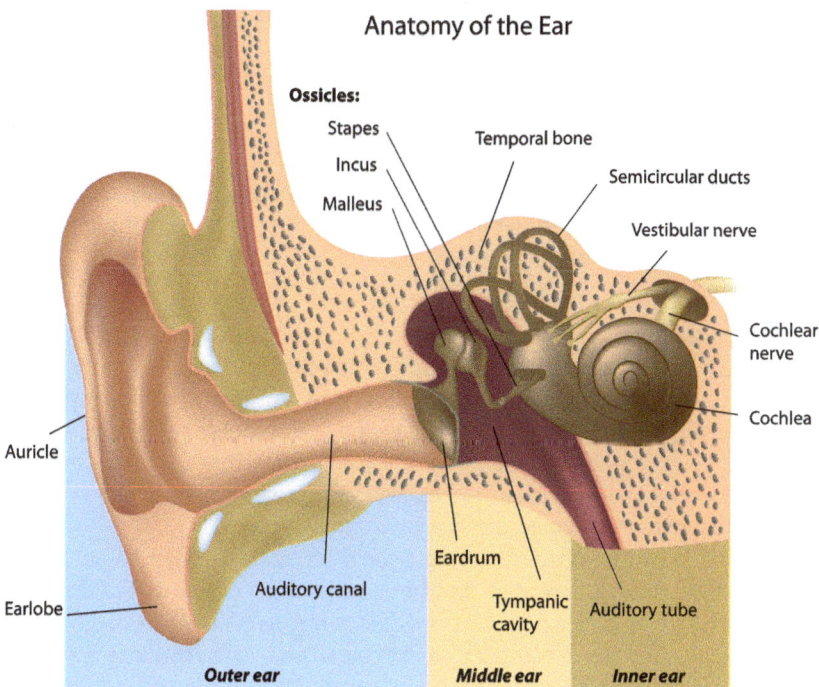

Anatomy of the Ear

**Fig 14.1** Cross-section to show anatomy of the ear

causing the eardrum at the end of the canal to vibrate and move a small chain of bones in the middle ear. The last bone in the chain hits the cochlea and makes the liquid in the cochlea move, stimulating nerve endings that communicate with the brain, and in this way we perceive the sound.

Two key considerations for sound creators are the **frequency** and **amplitude** of sounds.

## Frequency

The frequency of sound waves refers to the rate at which air pressure changes. For humans to hear air pressure changes as sound, the frequency of those changes must be within the range of our hearing. We call each sound wave a cycle and humans can detect sound waves of between 20 and 20,000 cycles per second. The more cycles per second the higher pitched the sound feels, and the fewer cycles per second the lower pitched the sound feels. Is it high like a bird tweeting, or low like an elephant rumbling? This is thinking about frequency.

Cycles per second are indicated using the measuring unit **Hertz**, abbreviated to Hz. Because the number is often quite high, once it goes over 1000 Hz it is divided by 1000 and given the term **kilohertz**, abbreviated to kHz. Thus 1000 Hz is 1 kHz and human hearing ranges from 20 Hz to 20 kHz.

Figure 14.2 shows the range of human hearing as red, orange and yellow sections, from 20 Hz to 20 kHz. Low frequencies from 20 Hz to around 400 Hz are **bass frequencies**, and high frequencies, or **treble frequencies**, are generally above 4 kHz. Inaudible sub sonic (also called infrasound) and supersonic (also called ultrasound) sounds are below 20 Hz and above 20 kHz respectively.

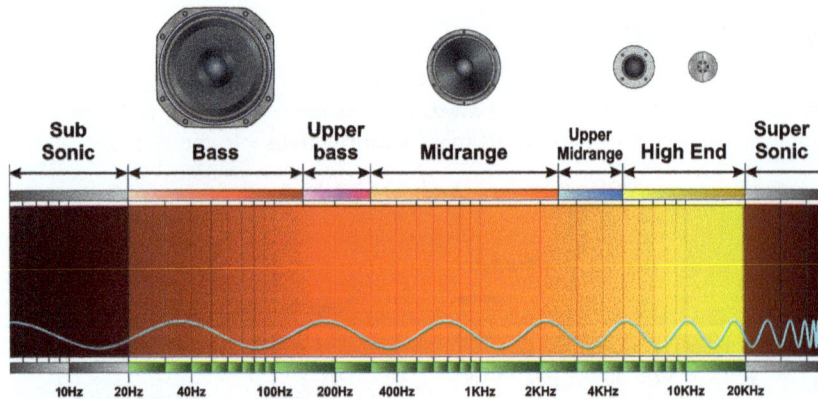

Fig 14.2 The frequency range of sound

**Frequency** (of sound) the rate at which a sound wave vibrates; high frequency equals high pitched sounds
**Amplitude** the strength of a sound wave; high amplitude equals loud sound
**Hertz (Hz)** unit of measurement of sound frequency
**Kilohertz (kHz)** unit of measurement of sound frequency
**Bass frequencies** low frequency sounds
**Treble frequencies** high frequency sounds
**Decibels (dB)** the unit of measurement of amplitude

## Amplitude

Amplitude refers to how loud a sound is – its volume. There are various measures of the loudness of sound that we see on our devices and sound equipment, but amplitude is usually measured in **decibels**, abbreviated as dB. The decibel is named after the inventor Alexander Graham Bell; this is the 'bel' part of decibel. The 'deci' prefix is a reference to the logarithmic nature of the scale: the higher the number, the higher the amplitude.

Normal conversation levels are between 50 dB and 70 dB. The sound of breathing might be as low as 15 dB whereas a jet flying overhead is often above 100 dB. Loud music concerts register as high as 110 dB to 140 dB, which is potentially painful and damaging to your ears. The sound wave diagram in Figure 14.3 shows that with no sound the amplitude of the sound waveform is close to zero, and that amplitude increases as the volume becomes greater.

If the highs and lows of the wavelength were to come closer together, the frequency of the sound would be higher.

When thinking about using different sounds, and knowing how loud they are in the real world, it can be very effective to play with these levels. For example, sometimes sound designers will make the sound of a telephone ringing louder than it would be in real life in order to highlight the anxiety that can be caused by a constantly ringing telephone.

## THE SOUNDTRACK

When most people speak about 'the **soundtrack**', they often mean the music that accompanies a film or video game. However, when digital media designers refer to the soundtrack they mean all of the different types of sound used in projects. These might be sounds that you record specifically for your project, such as voices and music. They might also include recordings of speeches or the sounds of machines that you find in sound libraries or in audio archives in museums, galleries or online. You might also invent sounds. Through considering, making and choosing these sounds, you are designing your project for sound. All of the sounds that you use in your project are known collectively as its soundtrack.

## PERSONAL RESPONSES TO SOUND

Each person's response to sound is different and depends on a variety of factors. For example, as we get older our perception of sound can change – prolonged exposure to noise can damage our hearing and limitations in hearing sound are common. What the sound designer hears and appreciates as a distinct sound might be just a noise to another listener. In addition, people respond to sounds in different ways depending on their culture, nationality, gender, age and more.

While there are no specific rules regarding sounds belonging to particular cultures, we know that some sounds have particular associations; the high pitched whistle of the 'shakuhachi' flute evokes traditional Japan; we associate guitar-led rock and roll music with American youth culture; the chiming of the Big Ben clock is a sound associated with London.

Some music may sound unpleasant to older people because it is created in new ways, while some music may sound alien to younger people because they have never been exposed to it. This can result in people describing the same soundtrack in opposite ways.

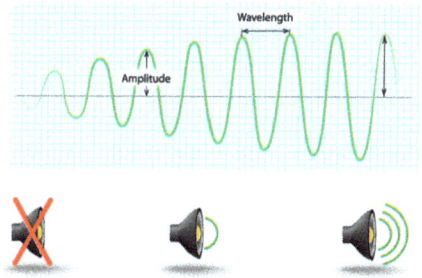

Fig 14.3 The wavelength and amplitude of sound waves

**Soundtrack** all sounds included in a digital media product

### Top Tip

Do not dismiss a type of sound because it is unfamiliar – rather, be open to listening and hearing a variety of sounds. Understand that sound and its enjoyment can be subjective. Listen for examples online. How does a Bollywood film sound different to one made in Hollywood, for example, or how does a film made in Denmark differ to one made in Nigeria? It is important to understand your audience, and to understand the ways that sounds make people feel.

### Skills Task: **Sound postcard**

Form a group of up to five people and give each person a postcard or piece of paper. On each postcard write a different location to explore; for example, a coffee shop, the library, a street corner or a bus stop. Each person goes to their location and writes descriptions of ten sounds they hear. Discuss what each person heard.

1. Are there things you can all hear?
2. Are the sounds unique to the area, to your town, or are they common sounds?
3. How do people describe the sounds? Do they use emotional or factual words?

### Top Tip

Learn to listen. While listening to sound, try to sit quietly without moving too much. Be comfortable. Try not to react immediately, but allow your thoughts to gather. How is the sound making you feel and what are the components of the sound you can hear? Is it high pitched or low, short or long, loud or soft? Write down your thoughts.

# 14.2 CATEGORIES OF SOUND

Sound professionals often think of the soundtrack as four, semi-formal categories of sound. These are:

- voice and words
- sound effects
- atmospheres
- music.

This is a great way to think about your projects and is an interesting way to investigate what other designers have done with their soundtracks.

## VOICE AND WORDS

These can be dialogue from a script said by an actor, a voiceover, a speech from an archive, lyrics from a song or words to a poem. They could, for example, be the vocal expressions of a character as they progress through a video game.

## SOUND EFFECTS

Sometimes called Sound FX, these are short sounds that usually give life to activities, for example, explosions, car crashes or footsteps. Working with recordings you make yourself, sounds from sound libraries, using synthesisers and more, you create the sounds that accompany the movement and actions of everything in your work.

**Foley** the process of creating and recording sounds (for example, footsteps) that match actions and images onscreen

Some of these sounds can be created through a method called **Foley**, named after its creator Jack Foley. In the late 1920s and early 1930s, the first films that included sound felt empty and hollow because the only audio they had was pre-recorded dialogue. Foley's solution was to re-create sound effects that were not recorded at the time of filming, such as footsteps, clothes rustling, punches, hits, stabs and more. Today, one 'Foley artist' using a few simple tools can make the sound of almost anything! In Figure 14.4, Foley artist Sue Harding is using water in a bucket to create the sounds of boats in a harbour. Most film, television and video games will likely have some form of Foley sound, and it is one of the most common practices of sound creation.

**Fig 14.4** Stills from the film *The Secret World of Foley* showing Foley artist Sue Harding at work recreating sounds of a harbour

# ATMOSPHERES

**Atmospheres** (sometimes called ambiance) are sounds long enough (perhaps as long as 10 minutes) to cover a whole scene or series of actions that tell us about the space your story occupies, whether a city, a forest or inside a machine. For example, a film that is set in a park 200 years ago would require the atmosphere of a park without any machine sounds, such as traffic or aircraft. So to record that sound you might travel to a park in a remote part of the world. You would set up your microphone(s), point them into the space and record a long form sound for a period long enough to cover the scenes in your film. Alternatively, you could go to the park with a sound recorder and microphone and record the atmosphere for 10 to 20 minutes then, during the editing process, cut out the parts of the recording you do not like and use effects to build the atmosphere so that it suits your images and story.

> **Atmospheres** sounds of long duration, that indicate where and when the action takes place

Atmosphere is often about establishing the scene, showing where and when the action is set. For example, a popular BBC TV series is shot in a very quiet studio, but in several scenes the characters are supposed to be in a restaurant in the bustling and noisy East End of London. To make the restaurant sound like it is in the East End, a sound recordist went there and recorded a long form sound of the area, simply placing a microphone in the street to capture the atmosphere. This was then added to the original film footage using editing software.

# MUSIC

Music is one of the most powerful parts of any project, but it can also be one of the most dangerous in terms of influencing your audience. You can tell people how to feel with music. When you think about the 1997 film *Titanic*, directed by James Cameron, you immediately think about the emotional music, composed by James Horner. The music includes flutes and string instruments to create a feeling of loss that recurs throughout the film, and those instruments are included in the film's signature song, Celine Dion's 'My Heart Will Go On'. A story, whether in film, on stage or in a game, is sometimes referred to as a melodrama because the tone of the melody (a musical term) leads the drama (thus melodrama) rather than other elements of the narrative.

Because music can lead our emotions so effectively, we hear a great deal of music in creative projects. Music could be commercial music or other

**Fig 14.5** The emotional music for the 1995 film *Titanic* added to the sense of loss in the film

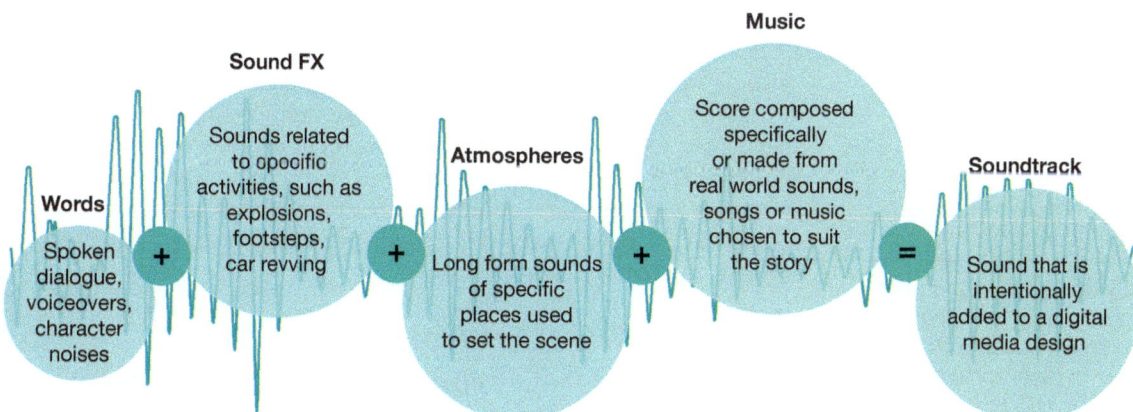

**Words**
Spoken dialogue, voiceovers, character noises

**+**

**Sound FX**
Sounds related to specific activities, such as explosions, footsteps, car revving

**+**

**Atmospheres**
Long form sounds of specific places used to set the scene

**+**

**Music**
Score composed specifically or made from real world sounds, songs or music chosen to suit the story

**=**

**Soundtrack**
Sound that is intentionally added to a digital media design

**Fig 14.6** Soundtrack categories

pre-existing music that you acquire the rights to use. Arguably more compelling is music that you have composed for your project. We call this music **score**. Score is deliberately composed to closely accompany your design. It creates a unique signature sound or theme that belongs to your project, and your project alone. For example, in Ridley Scott's film *Bladerunner* (1982), Vangelis' iconic synthesiser score made it a unique film that sounds like no other. Similarly, for Stephen Spielberg's film *Jaws* (1975), composer John Williams created a cello score that slowly, ominously builds to a crescendo as the shark hunts and then attacks its victims.

## DIEGETIC AND NON-DIEGETIC SOUND

Diegetic sounds are sounds that are made by something we can see in the images. If we see a car racing down the street we hear the car. A non-diegetic sound is one we can hear that is not in the picture. For example, a player in a video game might hear the car racing down the street before they see it. Experiment with sounds you can see and ones you cannot. If you have a window or door in your images, what sound can be heard through the door? Any of the four categories of sound – words, sound FX, atmosphere and music – could come from on or off screen.

You can begin designing your sound by thinking about how you might use, or not use, any or all of these four categories of sound. For example, using less music can leave your story open to greater interpretation because you are not giving your audience emotional cues to tell them how to feel. Sad music played over a sad scene is obvious and perhaps a good sad scene doesn't need the music for the audience to understand what is happening. In a video game with lots of car crashes and gunfire, the audience expects to hear sound FX so leaving the sound out of such scenes would feel strange. Make your choices based on the way the scene feels.

# 14.3 THREE PHASES OF SOUND CREATION

We have looked at the ways we perceive sound and considered the four categories of sound that you can include in a soundtrack. Now we will look at the three phases for creating sound that you will work through.

## RECORDING AND GATHERING SOUND

In this phase you record sounds, such as voices, atmospheres, effects and a Foley session, to create a **sound palette** unique to your work. It is much better to record too much than not enough, so that you have lots of different sounds to cut apart and edit together. You might also gather sound from audio libraries, such as the one at at the freesound website and other online and offline sources. Perhaps you could start with an atmosphere – where are you setting your story? Having an audio anchor such as this or sounds that tell the audience something about your narrative can help get you started.

**Score** music that is specifically composed for a particular project
**Sound palette** collection of sounds related to the narrative or setting
**Digital audio workstation (DAW)** any computer and software combination that allows you to edit, arrange and output audio

## EDITING AND MANIPULATING SOUND

In the second phase you use a **digital audio workstation (DAW)** or editing software to bring together all of your sounds in your timeline. You edit your sound down to what is useable and necessary. However, you might also manipulate and combine these sounds. Perhaps you will bring together the sound of a car engine and a lion to make the sound of a very powerful superbike. On one track of your DAW you can have the sound of the lion, and on another track, playing at the same time, you can have the sound of a car engine. By changing the volume of each you can make the sounds combine and they become a new sound!

## MIXING AND OUTPUT

In the final phase you will be thinking about where your final project will end up. Will it be on a hand-held device? Will it be for a console such as the Playstation™ or the Microsoft Xbox™? It might be multichannel audio or stereo (see below). If it is for television, you might need to meet the demands of the broadcaster; for example, they might ask you to fade out the sound before commercials, or ensure that an advertisement is slightly louder than the show the audience is watching. Mixing ensures that your sounds work together and that you are happy with the way your soundtrack contributes to your story. You will need to bring your sounds together in the software and balance the sounds – is the dialogue loud enough to hear over the music? Perhaps the footsteps need to be louder to show that your character is a large person or running heavily.

You will go back and forth with these phases – you might start by recording sounds, only to realise that the sounds you recorded aren't working when you cut them together, so you will try something different. Experiment and try new things!

> **Top Tip**
>
> When recording atmosphere sounds outside, be sure to listen with headphones and use a windshield or microphone cover to protect against wind sounds. On your recorder, a high pass filter (usually abbreviated in the menu to HPF) can help to remove low rumbles from traffic and wind.

### Skills Task: **Deconstruct the soundtrack**

Choose three scenes from films or video games that you like. Answer the following questions and then discuss in groups.

- What categories of sound (dialogue, sound effects, atmospheres and music) are present?
- What does each sound tell you about the story?
- How do the sounds make you feel?
- How does the sound change over time?
- What would you add, remove or change?

### Project work: **Producing sound palettes**

Produce three sound palettes that evoke a certain place. Record new sounds, borrow sounds from audio libraries or insert music. Play the sounds to a friend or family member. Answer the following questions about their reactions.

1. Do they know what place each palette is about? What was their response?
2. Is their response the same as you intended or did they think the place was somewhere different?
3. What sounds could you have included to make the palette more evocative of the place?

# 14.4 AUDIO TOOLS

## DIGITAL AUDIO WORKSTATION (DAW)

This is any device that allows the user to record, edit and output audio. Usually this is a computer running software such as Avid® Pro Tools® and some kind of USB-powered audio interface, such as the Focusrite Scarlett USB interface. DAW software will normally work without any external devices, and the functionality of the software is far beyond anything sound professionals imagined during the analogue era.

The term digital audio workstation (DAW) is inherited from the early days of digital audio, when more than just a computer was required to create digital audio. Today's low-cost software and hardware has meant making great sound is increasingly simple and affordable. Popular DAWs include Adobe Audition, Avid Pro Tools (available for free online in a version called Avid Pro Tools First), Logic®, REAPER and Ableton® Live™.

## SOUND RECORDING EQUIPMENT

For gathering sounds in locations and outdoors, ideally you should use digital sound recorders. These devices consist of a recording medium (usually a disk or a memory card), circuitry for boosting and improving the sound signal, and either a microphone or the ability to plug microphones into the recorder. Your school may have access to such recorders so learn how to use them. Another option when sound recording is to use a video camera that has the ability to record sound. As a last resort you can even use your smartphone; through practice you might be able to get a good result, and many companies now make add-on devices to help record better quality audio from a phone. A lack of the perfect equipment is no excuse not to try recording sound.

Sound recorders have a variety of styles and design features, but many of the controls will be consistent across different brands. Remember, you can also record directly into your computer using your DAW software. Sound recorders like the one in Figure 14.7 typically feature the following:

- Microphones – many recorders have at least two microphones to create stereo recordings, and some have more than two, which enables multichannel recordings. Many recorders, such as the popular Zoom and Tascam models, also allow you to attach further microphones, which can create better recordings.
- Headphone output – all recorders will have a headphone socket so that you can monitor what you are recording. It is essential that you listen while you record.
- Headphone level – this will usually be a dial or a lever that increases or decreases how loud you listen to what you are recording. Set it at a comfortable level for listening.
- Audio record level – you can control the sound level of the recordings you make. You should have them audible on the recording, but not so loud that they distort. Remember that this is a different sound level to the one for your headphones. The audio record sound level will normally be visually represented on the LCD screen of the recording device. Make sure you can see the sound levels in the screen.
- Menus – all digital sound recorders will have menus, usually accessed through an LCD screen that can control the sound file format (WAV, AIFF or MP3) and other details. Learn about your recorder by reading the manual and following online tutorials on the manufacturer's website or social media.

**Fig 14.7** A zoom recorder

Looking at the image of the zoom recorder (Figure 14.7) you can see the microphones on the top, the record button in red on the front, and the LCD screen, which shows the file name and the length of the file being recorded, and meters, which show the amplitude of the recording.

## SOUND FORMATS AND COMPRESSED AUDIO

There are a variety of sound formats available for digital audio. When you are recording and making sound, you generally want the highest possible quality. The highest quality sound formats are 'wav' and 'aiff' formats. These do not compress the sound and so they are called **lossless audio** file formats because they maintain the best possible detail and clarity of sound. Consumer formats, such as 'mp3', 'aac' and others that do compress the sound, maintain less detail and are therefore termed **lossy audio** formats, although they are generally sufficient for distributing your work to a wider audience. In the final stages of your digital project, when you are supplying it to your client or the audience, compressing audio files to make them more manageable makes sense.

**Lossless audio** digital audio formats that are uncompressed, usually used in professional contexts
**Lossy audio** digital audio formats that are compressed for ease of distribution, usually used in consumer contexts

| Lossless professional sound formats | Lossy consumer sound formats |
| --- | --- |
| • WAV files (file extension .wav)  • AIFF files (file extension .aiff) | • MP3 (file extension .mp3)  • AAC (file extension .aac) |

Despite being professional quality, wav and aiff files can vary in their quality. In a digital audio format the quality is determined by the file's bit depth, bit rate and sample rate, where sample refers to the amount of data in a recording. (In other contexts, 'a sample' is a small recording you manipulate using audio hardware or software.) High quality audio recorded, edited and mixed for professional use in your projects will have high bit depths, bit rates and sample rates. Consumer audio files, the audio formats that we generally use at home and on our digital devices, usually have lower bit depths, bit rates and sample rates. This makes these files more suitable for portable devices and easier to stream. While creating and editing, you will work at the higher rates of sound quality, but for your final outputs you will use lower bit depths, bit rates and sample rates, to make your files easier to distribute.

### Bit depth
Bit depth refers to the number of bits of data available for each audio sample. The higher the bit depth, the better the quality of the audio. CD audio is 16 bit, but higher standards are more common including 24 bit and 32 bit.

### Sample rate
Sample rate is the number of audio samples carried per second in an audio file. The higher the sample rate, the greater detail the sound file contains. A sample rate of 44.1 contains 44,100 samples per second.

### Bit rate
The Bit rate tells us how many bits of data are processed each second. For sound professionals, most sounds are recorded using a Bit rate of 24, and a sample rate of 48K.

**Top Tip**

We hear sound differently depending on the devices we use. The sound created on a laptop will sound different to that created by a sound studio. To understand how your sound will work, experiment with different devices. Listen to your sound on your phone, on your TV, and on your computer. How do they sound different? What could you change to help achieve your design goals?

**Genre sound** sounds and music associated with a particular genre of media

**Looped sound** sounds that are repeated seamlessly

**Temp sound** sound that you include temporarily, which might come from a variety of sources, that you will replace with sound you create yourself

# 14.5 DESIGNING SOUND

Having discussed the four types of sound, the three phases of creating sound and the tools that you will use, we will now move onto how you will decide what sounds you want to create.

## GENRE SOUND

When getting started, think about the kind of sounds that are most appropriate to your project and the meaning you want to convey. When planning this, gather and save sounds, and keep them backed up. You should make a plan and first ask yourself whether it is the right type of sound for the genre of media you are making. Sound designers refer to **genre sound** to describe sound types, sound FX and musical styles associated with certain styles of media. For example, laser gunfire and spaceship sounds belong to science fiction whereas simple electronic music that is played repeatedly (or 'looped') often accompanies puzzle or quest games, such as Super Mario Bros.™ series. This is known as **looped sound**. If you are making a horror film scene, you might want to have a Foley artist create a dramatic door slamming sound.

## CREATING A SOUND PALETTE

Just as you might use colour swatches and a mood board to experiment with how your project will look, you can do the same with sound. Gather sounds, atmospheres, songs and music from other films and whatever sources that have sounds that match your creation. You might be recreating a particular era in history, in which case you would look for signature sounds from that era – perhaps horses instead of cars, bicycles instead of buses. In doing so you will be creating your own sounds that have the feeling you are looking for.

You can base your sounds entirely on another video game, film or digital experience – using the sound from another work for inspiration, knowing that you are going to imitate or modify the sound that you have found. We sometimes call this temporary sound, which is shortened to **temp sound**. Remember that you can never use the exact sound recording from another work for reasons of copyright. The idea is to look for inspiration, and build up a group of sounds that you like.

## WORKING IN THE TIMELINE/TRACKLAY

Once you have gathered your sound palette of atmospheres, dialogue, sound effects and music, you need to arrange those sounds in a timeline or 'tracklay' using a DAW or editing software. It will look something like a checkerboard of sounds over time (see Figure 14.8). Sound engineers use the term 'tracklaying' much like a bricklayer might use the term 'bricklaying' to describe the process of building the components of a wall. If you organise your 'sound bricks' in a way that makes sense, either by type of sound or a system that makes sense to you, it will be easier to locate your sounds as you progress.

Figure 14.8 shows a project assembled in Avid's Pro Tools software. The voice and dialogue tracks are at the top, followed by sound effects, then atmospheres, and music at the bottom. Notice how long form atmospheres such as thunder and rain are elongated blocks of sound whereas short voice sounds are thin blocks of sound. Note also how individual sound files fade in and fade out (as indicated by the diagonal lines at the front and back of each individual sound) so that transitions between sections are smooth. Different parts of the overall tracklay are more or less dense – in the middle there are more sounds happening at once than at the end, which has fewer, quieter sounds, indicated by the sound files with less amplitude in the sound waveforms. In each different DAW, changing volume and other items are done using different menus.

**Fig 14.8** Sound project tracklay in Avid Pro Tools

# CHANGING SOUND USING PLUG-INS

When creating sound, you will often start with one simple sound and then manipulate it into something that better fits the meaning you are trying to convey. You can do this using plug-ins, which are software effects that work on sound samples in much the same way as guitar effects pedals change the sound of a guitar. Plug-ins enable you to do things like slow down or speed up a sound or change its pitch.

For example, in the film series *The Lord of The Rings*, many of the scenes are set in caves but were shot in studio spaces where the echo is not the same as in a real cave. To solve this problem the sound team added a plug-in reverb to the studio-recorded dialogue, to make it sound like the characters were in a cave. The film's sound designers also used a 'pitch shift' plug-in, to make some of the characters' voices deeper than the actors' voices.

Using plug-ins is one of the most exciting parts of sound work. You can turn the sound of a match being struck into the sound of a large explosion, or change the voice of a large man to sound like that of a small child. There are a few basic plug-ins you should learn how to use. Do not be afraid to experiment!

**Fig 14.9** The sound team for the film series *The Lord of the Rings* used plug-ins to re-create the sounds of being in a cave

## COMPRESSION

Compression is perhaps the most common effect used in sound design. You pass sounds through a compressor – an audio signal-processing programme or physical device – that reduces loud sounds and amplifies quiet sounds. This limits the affected sounds' **dynamic range** – or the difference between the quietest sounds and the loudest, which means the overall sound will not be as loud or as quiet as it was. For example, if you have a character whose voice was delivered by the actor as a whisper, or without much energy, you can increase the overall amplitude of the voice by adding compression. So what was a whisper can become as loud as the voices of characters who are speaking more forcefully.

**Dynamic range** (in digital audio) the range of the amplitude of the sound in your piece, from very quiet to very loud

## EQUALISATION (EQ)

This is the process of passing a sound through a filter that removes or enhances particular frequencies of a sound. So you could highlight the low frequencies or bass sound of an individual sound. You could also remove a high-pitched sound from a recording. For example, you might have recorded an interview with someone in the street, and there might be loud traffic sounds on the recording that make it difficult to concentrate on what the person is saying. This is a common problem. To solve it, you might use EQ to remove the traffic sounds. Because traffic is often quite a low frequency sound, and human conversation is a mid-range sound, it is possible to remove the low frequency sounds from the recording and therefore remove the traffic sounds.

## REVERB

Reverb is an electronically created echo. When we make sound in a space, the sound wave reflects off the surfaces of the space and comes back to us as an echo. Electronic reverb imitates that sound. So while your voice might have been recorded in a quiet studio, using reverb your voice could appear to be in a cave or a large concert hall. All of the DAWs have reverb as one of their most basic features, and you can achieve this effect using almost any editing software, as it is one of the most common sound effects.

## DELAY

Delay is similar to reverb in that it provides a kind of echo. However, rather than reflecting the sound, a delay repeats it. This can be done just once or repeatedly. Delay will repeat the sound being affected in different ways, depending on the settings in your software – the repeats could be fast and equal or slow and unequal. For example, if you listen to the Madonna's song 'Ray of Light' carefully, you can hear that the vocals repeat exactly what Madonna sings just after her original vocal. The delay is used later in the song on other instruments, passing different elements of the song through the effect. Delay effects became very popular in the 1960s. Among the types of music that used delay to great effect was dub music. For a good example, listen to the song 'Panic in Babylon' by Lee 'Scratch' Perry – every instrument is at some point passed through a delay effect.

## COMBINING PLUG-INS AND EFFECTS

As you combine plug-ins on a single sound, for example, a delay and compression, you will notice how adding one to another creates new sounds you had not expected. This kind of experimentation is at the heart of sound design. What happens when you try a pitch-shift effect with a delay, or a reverb and a delay together? These will create many exciting new ideas and inspire you to try new things.

There are many plug-ins made by different companies. Most plug-in manufacturers allow effects and plug-ins to be used for a trial period, usually a day or two, but sometimes up to a month. Experiment with them; try plugins made by iZotope, Waves and Avid.

### Skills Task: **Create an audio timeline**

Try to paint a picture using sound of where and when the listener is located.

- Record an atmosphere and import it into your timeline.
- Add some sound effects and perhaps some music.
- Make the piece at least one minute long.
- Using your software's export function, export a version of the timeline in a lossless format.

### Top Tip

Find sound inspiration through research. Listen to films from around the world, listen to old recordings in the library, search the internet, go to art galleries that have sound installations, go to archives in your town that specialise in certain ideas or periods of history. Keep notes, and try to keep a digital record of the sounds so you can listen to them.

# 14.6 OUTPUTTING FINAL SOUND

## MULTICHANNEL AUDIO

When you output sound in the final mix, you can send that sound out through multiple speakers. Any audio system that plays sound out of two or more speakers is technically 'multichannel audio', where channel refers to the number of speakers. Cinema systems and some home systems use multiple speakers to surround the audience so that they feel they are in the middle of the action; this is, known as **surround sound**. Figure 14.10 shows a home sound system that has multichannel audio output.

When making soundtracks, professionals can choose whether sounds come from behind, in front, to the left or right of the audience. Newer systems can even output sound from above or below the listener. For most of your work you will be working in stereo, but as you progress you might choose to make your sound more immersive by using more speakers.

In a nature documentary, for example, you might choose to have an atmosphere of a forest come from all of the speakers equally, making you feel like you are in the middle of the Amazon. You could make other sounds, such as the snarl of a jaguar, come from straight ahead, making it feel like the sound is coming from the screen itself.

Multichannel audio is described with reference to the number of speakers in an audio playback system. For example, stereo sound means there are two

**Surround sound** format that outputs sound from speakers on all sides of the audience

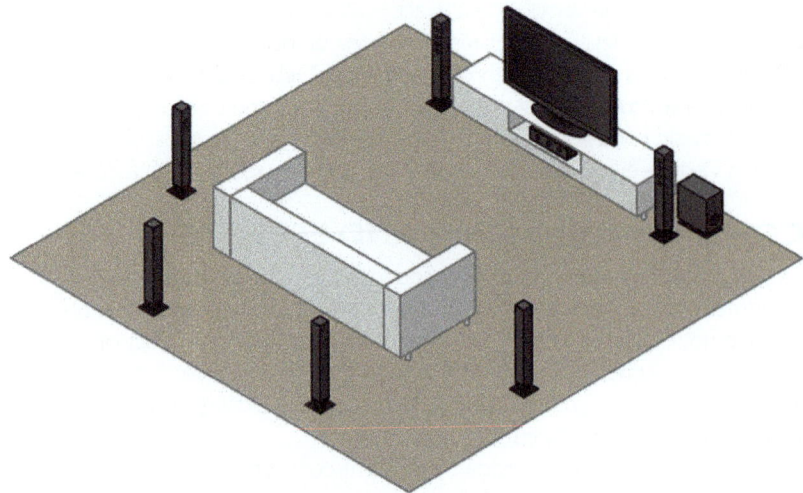

**Fig 14.10** A home sound system with multichannel audio output

speakers playing sound from roughly 20 Hz to 20 kHz ('full frequency') and no dedicated speakers playing sound at low frequency, between 20 Hz and 150 Hz. In other words, there is no bass speaker. Stereo systems are therefore represented numerically as 2.0. A 5.1 system would have five speakers playing at **full frequency sound** and one playing low frequency sounds – suitable for explosions or music with a lot of bass frequencies. For most of your work you will use stereo sound.

> **Full frequency sound** when a speaker system is capable of playing sound throughout the range of normal human hearing, from 20 Hz to 20 kHz

## Skills Task: **Identifying genre sound**

What kind of sounds might you use for each of these different genres of movies and video games?

- Game – a puzzle based 'sideways scrolling' game
- Movie – a cowboy movie based in the 'Wild West' of the USA
- Movie – a gangster movie set in Japan
- Game – a first person shooter set in a war

Research what sounds signify the genre of your chosen piece. How do each of these sounds make you feel? Present your findings to the group/class.

## Project work: **Building a memory in sound**

Think back to a time you remember well. It could be a holiday or the first day of school, a great game you played or a horrible visit to the dentist. Find or record five to ten sounds that remind you of that event.

- Create a new sound timeline using digital audio workstation (DAW) software, such as Adobe's Audition, Avid Pro Tools or Adobe® Premiere®.
- Arrange the sounds so they overlap and form an audio narrative telling the listener how you remember the event.
- Save different versions, changing the volume or amplitude of different sounds to change the way it feels.
- Export each version from the sound software as a .wav file.
- Play the audio files to the class or in small groups. Can they identify details of your memory?

Afterwards, discuss:

1. What happens when you change the volume of certain sections?
2. Do some sounds work better than others to evoke the time and space?
3. How do the different ways the sounds interact affect the way you feel?

## Case study: **Parkour safety app**

A group of Parkour (or Free Runner) artists wanted to make an app that would instruct people how to do Parkour more safely; an amateur free runner in London had recently had a serious accident. The artists and a professional camera team filmed a series of Parkour jumps and running sequences, a warm-up exercise and interviewed a safety expert and a psychologist. The team used lapel microphones to record the interviews and a microphone on a boom pole to record the Parkour artists' voices as they performed the sequences. The team then developed the app as follows:

**Fig 14.11** A Parkour artist performing

- They recorded an instructional voiceover in a sound studio, and matched it with the film material in the timeline of the editing software.
- One of the Parkour team, who was a musician, programmed an electronic dance track in Ableton Live, a popular digital audio workstation, to accompany the videos.
- They went to their filming locations and recorded atmospheres so they could create sounds for the background environments of the videos.

However, they found that the voiceover made a very exciting sport sound very dull, and identified some other problems:

- The sound on their videos contained a lot of wind noise and extra dialogue they did not need.
- The footsteps of the runners were recorded from body cameras they were wearing, and sounded heavy and awkward.
- The music was very loud, and overpowered the voiceover and the sounds of the runners.

To solve the problems, the team:

- removed the original sound recorded by the body cameras from the timeline; they had to create new sound for all the Parkour footage
- replaced the sound with an atmosphere – a light breeze on a summer's day in a park – from a sound library, making the videos calmer
- recorded one of the Parkour artists dancing across the floor of a ballet studio, as well as on concrete; they pasted these footsteps into the timeline to make the Parkour artists sound lighter and more like dancers
- they replaced some of the electronic music with a recording of one of the Parkour artists playing a cello very lightly.

These changes gave the videos within the app a more delicate feel, which more closely reflected the art they were creating with their Parkour moves.

### Further reference

- *The Sound Reinforcement Handbook* (Gary David and Ralph Jones, 1990)

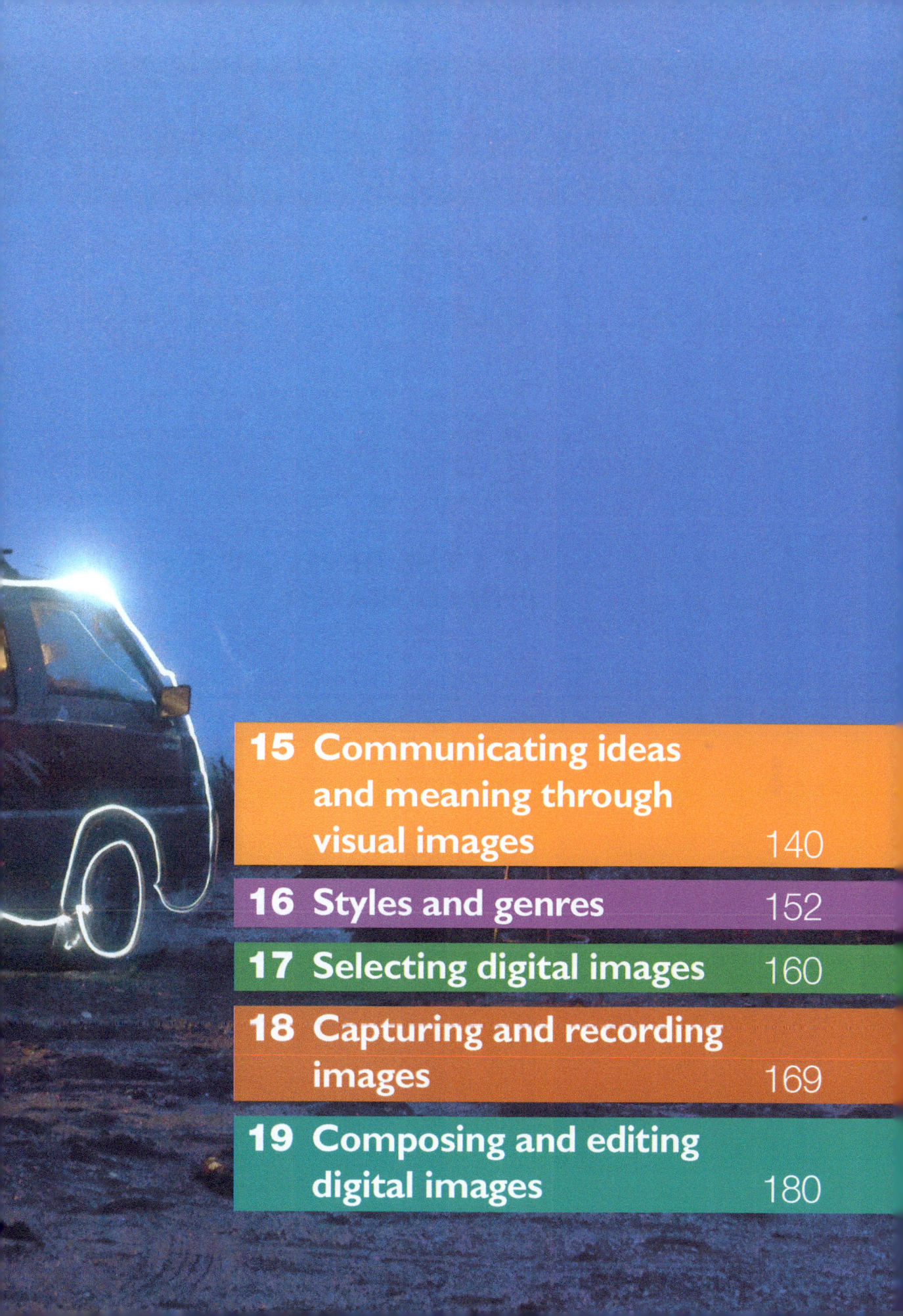

# 15  Communicating ideas and meaning through visual images

There is no doubt that photography has done more to change our perception of the world than any other visual medium. Since the invention of photography in the 19th century, it has quickly become the most important means of visual communication in the history of human society. In this chapter you will look at how photography has developed as a medium for Fine Art and for visual communication in a number of social, cultural and commercial contexts. You will also learn how digital photography evolved from analogue photography.

## 15.1 THE DEVELOPMENT OF PHOTOGRAPHY

Visual language has always shaped the way humans communicate with one another, from the earliest cave paintings created 40,000 years ago to the development in our time of photo-based social media platforms. However, it was the development of photography in particular that revolutionised the way we record and distribute information and ideas through images, by introducing a communication medium that was immediate and effective and also lasted over time.

The digital revolution of the last thirty years has resulted in photographic technology becoming more and more accessible and useable for

**Fig 15.1** One of the earliest examples of a pictograph on a cave wall; it shows people swimming

**Fig 15.2** Modern visual representation of Michael Phelps, an Olympic swimmer

non-specialists, while social media platforms have revolutionised the way we store, distribute and manipulate images. Anyone with a smartphone can now use photographs to distribute news and ideas (photojournalism), show and sell goods (advertising photography), record events in our lives (wedding photography) and communicate daily with friends, family and colleagues using visual media, such as Instagram, Snapchat and Facebook. This has been incredibly empowering.

The word 'photography' comes from a combination of the Greek words *photos* and *graphos*, and roughly translated means 'drawing with light'. Essentially it is a medium that mixes art and science: although the ideas and design behind a photographic image are artistic and creative, the method of creating and processing that image relies on physics and chemistry. The photographic process basically creates lasting visual images of real objects by recording the way they reflect light, either chemically (using light-sensitive **photographic film**) or electronically (using an **electronic image sensor**).

The origins of the photographic process are not clear-cut, since no single individual 'invented' photography as such. Instead it developed through a series of experiments and processes carried out in the late-19th century, based on the concept of the **pinhole camera** and the discovery that some chemical substances can be visibly altered by exposure to light.

In the early part of the 19th century, the Englishman Thomas Wedgwood made the first attempt to record a photographic image. He used a device similar to a pinhole camera to capture it, and white paper, which he had treated with silver nitrate, to record it. However, what he actually succeeded in capturing were the shadows of objects placed in direct sunlight, not images of the objects themselves. It wasn't until 1826 that a French inventor, Joseph Niépce, finally succeeded in capturing and fixing an image of the view from his window after years of experimentation with various light-sensitive chemicals.

> ### Link
> See Chapter 18, pages 169–179, for more information on how cameras work.

> **Photographic film** light sensitive film that captures photos in an analogue camera
> **Electronic image sensor** light sensitive plate that captures photos in a digital camera
> **Pinhole camera** very simple camera made from a box

**Fig 15.3** The first permanent photograph, *View from the Window at Le Gras* (1826) by Joseph Nicéphore Niépce

Niépce went on to experiment with the photographic process together with his partner Louis Daguerre. Complete instructions about the top-secret and complex technique they had developed using iodine and mercury vapour

**Daguerreotype** early type of black and white photographic image

eventually went public in August 1839 in France. These early photographic images became known as **daguerreotypes** and this was the most commonly used commercial photographic process until the late 1850s.

**Fig 15.4** An example of a daguerreotype

## Skills Task: **Make a pinhole camera**

Make a pinhole camera to understand how the photographic process works. You will need:

- a shoe box
- sheets of photographic paper
- a thin piece of metal, such as found in a soft drinks can
- electrical tape
- a sharp knife/scissors
- a needle

Method:

1. First, make sure there are no holes in the box and then paint the inside black. Seal the edges of the box and lid with the tape. Cut a small square opening in one end of the box. Keep the square piece for later.
2. Make the pinhole. Cut a square of metal from the can, slightly smaller than the side of the box. Make a hole in it with the needle then work the needle around to make it bigger.
3. Tape the pinhole behind the square opening in the end of the box. Centre the pinhole in the square.
4. Make the 'shutter'. Tape the square piece of card you saved to cover the pinhole from the outside.
5. Load the photographic paper. (You must do this in a darkroom.) Tape a piece of photo paper to the inside of the box, opposite the pinhole. Put the lid on the box. Make sure the shutter is closed.
6. Point the camera at the object you want to photograph. Hold the shutter open for 30 seconds (very sunny) to 4 minutes (very cloudy) then close. Go back to the dark room and take the paper out to develop the image.

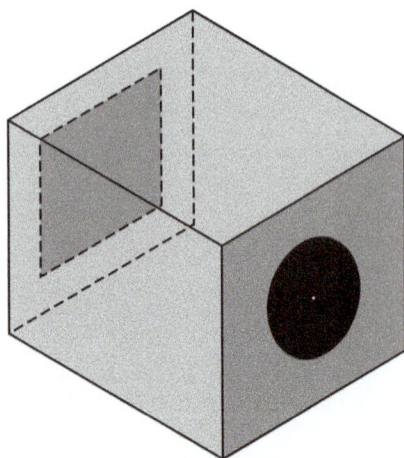

**Fig 15.5** A pinhole camera

# 15.2 PHOTOGRAPHY AND FINE ART

The history of photography has been shaped by its relationship with Art. Initially it was seem as a medium for representing people, objects and landscapes in a pictorial way, a sort of alternative to painting. There is evidence that the Master painters of the Dutch Golden Age, in the 17th century, used pinhole cameras to produce some of their very realistic, highly detailed works. As photography began to evolve, separate artistic styles and genres developed within photography in their own right.

## PICTORIALISM

One of the earliest uses of photography as Fine Art was in Pictorialism, an international style and aesthetic movement that became very popular during the late-19th century. The word Pictorialism refers to a series of techniques some photographers used to manipulate a straightforward photograph to create a very stylised, **painterly** image. Some of these were techniques used to construct the image (for example, theatrical and symbolic composition of the subjects and very dramatic lighting), while others were techniques used to develop it (for example, printing in colours such as **sepia** or dark blue, or applying visible **brush strokes** to the surface). In fact, most pictorialist images show a combination of all of these techniques. Artists, such as James McNeill Whistler, Henry Peach Robinson, Gertrude Käsebier and Harold Cazneaux saw photography not just as a means of recording the appearance of things but as a new artistic medium for creating atmosphere and conveying emotion and meaning. Above all, the Pictorialists were interested in involving the imagination of the viewer in the reaction to the image, not just the eye.

Fig 15.6 *Lollipops, a study of Mina Turner and her cousin Elizabeth* (1910) by photographer Gertrude Käsebier

**Painterly**  with the characteristics of an oil painting; stylised
**Sepia**  brownish colour sometimes used to print old monotone photographs
**Brush strokes**  visible lines created on the surface of a painting by the artist's brush

Skills Task: **Analyse the elements of Pictorialism**

Look at the example of a Pictorialist photograph in the section above (Figure 15.6). What mood and atmosphere do you think the artist was trying to convey in this image? Record your impressions about the following elements. Discuss your ideas in groups.

1. Composition
2. Lightning
3. Symbolism

## IMPRESSIONISM

A deep interest in photography was also important to the development of other late-19th century artistic movements. Many painters and sculptors began to use photography as a tool to help them prepare their work, for example, to record a model's pose or a landscape in particular weather conditions. Many of the great 19th century painters, including Delacroix, Courbert, Monet, Degas, Cézanne and Gauguin, took photographs themselves, used photographs by others and incorporated images from photographs into their work.

The Impressionists were particularly interested in trying to capture the impression of a subject or scene at a particular moment in time, rather

**Fig 15.7** *The Houses of Parliament, Sunset* (1903) by Claude Monet oil on canvas, National Gallery of Art, Washington, D.C.

**Fig 15.8** *The Houses of Parliament (Effect of Fog)* (1903–04) by Claude Monet oil on canvas, The Metropolitan Museum of Art, New York

**From life** working directly from a real scene or object without sketching first

than just representing its external form, and they usually painted **from life**. However, capturing certain effects of light could be difficult, as these often changed faster than the artists could paint them. The invention of photography helped artists by enabling them to record a scene in the moment that they could later use to paint from in the studio. It also allowed them to record the same scene in different conditions of light and weather on different days, and then to experiment with painting these different impressions that the same scene could convey.

In the early 1900s the impressionist artist Claude Monet used photographs in this way as the basis for a famous series of paintings of the Houses of Parliament in London. In it the same scene is represented many times in different weather conditions and at different times of the day. The buildings are reduced to silhouettes, while instead Monet concentrates on capturing the different effects of light on the scene, creating a different mood and atmosphere in each painting.

## MODERNISM

In the 1930s a number of experimental Art movements emerged where photography was no longer considered just a tool for documenting possible subjects, but instead became an important medium for innovative artistic expression in its own right.

Modern Art movements such as Dadaism and Surrealism developed as a reaction to the extreme political and social changes of the time. Artists in these groups were looking for new ways to interpret reality, new ways of seeing, and some of them turned to the new medium of photography as the most appropriate vehicle for this creative process. Developments in photographic technology, such as Leica's new range of sophisticated cameras, and in techniques, such as photograms (photographs made without the use of a camera or negative), allowed artists such as Man Ray, Iwao Yamawaki, László Moholy-Nagy and Hannah Hoch to experiment with surprising new techniques in visual communication.

'When the true qualities of photography are recognized, the process of representation by mechanical means will be brought to a level of perfection never before reached.'

'The illiterate of the future will be the person ignorant of the use of the camera.'

(László Moholy-Nagy, 1927)

Man Ray's photo *Glass Tears* (1932) (Figure 15.9) achieves a clarity and sharpness of focus that makes the viewer notice the details used to compose this unusual extreme close up of his wife. Shots such as this were made possible by the increasingly sophisticated cameras developed in the 1930s by manufacturers such as Leica.

In this disturbing **photo collage**, (Figure 15.10) Hannah Höch used details from a variety of photographic images of eyes to create a surrealist bouquet of flowers with the eyes as the flowers' centres. At the same time Hoch's work is a political commentary on the all-seeing, invasive control of people's lives on the part of the Nazi regime in Germany in the 1930s.

**Photo collage** image made from cut photographic images reassembled
**Photomontage** image made from various photographs superimposed on one another

Fig 15.9 *Les Larmes (Glass Tears)*, (1932) by Man Ray, gelatin silver print

Fig 15.10 *Bouquet of Eyes* (1930) by Hannah Höch, collage, Germanisches Nationalmuseum, Nürnberg, Germany

## FINE ART PHOTOGRAPHY

Also known as 'photographic art' or 'artistic photography', the term Fine Art photography has no universally agreed meaning or definition. Rather, it refers to a wide-ranging category of photographs where the intention is aesthetic (the value of the image lies mainly in its beauty) rather than scientific, commercial or journalistic. Generally speaking, in Fine Art photography the photographer, instead of merely capturing a realistic view of the subject, aims to produce a more personal, interpretive or evocative impression of it in order to encourage the viewer to see it differently.

Artistic photos have also been used frequently in photo collage, a sub-genre developed by artists such as David Hockney, and in **photomontage** by the Dadaists, for example, Raoul Hausmann and Hannah Hoch,

Surrealists such as Max Ernst and Pop Artists such as Richard Hamilton. By adapting the formal and compositional elements of visual art to the medium of photography, artists have been able to extend the visual vocabulary at their disposal and communicate artistically in new ways.

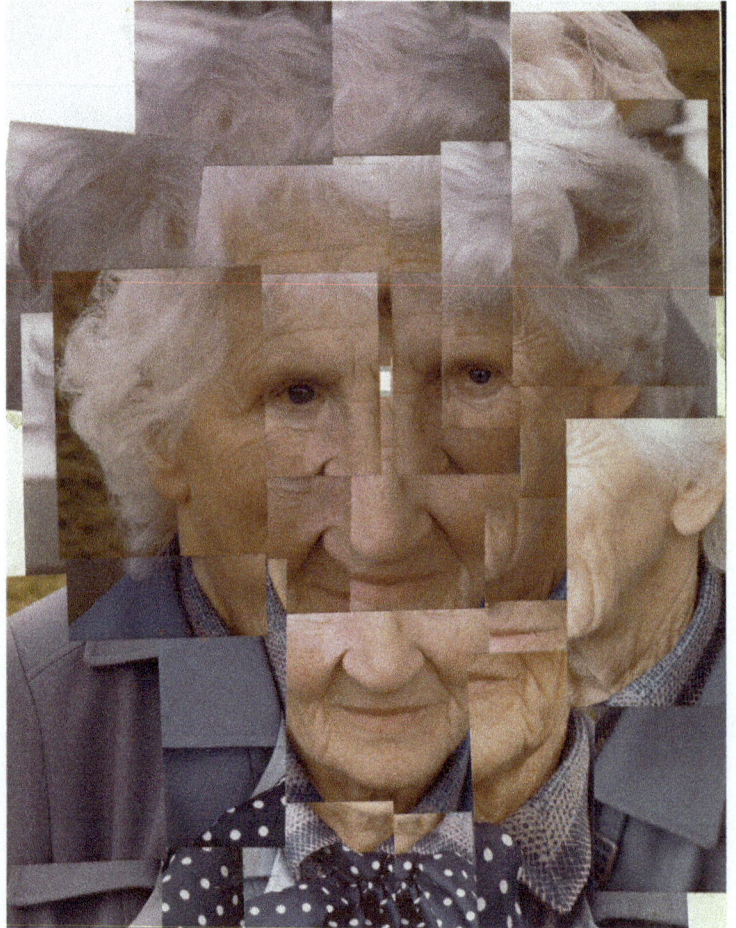

**Fig 15.11** *Mother I, Yorkshire Moors* (August 1985) by David Hockney, photographic collage

## Comprehension: 20th century artistic movements

Look at the timeline of 20th century artistic movements that made use of photography. Research each one online. Choose two example photographs to illustrate the style of each movement.

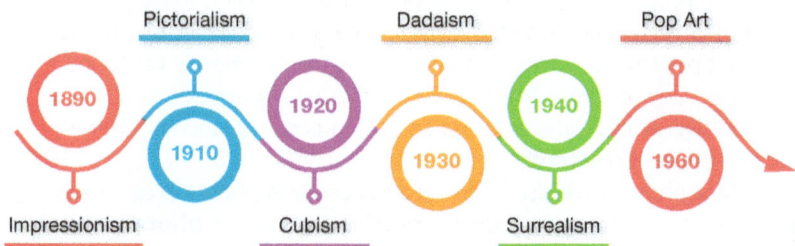

**Fig 15.12** Timeline of 20th century artistic movements

# 15.3 PHOTOGRAPHY IN SOCIAL AND COMMERCIAL CONTEXTS

In the years before World War I (1914–18), photographic technology developed rapidly and professional photographers were soon able to shoot images of a much sharper focus and finer quality. George Eastman's invention of the 'point and shoot' hand-held camera, marketed by the famous Kodak Company, meant that anyone could now capture spontaneous images easily, and advances in the development process meant photos could be developed more quickly.

## PHOTOJOURNALISM AND DOCUMENTARY PHOTOGRAPHY

Journalists were among the first people to see the advantages of this new visual medium and soon began using photographs to illustrate their articles in newspapers and journals. Consequently **photojournalism** (the communication of news through photographic images) began to emerge as a distinctive form of photography in the late 1920s. Some photographs, which were originally taken to illustrate important social or political events, were so effective in conveying the mood of the times in which they were shot that they became iconic, not just as social history but also as artworks in their own right. For example, the portrait photo, *Afghan Girl*, by esteemed photojournalist Steve McCurry, is often compared to the painting *Mona Lisa* by Leonardo Da Vinci because of the enigmatic expression McCurry has captured in the eyes of his subject.

Another famous example is Alfred Stieglitz photograph *The Steerage*, taken in 1907, which is now regarded as one of the most iconic photographs of the 20th century. In its sociological context it documents migrants arriving home in Germany after being refused entry to the USA, but it also has a narrative element, allowing the viewer from just the few details included to imagine the story, or stories, of the people shown in it. In an artistic context it expertly uses photographic techniques, such as **frame within a frame**, the **rule of thirds** and **leading lines** to compose the image and evoke contrasting feelings of hope and despair in the viewer's response. Because of the combination of all these elements it is regarded as one of the first and finest examples of the genre of documentary photography.

The Camera
that takes
the World !

**THE**

# KODAK

*No previous knowledge of Photography necessary.*

"YOU PRESS THE BUTTON, WE DO THE REST,"

(Unless you prefer to do the rest yourself)

AND THE PICTURE IS FINISHED.

Price from £1 6s.

**EASTMAN** PHOTOGRAPHIC MATERIALS CO. LD., 115-117 OXFORD-ST., LONDON, W.

SEND FOR PRETTY, ILLUSTRATED CATALOGUE, POST FREE.

**Fig 15.13** Advert for the first Kodak hand-held camera, 1893

---

**Photojournalism** news stories told through photographs
**Frame within a frame** use of elements within the subject itself to contain the central subject
**Rule of thirds** proportional rule governing positioning of main subject within an image
**Leading lines** elements of visual composition that lead the eye into a visual image

**Link**

See Chapter 19, pages 180–185, for more information on compositional techniques.

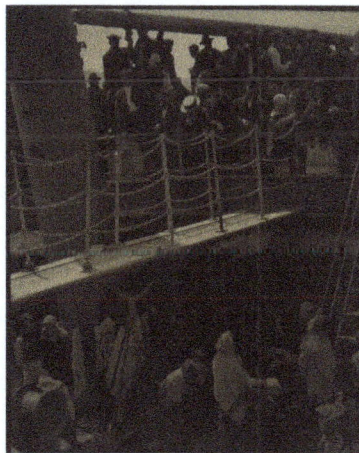

**Fig 15.14** *Sharbat Gula, Afghan Girl, at Nasir Bagh refugee camp*, Peshawar, Pakistan (1984) by American photojournalist Steve McCurry

**Fig 15.15** Alfred Stieglitz's *The Steerage* (1907) documents migrants arriving in Germany after being refused entry to the USA

**Fig 15.16** *Man Beside Wheelbarrow* (1934) by Dorothea Lange, photonegative; her images recorded the poverty and deprivation in the USA during the Great Depression

Through its use in journalism, people soon realised the narrative power of photography. A picture is a much more immediate and succinct way to tell a story than a written article, and it can often elicit a stronger emotional response.

During the 1930s, the period of the Great Depression in the West, some photographers began to use their work to document the terrible deprivation and poverty of the unemployed population in the USA. To call attention to the desperate circumstances of many of their countrymen, photographers such as Dorothea Lange started to publish uncompromising, disturbing images that hid nothing from the viewer. These photos had all the more power to shock because they were real: the photographer's art in the new medium of documentary photography lay in recognising the combination of ideal elements in a subject and shooting in the moment to capture that perfect image. These photographs did not aspire to imitate paintings as Pictorialist images had done; they were visual records of real, unadorned subjects, but the great documentary images were also Art, combining creative vision with expert use of compositional techniques.

*'The camera is a tool for learning to see.'*

(Dorothea Lange, 1936)

## COMMERCIAL PHOTOGRAPHY

Commercial photography basically means taking photos for commercial use – for business, for sales, for money. Commercial photography is often associated with advertising and product placement, merchandising and fashion. It is mainly used in promotional literature and on websites, but it is also used in corporate brochures, advertising leaflets, menus, advertorials and press photos (those that you insert when sending out press releases or mailings).

During the 1950s and 1960s, photography became a valuable marketing tool. As the advertising industry grew, it centred ever more frequently on the visual image as the most immediate and memorable medium to communicate a key message or the feeling and quality associated with a particular item or brand.

Advertising photography is generally used for promotional purposes to communicate an idea rather than to tell a story, as in Fine Art photography, or to comment on events, as in documentary photography. Its main purpose is to present an ideal version of the thing being advertised, in order to persuade the viewer that it is desirable and that they want or need it. If you want to sell a product, you certainly need to have great commercial photos. Either you want sharp, high quality idealising images to be printed in newspaper adverts or brochures, or you might need photos that focus on the design and functionality of the product for a user manual or operating instructions. The commercial photographer has to be particularly skilled in using a range of photographic techniques to edit and manipulate the image to ensure it exactly meets the brief of how the subject must be represented. An in-depth knowledge of the camera's technical features and capabilities is crucial, as is expertise in editing and manipulating images digitally.

### Link

See Chapter 19, pages 185–189, for more information on editing and manipulating digital photos.

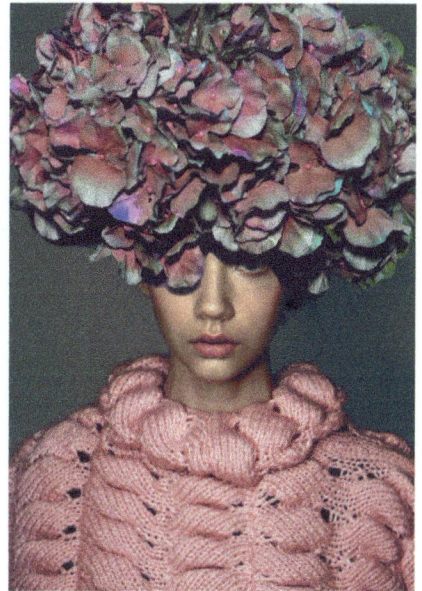

**Fig 15.17** Examples of advertising images: (top left) M&S lorry with appealing visual images of food; (top right) poster from the 'Think Small' campaign for Volkswagen, 1961; (bottom left) striking image of make-up brushes on black background; (bottom right) eye-catching fashion image

## Comprehension: **Different aims**

What are the differences in aims between photojournalism/documentary photography and commercial photography? Timing is an essential skill for photographers working in both of these genres to develop. Why? Makes note on the differences in aim for each point below.

- Lighting
- Scale
- Depth
- Timing

**Fig 15.18** US athlete Jesse Owens performing in the 1936 Berlin Olympic Games

# SPORTS AND ACTION PHOTOGRAPHY

Professional sports photography has a direct connection to photojournalism and developed in a similar way as illustration for reports on sporting events in the print media. The term 'sports photography' refers to the genre that covers all types of sports and action images and the particular techniques that are used to realise them.

Like all types of photography, great sports photography takes a lot of expertise and good equipment to produce, but the key skill in this case is timing. It is the sports photographer's job to look and anticipate where and how the action is going to unfold, and then be ready to capture it as soon as it starts.

This dynamic photograph (Figure 15.18) shows the sprinter Jessie Owens in the process of breaking the world record at the Berlin Olympic Games in 1936. At that time the Nazis were trying to use the international sporting event to demonstrate their idea of Aryan racial supremacy. These photographs were published all over the world and Owens was regarded as a hero to have performed so outstandingly in such a hostile, racist environment.

**Fig 15.19** An action shot of cyclists at the 2012 Olympics

## Comprehension: **Sports and action photography**

Look carefully at the image of Jesse Owens. (Figure 15.18)

1. What elements give the photograph its sense of dynamism and movement?
2. What effect does the background have on the main image?
3. What do you notice about the sharpness of focus in the different parts of the figure of Owens? What effect does this create?

> ### Project work: **Characteristics of photographic genres**

Choose **one** of the themes below and research how different photographers in different genres have represented it in the last 50 years.

- Childhood
- Animals and humans
- Climate change
- Fear

Choose six of your favourite photographs from those you have found, and make notes about why you think they are successful within your chosen genre. Explain your decisions.

# 15.4 AESTHETICS AND EMOTIONAL RESPONSES IN VISUAL IMAGES

Photography has become more and more accessible over the years; modern technological advances have enabled us to engage with photography with ease. The physical process of taking a photograph has changed dramatically but the mechanical basics remain the same; we still need a lens, a light source and process of visually capturing the moment.

Also the same, is that in the creation of an image the photographer is also creating an aesthetic experience for the viewer. Photography not only enables us to capture and record significant moments in time. It also conveys history, humanity and emotion. The phrase 'a picture is worth a thousand words' is just as true today as it was in 1913.

Today's fast-paced digital world enables us to digest information quickly, and allows social media platforms to thrive. Each photograph still coveys meaning and a wide of range of emotions, with the speed of social media allowing the viewer to experience a dozen different emotions with one swipe down their Instagram feed.

Just because you can now argue that emotional responses are evoked very quickly, it does still take skill and perseverance to enable that visual communication to happen. The professional practicing photographer needs to be:

- able to make visual and compositional decisions very quickly; to capture that split second of pure emotion.
- patient, dedicated and meticulous in preparation; to capture what could, for example, be a first or last natural occurrence or event.
- able to recognise and accept failure; to learn and adapt from previous aesthetic and compositional errors is very important.
- balanced and critical; to make sound compositional and aesthetical judgements enabling them to clearly and concisely communicate a visual message.

Have a look at some of the images in this section and consider how they evoke emotional responses. The photographers who created the portrait image *Afghan Girl* (page 147) and *Migrant Mother* (page 153) set out to create an aesthetic experience for their audience, as well as using photography to highlight social issues. Both images use the focus of the face, the eyes in particular in the image of the *Afghan Girl*, to convey sadness and despair. By using negative space to focus the images on their human subjects, the photographers have carefully considered the composition of their visual images to evoke the outcome they would like.

We have seen in the previous chapter how a range of different photographic genres developed over time, as people became more aware of photography's immense power and potential as a medium for visual communication. To thoroughly understand how photographers can work effectively within these different genres, however, it is important to understand the different techniques and processes that are used in each one, and in particular to build up a sound knowledge of the key elements of visual composition and how these are applied.

# 16.1 PORTRAIT PHOTOGRAPHY

Portrait photography is one of the most challenging genres to work in. Shooting a photograph that manages to convey a sense of the person's personality and presence, feelings and life experience, is a skill that takes considerable patience and dedication to develop. In fact, good portrait photography is not simply about learning techniques or choosing the right equipment – it is about developing the ability to really relate to your subjects and see beyond their face. In some cases it relies on making the person you are photographing feel comfortable, so they are prepared to reveal their true self for the camera. In others it is about capturing a particular look or momentary expression that gives the viewer an insight into the person. If a portrait photographer can achieve this, then he or she is able to capture a real sense of the person's essence, the thing that makes them unique. It is this aspect in a truly great portrait that elevates it from being just a technically perfect record of what someone looks like to the level of Art.

The American photographer Dorothea Lange's work, which was mostly done in the USA during the era known as the Great Depression in the 1930s, is a good example of how a photographer can relate to her subjects in this profound way and convey a sense of character and narrative. In fact Lange's work from this period is regarded as some of the best portrait photography ever **shot**.

Lange was asked to work with a government department called the Farm Security Administration, to document their attempts to tackle the terrible problems of poverty in rural areas of the USA during this time. Through her documentary work, Lange began to refine her techniques as a portrait photographer, capturing very poignantly the effects of the economic slump on individuals within the rural population. The photographs she took of the ordinary people she met in these communities provided not only documentary evidence of the shocking conditions she encountered, but also a series of beautiful and moving black and white portraits of working class Americans.

**Shot** photograph

One of Lange's most famous works is *Migrant Mother*, taken in 1936. In composing this image Lange expertly applied two compositional techniques to construct the image and give it visual impact: the rule of thirds and **leading lines**.

- The rule of thirds dictates where the photographer positions the main subject of the shot within the **frame**. In Lange's photograph the mother is not centred in the image, as we might expect. Instead Lange has chosen to position the face of the mother and the heads of her two children in the top third of the frame, slightly above the centre. This has the effect of drawing the eye into the composition.
- A leading line is then used to lead the eye through the image from bottom to top, from one element to another. Lange uses the diagonal line of the mother's forearm in the centre of the shot in this way, moving from her elbow in the bottom of the frame towards her face in the top third, and finally to her eyes, which are the main focus of the image. The gaze focuses on the mother's face (also the lightest part of the photo), noting the lines of tiredness and worry, the weather-beaten skin and the grim-set mouth. This diagonal leading line in the composition also bisects the frame into two symmetrical sections, each one mirroring the other, with the head of a child turned away from the viewer as he/she clings to the mother's shoulder.

> **Leading lines rule** the rule dictating the direction that the eye travels when viewing a visual image
> **Frame** border of the photograph

> ## Link
>
> See Chapter 19, pages 180–185, for more information on the rules of composition.

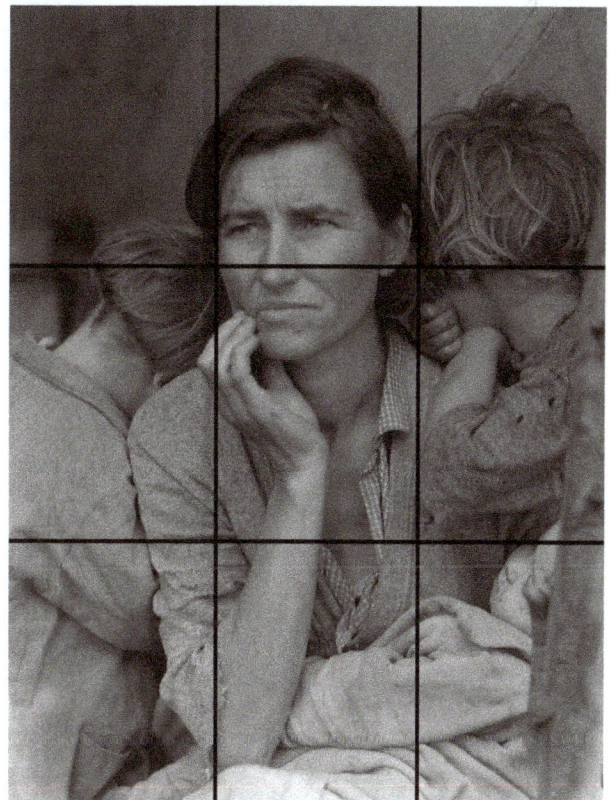

**Fig 16.1** *Migrant Mother* (1936) by Dorothea Lange; and right, showing the rule of thirds

Portrait photography requires a lot of creativity in order to achieve powerful, memorable portraits. Most of the best portraits involve an authentic representation of human emotion and expression that speaks to us all, whether the subject is a poor American farm worker, as in Lange's work, a scientist, a school child or a famous celebrity.

**Fig 16.2** American portrait photographer Annie Leibovitz in front of some of her work

**Fig 16.3** Untitled (1952/1955) by Seydou Keïta modern gelatin silver print

**Top Tip**

To gain an idea of the style and genre that most interests you, it is important to research different photographers. Portfolios of their work can be found online.

**Link**

See Chapter 15, page 143, for more information on Pictorialism.

One of the most famous contemporary American portrait photographers is Annie Leibovitz, who is known for her exceptional work photographing celebrities. She has worked for many well-known fashion magazines and pop-culture publications and many of her portraits have become iconic. Her use of bold colours, intriguing light effects and unique poses is what has ultimately helped her work become popular.

Rinko Kawauchi from Japan is best known for her serene and poetic photographs depicting ordinary moments in life, and is one of only a few celebrated female photographers in Asia and beyond. Rinko is also known for the creation of innovative photobooks.

Raghubir Singh is India's pioneer and master of colour photography, best-known for his vivid, complex, layered photographs of his home country. He is particularly interested capturing images about Indian identity.

The great African portraitist Seydou Keïta lived in Bamako, Mali, from 1921 to 2001. A self-taught photographer, he opened a studio in 1948 and started to specialise in portraiture. He soon gained a reputation for excellence throughout West Africa. His numerous clients were drawn by the quality of his photos and his great sense of aesthetics.

# 16.2 LANDSCAPE PHOTOGRAPHY

Landscape photography examines physical spaces within our world and deals with scale, sometimes showing vast scenes while at other times capturing microscopic subjects. Usually, the term landscape photography describes the photography of natural features, such as land, sky and water. However, it may also involve human-made subjects, such as fields, roads, walls or gardens, or sometimes architectural elements, such as individual buildings, industrialised zones or cityscapes. The subjects are most often seen from a distance, but landscape photographs may also include elements near the viewer in the foreground, sometimes even in close-up, to give the image a sense of scale through contrast. Some landscape photographs deal with natural features on a very small scale, examining them in microscopic detail to give the viewer a new perspective on the subject.

Ansel Adams was an American photographer who loved the wild places of the USA and the solitude and peacefulness he was able to experience being alone in such vast landscapes. For much of his life he travelled through the great untouched landscapes of the Sierra Nevada and Yosemite National Park using various small cameras such as the Kodak Box Brownie or the Hasselblad 35 mm to capture the grandeur and scale of these places.

In his early years he was inspired by the work of Alfred Stieglitz, who often tried to reproduce the effects of Fine Art in photography. Initially he copied many of Stieglitz's techniques, for example, hand-painting directly onto photographs to give them a more painterly effect (rather like the work of the Pictorialists in the early-20th century).

As Adams evolved as an artist in his own right, however, he rejected this sort of interference with the medium in favour of Realism. He worked primarily in large formats and used a variety of lenses to vary his effects, refusing to retouch his photos at all. He relied instead on compositional techniques such as the rule of thirds or the frame within a frame, where the elements in the landscape itself create a natural frame for the main subject. In the photograph *Half Dome, Mercer River, Winter*, Ansel uses the trees on either side of the shot, plus the lake in the foreground, to create an inner frame. This draws the eye in to focus on the mountain, his main subject, and gives the image a sense of scale and grandeur.

Ansel also frequently worked in black and white rather than colour, expertly using standard photographic techniques such as **heightened contrast** and **sharpened focus**, to give scale and **texture** to his subjects.

**Link**

See Chapter 11, page 113, and Chapter 19, 180–185, for more information on compositional techniques.

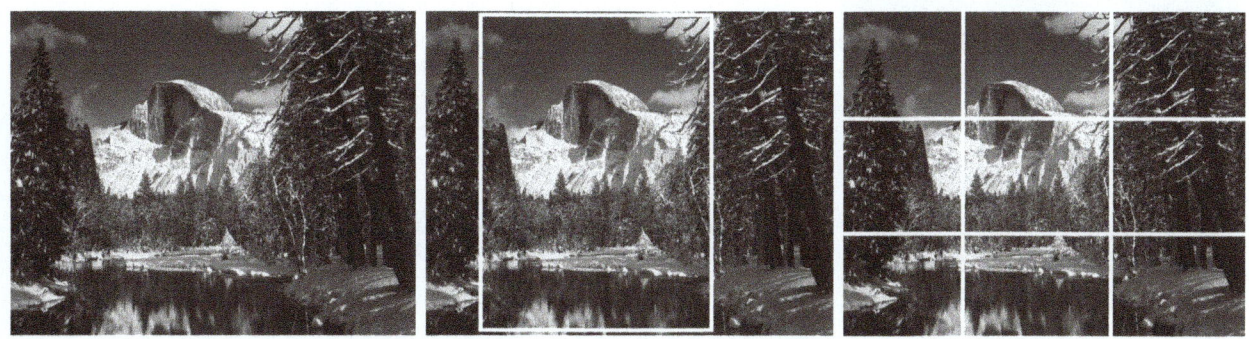

**Fig 16.4** *Half Dome, Merced River, Winter*, Yosemite National Park, California (c.1938) by Ansel Adams, gelatin silver print; also showing frame within a frame (centre) and leading lines (right)

## Skills Task: **Analysing features of landscape photography**

Choose two other examples of Ansel Adams' landscapes.

1. How many of the compositional techniques can you recognise in each photograph?
2. What effect is achieved by using each technique?
3. What do you think about when you look at each image? Reflect on how each one makes you feel.

**Heightened contrast** increasing the intensity of the light and dark areas
**Sharpened focus** increasing the resolution and quality
**Texture** materials the subjects are made of
**Tone** intensity of light and shade

# 16.3 STILL LIFE PHOTOGRAHY

Still life photography essentially shows inanimate subjects, mostly individual objects or small groups of objects that are somehow linked, such as food, flowers, household items or even sports equipment. Most still life photography is used in advertising or publishing, whether as a complete image in an advert or book cover, or as part of an overall page design or on product packaging.

Good still life photography looks simple, but in fact it is often very complicated to set up. More than in other photographic genres the still life photographer has control over the composition of the shot, but is often required to photograph the subject in a very particular way. To some extent it can be said that a still life photographer makes the photograph, rather than takes the photograph, choosing colours, textures, sizes, shapes and possibly backgrounds that work together visually, to carefully set up the shots. Still life photographers therefore need to have a very detailed understanding of lighting techniques, the psychology of colour, how **tone** and texture work in

**Link**

See Chapter 2, pages 19–21, for more information on the basic elements of visual design.

**Fig 16.5** An example of compositional food photography

an image, and the effect of **depth of field**, and know how these can be used to enhance the image.

David Griffen is a still life photographer who works for some of the most prominent award-winning restaurant chains in the UK, including those set up by Rick Stein and Paul Ainsworth. Griffen's work focuses on making his subject matter, in this case food, look delicious and appetising as well as beautiful and artistic. The shots that he takes are mainly used in food magazines, newspapers and supplements, and on social media sites.

Griffen often uses unusual compositional techniques such as the Fibonacci sequence to present his subjects as dynamically and interestingly as possible. Fibonacci sequence as the organising principle also makes a harmonious composition of the elements that is easy for the human eye to process and therefore pleasing to look at.

**Depth of field** the distance between the closest and furthest object that is in sharp focus

## Top Tip

The Fibonacci sequence is a mathematical sequence where each new number is the sum of the two numbers before it. Starting with 0 and 1, the sequence goes: 0, 1, 1, 2, 3, 5, 8, 13, 21, 34, and so on. The sequence is known as 'nature's numbering system', as it appears everywhere in nature, from the arrangement of stripes on a seashell to the pattern of petals in a flower. When used in visual design, this relationship of proportions creates a composition that is very harmonious and aesthetically pleasing.

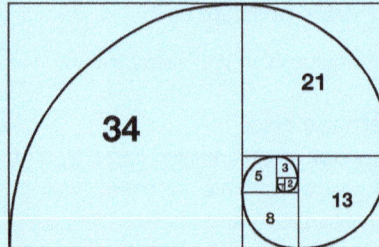

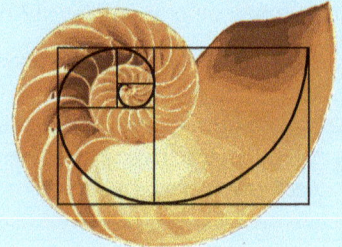

**Fig 16.6** The numerical proportions of the Fibonacci sequence as related to a shell

## Skills Task: **Analysing still life photographs**

Consider the three examples of still life photographs opposite (Figure 16.7). Make notes about how the photographer in each case has used the following techniques.

- Lighting
- Colour
- Depth of field
- Texture

Reflect on which image you like best. Explain your choice.

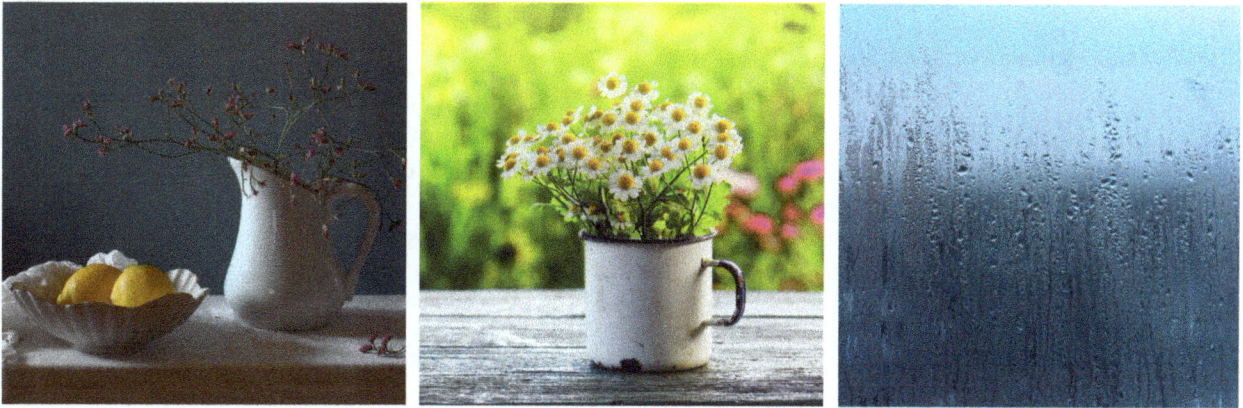

**Fig 16.7** Examples of still life photography showing effective use of lighting, colour, depth of field and texture

# 16.4 DOCUMENTARY PHOTOGRAPHY

Probably the most widely used photographic genre is documentary photography, which records aspects of real life and invites the viewer to reflect on them. Documentary photography usually follows (or implies) a 'story' about its subject over a period of time, as opposed to the real-time instant recording of breaking news and events that photojournalism focuses on. These two types of photography are intimately connected, however.

Documentary photography is an extremely effective vehicle for highlighting stories that aren't widely known or understood, and is often used in reportage about social issues. It is frequently used to tell longer, more involved human-interest stories, often documenting the effects of wars, natural disasters and deprivation, although it does sometimes tell happier stories. Compelling visual imagery of this type has been able to greatly influence public opinion and create real political change in the last sixty or seventy years, and combined with the power of the internet in more recent times, it has changed history. For example, photographs depicting a young Syrian boy who drowned in the Mediterranean Sea trying to reach Europe in 2015 brought the Syrian conflict and the European refugee crisis to the attention of the world in a more disturbing and immediate way than tens of news articles had managed to do; it also helped to change public attitudes to what was happening in Syria, eventually leading to international condemnation of the conflict there.

Great documentary photographers work to develop strong relationships with the people, or sometimes animals, they are photographing, in order to gain real insight into their subjects that will help them to take powerful photographs. They also always try to ensure that their work doesn't jeopardise the safety or security of the people they are photographing.

Robert Frank was a Swiss documentary photographer who became extremely influential in the mid-20th century. He started out as an industrial photographer, then moved into fashion photography when he emigrated to the USA in 1947. However, he always wanted to do more challenging work and this led to him experimenting with other genres and eventually shooting his most famous work, a documentary series called 'The Americans', between 1955 and 1956. Frank's photographs expertly capture a unique view of

16: Styles and genres

> **Rule of odds** rule that says an odd number of subjects in the foreground of an image is more pleasing than an even number
>
> **Left-to-right rule** the direction that people in the West 'read' a visual image
>
> **Juxtapositioning** contrasting different subjects by placing them next to each other

American life in the 1950s from an outsider's perspective, combining social commentary with aesthetic mastery. 'The Americans' has become one of the most iconic photographic documentary series. In this photograph from the series, *Main Street – Savannah, Georgia*, shot in 1955 (Figure 16.8), Frank used various compositional techniques to compose the image. In particular he made expert use of the **rule of odds**, the **left-to-right-rule** and **juxtapositioning**.

In this visually complex scene, Frank's use of composition has been carefully designed to lead the eye towards his main point of interest – the relationship between the young man and woman in the bottom right-hand side of the photograph. The disdain for the young Black man in the young White woman's eyes is there for all to see, and by highlighting this through the way the viewer reads the image, Frank is able to capture the 'story' of racial segregation and tension in the USA in the 1950s in a single, powerful image. There is a lot going on in the shot, with various elements fighting for visual supremacy. Taken from a different angle, distance or height, the image would not have been as effective, but Frank pulls it off through his use of the rule of odds and the left-to-right rule.

The rule of odds states that framing your subject with two surrounding objects (thus creating an odd number of three) gives balance and harmony to an image – the human eye tends to prefer balance and feels comfortable with

**Fig 16.8** *Main Street – Savannah, Georgia* (1955) by Robert Frank, gelatin silver print; Frank makes use of various compositional techniques

groupings of three. An even number of subjects on the other hand produces visual symmetry, which can appear less natural in a naturalistic composition. In this photo there are five main people in the front row, which highlights the woman in the middle. The eye then jumps right to the Black man and then further right to the White woman looking at him. This is because, as Frank knew, in the Western hemisphere people tend to 'read' pictures from left to right, following the same direction in which we read text. Experts on visual perception claim that pictures where the 'flow' of the image is left to right (subject looking, pointing or moving to the right) feel more tranquil, whereas right to left images create more tension. In Frank's photo the eye moves first from left to right, creating a sense of security, then is surprised into reading back to the young man, right to left, following the line of the last woman's gaze. This creates a disturbing feeling of tension and invites the viewer to compare the man to the rest of the (White) subjects in this area of the frame, in this way juxtapositioning (or placing side by side to emphasise contrasting characteristics) the people in the foreground.

## Project work: **Photography and analysis**

Decide which of the genres described in this section you would prefer to work in – portrait, landscape, still life or documentary photography. Choose a subject that has particular significance for you. Note down which compositional techniques you learned about in this chapter would be most appropriate to this type of subject. Make a plan, then take some initial shots. Answer the following questions about your image.

1. Why did you choose this subject?
2. What message do you want to convey about it?
3. Which parts of the subject did you want to draw attention to?
4. What compositional techniques did you use to do this?
5. Which techniques do you think you used most/least successfully? Why?

### Link

See Chapter 17, pages 160–162, for more information on planning when taking shots.

# 17 Selecting digital images

In the previous chapter you explored a range of different photographers, the genres they are most commonly connected to and the most commonly used photographic compositional rules they have developed. In this chapter you will start to understand more about modern photography and digital image selection. You will explore the purpose of image selection, file formats and how to start editing photographs.

Anyone can take a photograph, but as we have discovered in previous chapters, it is a combination of photographic skill and compositional understanding that makes a good photographer. In the same way, anyone can select and edit a photograph; however, it takes those same skills to be able to identify a good photograph from a poor one, and know where or how to edit a photograph if required.

## 17.1 IMAGE SELECTION – YOUR OWN PHOTOGRAPHS

Deciding on and selecting the best photographs you have taken is a skill that is often underestimated. In a creative and visual sense you are looking for the images with the most potential, and this is a process that can take time and patience but that improves with experience. It is important to really look closely at all the possible images you have; photographs that have been discarded at first can often reveal hidden treasures later, once the editing process begins.

The key to successful image selection and editing is having a good plan and a sound understanding of what you want to achieve. Any new or budding photographer expecting to emulate the work of Robert Frank or Dorothea Lange without a plan as to what they want to capture, will only be disheartened with the results!

There are four key stages to work through when selecting your photographs:

1. Planning your aims
2. Taking some initial shots
3. Taking further shots with more purpose
4. Assessing quality

### Stage 1: Planning your aims

First, you need to define your goals: what do you want to achieve with these images? By defining your goals clearly from the outset you will be able to make informed choices about the locations, people, objects and compositional aspects to use in your work. You will also be clearer about what sort of mood or emotion you want to capture and what the **purpose** or 'message' of your final image should be.

**Purpose** the message, emotion or atmosphere an image is trying to convey

## Stage 2: Taking some initial shots

Once you have chosen your subject, take some initial 'loose' spontaneous photographs, not really focusing too much on composition. Get a feel for the space, the location, the people or objects you are working with and become familiar with them. Explore different angles, light conditions and ways of looking at them. From your first initial **photoshoot**, examine all your photographs and select some images that you think work well. Try to analyse why they are successful – how did you achieve the effect? Is it down to the composition, the light, the textures or the expression on someone's face you've managed to capture? Start to think carefully about formal elements, such as light, contrast, tone, form, line and colour. Identify the best points of each successful image, but also look back through the discarded shots and see whether you can identify some 'hidden treasure' that you may have overlooked first time round. Make notes to document your reasons for selecting these shots.

> **Photoshoot** collection of shots of one subject
> **Critique** analyse critically

**Fig 17.1** Taking some initial shots outside with a digital camera

## Stage 3: Taking further shots with more purpose

Once you have your initial shots, go back to the subject another two or three times and take a further series of photographs with more purpose. To do this, start from your plan again and decide how you need to amend it to get what you are aiming for. Think more about techniques this time and try to build on the things you did that were successful in the initial photoshoot. After each shoot, go through the shots you've taken, selecting the ones you think are the best. By the time you've collected all of your best work from two to three photoshoots you should have between five and twenty images that could be used as the final photograph or photographic series.

## Stage 4: Assessing quality

You should now only be working with a small percentage of all the images that you've captured. (If, after your selection process, you still have a very large amount of photographs, you probably need to be more critical about your work.) Go back and look at your plan and remind yourself of your overall purpose then assess and **critique** your best photographs properly. You can do this using software packages such as Adobe Photoshop and

> **Image resolution** the number of pixels that form an image, determining its quality

Adobe® Lightroom®, looking in particular at aspects of colour, composition, tone and texture. Zoom in on your subjects to identify any small defects in the **image resolution** or quality. Remember that the most important thing to consider when examining a photo objectively is whether it communicates your purpose or message effectively. Ask yourself whether the viewer will understand from the image in question what your aims are. Evaluate whether the techniques of composition and lighting that you've chosen really contribute to the effectiveness of the image. Be honest and critical. If the answer is no, then you will need to reject that particular photo and consider others.

**Fig 17.2** Consider the differences between these four images of the same location, each taken with different lighting effects

### Top Tip

Always note down your thought processes when critiquing your own work. Record the reasons you felt an image was good and should be selected, or not so good and should be rejected. This will help you to develop better photographs more quickly in future and will also help your tutors assess the development of your work.

### Project work: **The stages of image selection**

Practice working through the first three stages of the process described above. Choose a subject and follow these steps:

- Begin by defining your goals. Write a short 100-word description of why you chose this subject and what you want to achieve with your final image(s).
- Take an initial series of shots – at least 20 photographs – and critique them. Record this process by taking notes of your observations about the photos.
- From your initial photoshoot, select what you think are the five best images. Explain why you think these images are the best.

# 17.2 IMAGE SELECTION – USING OTHER RESOURCES

Designers often need to source photographic images that aren't their own. This may be as inspiration, for example, images on a mood board for an advert, or as part of a design for a particular project, for example, images of products to be used on a product catalogue on a shopping website. Online photo libraries are a great resource for finding what you are looking for, and there's more than just beautiful photos in their archives – lots of professional designers use sites such as Shutterstock® for textures, icons, maps, flags, backgrounds, 3D renderings, video clips, and more. However, if you are not careful about sourcing **third party photos** and **stock art**, you could be infringing copyright laws and risk being prosecuted.

In order to comply with the complex legislation around reusing third party images, here are a few useful tips.

## REQUESTING PERMISSION

Make sure to ask permission to use a third party photo before reusing it. It is not okay to copy and paste photos directly from a search engine image search (for example, Google Images™) and do what you like with it – you must find out the **original source** (the place where the image first appeared and/or the person who took the photo) and request permission to reproduce it.

Getting this information depends on where you found the image. Images from magazines or newspapers often include the **copyright holder's** information under the image or at the back of the publication. Sometimes, if the image was provided by an agency, the agency will be credited rather than the photographer. If there is no credit line the next step is to contact the publisher. The publisher's contact details may be listed in the publication, or you can use a search engine to find them.

Finding the copyright holder's details in an online publication is easier than from a printed publication. Again, start with the credit line on the image. In online publications or websites these credit lines are often links that take you back to the original source of the image.

If you find an image using a search engine such as Google, there are a couple of ways to find the copyright details. If you select an image in Google Images, it will load some information about the image to the right-hand side, including the website the image is hosted on along with any captions and the image credits. If the image credits aren't shown, check the website that is hosting the image, as this may contain details about who owns it or where it was sourced.

## BUYING STOCK ART

Commercially reusable visual images are widely available from sites such as iStockphoto by Getty Images or Shutterstock. However, there is a set procedure to follow when sourcing images from these sites. It is important to get permission from the site to reuse one of its images and this generally involves paying a small **licensing fee**. You should always get the proper licence for any stock image that appears in your work, even if it is part of a portfolio or a **screenshot**.

> **Third party photos** photographs taken and published by others
> **Stock art** images available from paying image libraries
> **Original source** the person who created the image
> **Copyright holder** the person or agency who owns the image
> **Licensing fee** money paid to image libraries to reuse their images
> **Screenshot** a digital image that shows the contents of a computer display

**Fig 17.3** Getty Images is one example of a stock photo agency

## USING CREATIVE COMMONS MATERIAL

Many amateur and professional photographers are willing to let other people display their work for no charge, using the Creative Commons licence. This type of licence dictates what other users can do with the image. For instance, some do not mind commercial uses of their work as long as they are credited as the originators of the image.

## SIGNING UP FOR A SUBSCRIPTION SERVICE

If you need to use a lot of news-oriented images, such as photographs of celebrities or sports events, in your work, it may be worthwhile paying for membership with a subscription service, such as AP Images, Reuters Pictures or Getty Images. This gives you permission to search and reuse photos from their vast image archives. The downside of these services is that they can be expensive.

## WHAT TO LOOK FOR IN A THIRD PARTY IMAGE

Here are a few simple tips that can help you find the images you want from photo libraries such as Shutterstock and Alamy.

### Tip 1: Watch for recommendations

As a starting point, check out photos that look good on wide-screen websites in the web-friendly section of some image-sourcing sites. For example, Shutterstock has a 'web-friendly photos' lightbox feature.

You will also often see footers for 'Related searches,' 'Same model' and 'Similar images', which will lead you to similar photos related by theme or subject, and so on. Alternatively, click on any contributor's name to see more of their work.

### Tip 2: Adapt your search terms

If your search terms produce thousands of results, try arranging them in a different order. The tabs at the top of your search results page should let you do this.

### Tip 3: Use the advanced search options

Most search engines also allow you to search for images according to whether their format is portrait or landscape. They will also give you the option to change the format of an image you like, if it is not in the format you need.

---

### Comprehension: **Using third party photographs**

1. How can you find out the original source of a photograph in a magazine?
2. Where can you find this information for an image from a website?
3. What is a licensing fee for stock art?
4. Can you use an image with a Creative Commons licence for commercial purposes?
5. What type of service is Reuters?

---

Skills Task: **Photo selection**

**1.** Choose **one** of the briefs below. Use a free image sourcing website to make a photo selection of five possible images for it.

- Brief 1: image to illustrate the term 'family holiday'. Photo of a family, two parents and two children, enjoying themselves on holiday together on a summer's day. The parents should be in their mid-40s, the kids around 10 years old, and they should be doing an activity together, for example, cycling. The image should have a sense of fun and relaxation.
- Brief 2: photo to convey the freshness of the produce from our client's supermarket fruit and vegetable department. Image of perfect, ripe, colourful and delicious looking fruit or vegetables. Produce should look delicious, tempting and make viewer want to eat it.

**2.** Now look at the images your classmates have chosen. Which do you think are the best? Why?

---

# 17.3 STORING FILES – FORMATS AND RESOLUTION

Understanding file formats and digital resolution is essential to presenting your images in a professional way, whether they are photos you have taken yourself or images you have downloaded and want to edit or adapt. File formats define how we can use digital files, either for selection or use.

There are two different types of images generated digitally: bitmap files and vector files.

**Bitmap images** are the file format that most digital photographers use for editing and retouching images. They require a high resolution and appear 'smooth' on screen, but are actually made up of thousands of individual **pixels** on a grid system. If the resolution is lowered, the image will appear blurry.

**Vector images** are based on **vectors** that connect nodes on the screen, in this way creating polygons. These are used instead of dots to create the image. Vector files maintain their sharpness even when the image is enlarged. Graphic designers and illustrators mainly use this file format.

Good photography depends on the photographer using the right file format for the job. High quality digital resolution will give a sharper, clearer photograph but creates a bigger, heavier file. Low resolution photographs will appear pixelated and blurry but can be used for initial photo selection to compare a range of images where detail is less important.

Digital resolution is measured in DPI and PPI.

- DPI (dots per inch) refers to the number of dots of colour in one square inch of paper when images are printed out. The more dots in the image, the higher the quality of resolution.

**Link**

See Chapter 4, pages 37–39, for detailed information on pixels and vectors.

**Bitmap image** a digital image comprised of dots
**Pixels dots** of colour that form a digital image on-screen
**Vector image** digital image comprised of vectors
**Vectors** lines forming 3D geometric shapes that are used to form digital images on-screen

- PPI (pixels per inch) describes the pixel density of a digital image displayed on a screen, such as a laptop, smartphone or tablet.

| DPI resolution scale | Image quality |
| --- | --- |
| 300 DPI+ | Resolutions of 300 DPI or above are used to print images on paper. |
| 150 DPI | Mid-range resolution; often used to print samples/test pieces. |
| 72 DPI | Screen resolution, not for printed work, used in web editing and publishing. |
| <72 DPI | Anything below 72 DPI will look pixelated on screen. |

### Top Tip

Printing out a 72 DPI image will result in your work looking very pixelated and blurry on paper. This is because the printer you use will be calibrated to automatically print at 300 DPI or above. Effectively the printer will 'stretch' the dots of colour from the 72 DPI image and this allows the white paper to show through and the dots to blur.

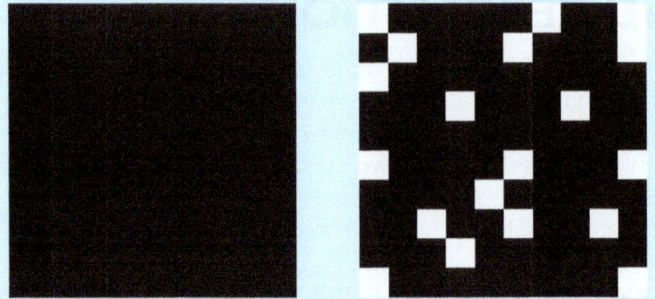

**Fig 17.5** Note the difference between a printed 300 DPI image (left) and a 72 DPI one (right) – the printer 'stretches' the coloured dots in the 72 DPI image

**Fig 17.4** Two images to show the difference in resolution between a printed 300 DPI image (top) and a 72 DPI one (bottom)

Different file formats are needed in order to structure data differently for different uses or outcomes. A useful analogy is how goods are displayed in a department store: originally items are delivered to the store tightly packed and carefully stowed away; when they are ready to be sold, the items are unpacked and displayed for sale in different ways, as is most appropriate to the type of goods themselves and the sort of customer that might buy them – some items will be displayed in packets on shelves, while others will be displayed on hooks on rotating carousels, in shop windows or on a mannequin. File formats are similar to packaging for transit – they compress the images and package them to allow them to be 'transported'; when the user needs to access the image it can be easily accessed and unpacked in perfect condition and fit for purpose.

The most commonly used bitmap file formats for digital photography are as described in the table, opposite.

| File type | Use |
|---|---|
| TIFF (Tagged-Image File Format) | Used when a high-resolution photographic file is needed. Typically used for printing. |
| JPEG (Joint Photographic Experts Group – web and print ready file) | This is a **compressed** file. JPEG files can be created at a variety of compression levels; more compression = lower quality. They are used for web design and printing, but for printing it is important to know the exact resolution of a JPEG file to decide whether the image is of the high quality required. |
| GIF (Graphics Interchange Format) | A small, limited-colour file that is used for on-screen viewing only, when a very small file with just a few solid colours is needed. Used for developing small animations. |
| PNG (Portable Network Graphics) | Essentially designed to replace the GIF file format, this file type has more colour options than a GIF file. It is also used for on-screen viewing. |
| PSD (Photoshop Document) | A PSD is a **layered** Photoshop file. In Photoshop image files default to PSD format, which is used mainly for editing. To save and then use the image in other formats, the file must first be **flattened**. |
| EPS (Encapsulated PostScript) | Although this is really a vector art file format, if an image is saved in Photoshop as an EPS file, it is similar to a TIFF file and can be used in the same way. |

**Compressed**  file type used to store images at low resolution
**Layered**  file type used to separate different elements of an image
**Flattened**  process of file conversion to make layered files usable

## Comprehension: **Image resolution**

1. What do DPI and PPI stand for?
2. What does the term 'resolution' mean?
3. What is the difference between a Bitmap file and Vector file?

## Skills Task: **Image file formats**

Look at the three situations described below. Which file format would you choose for the image in each case? Explain your reasons.

1. A photograph to illustrate an article about roses in a gardening magazine.
2. A selection of twenty portraits using a selected model of your choice, to present to a client as part of your research for a photo story in an English language textbook.
3. A group of three landscape shots for a tourism website.

## Case study: **Landscape photography planning**

Landscape photography is, at its simplest, the process of finding a great location, creating an arresting composition, and capturing the image in great light. A successful photograph is normally a combination of planning and a certain amount of good fortune with the weather and the quality of the light.

To maximise the chances of taking a good photograph, you must plan carefully. There are a few items to help in this process:

- a map
- a tablet with the Photographer's Ephemeris®, sometimes Google Street View™
- the Highways Agency traffic camera website (and sometimes other webcams)
- a Satmap Active 12 GPS.

The planning process starts by using knowledge of the local area and finding a good map. You will need maps that give a detailed idea of the landscape; paper maps are often better for planning, as they cover a wider area. With practice it is possible to visualise the sort of view to be seen from a location, and evaluate possible issues such as woodland blocking the view or an inconveniently located building.

The Photographer's Ephemeris is a useful planning tool, as it contains a map with a display showing sunrise and sunset times and angles. The programme superimposes the sunrise and sunset times and angles on a configurable map. It also shows the sun direction at any chosen time of day, and the corresponding length and direction of shadows at the same time. For planning purposes the date can be changed. This allows for planning when the sunset will occur at a particular angle at any chosen location.

As an added bonus, the Photographer's Ephemeris also shows moonrise and set times and angles, and the times of the various types of twilight. This can be extremely useful in planning night photography in cities or countryside, and in setting up astrophotography shoots. Google Street View is also a useful tool for understanding the area you may see.

All of this initial work can be completed days before a shoot. On the day before the shoot, check the weather. It is also worth looking at the rainfall radar history and forecast, and any webcams around the area you are planning to visit. The weather in one area can be radically different to another, even on the same day, particularly if you are going up or down hills and mountains.

Once in the field, it is important to keep an eye on the broader weather conditions to take advantage of any opportunities. A Sat Nav or Google Maps™, can be used to navigate to the locations you have planned to visit, and can also be used to estimate the time required to reach alternative viewpoints if you need to change your plans.

Planning helps, but it is only part of the process of taking landscape photos. Making the best of the location and conditions is equally important, and waiting (sometimes for a long time) is vital to capture the decisive moment when the view is at its best.

(Courtesy of Paul Heaton. Paul Heaton is UK-based landscape photographer.)

**Fig 17.6** Landscape photos by Paul Heaton. Getting the perfect landscape shot requires careful planning so you can make the best of location and conditions

## Learning Aims

By the end of this chapter you will be able to:
*   Understand how DLSR cameras work
*   Understand how point-and-shoot cameras work
*   Understand some of technical features to use in your photos

In the previous chapter, you looked at the features to consider when selecting digital images, as well as simple editing techniques such as cropping and digital resizing. In this chapter you will start to understand more about capturing and recording digital images, the various tools that are available to do this, how they work and how to use them.

# 18.1 HOW CAMERAS WORK

It is often difficult for students to decide which camera to use for their work, as there are so many different types of camera available with a wide variety of features (and prices!) to choose from. Fortunately, nowadays even the most technologically advanced cameras are fairly straightforward to use – indeed, most of them can be used like a basic **point-and-shoot camera**. However, there is also an infinite amount of hybrid cameras, tools and additional components available. All this kit can become quite confusing, so let's take a look first at how a camera works, and then consider some of the basic features available on most models and what they can be used for.

## HOW CAMERAS WORK

In a traditional, non-digital camera there is a convex lens in front of an aperture, a space that light passes through and that can be opened and closed by a shutter. The lens focuses the light rays reflected from an object onto a light-sensitive surface inside the camera (photographic film) during a timed **exposure** (the period of time that the aperture is open). This produces a **negative** image of the object on the film, which is then processed using special chemicals to give the final photographic image.

A digital camera works in much the same way, but instead of photographic film inside it, an electronic image sensor records the light rays coming through the aperture as a series of **electrical charges**. These are processed as pixels

**Point-and-shoot camera** an automatic camera
**Exposure** the amount of time the aperture remains open for
**Negative** the reverse image produced on photographic film
**Electrical charges** the light signals that create a digital photograph

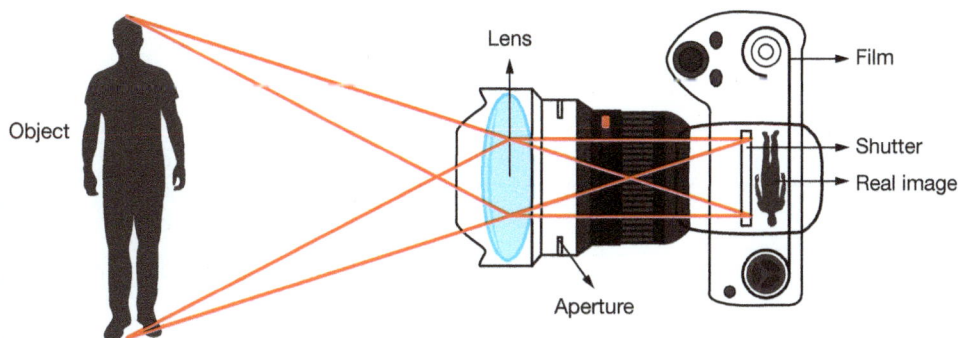

**Fig 18.1** How a traditional photographic camera captures an image

**Digital image file** the method used for storing digital photos

and the pixelated image is stored as a **digital image file** inside the memory of the camera. This file can then be displayed as a photo or digitally processed using editing software and used in a variety of digital or print formats.

## Comprehension: **Digital camera workflow chart**

Using the following terms, create a flow chart showing how a digital camera works:

- Lens
- Shutter
- Aperture
- Electronic image sensor
- Digital image file

**Top Tip**

Compact cameras are especially useful for taking initial shots on a first photoshoot when you begin to explore ideas and locations related to your plan, before you start refining your work.

# 18.2 CAMERAS AND ACCESSORIES

## THE COMPACT CAMERA

These cameras are easy to use and carry around because of their size, and they are usually quite reasonably priced to buy. Many of them now have a range of useful and easy to use features.

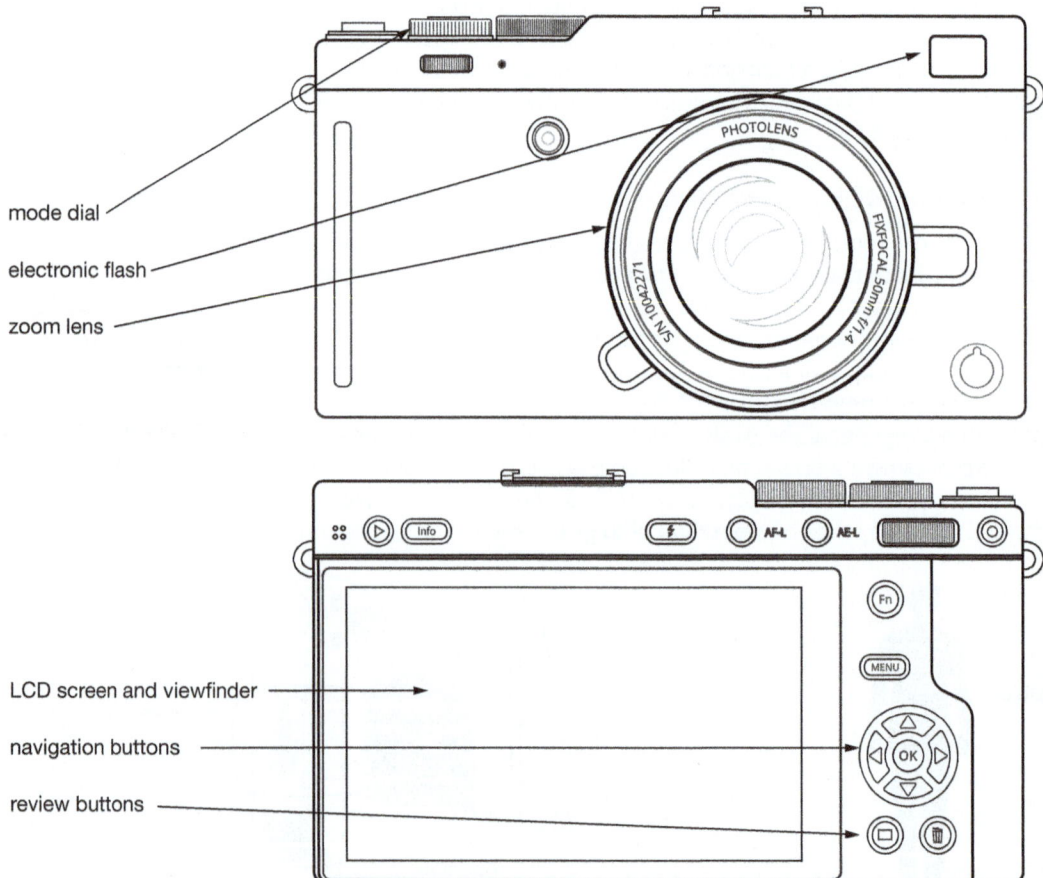

mode dial
electronic flash
zoom lens

LCD screen and viewfinder
navigation buttons
review buttons

**Fig 18.2** A compact camera

## 1: Zoom lens

Zoom lenses can vary greatly in quality and magnification depending on the camera. They are useful for focusing in on a particular part of the subject or experimenting with viewpoint.

## 2: Viewfinder

Compact cameras use what is called an **electronic viewfinder** (EVF), which attempts to re-create what an SLR camera's viewfinder would see by using the electronic image from the sensor.

## 3: Electronic flash

This usually has a function that allows you to choose whether you want the camera to flash automatically when the light level falls below a certain value or to be able to operate the flash manually yourself. Many compact cameras feature a pop-up flash. While this may not as versatile or as strong as an external flash, it can still be useful in different situations.

## 4: Mode dial

Most compact cameras now have a dial (or sometimes buttons) that allow the user to navigate through the camera's various **modes**, such as portrait, landscape, still life or moving image. These are usually indicated by icons on the dial and allow you to select the best mode for the subject you are trying to photograph. The camera then automatically selects the default settings for shutter speed, ISO, and so on (see below) that are best for the type of subject you've chosen, so you do not have to adjust these.

## 5: LCD screen

Not all basic cameras have a LCD screen but most recent models will have one. It is often used as a viewfinder, to select the composition and for framing the shot. The LCD screen can also be used to view the shots you've taken, which are stored in the memory (**camera roll**). In some cameras it is also used to select different options from the menus to edit your photographs in a basic way. For example, you can often crop shots, convert images to black and white or sepia, or correct 'red eye' reflections in portraits.

## 6: Review button

This allows the user to move back and forth through the photographs on the camera roll, delete shots, copy them or print photographs when the camera is connected to a digital printer.

## 7: Navigation buttons

These buttons are an additional option on some compact cameras to move through the camera's various modes and menus.

## 8: USB port

A USB port is a standard cable connection interface for computers and other electronics devices. USB stands for Universal Serial Bus. Connected USB devices allow the transfer of digital data through USB cables.

# THE DSLR CAMERA

The DSLR (digital single lens reflex) camera offers a more professional range of features, capabilities and accessories than a compact camera. However, it requires more knowledge and skill on the part of the photographer to use it effectively. DSLR cameras are also much more expensive than compact cameras, and you may have to buy additional kit to use with them, such as interchangeable lenses

**Electronic viewfinder** large viewfinder in body of a digital camera
**Modes** types of photography (for example, portrait)
**Camera roll** all the photos stored on a digital camera

or an external flash, which will push the costs up even further. Many of these accessories are interchangeable and can be used with different models of DSLR camera, but because of their high quality they are usually expensive.

What exactly does it mean for a camera to be SLR (single lens reflex) rather than compact (point-and-shoot)? The main differences are related to these three features:

- viewfinder mechanism
- fixed versus interchangeable lenses
- camera sensor size.

### 1: Viewfinder

Unlike a compact camera, with an SLR camera what you are seeing through the viewfinder is the same light that will reach the camera's sensor when you press the shutter button. (The flipping up of the internal mirror when you press the shutter button is what makes the characteristic 'clicking' sound associated with SLR cameras.) If your work requires seeing exactly the light that will be captured in the finished shot, then you should use an SLR camera. With a compact camera, the viewfinder mechanism tries to estimate what light will reach the sensor, so it is potentially not very accurate.

### 2: Interchangeable lenses

DSLR cameras allow the user to switch between different types of specialised lenses, such as **ultra-wide angle lenses**, **fish-eye lenses** and **extreme telephoto lenses**, which give more creative options. It would be impossible to design a single lens that could capture all types of shots without compromising on quality and portability. In practice, being able to use different lenses means you have the potential to achieve better image quality because the lens will have been specifically designed for the task in hand. For example, for a portrait, a photographer might use a wide aperture lens to create a smooth, out-of-focus background and isolate the subject in the shot. Alternatively, for a shot of architecture they could use an ultra-wide angle lens that causes straight lines to appear curved, therefore allowing all of the building to appear in the shot.

### 3: Camera sensor size

In general, compact cameras have much smaller camera sensors than SLR cameras and this has a noticeable impact on image quality. For the same number of megapixels (1000 pixels), larger sensors have much larger pixels than a compact camera. This increased light-gathering area means that the pixels are more sensitive to tiny amounts of light, resulting in less 'image noise' than in a shot taken with a compact camera. Another consequence of having physically larger pixels is that SLR cameras can usually capture a greater range of light to dark (**dynamic range**). For example, this can help preserve more details in the deep shadows in a particular shot.

## OTHER TYPES OF DIGITAL CAMERA

Most smartphones and tablets now have fairly good quality cameras installed on them and the technology is improving all the time, providing increasing digital resolution options, editing techniques and creative freedom. Because of their portability and convenience (you almost always have one to hand) these types of camera are particularly useful for spontaneous, unplanned shots and initial photoshoots on a project. The functionality is extremely intuitive, so they are general easy to use.

**Ultra-wide angle lens** lens for taking big landscape shots
**Fish-eye lens** a lens that gives a curved, distorted view of a wide scene
**Extreme telephoto lens** a lens for focusing on small details from far away
**Dynamic range** (in digital photography) the range of light and shade a camera can capture

### Top Tip

'Image noise' appears in digital photographs as random speckles on an otherwise smooth surface. It can significantly reduce the quality of an image. Although image noise often detracts from an image, sometimes photographers use it deliberately to add an old-fashioned, grainy effect to a picture reminiscent of early analogue photos.

| Camera type | Advantages | Disadvantages |
|---|---|---|
| Compact camera | • Cost<br>• Size and weight<br>• Portability<br>• Ease of use | • Lack of real viewfinders<br>• Less control to manually refine shots<br>• Image quality |
| DSLR camera | • Quality and resolution<br>• Manual overrides allow greater control and choice of effects<br>• Opportunity to upgrade accessories/ features<br>• Size of photographs (allows you to take good quality, large resolution photos) | • Weight<br>• Size<br>• Complexity |
| Smartphone/tablet camera | • Size and weight<br>• Portability<br>• Ease of use<br>• Greater opportunity to share photographs quickly<br>• Integrated software allows you to edit on the go | • Limited battery life<br>• Poor quality shots in low light<br>• Poor zoom functions<br>• No manual control<br>• Weak flash<br>• Cost |

## Comprehension: **Features of a DSLR**

Label the picture of a DSLR camera with the correct words for these five features: electronic light sensor, aperture, shutter, viewfinder, interchangeable lens.

**Fig 18.3** A DSLR camera

## Project work: **Taking 'selfies' with a difference**

Follow the instructions to take a series of 'selfies' (photographs of yourself on a smartphone, taken with no real thought about composition or quality). At the end of this process you should finish with the 'best ever' selfie!

1.  Make a plan. Choose 10 different locations to take your selfies in.
2.  Think about everything you have learned so far about composition (rule of thirds, triangles and angles, leading lines). Decide which ones you'd like to use in your selfies.
3.  Record your choices in your plan and add some notes explaining your reasoning for using each one.
4.  Take an initial group of shots in each location.
5.  Go through the selection process highlighted in Chapter 17 and decide which shots are the best.
6.  Go back to those locations and improve on your use of the compositional techniques you chose for the shots.
7.  Choose the best three shots from your photoshoots.

# 18.3 TECHNICAL FEATURES

Some of the key technical features of a camera that you can experiment with in your photography are the aperture, f-stop and ISO. These control the speed and quality of light that enters the camera and can be adjusted to take different types of shots and to produce different effects.

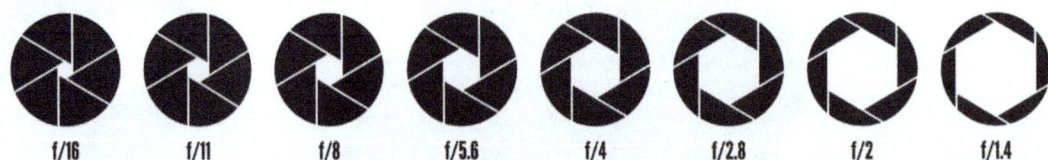

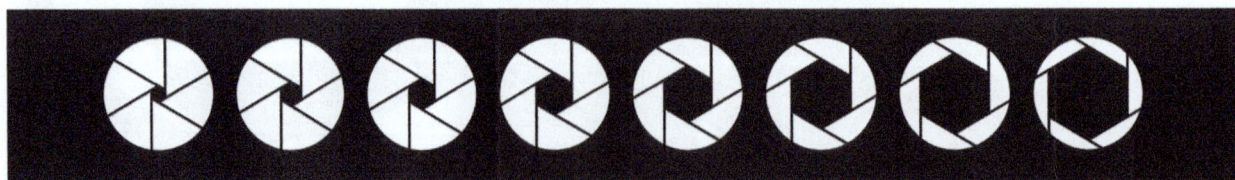

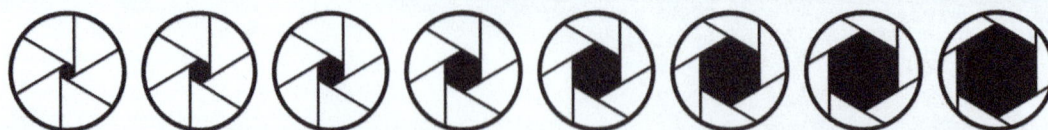

| f/16 | f/11 | f/8 | f/5.6 | f/4 | f/2.8 | f/2 | f/1.4 |

**Fig 18.4** Apertures and f-stops

# APERTURE

The aperture controls the **shutter speed**, which in turn controls your camera's sensitivity to light and the amount of light that enters through the lens. The aperture is designed like the human eye, or specifically the pupil of the eye. It is actually a small set of **blades** behind the lens that open and close to control the quantity of light. The blades create an octagonal shape that can be opened or shut to varying degrees. Shooting with the aperture wide open allows more light to enter the camera, while shooting with the aperture almost closed allows only a tiny ray of light to enter the camera. Depending on which lens you are using, this will allow you to take sharper photographs with a greater **depth of field**.

**Shutter speed** the speed at which the shutter opens to expose the electronic sensor to light

**Blades** components of the aperture cover

**Depth of field** the range of distance in front of and behind an object which is in focus

**Focal length** distance from which the camera can focus on an object

# F-STOP

The f-stop (or f-number) is an optical system that controls the focus of the lens. It is calculated by dividing the **focal length** of the lens by the diameter of the aperture. Focal length refers to a lens's depth of field – the width and height of the area that a particular lens is able to capture. (This information is often printed on the camera lens itself.)

F-stops and aperture are effectively the same thing: the f-stop number dictates the diameter of the aperture that the light passes through into the camera. The higher the f-stop, the more closed the hole is and this allows less light into the camera. If you set a lens with a 100 mm focal length to an f-stop of f/10, the aperture of the camera will have a diameter of 10 mm. Doubling the f-stop number halves the size of the aperture opening, so moving from f/10 to f/20 will decrease the size of the aperture from 10 mm to 5 mm.

Photographers select different f-stops to capture specific elements within their photographs while also taking into consideration the light conditions they are working in. For example, in low light you would select a lower f-stop, for example, f-2, to allow more light into the camera and capture greater detail in the image. Alternatively, if you wanted to take good quality shots of a bird taking flight while still capturing some of the depth in the background, you would choose a lower f-stop number such as f5.6, to allow light to enter your camera faster. This would help avoid the problem of motion blur and produce sharper images.

**Fig 18.5** Choose a lower f-stop number to capture birds in flight

# ISO

In very basic terms, ISO controls the speed and quality of your camera's sensitivity to available light. ISO stands for International Standards Organisation, and refers to a particular standard of sensitivity to light – the lower the ISO number, the less sensitive the camera is to the light. The component within your camera that can alter its light sensitivity is the camera's electronic light sensor. This is responsible for gathering light and transforming it into an image. More expensive cameras usually have better sensors, allowing them to produce better quality photographs.

ISO numbers start from 100–200 (Base ISO) and increase in value in sequence, each number being double the one before: 100, 200, 400, 800, 1600, 3200, 6400, and so on. Effectively each time the value increases it doubles the sensitivity of the sensor, so ISO 200 is twice as sensitive as ISO 100, while ISO 400 is four times more sensitive to light than ISO 100, and ISO 1600 is sixteen times more sensitive to light than ISO 100, and so on. At ISO 1600 your camera needs sixteen times less time to capture an image than a camera at 100 ISO.

**Link**

See page 172 in this chapter for more information on a camera's electronic light sensor.

**ISO speeds**
- ISO 100: 1 second
- ISO 200: 1/2 of a second
- ISO 400: 1/4 of a second
- ISO 800: 1/8 of a second
- ISO 1600: 1/15 of a second
- ISO 3200: 1/30 of a second

## Case study: **Light painting**

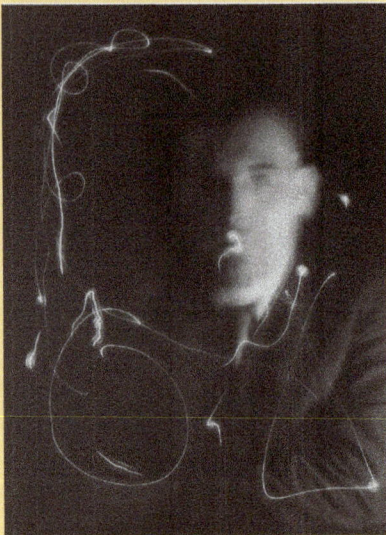

**Fig 18.6** Man Ray's *Space Writing (Marcel Duchamp)* (1937) selenium print

**Fig 18.7** A modern light painting of orbs on a train track at night

Light painting is produced by shooting in low or dark light conditions while experimenting with ISO and f-stops, and is used for both scientific and artistic purposes. The technique dates back to 1889, when Étienne-Jules Marey and Georges Demeny traced human motion in 'Pathological Walk From in Front'.

Man Ray was the first artist to use light painting as an art form. He used light painting to create what was, in essence, a sophisticated selfie in 1935. For many years, people thought he had used the technique just to demonstrate light swirls and lines – it was discovered in 2009 that this was actually his signature.

Up until the 1970s, the technique was known as light drawing; it wasn't until 1977 that the technique became known as light painting. Dean Chamberlain, working at the Rochester Institute of Technology, created the idea of light painting by using hand-held lights to selectively illuminate and/or colour parts of the subject or scene. Photographers have worked with light painting in varying ways, from Vicki DaSilva's text light graffiti works to Pablo Picasso's work on light drawings with Gjon Mili.

Light painting has been a popular form of photography for many years, due to the level of creativity it requires but also because it can offer photographers the opportunity to mirror some of the traditional characteristics of painting, such as superimposition and transparency, which can easily be achieved by moving, adding or removing lights or subjects during or between exposures.

The technique has increased in popularity since the increased availability of DSLR cameras, and is now so popular that it is displayed at various festivals around the world. As befits its name, light painting relies heavily on accessibility to light sources, so has increased in popularity since the advent of more portable light sources. You have also probably seen light painting on social media without even realising this technique was being utilised; for example, when you see images where photos include words written by sparklers, you are seeing light painting in action.

### Project work: **Light painting**

A creative and fun outcome of working with light and camera settings is light painting. It takes practice and patience but the results can look spectacular! Follow these steps to produce a simple light painting of the letters of the alphabet.

1. You will need the following equipment.
   - a DSLR camera
   - a tripod
   - a cable release (this allows more manual control of aperture and shutter speed; if you do not have a cable release, please make sure your camera mode is either set manual or bulb mode)
   - a torch or light source
   - a stopwatch.

2. Make sure you have a high f-stop selected; you could start with F/4 and adjust the f-stop if you feel that you need more or less light.
3. Select a low ISO setting, ideally around 100.
4. Draw the alphabet in light and capture it photographically. Start by trying one letter at a time.
5. Practise shooting and re-shooting the letters, to get used to the camera's tools, while also adjusting and experimenting with f-stop and ISO to get the right results. Aim to start with a 30–60 second long exposure.
6. Take lots of shots and refine your work until you have selected your final photographs.
7. Explain the process and why you have chosen your final images.

Note: Remember that when it comes to having a smaller aperture or f-stop, each stop you close down doubles the amount of time you need to be painting and exposing. So, for example, a 60-second exposure at f/4 or f/5.6 could become an 8-minute exposure at f/16.

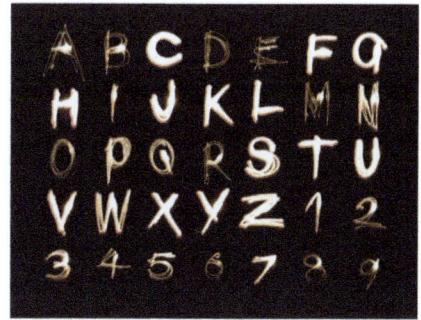

**Fig 18.8** A light painting of letters of the alphabet

# 18.4 SETTING UP A STUDIO

A photographer's studio set-up doesn't have to be overly complicated. However, there are essential items every photographer should have in their studio set-up to get started:

- a backdrop and support stand
- light sources
- a camera
- a model or other subject.

### Backdrop and support stand
Most **backdrops** come in the form of a roll of paper. They are available in a variety of sizes and colours. You will need support stands and a pole to keep the backdrop in place. If you do not have one, try a large sheet or piece of self-coloured fabric.

### 2: Light sources
There are two kinds of lighting: **flash heads** (also called strobes) and continuous lighting. Strobes are generally used for still photography.

**Backdrop** screen behind model/subject
**Flash heads** controls for flashlights

**Fig 18.9** It is important to select the most appropriate equipment, for example lights

**Light stands** supports for lights
**Diffuser** box that makes the light appear softer
**Snoot** attachment that focuses light on one particular area
**Reflector** attachment that intensifies the light

The power of the flash is controlled using buttons on the flash head. Continuous lighting can be used for either stills or videos. A strobe light gives a quick burst of bright light, freezing the action for a sharper image. It is also brighter, so you can use smaller apertures for greater depth of field.

It is highly recommended that you also use a **light stand** for each of your lights, for greater control and for health and safety in the studio. You should also use your lights with a **diffuser**, such as a softbox. This softens the light so the shadows are less harsh. The angle, height and distance of the main lights are vital to getting the look you want.

If you are photographing a model you may wish to have a second light source positioned behind the model with a **snoot** attached. A snoot effectively concentrates the light on a specific area of the composition and creates a further separation from the backdrop. It could be used to highlight the hair or facial features of the model, for instance.

A **reflector** may be used to bounce light back from the main light into the shaded side of the subject's face. This ensures the shadow is still there to define the shape of the face but is not too dark. Reflectors can range in size but are usually coloured white, silver or gold.

### 3: A camera

Normally in a modern studio it is recommended that you use a DSLR camera, as it will give you more control and allow you to connect your lighting tools to the camera. This can be done through a sync cable if your SLR has a PC socket, or with wireless triggers. In a controlled environment such as a studio, you are best switching to manual mode.

### 4: A model or other subject

As a first attempt, try to get someone you know – a friend or a family member – to model for you. This will leave you free to concentrate on experimenting with setting up your studio. It is a good idea, though, to brief your model on what your aims are. This will help them to find an appropriate pose and feel comfortable during the photoshoot.

## Skills Task: **Setting up a studio**

Follow the steps below to plan the set-up for your photographic studio.

Measure the room in which you will be setting your studio up.

Carefully draw it to scale and make several photocopies.

Experiment with where you would place the backdrop, lights, reflectors and diffusers, and so on in different versions of your studio.

Select the plan you think works best for your aims.

Collect your equipment and position it in the space according to your plan.

Ask a friend or a family member to model for you. Experiment with camera angels, lighting angles and distances, move your studio around to compare what works best in terms of the quality of the shots you take.

Make notes of your thoughts and processes throughout this task.

## Project work: **Photoshoot**

Now that you have set up your first studio and experimented with lighting and other studio equipment, use your studio for a more refined photoshoot. Choose **one** of the five themes listed below.

- Nature
- Time
- Transition
- Elements
- Construction

Experiment with different props, textures, styles and colour schemes to capture and visually communicate your chosen theme. You may wish to develop some initial research, mind maps, mood boards, and so on to get a better feel for your theme.

Take a series of experimental photoshoots to improve and further refine your work, analysing your style and technique and following the process outlined in Chapter 17. At the end of this process you should have a really well refined photograph or series of photographs that will fully communicate your chosen theme.

# 19 Composing and editing digital images

## Learning Aims

By the end of this chapter you will be able to:
- Identify and use the basic elements of photographic composition
- Use the basic digital tools in image editing software
- Understand the concept of layers and how to use them
- Understand how to adjust image tone

In the previous chapter we learned more about the different types of camera available today and the key terms and features of the modern digital camera. We also explored some experimental photographic techniques such as light painting while also revisiting previous learning from past chapters on photographic planning and composition.

In this chapter we will start to understand more about composing good shots, then editing and re-touching the photographs you have taken. We will look in more detail at the basic elements of photographic composition and explore the possibilities of digital editing software such as Adobe Photoshop, including working with layers, curves and levels, colour refinements, and basic re-touching techniques.

# 19.1 COMPOSING YOUR SHOTS

There are no fixed rules in photography, but there are a number of established guidelines that can help you enhance the impact of your photos. These guidelines will help you take more compelling photographs, lending them a natural balance and drawing attention to the important parts of the scene, so leading the viewer's eye through the image.

## ASPECT RATIO

Aspect ratio refers to the ratio between the height and the width of a screen used to display any visual image. While this was an important part of film making in the past (due to the standardisation of television and movie theatre screen sizes), it is now less relevant thanks to the vast array of screen sizes available.

## VIEWPOINT

Before starting to photograph your subject, take time to think about where you will shoot it from. The viewpoint has a massive impact on the composition of a photo, and as a result can greatly affect the message that the shot conveys. Rather than just shooting from eye level, experiment with different viewpoints, such as photographing the viewpoint from above, from down at ground level, from the side, from the back, from a long way away, from very close up, and so on, and see how it changes the viewer's response to the subject.

## RULE OF THIRDS

Imagine that your image is divided into nine equal segments by two vertical and two horizontal lines. The rule of thirds says that you should position the most important elements in your scene along these lines, or at the points

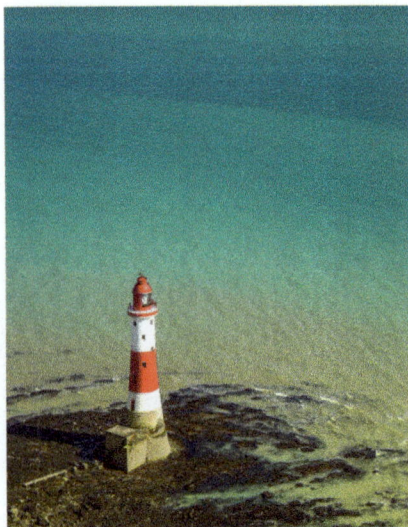

**Fig 19.1** The viewpoint has a massive impact on the composition of a photo

where they intersect. Doing so will add balance and interest to your photo. Some cameras even offer an option to superimpose a rule of thirds grid over the LCD screen, making it even easier to use.

Playing with expectations around the rule of thirds can create interesting effects. For example, positioning the main subject of your image in one the boxes other than the central one creates a different relationship between the subject and the rest of the image. In the example in Figure 19.1, doing this has created a sense of isolation and remoteness around the lighthouse, which is very appropriate to the message of the image.

When composing your work using the rule of thirds, it is also important to consider the positive and negative space within the image you have selected. By thinking about what will be the positive space (the focus) of your photo as well as the negative space (the background) you will be able to make a positive visual statement with much more clarity. It will also help the audience to interpret what you intended by the composition.

**Fig 19.2** Composing an image in line with the rule of thirds can add balance and interest to your photo

## LEADING LINES

When you look at any visual image the eye is naturally drawn along 'lines' created by the relationship of one visual element to another. By considering the scale and volume of each visual element within your shot, you can create these lines in your composition. You can affect the way the viewer looks at the visual elements within your shot 'pulling' the viewer into the picture, towards the subject, or lead them on a journey 'through' the scene. Lines of composition can be straight, diagonal, curved, zigzag or **radial**, and each type can be used to enhance photographic composition.

**Radial line** line that passes through the centre of a circle, cylinder or sphere

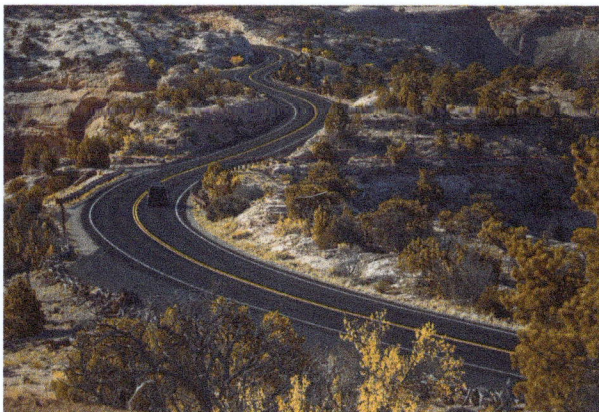

**Fig 19.3** A photo with very strong leading lines will draw the eye in and through the image

## Skills Task: **The rule of thirds**

Choose a digital photograph that you like. Draw the nine-box grid for the rule of thirds over the top of it using an editing programme such as Photoshop and note where the main subject is positioned. Is it at the intersection of two lines?

Now try making these changes to the image and note down the effect they have on the viewer's response to the photo:

1. Zoom out so that the main subject is now positioned inside just one box
2. Add another object in one of the empty boxes in the grid.
3. Zoom in, so that the main subject occupies almost all of the boxes in the grid.

## BALANCING ELEMENTS

Placing your main subject off-centre, as with the rule of thirds, creates a more interesting photo. However, it can leave a void in the scene that may make it feel empty. To avoid this you should balance the 'weight' of your subject by including another object of lesser importance to fill the opposite space.

**Fig 19.4** Notice how the signs on the left and right bring balance to this image

## SYMMETRY AND PATTERNS

**Symmetry** where different parts of an object/image are balanced in shape and the same size

### Link

See Chapter 10, pages 93–94, for more on the golden ratio.

We are surrounded by **symmetry** and patterns, both in nature and in our human-made world. The human visual sense is attracted to symmetry and sub-consciously responds to certain patterns. For example, the symmetry created by the golden ratio, a geometric relationship between two quantities of 2:1 of the larger quantity to the smaller one, when it is used in architecture or design, makes us feel calm and positive. Symmetrical compositions can be very powerful, particularly in situations where they are unexpected. Another great way to use them is to break the symmetry or pattern in some way, which introduces tension and a focal point into the image.

**Fig 19.5** This photo of the front of a building provides a good example of visual symmetry

## BACKGROUND

It often happens when you take what you thought would be a great shot, that the final image lacks impact because the subject blends into a busy background. The human eye is excellent at distinguishing between different elements in a scene, whereas a camera has a tendency to flatten the foreground and background, and this can often ruin an otherwise great photograph. This problem is easiest to overcome at the time of shooting – pay close attention to the positive and negative space of your composition and ensure that your shot is meeting your intention. Look around for a plain, unobtrusive background and compose your shot so that the background doesn't distract from the subject in the foreground.

**Fig 19.6** The subject is highlighted in this photograph because of the plain, unobtrusive background

## DEPTH

Because photography is a two-dimensional medium, you have to choose your compositional elements carefully to convey the sense of depth that was present in the actual three-dimensional scene. You can create depth in a photo by including objects in the **foreground**, middle ground and **background**, which will give a sense of **perspective** leading off into the distance from the viewpoint.

Another useful composition technique is **overlapping**. This is where you deliberately partially obscure one object with another. The human eye naturally recognises these layers and mentally separates them out, creating an image with more depth.

**Fig 19.7** The use of receding layers in the foreground, middle ground and background creates depth in this landscape shot

## FRAMING

The world is full of objects that make perfect natural frames, such as trees, arches and holes. When framing shots think about the positive and negative space in your shot. This will help focus the image and allow you to better understand how to use framing techniques within your work. By placing natural frames around the edge of the composition you help to isolate the main subject from the outside world. The result is a more focused image that draws the viewer's eye naturally to the main point of interest.

**Fig 19.8** Natural framing can be achieved by using features of the surrounding landscape

## FILE NAMING

When naming and saving your images and files, try to maintain a level of relevance to either the project you are working on or the content of the image in some way. You might consider saving the image file as a reduced size image, also known as a **thumbnail**, to easily refer back to. This makes searching and organising your images and files much easier.

Choose **one** of the two photographs below. Analyse its composition according to the rules of composition described in this section. Which do you think have been used to compose this image? Explain how you think they have been used.

**Fig 19.9** Which rules of composition have been used to compose these images?

# 19.2 EDITING AND MANIPULATING IMAGES

Once you have taken your photographs, you need to think about how to present them appropriately for the context you want to use them in. In this section we will look at some of the basic techniques for editing digital photographs, so that you can tailor them to context.

## CROPPING AND TRIMMING

There are two main reasons why you will need to crop or trim a photograph:

- In the editing of the final photograph you might wish to focus on a specific aspect of the image and cut away other details or background areas that aren't relevant to this aim.
- You might want to even up the composition of an image by centring the subject better within the frame. In this case you will need to trim the area around the subject to achieve better symmetry.

In the example in Figure 19.10 – a portrait shot – the photographer wants to focus on the girl, particularly her face and expression, and the background is not important.

Cropping or trimming digital photographs can be easily done by selecting the appropriate tools in editing software such as Adobe Photoshop. The programme will allow you to draw an outline around the part of the photograph you want to keep and eliminate everything outside of that.

## RESIZING

If you simply want to resize a photograph within a digital document so that its physical size on the screen is enlarged or reduced, you can use the commands in the Picture Format menu in most basic editing software. Simply change the dimensions of the image in the boxes in the Image size menu and drag it into the desired position in the document.

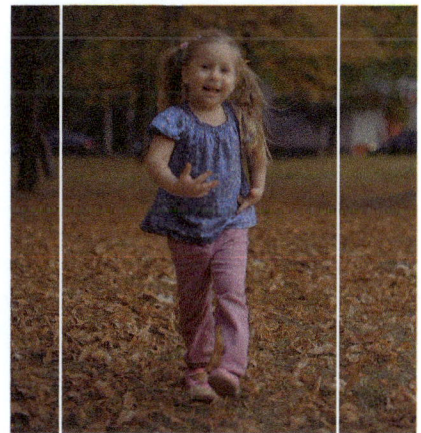

**Fig 19.10** The cropping of this image brings the focus in on the child

However, if you want to use your image as part of a mobile app or on a web page, you may need to resize it digitally, which can be more complex. Normally it is not possible to make a digital photograph larger or smaller without affecting the pixel density, which in turn can impact on the resolution and quality. However, you can effectively resize digital images by working with the overall file size.

File sizes are defined in bytes. A bit is the smallest unit of data that can be stored on a computer and 1 byte = 8 bits. All files sizes are described in numbers of bytes – kilobytes, megabytes, gigabytes, and so on. As a general rule the higher the number of bytes used in the file format to store the image, the better the quality of that image when it is opened and displayed.

Depending on the use you want to make of the image, you can choose to store it using a particular file format of a certain byte size. Remember, it is not always appropriate to choose the biggest type of file with the highest quality resolution. For example, if you need to use the image on a website, you may decide that the JPEG format with its reduced byte size is actually fine for your intended use. JPEG files are quicker for the end user to download and view online, even if the resolution is not very sharp, and this is an important consideration for images for use on the web. However, if you intend to use the image in a print format such as a magazine, you will probably opt for a format like TIFF. This format takes up many bytes of storage but guarantees the very high quality resolution needed for print publishing.

## Link

See Chapter 17, pages 165–167, for more information on file formats.

## ADJUSTING TONE AND COLOUR

These elements of a digital photograph can be corrected using a software package, such as Adobe Photoshop or Adobe Lightroom. The tools in these programmes enable you to make adjustments to colour balance and tonal balance (the amount of white in a colour), and the light and shade captured in your image. For example, using Photoshop you can refine the intensity of the

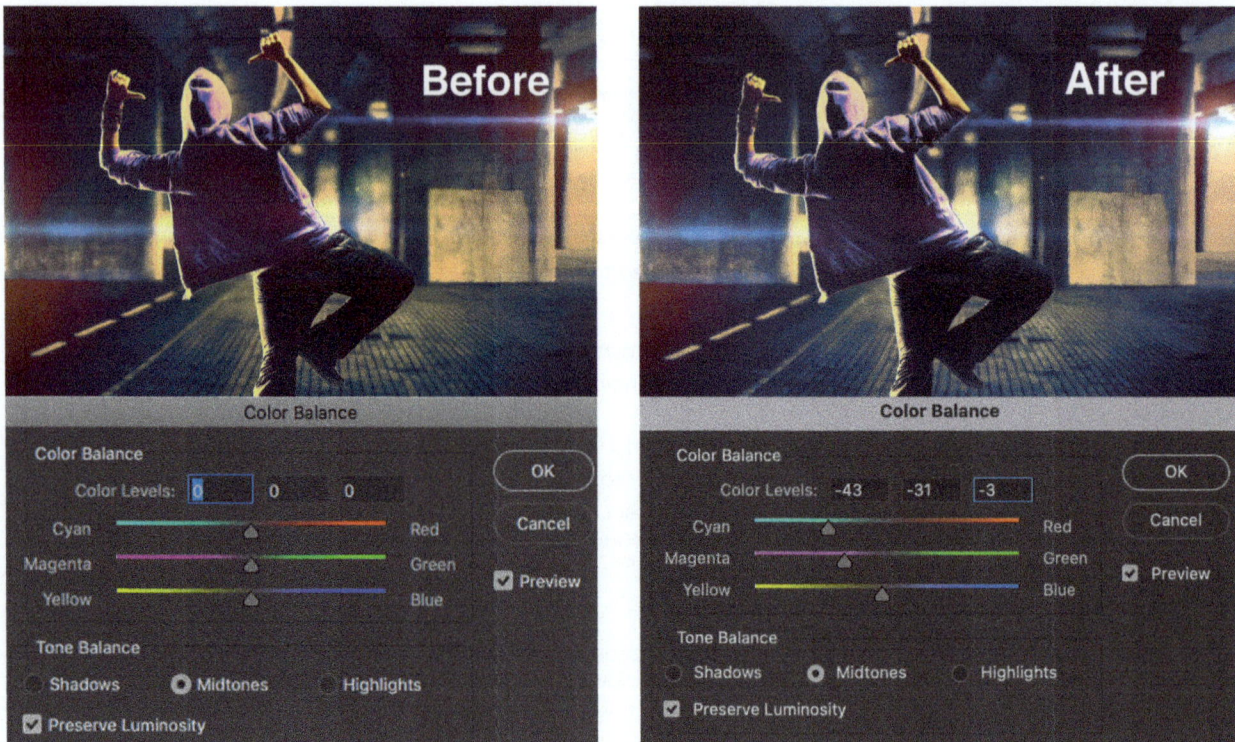

Fig 19.11 'Before' and 'after' adjusting tone in Photoshop

colours in different parts of your photograph separately, which can help to highlight or improve certain parts of the image. Simply adjusting the contrast between highlighted and shadowed areas in an image can often increase its power. In the example in Figure 19.11, Photoshop has been used to adjust the tonal balance of the shadows, mid-tones and highlights in the photo separately. Compare the adjusted version to the original one.

The table below provides a useful quick reference to help you decide which colour model to use.

| RGB | CMYK |
|---|---|
| • Websites<br>• Animation<br>• Film<br>• Digital advertising<br>• Social media | • Printed advertising, including: Leaflets / Posters / Billboards<br>• Packaging<br>• Newspapers<br>• Magazines<br>• Book covers |

## CORRECTING IMPERFECTIONS

Cloning is a great technique for repairing and refining images and is available in photo-editing software. Although it is one of the most widely used techniques in any photo editor's toolkit, it does take a lot of practice to get flawless results.

There are two different ways of cloning an image:

- The first technique requires you to substitute pixels from another part of your original image or from another image. For example, you could retouch **glare** in a person's left eye in a portrait shot by copying pixels from the right eye. Alternatively, you could replace the person's eye with a dog's eye from a different photograph!
- The second technique requires you to displace and move pixels using the **clone stamp tool**, **patch tool** or **healing brush tool** in Photoshop. (These tools will be available in other software programmes but may have slightly different names.) When displacing pixels and using cloning tools, these techniques help you get the best results:
  - Use soft or feathered edges and low opacity in areas of colour gradient or smooth tonal changes.
  - Use hard edges and 100 opacity in areas in which there are defined edges or hard colour and tonal changes.
  - Try to avoid smudging effects.
  - Use as few brush strokes as possible to avoid reparative patterns.

### Skills Task: **Understanding digital resizing**

Imagine that you have been asked to supply images for each of the following products.

- a website
- a printed advertising campaign
- an animated gif.

Explain how you would save and possibly resize imagery for each of the final outputs listed above.

**Top Tip**

When using the colour balance tool in Photoshop you will notice that you have different colour options – red, green, blue, cyan, magenta and yellow. Remember you should use different colour models to edit visual images according to the final use you want to make of them. For example, if you want to print your photo, you should finalise your work in a CMYK colour model. Alternatively, if your work is to be presented in a digital format, you should prepare your work in an RGB colour model.

**Link**

See Chapter 11, pages 104–106, for a more detailed explanation of colour models.

**Glare** the shine of a harsh uncomfortably brilliant light
**Clone stamp tool** option for cloning and moving pixels in a digital photograph
**Patch tool** option for cloning and moving pixels in a digital photograph
**Healing brush tool** option for brushing in more pixels in a digital photograph

# WORKING WITH LAYERS

Image editing software also gives the photo editor the possibility to work with layers – images laid on top of one another to compose the final complete image. Using layers is probably the most important skill to master when working with software such as Photoshop, because it gives you immense flexibility and enables you to apply a vast range of techniques and effects.

You can think about layers as physical layers of acetate, like those used with an overhead projector, each one with a different element of the complete composition printed on it. These layers sit on top of each other, or even merge with one another as layer blends, to create the complete final image.

## Working with layers in Photoshop

There are five basic steps to starting to work with layers in Photoshop.

1. Open the editing software programme. Select an image from an existing folder or the desktop and open it in Photoshop.
2. Notice that your image is called Background. To select a new layer you must select the Layers dialogue box.
3. Click on the top right-hand corner of the box to open another dialogue box with lots of options and select New Layer.

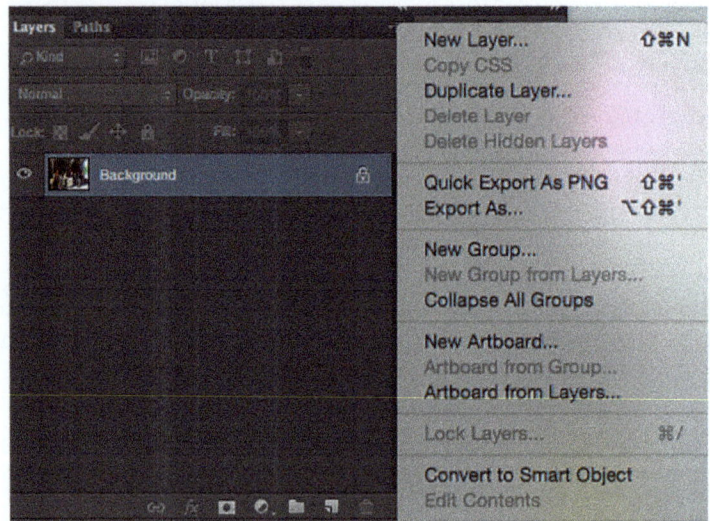

**Fig 19.12** Photoshop interface for creating new layers in a digital photo

4. You will see a box that allows you to name your new layer. (Always name your layers clearly – this will mean you do not lose track of your work if you are working on an extensive re-touch with many layers.)

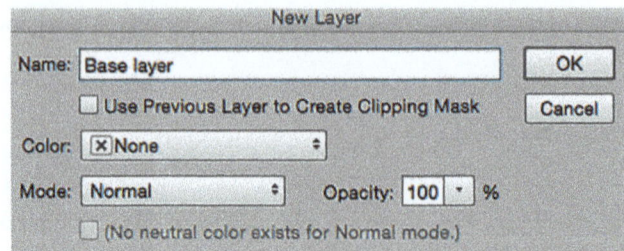

**Fig 19.13** Photoshop interface for naming new layers in a digital photo

## Top Tip

Always copy the files you want to use onto your computer when working with external devices or universal storage buses (USBs), because your image files can easily corrupt when transferring to and from external devices.

**5.** You should now have two layers within your Layers dialogue box. Follow the same procedure to create further layers.

## IMAGE TONE CONTROL

In applications such as Photoshop, you can also apply effects called 'Levels' and 'Curves', which are used for the single most important editing task: image tone control.

When you have a photograph that has less than perfect contrast (that is, the contrast is either too low or too high), you need to apply some form of tone control. Both the Levels and the Curves commands allow you to alter the black and white end points in the tonal range of your image. Adjusting the end points enables you to change the overall contrast of a photograph. The method followed and final effect is the same whichever of the two you use, and both of them also allow you to change the appearance of the intermediate or grey tones in between the black and white end points.

There is, however, an important difference between the two commands:

- Levels adjustment is linear and proportionally changes all of the tones in the tonal range.
- Curves adjustment is geometric and allows you to choose which portion of the tonal range you want to adjust.

Learning to use Curves rather than Levels is more complex, but will elevate your editing skills to a professional level.

# Part 3B

## Moving image

# 20  Communicating ideas and meaning through moving images

**Learning Aims**

By the end of this chapter you will be able to:
* Understand different moving image formats
* Understand how audiences relate to moving image products
* Prepare the type of moving image product you want to design
* Understand contemporary creative practice for creating meaning through moving image

The term 'moving image media' covers a vast range of digital media design products, from a 30-second screen advertisement for a holiday resort to a short educational animation for schoolchildren or a three-hour Bollywood blockbuster.

In this chapter you will learn about how to convey ideas and meaning through the use of moving images. You will investigate different moving image formats and think about the impact on the audience of your decisions as a designer. You will look at specific examples of how meaning can be created through the use of film-making and editing techniques.

## 20.1 MOVING IMAGE FORMATS

A moving image can take many different forms. In this section you will learn about the formats you might design. You will also learn how each format communicates ideas and meanings in a particular way. The audience for an animated internet commercial, for example, will have very different expectations to people sitting in a cinema to watch an epic film. Each format has a particular language; in this chapter we will explore how each connects with its respective audience.

### ANIMATION

Animation allows you enormous creative freedom, because you can depict surreal or fantastical worlds that are impossible to show on film. Japanese film-maker and animator Hayao Miyazaki creates worlds and structures in films such as *Spirited Away* and *Howl's Moving Castle* on a scale that would be impossible using conventional filming techniques. If you can draw it, you can show it. The drawback of animation is that it can be extremely time consuming to produce. Standard animation, for example, requires at least 24 images to be drawn for every second of footage.

### DIGITAL FILM-MAKING

Digital film-making has become much more accessible, such that today you can make high-quality films using a DSLR camera and a laptop with free or inexpensive editing software such as Media Composer® First. Once you have made your film, you can easily show it to your audience through free online

**Link**

See Chapter 21, for a detailed explanation of 2D animation.

streaming services, such as YouTube or Vimeo, and promote it using social media. It is possible to set yourself up as a digital film-maker for as little as $1000; $500 for a DSLR with HD video recording capability and $500 for a laptop capable of video editing. Because our brains process imagery much faster than text, because we recall more information from visual imagery, and because film can convey body language, personality and emotion accurately, it is great for getting your audience's attention and holding it.

## COMBINING DIGITAL FILM-MAKING AND ANIMATION

It is now possible to create animations that fit into live action film and vice versa. Combining film with digital effects or computer generated imagery (CGI) is now common practice. A good example is when film director Peter Jackson used his visual effects company WETA to create the character of Gollum for his *The Lord of the Rings* trilogy of films. This entirely animated character interacted closely with the live actors in a number of key scenes. In these scenes, the actor Andy Serkis played Gollum while wearing a blue suit. The film's editors then edited out Serkis from each frame of the film but kept his movements and actions. They then replaced Serkis with the animated Gollum, to make it look like the animated Gollum moved naturally.

    To make an animated element and live action scene appear together, you need to blend the different layers of animation and film footage into a **composite**, as seen in Figure 20.1. You would usually do this through the following process:

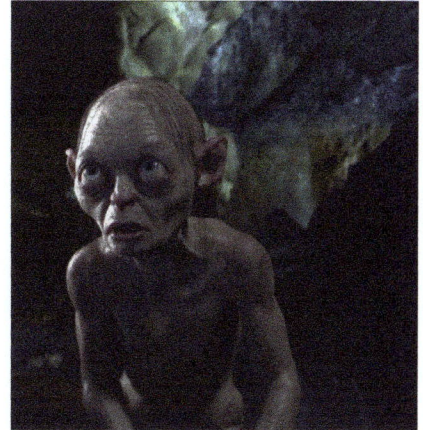

**Fig 20.1** A CGI-animated character, Gollum, is composited onto a real background in Peter Jackson's *The Lord of the Rings* trilogy

- Extract each shot from the scene, so that it stands alone as a video clip, and insert it into compositing software (such as Flame®, Nuke™ or After Effects®). This layer will become the background of your composite clip.
- On the next layer, insert the animated footage or VFX (visual effects) layer.
- On a third layer (above both the filmed clip and the animated footage), create a **grading layer** that affects the look (through filters or lighting or atmospheric elements such as mist or cloud) of both the live and animated layers. Now all the animation and film elements look like they belong in the same world.

> **Composite** the final completed image sequence made from a series of layers
> **Grading layer** a layer that sits on top of the animation and live action layers that gives a moving image sequence a particular look

# 20.2 PREPARING MOVING IMAGE DESIGNS

There are some fundamental questions you should ask when preparing to design a moving image product:

- What is your purpose?
- Who is the audience?
- How and where will your product be presented?

## DEFINE YOUR PURPOSE

Before starting a moving image project, you must define what you are trying to achieve. What audience reaction do you want? You might want to inform people or provoke discussion on a controversial topic, or encourage people to buy something or simply entertain them. It is sometimes difficult to design a media product that balances commercial and artistic purposes. Purely commercial clients may just want to please their audience by conveying easily recognisable, comforting or 'safe' ideas and meaning. By contrast, purely artistic clients may want to challenge their audience by presenting ideas that make them feel uncomfortable. Most moving image media lies somewhere between these extremes. For the digital media designer this means balancing these tensions by defining very clearly with your client your design purpose and acknowledging that the client is in charge of this process.

## KNOW YOUR AUDIENCE

Perhaps the most important consideration for a moving image designer is the audience. An audience may be categorised in terms of demographics (age, socio-economic background, ethnicity, gender) but it is often more useful to look at what moving image products the audience may have watched previously and plan accordingly. Moving image production is a triangular relationship between the client, the designer and the audience.

When a designer makes a product they have to consider what the audience might expect. For example, each culture has its own particular response to stories and genres. Modern Japanese audiences have a particular relationship with disaster movies showing urban destruction and its environmental impact (such as 'Godzilla-style' monster movies) that link to the nation's experience of the atomic bomb attacks at the end of World War II. American audiences have a particular relationship with the myth of the hero from outside the community saving a vulnerable town or family but then forging ahead into the West onto their next adventure, which links to popular perceptions of the way the western territories of the United States were explored and settled.

If you are making a genre film that has particular characteristics and conventions, the audience will have cultural references that will create expectations. For example, the costume in a Bollywood movie is likely to reflect cultural traditions, while Bollywood characters traditionally do not kiss on screen. If you meet these expectations then the audience is likely to be satisfied.

Having said this, sometimes you may want to challenge and subvert expectations. This way the audience may be shocked or pleasantly surprised, making your product more memorable and thought provoking. For example, horror movies about vampires today have radically changed the way they present their main characters.

The three images in Figure 20.2 show the classic horror character Count Dracula from three different eras of cinema. Top, Max Schreck plays the Count in F.W. Murnau's silent film *Nosferatu* (1922). Without sound, the supernatural and ominous presence of the character had to be portrayed by the movement, costume and physicality of the performance. This would seem a very melodramatic and unusual performance to modern audiences. Christopher Lee (centre) played the same character for the Hammer Horror franchise years later in 1958 and was able to use a wider range of acting techniques and subtlety in his performances that was popular with the audiences of the day. However, today this style would appear unusually formal and theatrical – modern audiences might expect a more subtle, realistic or 'human' style, as seen in Gary Oldman's performance as Dracula (bottom) in Francis Ford Coppola's 1992 version of the story.

**Fig 20.2** Dracula through the ages (from top to bottom): Max Schrek in *Nosferatu* (1922); Christopher Lee in *Dracula* (1958); Gary Oldman in *Bram Stoker's Dracula* (1992)

Franchise movies are even more loaded with audience expectations than genre movies. For example, the James Bond franchise has expected conventions, such as:

- glamorous, colourful locations filmed in a way that presents the locations as exotic and romantic
- powerful villains that control a criminal network
- pre-title sequence with rapid action scenes
- animated title sequence combining silhouetted figures and icons
- advanced weaponry, gadgets and technology.

If you watched a Bond movie that failed to offer any of the expected conventions you might be disappointed – or delighted to see changes in the franchise.

**Fig 20.3** Daniel Craig as James Bond in *Skyfall* (2012), looking out over an iconic London skyline

## CONSIDER YOUR PRESENTATION FORMAT

People watch moving image designs in diverse ways, whether on a cinema screen, a mobile phone or an art gallery wall. It is important to consider the presentation format in detail because it has a large impact on numerous design elements, such as shot selection and duration, soundtrack, lighting and visual effects. For example, if you were designing for a cinema screen you would likely include 'cinematic' features such as wide shots showing landscapes and large-scale events (think of the classic Hollywood Westerns depicting the canyons and rock formations of Monument Valley). Alternatively, if you were designing for television you might include more filming in studio sets (common in soap operas and situation comedies) and use more close-up shots in order to focus on dialogue between characters that develops the story quickly.

The presentation format will influence the duration of your product. If you were creating a TV commercial, you would need to design a short (up to 30 seconds) engaging product that conveys ideas and meaning very quickly. If you were designing a video for social media you would probably limit the duration to about four minutes or less. If you were making a movie for the cinema you know the audience would expect to be entertained for at least 90 minutes.

Where your moving image product will be displayed will also have an impact on your soundtrack. For example, the broadcast standard for UK television requires a 'dynamic range' (the difference between the loudest and quietest audio on the broadcast product) of around 6 decibels (dB). This is because some television speakers on cheaper sets are unable to cope with a wider range. The loudest explosion in a TV broadcast can only be 6 dB louder than the quietest whisper. A Dolby Digital presentation in a cinema, however, has a dynamic range of around 20 dB, thereby allowing for a much more interesting and complex soundtrack.

The brightness and detail of images also need to be considered in terms of the final presentation formats. For example, cinema projectors can show visual effects in high levels of detail, so if a product is designed for the big screen it will need to have that level of quality.

### Skills Task: Decoding film conventions and messages

Working in small groups, choose a franchise or genre movie, such as a Bollywood movie or a Manga-inspired animated film, and list the characteristics, conventions and audience expectations. Consider the ways the film has sent the audience coded messages. Create a presentation to demonstrate the codes and conventions of your group's movie to the rest of the class.

# 20.3 CREATING MEANING THROUGH MOVING IMAGE

There are many ways to create and communicate ideas and meaning with moving image designs, both directly and indirectly. These include the elements of *mise en scène*, filming techniques, the characters' appearance and dialogue, and editing techniques.

## AESTHETICS AND EMOTIONAL RESPONSES IN MOVING IMAGE SEQUENCES

As the designer, the aesthetic experience within any moving image is controlled by you. By making careful decisions about the different aspects of a shot you can choose to create a particular set of emotional responses within your audience; making them feel sympathetic, scared, elated, disgusted, detached, conflicted or many more emotions of your choosing. Throughout your work you should consider what emotion you are trying to elicit from your audience.

During the final sequence in *The Florida Project* (2017), the character of Moonee (Brooklynn Prince) is trying to explain that she is being sent away. The designer of the film manages the scene to force an emotional response from the viewer. The director, Sean Baker, uses a number of different tools effectively to generate an emotional response from the audience. The film has set up a narrative so that the audience is familiar with the confident character of Moonee; in this scene she is upset to the point where she is finding it hard to speak. This contrast ensures that the audience feels as upset as the character. This is an example of using narrative to evoke a response.

The director has chosen the type of shot carefully. He has used a close-up, point-of-view shot so that the focus is on the actor's face, and so her emotions. No soundtrack is used in the scene, adding to the focus on the dialogue and increasing intensity. Finally, the fact that film-maker does not cut away with an edit from this difficult to watch shot for an uncomfortably long time promotes a feeling of sympathy with the character.

When creating moving image sequences, you can convey emotional subject matter to provoke different emotional responses from your audience. You can use audio, music, editing rhythm, lighting, costume, dialogue or the type of camera shot to convey emotion. The best moving image sequences knowingly use the different options available to purposefully create an aesthetic experience that leads to emotional responses from their audience.

**Fig 20.4** Willem Dafoe and Brooklynn Prince in an emotional scence from *The Florida Project* (2017)

## MISE EN SCÈNE

To communicate ideas and meaning, you start with the *mise en scène* – a French phrase that translates roughly as 'the arrangement of elements on stage': the scenery, the actors, their make-up and costume, their movement, the lighting. In the digital context, the *mise en scène* refers to how the world has been created to communicate ideas, directly or indirectly, to the audience.

For example, think about a film in which the characters arrive at an abandoned house at night, with thunder and lightning sound effects. The **direct communication** shows the characters have arrived at a house, there is a thunderstorm, and that it is night-time. The **indirect** (symbolic) **communication** uses the fact that the storm is raging as the characters arrive at the house to suggest that the scene is going to be dramatic or scary, because this is a common metaphor in thriller or horror films. The film uses the audience's expectations and memories of such scenes to convey meaning.

> **Direct communication** where an audience understands a message directly, for example, we hear gunfire meaning someone has shot a gun
>
> **Indirect communication** where a message is decoded by an audience, for example, we see a gun, we deduce the person with the gun is a criminal or police officer
>
> **Shaky-cam** filming technique where the camera movement (shaking) alerts the audience to the fact that someone is holding a camera

## FILMING TECHNIQUES

Moving image creators also convey ideas and meaning through filming techniques, such as portable cameras, video effects and multiple camera angles. For example, Paul Greengrass's Jason Bourne films use a frenetic, '**shaky-cam**' technique throughout. This technique is both practical (allowing the film-maker a high degree of flexibility in capturing the action) but also gives the films a particular mise en scène — one that appears to indicate that the action is being captured by a documentary film-maker with a hand-held camera who just happens to be on the scene when the action unfolds. This technique gives the films a sense of gritty realism that other big budget Hollywood action films have since imitated.

Another way to create a particular atmosphere or meaning is to unexpectedly mix different media, for example, by placing a filmed sequence in the middle of an animation or by superimposing animated elements onto film. This can add a surreal, fantastical or dreamlike quality to the action, which may mirror the emotional state of the characters.

## CHARACTERS

Characters' appearance, actions and dialogue are of course central to conveying meaning. For example, the opening sequence to *Casino Royale*, which introduces Daniel Craig as the 'new' James Bond, shows Bond assassinating someone. In previous Bond movies the hero would have easily, skilfully eliminated his target, perhaps even making a joke afterwards to divert the audience from the cold-blooded violence. However, in *Casino Royale*, Bond really struggles to deal with his victim in a messy and desperate fight sequence, shot using a grainy, high contrast black and white film stock rather than the normal glossy colour. The grittier, unglamorous design of the cinematography and the fight choreography challenged the audience and signalled to them that the Bond franchise was moving in a different direction, presenting Bond as more violent, flawed, vulnerable, and therefore more human.

You can also change how your characters and story are presented in order to convey ideas and meaning more effectively. For example, you might have a fictional character turn and talk directly to the camera, as though addressing the audience, as Audrey Tatou does as Amélie in Jean-Pierre Jeunet's film of the same name (2001), and as in the final moments of Federico Fellini's *Nights of Cabiria* (1957).

## EDITING TECHNIQUES

Moving image practitioners, for example, documentary film-makers, always create considerably more footage than the audience sees, and so they must do a lot of editing. Documentaries commonly feature interviews with people affected by the subject of the documentary, gang members, for example, and this generates a lot of footage that must be edited to develop a coherent message.

In this editing process, you start by showing the interviewee in close up, then **cutaway** to show something else such as **B-roll footage** – film clips associated with the subject matter, gangs on street corners, for instance – while continuing to play the audio of the interviewee speaking. This enables you to **splice** together different sections of the interview while giving the impression the interviewee is speaking continuously. Finally, you cut back to the interviewee in close up again to finish. Imagine the following interview recording.

**Cutaway** a shot used to show the audience some information about what is being talked about (also used to cover edits in spoken sequences)
**B-roll footage** footage shot in secondary filming sessions (without the cast or main contributors), used for cutaways and establishing shots
**Splice** to join together two clips of footage, such as two separate sentences in a documentary interview

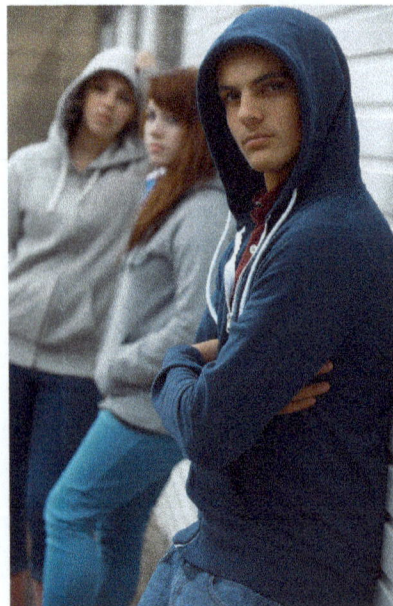

'Yeah! See it's like **the crew**, yeah, the crew here, **my boys, they're my real family**, you know? You need to get it out there what it's like, living on the street and you know, **nobody's going to tell this story like me, I'm representing this place**, this world so you can see how things be. You feel me?'

**Fig 20.5** Sometimes you will need to significantly edit the footage from an interview

To edit this footage:

**1.** Identify where the interviewee gives a clear and coherent message. The main ideas he wants to get across are (a) how close he feels to his fellow gang members and (b) that he is a credible witness of gang life. To express this concisely you only need to retain the words in bold.

'The crew | my boys, they're my real family | nobody's going to tell this story like me, I'm representing this place.'

**2.** Remove the unwanted footage by cutting at the start and end of each unwanted (non bold) section and closing the gaps between the useful sections, leaving you with a continuous piece of audio that conveys the message as below.

The video will have visible edits where you have removed footage (these are called **jump cuts**) and will be shown by vertical lines along the clips in the timeline window of your editing software.

> **Jump cut** a visible cut in a sequence of footage that tells the viewer the sequence has been edited

**3.** Insert B-roll footage that reflects the interviewee's words (for instance, the gang socialising together) immediately after the word 'crew' and end it after the word 'family'. This is your cutaway.
**4.** Cut back to the interviewee starting from the word 'nobody's'. You would now have a clear, coherent message reinforced by footage that depicts the closeness of the group.

Choosing how to edit interviews depends on your expectations of the audience. Most film-makers want to make watching a documentary easy and use the cutaway option described above to smoothly move from one part of the interview to another and therefore clearly and concisely communicate ideas and meaning.

However, others do not feel that the audience should be given such a smooth ride. British film-maker Nick Broomfield, who has made several award winning documentaries, such as *Biggie & Tupac*, *Kurt & Courtney* and *Aileen: Life and Death of a Serial Killer*, often features interviews without cutaways so the audience can see the edits. Broomfield does this because he argues that covering the edit gives a false representation of the interview and his methods create a more realistic or authentic experience for the audience, which promotes trust between audience and film-maker.

Alternatively, documentary film-maker Adam Curtis (*The Power of Nightmares*, *The Century of the Self* and *Bitter Lake*) produces films that appear to deliberately challenge the audience with an abruptly intercutting montage of related footage (filmed and sourced from archives) that creates a disorientating effect. This forces the viewer to listen closely to the narration to follow the story being told.

> **Project work:**
> # Editing interviews
> Imagine you are the film-maker of a documentary about your school. Interview several classmates on camera about what they think of life at your school. Ask some difficult questions. Film some B-roll footage of school life. Then edit the interviews using both the cutaway method and the Nick Broomfield method described above. Discuss which method you think is more effective at conveying meaning.

## Case study: **Paul Greengrass – from TV documentary to Hollywood**

Paul Greengrass is a British film-maker born in 1955. He began his career as a documentary film-maker for the British TV programme *World in Action*, which combined current affairs with social realism. Greengrass reported from difficult, hostile environments such as inner city areas and war zones, which heavily influenced how he used a camera to tell stories.

Greengrass believed that filming life as it happened, and reacting to fast-moving, unpredictable events, overruled the formal requirements of setting up steady camera shots (using a tripod). Instead he used hand-held cameras, developing the shaky-cam style for which he is famous. He moved on to creating dramatised documentaries, or 'docudramas', such as *The Murder of Stephen Lawrence* and *Bloody Sunday*, in which he directed actors to research the real-life characters in the story and then improvise and react to real-life events 'in character'.

Greengrass brought his documentary filming style to Hollywood when he directed *The Bourne Supremacy* in 2004 and has made two further Bourne films. He gives the audience the impression that they are watching real events via a camera crew scrambling to keep up with the action. Hand-held shots zip around real locations, trying to keep up with the characters as they run, jump, fight or drive. He often uses zoomed shots from across a street and shots go out of focus as characters move too quickly for the camera. This style breaks the formal conventions of film-making and places the viewer at the heart of the action, as if they are witnessing it or trying to capture it on their smartphones.

In a famous scene from *The Bourne Ultimatum*, Greengrass filmed in Waterloo railway station in London (see Figure 20.6). The station remained open and full of commuters. To create space for his film-making, Greengrass set up a fake camera crew at one end of the station, where curious people moved to look. Meanwhile the real film crew were shooting at the other end of the station. The fact that the scene is shot with real commuters and in a real location gives it a greater sense of realism than a series of set-up shots.

Greengrass's success has led to many film-makers copying the raw 'documentary' style of his film-making. Each subsequent Bond film since the release of Greengrass's Bourne films has used his techniques and he has become one of the world's most influential film-makers.

**Fig 20.6** On the set of the 2007 film *The Bourne Ultimatum* (from top to bottom): film-maker Paul Greengrass discusses a scene; Matt Damon as Jason Bourne; Paddy Considine as Simon Ross

### Further references

**Books**
- *Cinematic Storytelling* (J. Sijll, 2005)
- *Guerilla Film Makers Handbook* (C. Jones, 2006)
- *Voice & Vision: A Creative Approach to Narrative Film and DV Production* (M. Hurbis-Cherrier, 2011)

# 21 2D animation

## 21.1 CREATING 2D ANIMATION

Animation is the creation of movement by rapidly presenting a sequence of still images or photographs, known as **frames**. If the sequence is displayed at a speed of less than 12 frames per second (**fps**), the human eye sees individual still frames. The eye sees an image and the brain stores it for one-tenth of a second before replacing it with the next image. When animators increase the number of images shown to somewhere between 12 and 24 per second, however, the eye cannot capture individual images and so the brain is fooled into thinking the images are moving, as when you look at a flip book. This phenomenon is known as **persistence of vision**.

In this chapter you will learn about the principles of good 2D animation, the techniques, processes and tools required to create animated characters and backgrounds, and how to create your own animation.

However, first it is important to understand that it is not the individual drawings that create a believable and appealing animation, but the quality of the idea and image sequence as a whole. A series of sketchy, badly drawn frames can create a beautiful flowing animation just as a series of detailed, well-drawn frames can create a bad animation.

Making a traditional hand-drawn animation generally requires many images. For example, if you wanted to create a one-minute animation running at 24fps you would need to produce 24 images per second of film. So that is 24 × 60 = 1,440 images!

To reduce the workload, animators use a technique called **shooting on twos**, whereby each image is displayed on-screen for twice the amount of time. By using two frames per image instead of one, the animator halves the workload. This can often be seen in Japanese animation, or 'Anime'. If you look carefully you will see that when Anime characters speak their facial expressions often do not change much. This is because Japanese animation contains a lot of dialogue and would result in a lot of work to draw expressions to match everything the characters say at 24fps. Animators in Japan shoot at 12fps to reduce the workload.

### CREATING TRADITIONAL 2D ANIMATION

Creating 2D animation, such as that produced in the 1940s and 1950s by Walt Disney, requires patience, plenty of time and a series of steps including idea generation, a script and storyboarding. Lead or senior animators draw the **key frames** – the important poses, actions or expressions that tell a story or emotion. Other animators then add further **in-between frames** and backgrounds, such as scenery or buildings, to the frames on a separate

**Frames** single still images used in sequence to create an animation

**Fps** frames per second presented to the viewer, between 12fps and 24fps for animations

**Persistence of vision** the illusion of continuous motion created when we see a rapid sequence of still images

**Shooting on twos** showing each frame on-screen for double the amount of time

**Key frames** frames are single still images used in sequence to create an animation; key frames are the most important poses, actions or expressions

**In-between frames** frames are single still images used in sequence to create an animation; in-between frames link or transition between the key frames

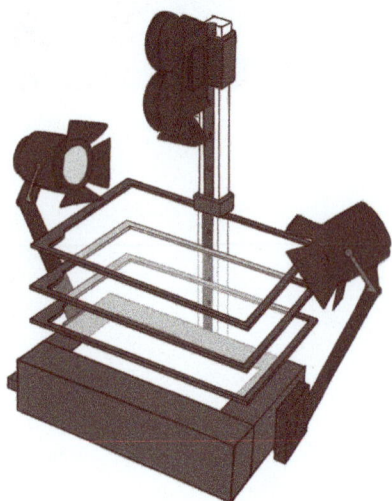

Fig 21.1 This specialist camera and lighting set-up allows for recording of hand-drawn animation on multiple planes

sheet of paper. Backgrounds designed to move are drawn on longer sheets of paper, allowing the animator to slide the whole background one frame at a time to give the illusion of camera movement. Once all frames and backgrounds are complete, these are arranged in **image layers** below **a rostrum camera** raised above several panes of glass, as in the image below. The background drawing is placed on the bottom layer and the characters or props on the layers of glass above.

The lead animator sets the animation timing using a **dope sheet** (see Figure 21.2). This is an essential document in animation production that describes an animation sequence, showing each action and how many frames that action will be on-screen, which drawings or layers are included and in what order, which sounds are required, and how the camera is positioned. The animator will use the dope sheet to film each frame and add them to editing software as a sequence, along with sound. The final outcome is a **rendered animated** film – rendering describes frames played in sequence at a frame rate of 12–24 per second.

| Animator: *J Bloggs* | | | | | | |
|---|---|---|---|---|---|---|
| Production: *Road rage* | | | | | | |
| Scene No: *1* | | Sequence No: *1* | | Length: *10 seconds (24fps)* | | |
| Frame | Action | Sound | 2nd layer (Car) | 1st layer (Man) | Background Layer | Camera |
| *1–120* | *Man driving car* | *Ambient road* | *x* | *x* | *x* | *Close up of car* |
| *121–180* | *Man driving car* | *Interior of car/radio* | | *x* | *x* | *Close up of man inside car* |
| *181–240* | *Man driving car* | *Wheels on road* | *x* | | *x* | *Close up of wheels* |

Fig 21.2 The lead animator sets the animation timing using a dope sheet

Skills Task: **Produce a flipbook animation**

Take 24 sheets of A5 or A6 paper to create a flipbook. Draw a ball on page one at the bottom of the page. Then on each subsequent page draw the ball slightly higher, with the ball at the highest point on page 24.

1. Flip through all 24 pages in one second. You have animated the ball at 24 frames per second.
2. Remove all even numbered pages. Flip through the remaining 12 pages in one second. Your animation is now at 12 frames per second, as if 'shooting on twos'.
3. Contrast the two animations and discuss any differences between them.

## CREATING DIGITAL 2D ANIMATION

Creating animation digitally is much the same as the traditional method; idea generation, character design, storyboarding and dope sheets are all still essential. The main difference is that you draw directly onto the screen using a **graphics tablet** instead of using paper or plastic acetate. A graphics tablet is an input device much like a mouse, except it consists of a pen-like stylus and

**Image layers** different images arranged together to create a single image

**Rostrum camera** camera used to shoot animation, which is placed above multiple panes of glass displaying the image layers

**Dope sheet** document that describes the key details of an animated sequence

**Rendered animation** a sequence of frames played back at 12–24 frames per second (fps)

**Graphics tablet** computer input device for hand-drawing images, graphics and animations that uses a pen-like stylus a plastic slate to draw onto. It allows you to hand-draw frames with a fluid motion, and most digital animators prefer it to using a mouse.

Software, such as Toon Boom, Photoshop, After Effects and Flash®, allow the animator to draw on a digital canvas. Benefits include the ability to erase mistakes with a click and to save the work in a high quality format at any screen size. These digital software applications also allow for fast copying of layers and backgrounds and immediate control over the timing and spacing of the animation.

Some applications also have tools such as **onion skinning**. This generates a faint ghost-like image of the previous frame, which the animator can use to help draw the next frame while easily maintaining continuity.

Another benefit of these software programs is **tweening**. This enables the animator to draw a shape on frame 1, then draw the same shape but in a different position on frame 10. The software then calculates the movement of the shape during the eight in-between frames and draws these automatically.

These programs can also use scanned hand-drawn animations, digitally trace the drawing and colour each image automatically. This allows for faster production and easy access to saved files for reuse in other scenes. The individual frames can also be manipulated beyond what is possible traditionally, magnifying, rotating and flipping with a few clicks of the mouse.

The more advanced software applications for 2D animation allow the animator to add bones to their character drawing and then animate the character by manipulating these bones. The benefit here is the ability to save the animation from these bones and place that animation on a second character with a similar bone structure. This means when the animator has perfected a piece of movement such as a walk cycle, it can be placed on other characters within seconds.

> **Onion skinning** technique whereby frames are made translucent, enabling the animator to see several frames at once and draw the next frame in the sequence more easily
>
> **Tweening** process whereby in-between frames are automatically completed and inserted by software

# 21.2 PRINCIPLES OF ANIMATION

Walt Disney Studios animators Frank Thomas and Ollie Johnston developed the 12 basic principles of animation in the 1940s. Many other animators from both Western and Eastern traditions use them as a bible for best practice animation. The 12 principles are detailed below.

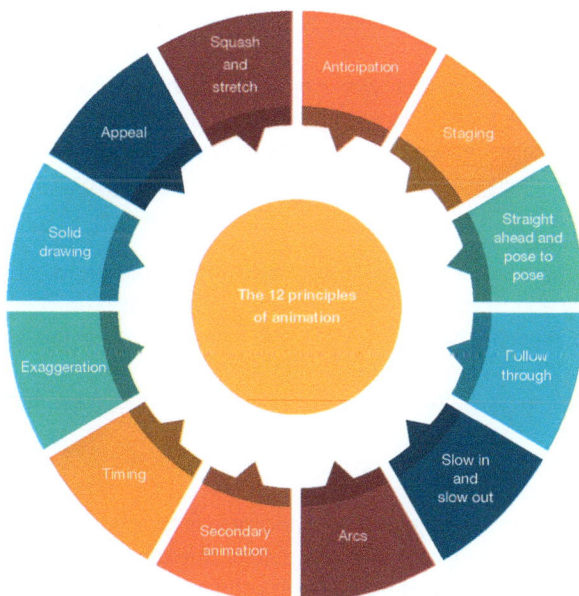

**Fig 21.3** The twelve principles of animation as described by Walt Disney animators Frank and Ollie Johnston

## Squash and stretch

To show the speed, momentum, weight and size of an object or character as it moves, you make it flatter (squash) or longer (stretch). For example, whether you draw a ball flatter or squashed as it hits the floor shows whether the ball is soft like a water balloon or hard like a bowling ball. However, when squashing or stretching an object you must ensure the size of the object remains the same. This means if a ball hits the floor and squashes in the Z-axis (vertically) by 10 per cent, it must stretch in both the Y- and X-axis (horizontally) by 5 per cent each. If you do not apply this rule your object or character will appear to grow or shrink instead of squashing or stretching.

## Anticipation

This prepares the audience for a major action that the character or object is about to perform. Each major action is preceded with specific moves that hint to the audience what is about to happen. For example, if your character is going to jump directly up in the air, they should first crouch down to build tension and energy in their legs. Animating the character jumping without the crouch and anticipation will result in a less convincing and less realistic animation.

## Staging

This refers to the presentation of an idea so it is clear. The main action of the scene should be very clear and simple; it should not be upstaged by anything else. Consequently, you must animate and position each character or object correctly so the audience is not confused as to where to look. Scenes are equally important to stage correctly. For example, if you want to set a scene for a poor home then ensure the floors are stained, there are holes in the walls, peeling wallpaper and broken windows. Do not include anything that contradicts the scene, such as a new TV or fancy picture frames.

## Straight ahead and pose to pose

These are different methods for creating animation.
- The straight ahead method draws each frame one after the other. Straight ahead works best for animating elements, such as water, hair, wind or fire because their unpredictable movement makes it difficult to draw key frames.
- The pose to pose method works by first drawing key frames at intervals throughout the scene. This ensures timing and spacing is correct. You then complete the in-between frames. Pose to pose gives the animator a better idea of the timing of a scene earlier in the animation process.

## Follow through

This refers to the effect when the main part of the character or object stops moving and all other parts continue moving to catch up. Think of shampoo commercials where a woman's head stops and her hair continues moving to catch up with her head. Similarly to squash and stretch, the amount of follow through you give to an object shows its mass, stiffness or flexibility.

## Slow in and slow out

This refers to a moving object. A good example is an accelerating car, which then slows and comes to a stop. To be realistic, the car must gradually gain speed. This is the car 'slowing out'. Likewise, the car will gradually slow down before stopping; this is the car 'slowing in'. An animation with slow in and slow out will have more drawings/frames at the starting pose, fewer in the middle and more drawings near the next key pose. Fewer drawings make the action faster and more drawings make the action slower. If the object being animated moved at a constant speed between the first and next pose it would look too mechanical. Only robots move in such a way.

## Arcs

All human or animal actions with few exceptions follow an arc that moves on a curving trajectory. Arcs give animation a more natural action and better flow, so you should add them at every opportunity. In the example in Figure 21.4 Image A has very little arc in the hand wave and would appear robotic. Image B has a much more fluid arc and would give a more human, natural feel to the movement.

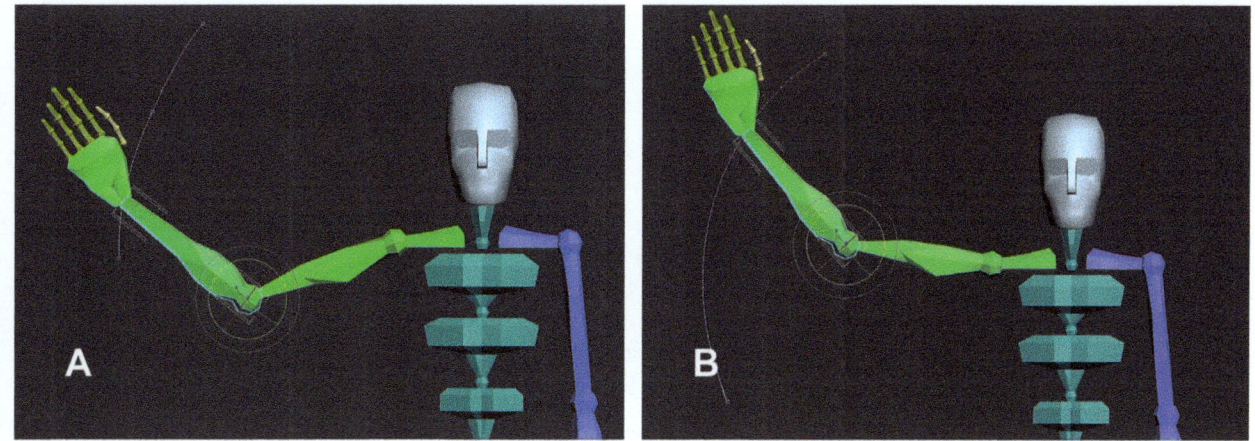

**Fig 21.4** Image A has little arc in the hand wave and would appear robotic. Image B has a more fluid arc so the movement would appear more natural

## Secondary action

This is an additional action in a scene used as a supplement to the main action in order to reinforce it. Secondary action is not to be confused with overlapping animation or follow through. An example of secondary action is in Anime cartoon *Dragon Ball Z*. When a character jumps into the air the animator adds secondary animation by cracking the floor as they leap. This emphasises the strength of the character and the jump.

## Timing

More drawings between actions slow the action down; fewer drawings make it faster. The same action with more or less frames will convey a different message. For example, extending an arm with an outstretched hand over four frames will appear very fast, perhaps as if the character is slapping someone. Increase the amount of frames to 10 and the action will appear slower, and the character could be pointing out directions.

## Exaggeration

Exaggerating a drawing means the action is made more convincing by showing it in a more extreme form. For example, if a character is sad, the facial expression can be exaggerated to include a build up of tears and a larger frown, the body could be hunched over with arms drooping to the ground. Exaggeration is the ability to push the boundaries of a drawing to deliver the message to the audience more clearly.

### Solid drawing

Solid drawing means drawing in three-dimensional space to give characters and objects volume and weight. This means use simple geometric shapes, such as spheres, cubes and cylinders, when drawing, not flat circles, squares and rectangles. Figure 21.5 shows a solid drawing of a cube and Figure 21.6 a flat drawing of a square.

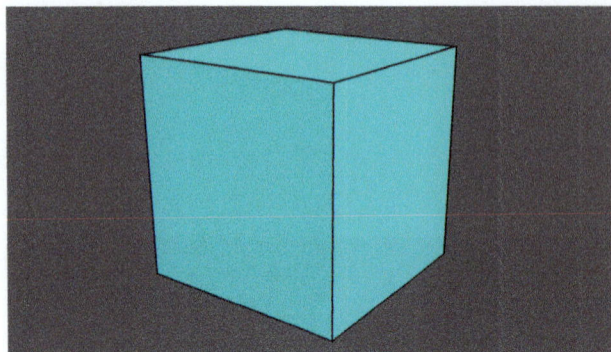

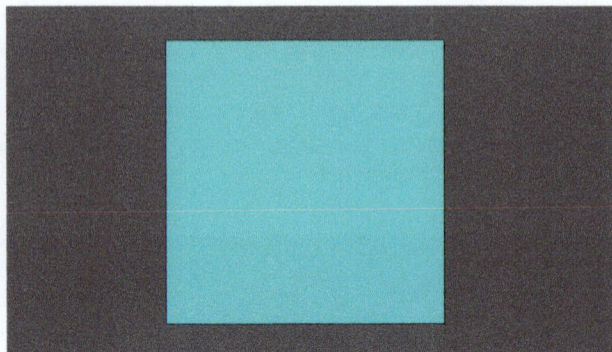

**Fig 21.5** A three-dimensional cube, demonstrating the principle 'solid drawing'   **Fig 21.6** This two-dimensional square is an example of a flat drawing

### Appeal

This refers to the charisma of the action and character. The appeal of a character relates to whether they are drawn in such a way that they are easily recognisable as a certain type. For example, a villain may have a personality drawn into them that the audience can relate to, such as Bart Simpson from hit TV series *The Simpsons*.

---

Project work: **Create a 2D animation**

Start with a simple object, such as a ball or cube, and animate this object using the animation principles. You could do this by creating another flipbook or by using a graphics tablet and software programme. An idea to animate could be:

- A ball slowly rolls towards a gap in the floor, using slow in and slow out. It stops right on the edge, perfect timing. It squashes with anticipation to jump over the gap and arcs into the air stretching as it does. A small piece of the floor breaks apart from where the ball jumped (secondary action) before the ball lands with an exaggerated squash and a stretch on the other side of the gap, maintaining its solid drawing throughout.

---

# 21.3 CHARACTER DESIGN

## PERSONALITY

Designing a character for animation has as much to do with developing personality traits and giving the character a backstory as it has with putting pencil to paper or pen to graphics tablet. Characters with personality tend to be successful because the viewer sees something in that character that they recognise and is therefore able to empathise and engage with them. Feeling such empathy is often why we support the underdog or the hero. For example, a superhero who can fly, shoot fire from their eyes and bend steel is not necessarily that engaging but a superhero with amazing powers who also has a family and children, works in a meaningless job and is experiencing a midlife crisis, such as Mr Incredible from the animated film *The Incredibles*, may be more interesting.

This is why you should always research and develop your character's backstory. Engaging characters have a **story arc**, meaning they are on a journey from a state where they are emotionally or physically challenged or frustrated towards a state where they are fulfilled. For example, the cowboy toy Woody in the animated film *Toy Story* lost his status of favourite toy and started losing confidence, behaving badly and alienating his friends. However, through his heroic adventures he regained his position, self-belief and popularity.

**Story arc** the emotional journey a character takes in a story

## BODY TYPES

Characters come in all shapes and sizes, so it is very important to distinguish your characters by varying their body shapes. If you ignore this and simply add clothing to your character you reduce their individualism and personality. If you create a young teenage character with a pretty face, average height, perfect nose and smart clothes, the audience will not remember them. Vary the body type, the size of the head, hands, or feet.

For example, in Figure 21.7, the artist has given each robot personality. The blue robot with a wheel would be speedy, but how does it pick anything up? The green robot with a wheel has much more useful arms. The three-legged red robot looks slow, but with such a large head it is perhaps very intelligent. Physical traits tie in with personality.

**Fig 21.7** Consider how the variations in body type contribute to the 'personality' of each of these robotic characters

## CONTINUITY

In live action films, continuity ensures that clothing, placement of objects and actors are logically correct from scene to scene according to the narrative. Continuity in animation also concerns the way the character or background is drawn from frame to frame, known as **solid drawing**. For example, if a character is animated to bounce a ball, the ball must be the same size throughout the bounce sequence, as in Figure 21.8.

**Fig 21.8** The trajectory of a falling/bouncing ball, including spacing

A character should also follow this rule, maintaining the same width and length of limbs, hairstyle and colour of clothing in each frame to ensure the animation is both believable and fluid. To ensure that a character is drawn correctly from all angles, animators use a **character turnaround** (sometimes called a character sheet). This is generally a series of images from all angles of the character, as in the image below, which allows each animator to understand the character's proportions and style.

**Solid drawing** drawing in three-dimensional space that gives characters and objects volume and weight
**Character turnaround** series of drawings that show the proportions of a character or object from many angles

**Fig 21.9** Character turnaround: seeing the character from all angles in the horizontal axis

### Skills Task: **Create a character design**

Using the information in this section, draw six robot, fantasy or superhero characters of your own, each with different body types. Remember to vary the limbs and torso sizes.

Then, in a small group, analyse each other's characters. Write one or two key words that sum up or describe each character.

The lead animator draws the character turnaround, which is then checked and agreed by the director and publishers. All animators working must then use this when drawing and/or animating the character. This ensures that the details that make up this character (in this case large round head, bushy hair, short legs) are always the same.

To create a character turnaround, follow these steps:
- Draw your character from a front view to the left of the page.
- Draw faint horizontal lines from key areas, such as the top of the head, eye, ear, nose and mouth line, chin, shoulders, waist, knees and feet.
- Draw left facing, back facing and three-quarter views of the character using the horizontal lines as guides for proportion.

Take a sheet of paper or use a software application to draw your favourite robot, fantasy or superhero character from the previous task. First draw a front view. Then try the following, while keeping the continuity of the character the same:

1. Draw the character from a side view.
2. Draw the character from behind.
3. Draw the character from other angles
4. Draw the character moving/running/flying facing right.

# 21.4 CREATING BACKGROUNDS

The background to an animation is generally static and a more conventional picture used to place characters in a specific location. Backgrounds can consist of more than one layer, to give the illusion of perspective. For example, in Figure 21.10, there are four layers to the background, which can be seen in the bottom right. Each layer has transparent sections shown with blue and white boxes.

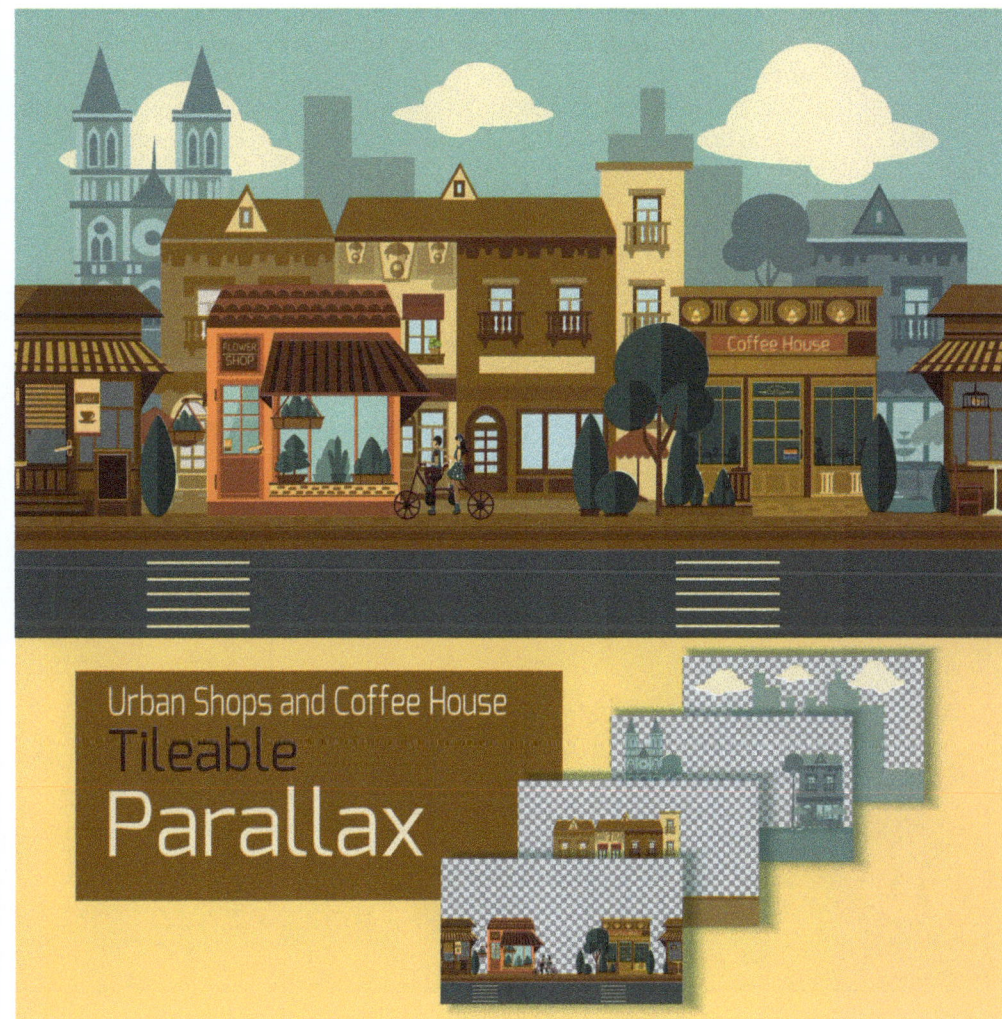

**Fig 21.10** A parallax background environment made up of four separate layers

**Parallax effect** technique that uses layered backgrounds moving at different speeds to create the illusion of perspective and movement

**Tiled images** images that can be seamlessly repeated horizontally or vertically

When these four layers are placed on top of one another, the result is the image at the top. The two desaturated (colourless) layers are furthest away from the camera.

To trick the audience that a camera is panning across the scene to the right, the two desaturated layers would move from right to left slowly, the brown pavement and four buildings would move a little faster, while the shops, trees and road would move the fastest. This would give an illusion of travelling past this view at speed, perhaps looking out of a car or train window, known as a **parallax effect** – the background images move slower than the foreground images, creating the illusion of depth and immersion.

Note how the building with the striped awning appears at both the right and the left edges of this background. These are **tiled images**, meaning the original image can be repeated horizontally (or vertically) seamlessly.

In this example, tiled images are created by making sure that, if part of a building is cut off on one side of the image, the section of the building that is cut off is placed on the other side of the image. When the camera pans across, it will appear as though the building is intact. When you create a tiled image, photocopy your drawing and place the original and the copy side by side like wallpaper. Do they appear seamless? If so, you have a tiled image. A great example of this in cartoons is *Tom and Jerry*; they would chase each other past the same window or door multiple times without the audience really noticing the same background image being repeated.

To create your own parallax background in Adobe Photoshop, for example, for hills of varying heights, as in Figure 21.11, follow these simple steps:

- Start with a transparent background. (File>New>Background contents: Transparent)
- Then add a new layer (Layer>New>Layer) and draw the furthest away asset in the viewport area (highlighted in red). In the example below it is the sky, the bottom layer of the layer stack (see the yellow box).

**Fig 21.11** Creating a parallax background in Photoshop using five layers

- Then add a new layer (Layer>New>Layer) for each asset in the drawing, in this case background, farground, midground and foreground. Photoshop arranges these so that the closest (foreground) is at the top of the layer stack.

This method allows you to move the foreground and midground layers faster than the background and sky, thereby generating a parallax effect.

To make the landscape move you must ensure each layer can tile horizontally. To do this, move the image to the left of the Photoshop viewport, so you can see the right-side edge of the image. Then, holding the 'Alt' key down and with the move tool activated ('V' on keyboard), drag a copy of the image and line its left-side edge with the right edge of the original. In Figure 21.12, the original image has been copied twice; the yellow lines show where the image is repeated.

**Fig 21.12** The completed parallax background tiled horizontally three times

To animate the background you will need to take the following steps in Photoshop, as illustrated in Figure 21.13. One important note: the software will only show you what is visible by the camera, shown in the image below by a red box.

- Enable the motion tab (the green box). You should then see a timeline window at the bottom of the application (outlined in yellow, marked '2'). This window includes layers with the same names as those you previously created.
- Each layer in the timeline window has a drop-down menu with options to place key frames for position, opacity and style (orange box). Select 'position'.
- Move the time slider (highlighted with a blue box) to the start of the timeline (on the left, marked 0:0). Click the clock symbol next to the word 'position'. This places a key frame here and activates the auto key frame tool (orange box).
- Move the time slider to the end of the animation timeline (to the right, 05:00) and reposition the layer shown in the main application window (marked '1') by dragging it to the left within this window. Photoshop will automatically set a new key frame for this new position.
- To check whether you have animated this correctly, press spacebar to play the animation.

Repeat this for all layers of your scene, remembering to move layers closest to the camera more to the left than those further away.

**Fig 21.13** The workspace for animating in Photoshop

---

## Skills Task: **Design your own background**

Design your own background for an animation using a software application such as Photoshop. The background can be a city or the countryside. Try ensuring the following is included for best effect:

1. Add layers to give depth and ensure there are transparent areas on each layer.
2. Desaturate the furthest away layer to emphasise distance.
3. Make sure each layer tiles horizontally.

---

## Project work: **Animating your character and background**

Now animate the character you created earlier on the background you drew in the previous Skills Task.

1. Use your background layers and animate them individually, moving from right to left. Remember the further away the layer the slower it should move.
2. Place your character on the top of the layer stack and animate it moving slightly up and down, as if running, flying or rolling over an uneven surface. There is no need to move the character left or right, as the background is moving and tricking the eye into believing the character is moving.
3. Animate the character's legs, arms or accessories to emphasise motion. For example, if the character has a scarf or antenna, this could be pulled backwards as though blowing in the wind.

## Case study: **dotGEARS**

dotGEARS is a Vietnamese game development company founded by Dong Nguyen. It creates child-friendly, extremely difficult, arcade-style mobile phone games.

dotGEARS is best known for developing the mobile game Flappy Bird. This uses the same parallax scrolling techniques described in this chapter and is an excellent example of using simple graphics, limited animation and backgrounds to maximum effect. The player controls a bird, tapping the mobile phone screen to flap the wings and fly between columns of green pipes without hitting them. After the success of Flappy Bird, dotGEAR has gone on to produce the Swing Copters and Swing Copters 2 games, which also make use of the seamless tiling backgrounds and parallax views but in a vertical format, as opposed to the landscape format of Flappy Bird.

Whether scrolling backgrounds vertically or horizontally, designers such as dotGEARS use the same technique, creating seamless tiling images. To successfully create a horizontally tiling image, as described above, you must ensure the right edge of the image matches the left edge of the same image. Developers at dotGEARS used this technique when creating the backgrounds for Flappy Bird and Swing Copters.

In the case of Flappy Bird, the brown ground and green grass are the forefront layer, which moves at a faster rate to show the speed that the bird is travelling. The trees, buildings and clouds are in the background, moving at a slower speed to give an illusion of depth. Both foreground and background layers are tiling images. The pipes are repeated as the bird flies through them and random heights are programmed to each set of pipes, to increase the difficulty of the game.

**Fig 21.14** An example of the Flappy Bird interface

## Further references

### Books
- *Acting for Animators* (E. Hooks, 2011)
- *The Animators Survival Kit* (R. Williams, 2009)
- *Drawn to life: 20 Golden Years of Disney Master Classes* (W. Stanchfield, 2009)
- *The Illusion of Life: Disney Animation* (F. Thomas and O. Johnston, 1997)
- *Timing for Animation* (H. Whitaker, 2002)

# 22  Stop motion animation

In this chapter you will learn about stop motion animation, and explore and experiment with materials, techniques and processes to plan and create your own stop motion animation.

## 22.1 HOW STOP MOTION ANIMATION WORKS

Any moving image product is made up of a series of still images, or stills. When the stills are played rapidly in sequence we cannot see each individual image and our brains see one continuous moving image, an effect known as persistence of vision.

Stop motion animation works by moving an object, for example, the arm of a clay model, very slightly and capturing a still image of the object using a camera (see Figure 22.1). You then repeat the process for each motion you want to show, such as the model raising its arm. Such an action will require you to take more or fewer photographs depending on how fast you want your model to raise its arm. When you put all the still images in sequence using digital editing software, it creates the illusion of continuous motion. You can animate anything using this technique, although dolls with movable joints, clay or **Plasticine**® figures are commonly used because they are relatively easy to manipulate and reposition.

**Plasticine**  synthetic modelling clay used to make figures and objects for animation

**Fig 22.1** Plasticine figures being manipulated for stop animation

214

Traditional stop motion animation used film cameras that required the film to be processed, which was very time consuming. Digital cameras now enable much quicker stop motion animation, and through the **live view** feature on many DSLRs you can see previews of how your **stills** will look in sequence. Tim Burton's film *Corpse Bride* (see Figure 22.1) was the first stop motion animation to be shot using digital cameras.

**Fig 22.2** A still from Tim Burton's film *Corpse Bride* (2005) – the first stop motion animation shot using digital cameras

# 22.2 PLANNING A STOP MOTION ANIMATION

## IDEA GENERATION

The first stage of any animation project is generating good ideas. However, because stop motion animation requires you to take a lot of still images to show even the smallest movement, you should keep it simple at first. You may find it useful to set yourself a time limit for generating ideas. Be practical about what is achievable. Your animation will be played at 24 frames per second (fps) so be aware that even a one-minute animation will require a lot of preparation. As your skills develop you can progress to more complex animations. Later in this chapter we will discuss how many stills you will need, but at this stage focus on your idea or story.

As discussed in previous chapters, you can use visualisation techniques and tools to represent your ideas, for example, mind maps, mood boards and storyboards. When doing this, some basic questions to consider are:

- What characters and objects will you create?
- How will you show their motion using drawings, models, dolls or clay/ Plasticine figures?
- Will you need backgrounds?
- Will you need any other props or objects?
- Will you need audio, such as voice, music or sound effects?

First, draw a mind map with all your associated ideas and then use that to create a mood board with images, objects, textures, materials, words or quotes that communicate your ideas and the atmosphere or genre you want to represent.

**Live view** feature on many DSLR cameras that enables video playback of a sequence of still images
**Stills** individual photographs, or individual frames of a moving image product

Finally, plan your animation using a storyboard, showing the important characters, objects, motions, camera angles and other key elements. You do not have to include every scene, but it is very important to clearly indicate time and key scenes and key motions to be included. You can make a hand-drawn storyboard or create one using digital drawing tools.

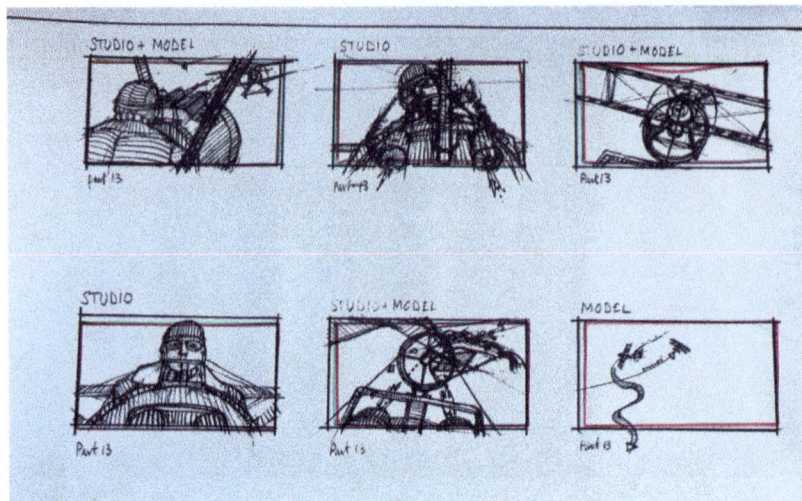

**Fig 22.3** A hand-drawn storyboard for a stop motion animation

### Skills Task: **Analyse Corpse *Bride***

Research the stop motion animation film *Corpse Bride* by director Tim Burton. Write a short essay about the stop motion animation techniques used in the film, how long the film took to make and how the scenes, models, props and other objects were made. Discuss what mood was portrayed and how this atmosphere was created.

### Project work: **Generate animation ideas**

In 15 minutes, devise three ideas for a one-minute stop motion animation; this could be based on your daily life or a dream, a fictional character, a hobby or a holiday. Draw a mind map of your ideas then use it to create a mood board. Finally, create a list of all of the assets that you will need.

# 22.3 CREATING STOP MOTION ANIMATION ASSETS

## ANIMATION SETS

The first thing you need to think about when you start to create your animation is your set. The set is the environment where your animation will exist and the place where all the action will happen, similar to a stage (see Figure 22.4). Decide on the size and nature of your set before you make your models and props. This will help you understand what size your models and props need to be. Your set could be a 2D photographic backdrop or a 3D mini-set inside a shoebox, or even a combination of both. Use your mood board and storyboard to identify what you need.

Creating your own images for your animation set is always a good idea. These could be a photograph of a location, such as a park or a **backdrop photo** (see Figure 22.4) or painting that you create; the important thing is to remember to plan enough time to create these and enough time to experiment and rectify any mistakes. You will need to consider the size and colours of your images as early as possible and make sure you create or edit these appropriately, so they fit the animation set dimensions and colours.

**Backdrop photo** photographic image showing the background environment or scene

**Fig 22.4** Digital backdrop image to be used in a stop motion animation

**Link**

See Chapter 17, pages 163–165, for more information on sourcing photographic images that aren't your own.

**Top Tip**

Add depth and perspective to your animation set by using different tones and shades of colour, for example, by making the foreground of your set darker and the background lighter.

It is also a good idea to use existing materials, such as royalty free images from an image library. You must consider the suitability of these for the size of your set and research thoroughly any terms and conditions attached to using other people's images.

## MAKING MODELS AND PROPS

Making models and props for your animation is exciting, but it can be very time consuming. The stars of your animation can be made out of any materials you like, but remember that they must be flexible enough so that you can make small adjustments to their position accurately for every frame of motion you capture. They should be able to stay in position without being held or supported, but if that is not possible you need to ensure that any support you give them is not visible when you take the photographs.

### Clay models

There are many types of modelling clay that can you use (for example, Plasticine, putty, plaster, ModRoc); you will need to experiment with different types to see what works best for your model. You may also need to use more than one type, depending on the model or prop you want to create. Try to keep your models as strong as possible; you do not want parts of your models breaking off or being damaged while you are creating your animation. Remember that you will be touching these models a lot, so choose modelling clay that can sustain a lot of handing. You may also need to reinforce some models by building them around a solid structure, such as a wooden or wire frame

**Fig 22.5** The models for your animation must be flexible enough to allow for very small adjustments to be made

or some other hidden support. You are likely quite familiar with this form from Aardman features, such as *Wallace and Gromit* and *The Pirates! In an Adventure with Scientists!* or even the children's animation *Pingu*.

**Fig 22.6** Stop animation characters Wallace, Gromit and Wendolene from the Oscar-winning *A Close Shave* (1995) by Aardman Animations

### Paper models and props

Paper and card models (see Figure 22.7) are a quick way to build your animation and can create a very distinctive or **stylised** effect. You can keep these models as strong as possible by coating them with a clear varnish or using hidden supports for them to lean against. A good way to enable movement for paper models is to create separate parts, which are attached using split pins. This will mean you can create movement for limbs and/or any objects you want your characters to carry.

To make best use of your paper or card models, use both sides in your animations. Examples of this can be seen in the work of Yuri Norshteyn and in the cartoon series *Charlie and Lola*. The first episode of *South Park* was filmed using paper cut-outs, before moving to computer software, and this style is still reflected in the appearance of the characters.

**Stylised** having a clearly non-naturalistic style; conforming to a particular style

**Fig 22.7** Clothing designs for paper models

## Papier-mâché models

Papier-mâché is a very useful technique for creating models and props. It is inexpensive, as it recycles different papers, such as newspaper, magazine, wrapping paper or wallpaper. The technique involves dipping strips of paper into glue such as wallpaper paste and sticking them onto a frame or other object in layers and allowing them to dry and harden into the desired shape. You can use the technique to cover hard surfaces as well as create solid models. Once dry, the surface is easy to paint and protect using a clear varnish, depending on the effect you want to achieve. You can also add materials to the paste, such as sand or glitter, to make different textures.

**Fig 22.8** Painted papier-mâché model cars

### Skills Task: **Practise making models**

Design a character for a stop motion animation. Make three different models of that character using clay, paper or card and papier-mâché. If you prefer you could also complete this exercise using three different characters.

## 3D PRINTING

A relatively new way to create models for stop motion animation is to use 3D printers. *Coraline* (2009) was the first film to use this technique, with films such as *ParaNorman* (2012), *The Boxtrolls* (2014) and *Kubo and the Two Strings* (2016) following and refining the style further. Computers design and model each character, creating a variety of different facial expressions. These are then printed out using 3D printers and filmed in the traditional way, or using 3D cameras. This way of creating models requires high-end technology at present, but as 3D printing becomes more commonplace this technique may be something you can experiment with.

**Fig 22.9** A scene from the animated film *ParaNorman* (2012), directed by Chris Butler and Sam Fell

## AUDIO ASSETS

Using sound in your animation can really bring your work to life and may include some or all of the following:

- background sounds to create an atmosphere or set the mood
- sound effects, for example, door knocks, bells ringing or car horns
- voiceovers or characters' voices
- music.

You can record sound using a computer, a hand-held microphone or your mobile phone. Basic sound editing software will allow you to edit the audio and prepare it for your animation scenes. Free audio editing software is available online from various providers including Audacity and WavePad®, and you can find free sound effects online at websites, such as AudioMicro, Freesfx and ZapSplat. Remember to include any audio on your storyboard and in your script.

**Link**

See Chapter 14, for more guidance on using audio.

---

**Project work: Creating assets**

Using the list of assets that you created in the previous Project work activity, decide what assets you can find elsewhere and what assets you will need to create. Then make an asset collection/production plan, allocating time for tasks, such as searching for and printing images, making animations sets and models or editing audio. Finally, create your assets.

---

# 22.4 CREATING A BASIC STOP MOTION ANIMATION

To start animating your assets, you need a digital camera, tablet or your mobile phone to photograph each frame of your animation. Make sure your device has enough memory space to store a lot of images. Once you have all of your images, you will need a digital software application to bring them together in a timeline, as in Figure 22.10. There are numerous software applications you can use, from providers such as Adobe, Dragonframe® and Zu3D.

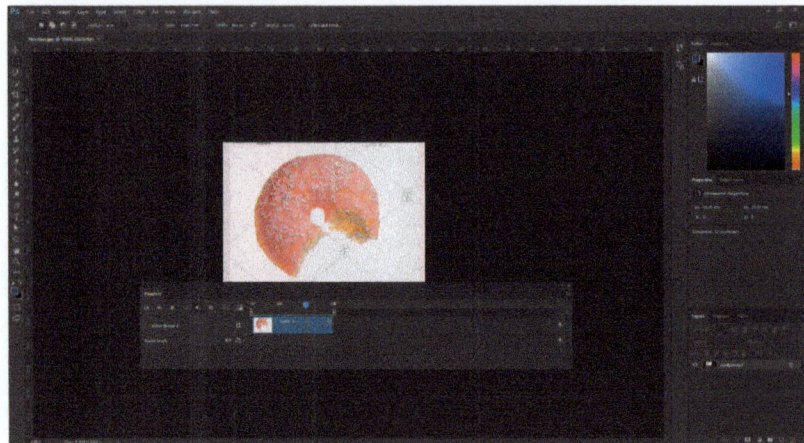

Fig 22.10 A timeline in stop animation software showing an imported single image of a donut

Whatever device you use, make sure that it is stable, so that each image will be consistent in terms of the frame size and set up. You must avoid your camera moving every time you take a picture, as this will ruin the illusion of motion. One way to ensure this is to use a tripod. This can be a professional tripod or anything that will hold your camera still. You will also need to consider the angle from which you capture your frames: will these be face on, from above or a combination of camera angles? Your storyboard will help you plan these angles.

### Skills Task: **Stabilising your camera**

In small groups, practise making a tripod or stand for your camera or camera phone using books, boxes or any other objects that help keep it still. You may need to temporarily fix it in place with sticky tape or another form of adhesive. Take some photographs of an object to test your solution and make sure there is no obvious change in the shots. Compare the results with those of other groups.

### Top Tip

If you are using a tripod, mark the location of the legs of the tripod using masking tape or another visible marker, so you know exactly where to place the tripod each time you take a photograph.

Once you have practised taking some stills, you can start to create your animation using your storyboard and the assets that you have created. Follow these basic steps:

- Step 1: Set-up the first scene with your set, models and props and take a picture. Take two pictures for each frame, as this will help keep the animation smooth.
- Step 2: Make one or more small adjustments to the scene, for example, by moving a model or prop or by changing a backdrop image. Keep changes as minimal as possible. The bigger the changes between frames, the jerkier the animation will be; the smaller the changes between frames the smoother the animation will be. Be careful not to make any adjustments to anything in the scene that should not move! Again, take two pictures.
- Step 3: Repeat steps 1 and 2 until you have enough changes in the scene to create some motion when you bring all of the frames together. A rough but useful guide is to make 12 adjustments in the scene (captured twice) to create about one second of animated movement.
- Step 4: Transfer your images to your computer with an animation software package. Create a timeline in the software and import your images into the timeline in the correct numerical sequence, as in Figure 22.11. Each image will sit in one frame of the timeline only; remember, you have taken two pictures of each frame so put them side by side on the timeline.

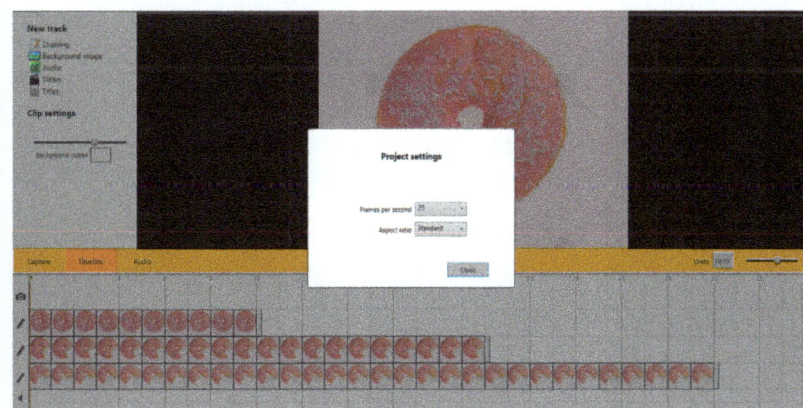

**Fig 22.11** A timeline in stop motion animation software showing a sequence of imported images of donuts to create movement

- Step 5: Set the frame rate on your timeline to 24fps (the standard rate for most animation). This controls the speed of your animation. Play your timeline and identify any frames that you want to delete. If there are any you want to play for longer, copy the frame and paste it immediately after the copied frame on your timeline.
- Step 6: Add sound. Import any sound effects or music in the same way as you imported images. Add a sound channel to your timeline if there is not one already visible.
- Step 7: Edit your sound. The sound channel will enable you to edit the sound, such as fading it in at the start of a scene or increasing the volume to create a dramatic effect (see Figure 22.12). You can have multiple sound channels, to enable you to have background music as well as character voices or sound effects such as a ringing telephone. Make sure you match the timing of the sounds to the action. Sound will have a big impact on your animation and can create drama and atmosphere; however, it can also detract from the animation if done poorly. Use clear, high quality sound or your audience will be distracted.

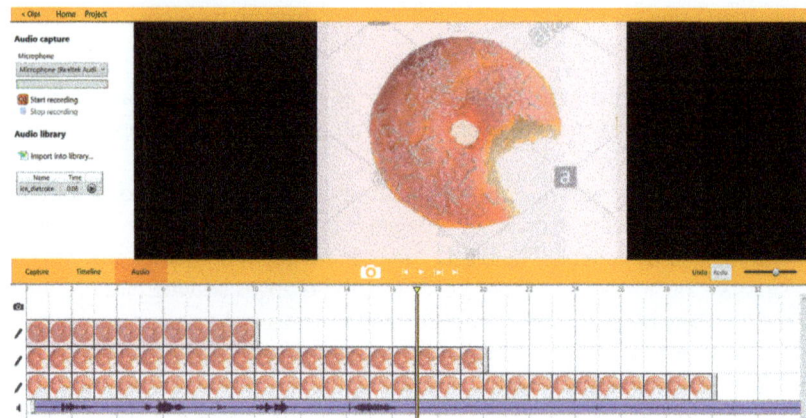

**Fig 22.12** Editing sound using the sound channel in stop motion animation software

## Project work: **Produce a stop motion animation**

Using your storyboard and the various assets that you have created in previous Project work activities, create your stop motion animation by following the steps described above.

## Further references

- *Fluid Frames: Experimental Animation with Sand, Clay, Paint and Pixels* (C. Francis Parks, 2016)
- *Stop-motion Animation: Frame by Frame Film-making with Puppets and Models* (B. Purces, 2016)

# 23 3D animation

## 23.1 PRINCIPLES OF 3D ANIMATION

Animating in 3D is very different to its 2D counterpart. While some principles crossover, such as squash and stretch, timing, spacing and the fundamentals of storytelling, there are significant differences. For example, with regard to frame rates: with 2D animation you can go below the industry standard of 24fps in certain situations, as discussed in Chapter 21; however, this is not possible in 3D animation, because if a 3D character is still, it appears lifeless. Therefore, in 3D animation you must keep to 24fps and use **moving poses**, even when the character is in a still pose for some part; to keep the character alive, hair or clothing needs to keep moving slightly. 3D animators must also keep limbs moving regardless of the position of the character, particularly in gaming environments. In 2D animation if an arm is not in view because it is obscured, the animator does not need to draw that arm. In 3D animation, however, the player/viewer can rotate the view to see the obstructed arm from another angle, so that arm must also be animated.

> **Moving poses** small movements such as blinks or hair moving in the wind that give life to animated characters who are not moving

## 23.2 3D ANIMATION PROCESS

### 1. Storyboarding
Animation studios generally begin the process of creating an animation by storyboarding. This is covered in previous chapters but is essentially the same process of organising illustrations in a sequence that explains visually what particular scenes will include. Figure 23.1 is an example of a storyboard from a Bollywood movie.

> **Link**
>
> See Chapter 5, page 54, for more information on storyboarding.

**Fig 23.1** An example of a storyboard

Create your own storyboard using 6–8 drawings. The topic for your scene can be one of the following:

- A child opens a box she found when in the woods; what is inside shocks her.
- A scientist drinks his own potion and begins to change physically.
- A soccer player scores the winning goal.

## 2. Reference

Reference involves gathering reference video from sites such as YouTube or filming yourself or someone else acting out the scene in real life. This might sound embarrassing, but it is absolutely necessary – even the professionals at DreamWorks and Pixar do this. A big mistake amateur animators make is assuming they know how to animate a certain pose because they have seen it before or done it. Reference is essential.

## 3. Key frames

Study the reference video and then position your characters or objects into the key frames. The key frames are the most important frames in the animation. If a viewer saw only these frames, they would understand the scene and the character's actions. These key poses should also be timed correctly, with the software package being set to **stepped animation** or playback. This means the computer will not 'fill in' the frames between each key frame, but rather stay on the pose until the next key frame.

For example, imagine animating a character taking a bite from a sandwich. The key frames/poses would be:

- Key Frame 1: **Initial pose** – character holding sandwich, looking down at it
- Key Frame 70: **Extreme pose** 1 – character holding sandwich in the air with an open mouth and wide smile
- Key Frame 110: Extreme pose 2 – sandwich in mouth and character's squashed face, eyes closed
- Key Frame 150: **Final pose** – character holding sandwich smiling, eyes remain closed showing happiness

## 4. In-between frames

You then have to pose the character for the in-between frames:

- Key Frame 1: Initial pose
- Frame 40: In-between – character lifting sandwich into the air
- Key Frame 70: Extreme pose 1
- Frame 80: In-between – character moving sandwich towards their mouth
- Key Frame 110: Extreme pose 2
- Frame 140: In-between – character removing sandwich from mouth
- Key Frame 150: Final pose

## 5. Splining

Next comes **splining**, where you allow the computer to fill in the empty frames and then you add in subtle 'details' to bring life to the final animation. For example:

- Key Frame 1: Initial pose
- Frame 10: In-between
- Frame 20: Character's pupils dilating with pleasure. Detail.
- Frame 40: In-between – character lifting sandwich into the air
- Frame 50: Eyebrows raised. Detail.
- Frame 60: In-between

**Stepped animation** software setting that keeps a character's pose the same from one key frame to the next
**Initial pose** starting pose or beginning of a scene
**Extreme poses** the most important frames/poses of the scene
**Final pose** the pose or frame that ends a scene
**Splining** method of instructing software to fill in the animation between key frames with in-between frames

- Key Frame 70: Extreme pose 1
- Frame 80: In-between – character moving sandwich towards their mouth
- Frame 90: Character licking lips before the bite. Detail.
- Frame 100: In-between
- Key Frame 110: Extreme pose 2
- Fame 120: In-between
- Frame 130 – Eyelids squashed as character chews. Detail.
- Frame 140: In-between – character removing sandwich from mouth
- Key Frame 150 – Final pose
- Frame 175 – In-between
- Frame 200 – Part of the sandwich filling falls out. Detail.

## 6. 3D modelling

Once you have done your reference work and created your frame sequence, you then start modelling the three-dimensional characters and objects you need using software programs, such as Maya, 3ds Max® or Blender. This is discussed in detail in the next section. You will find 3D modelling in various industries including games, virtual reality, motion pictures, medical imagery, TV, marketing and manufacturing.

> ### Project work: **Preparing reference material**
>
> In a group, choose one storyboard drawn in the previous Skills Task. Then film each group member acting out the key poses/frames in the storyboard. Notice how each of you will act the scene slightly differently to one another; this is why reference is necessary. Choose the best reference and prepare a document recording the poses that would work best for:
>
> - key frames
> - in-between frames.

# 23.3 3D MODELLING

Every 3D model is created from **primitive objects**. Primitives can be anything from:

- a single point (called a **vertex**)
- a two-dimensional line (an **edge**)
- a curve (a **spline**)
- two-dimensional shapes (**faces** or **polygons**)
- three-dimensional objects (**meshes**).

## USING 3DS MAX SOFTWARE

This chapter uses 3ds Max software to illustrate examples. Students can go online and access this software free of charge.

Figure 23.2 shows a screenshot with the most important areas colour coded.

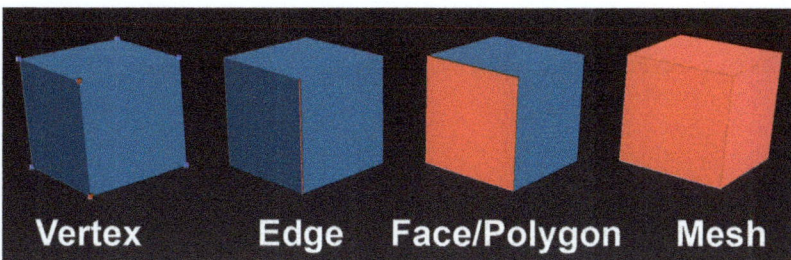

**Vertex    Edge    Face/Polygon    Mesh**

**Fig 23.2** The red highlights show examples of a vertex, edge, face/polygon and mesh

**Primitive objects** standard 2D and 3D points, lines and shapes used to create 3D animation
**Vertex** a single point of a 3D model
**Edge** a line that joins vertices
**Spline** a flexible curve that can also be manipulated to create straight lines and corners; they allow artists to draw shapes in two dimensions that can later be turned into three dimensions
**Face** a 2D shape, for example, triangle or square, formed by three or more edges
**Polygon** a 2D shape, for example, triangle or square, formed by three or more edges
**Mesh** a collection of vertices, edges and faces that defines the shape of a 3D object

- Refer to Figure 23.3. Beginning in the far top left, you will see a green/blue number 3, which is your File menu, used for opening a new scene, saving a scene and loading a scene.
- Directly below this is the main toolbar with Undo/Redo buttons highlighted in red.
- The four icons highlighted in blue are the most used: Select, Move, Rotate and Scale.
- There are four viewports, numbered 1–4. When using a viewport, use the View cube (highlighted in purple in viewport 4) to change the viewport angle or rotate around 3D objects.
- The area shaded in purple is the Animation toolset, containing the frames available, the time slider, and a large + used to set a new key frame.
- There are also Rewind, Play, Pause and Fast forward buttons.

## DRAWING PRIMITIVE OBJECTS

To draw primitive objects, first click the Create tab (large + sign highlighted in yellow) then select the Primitives tab below (highlighted in green), which shows the primitives you can draw.

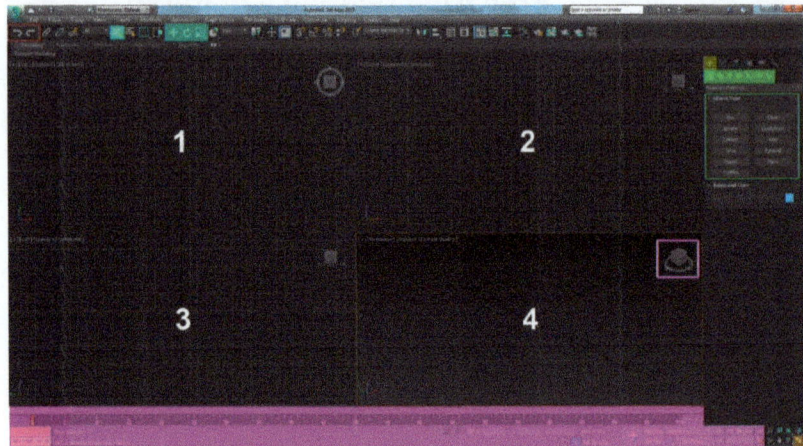

**Fig 23.3** The workspace for 3D application 3ds Max

### Skills Task: **Drawing primitive objects**

Using 3ds Max or equivalent software, use the Create tab followed by the Primitives tab to draw a variety of 3D primitive shapes into the viewports. Practise moving, rotating and scaling these primitives. Also experiment with the keyboard and mouse controls for panning, zooming and circling (or 'orbiting') the view/camera around the primitive you have drawn on-screen.

## TYPES OF 3D MODELLING

There are three distinct ways to model objects in 3D software applications:
- Box modelling
- Poly/Edge modelling
- Spline modelling

Most designers will find one method easier than the others and use that method each time. Although typically determined by the designer's preferred choice, the type of object being created also influences the method used.

# Box modelling

Box modelling is one of the most popular methods of 3D animation. You begin with a primitive object, such as a cube or sphere. By subdividing the object you can add more edges and therefore more faces/polygons, which can be extruded and manipulated in terms of position, rotation and scale. This allows you to gradually create the mesh you desire. This method proves very efficient for creating a basic shape quickly.

To give a mesh more detail, you subdivide the primitive object to add detail. This process is repeated until the mesh contains enough detail and the object is identifiable. However, if not modelled with care this method can lead to a poor model that may not deform (subdivide) correctly when animated. Creating organic and hard surface models is possible with this method, but shapes with precise curves will prove more difficult.

To box model a foot, you would start with a cube. Subdivide the cube by giving it five length segments, three width segments and one height segment, as seen in Figure 23.4. The area for subdividing/adjusting segments is highlighted with a red box.

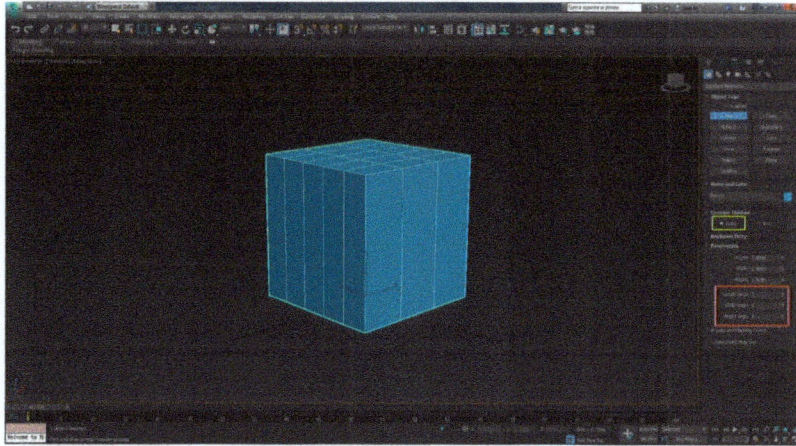

**Fig 23.4** Subdividing a cube in 3ds Max

The next step is to convert the cube into an editable polygon mesh. This will allow you to move and manipulate the mesh by moving vertices, edges or faces. To convert the mesh: Right click > Convert To > Convert to Editable Poly, as seen in Figure 23.5.

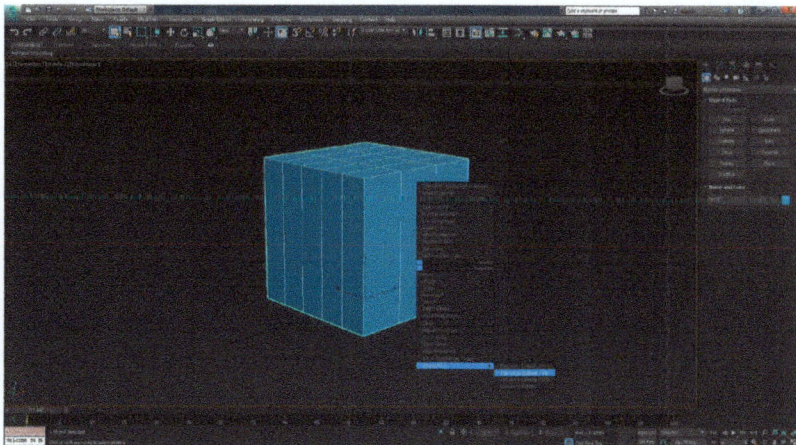

**Fig 23.5** Converting the cube into an editable polygon mesh

Now you can select the mesh's vertices by pressing 1 on the keyboard. You can then click on each of the vertices you wish to move, holding down Ctrl to select more than one at a time. Select the top front row of vertices and move these down, as in Figure 23.6.

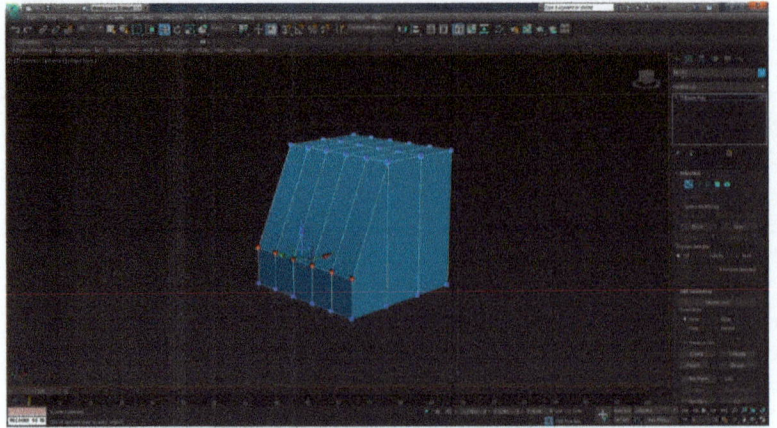

**Fig 23.6** Selecting the mesh's vertices

You can then select all the vertices on the front row and move them forward using the Move tool (press 'w' on the keyboard), as in Figure 23.7.

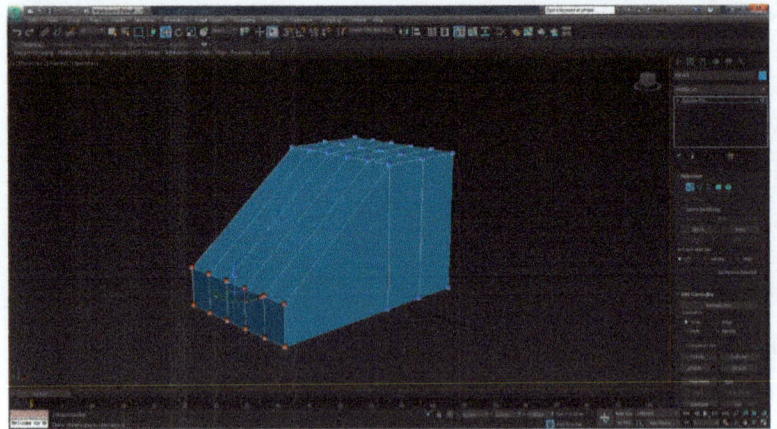

**Fig 23.7** Selecting all the vertices and moving them forward using the Move tool

Next, adjust each vertex by selecting and moving it to resemble a foot. In Figure 23.8, the outer edge vertices have been moved down while the top set form a more circular shape for the ankle.

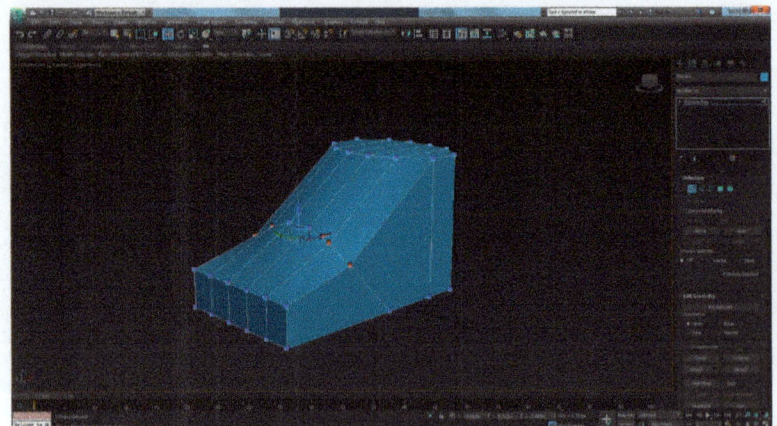

**Fig 23.8** Adjusting each vertex by selecting and moving it to resemble a foot

The next step is to create the toes using the **Bevel** tool, which is highlighted with the green box in Figure 23.9. To access this tool you must first select the faces/polygons you wish to extrude. Begin by pressing '4' on the keyboard to activate Face selection mode. Then select each of the five front faces (holding Ctrl to select all), click the settings box next to the Bevel button and manually adjust the type of bevel, the length of the extrusion and the amount of bevel applied. You must ensure the type of bevel is 'By Polygon'.

**Bevel** software tool that enables a designer to extrude a face/polygon and scale it simultaneously

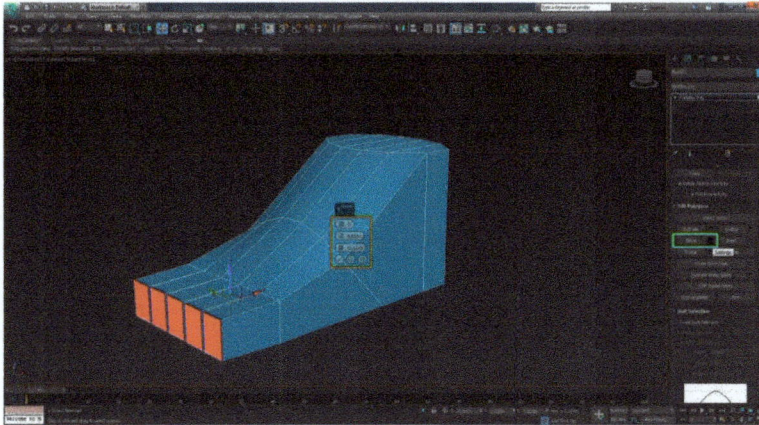

**Fig 23.9** Creating toes using the Bevel tool

The final step is to adjust the length of each 'toe' and to scale each toe according to reference. See Figures 23.10 and 23.11, for example.

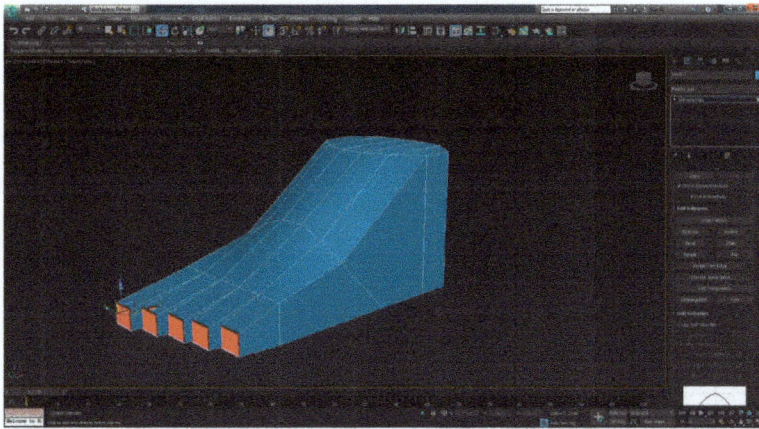

**Fig 23.10** Adjusting the length of each 'toe'

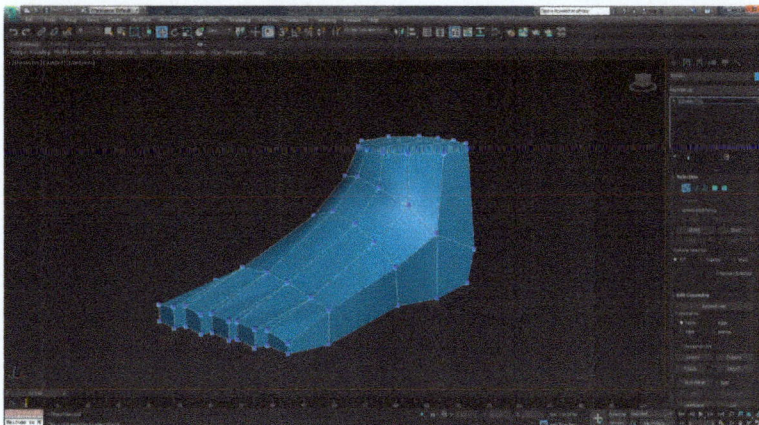

**Fig 23.11** Adjusting 'toe' scale

229

**Quad** a four-sided polygon/face
**Tri** a three-sided polygon/face
**N-gon** a polygon/face with more than four sides
**Plane** a flat four-sided polygon/face

When box modelling, you must start with an accurate primitive. If it is inaccurate with regards to scale or style, changing this once you have added lots of detail will be problematic. Use as few polygons/faces as possible before dividing the surface to add more detail. To efficiently model an asset, aim for a low overall amount of polygons/faces. Of those you do use, try to keep as many of them four-sided as possible, as this helps to keep the model looking smooth and even. Four-sided faces/polygons are called **Quads**, three-sided ones are called **Tris**, while five-sided ones are known as **N-gons**.

## Skills Task: **Create a box model**

Using the instructions above, create your own simple 3D asset. This could be the foot as described in this chapter or a simple boot, house, hand or something similar. Keep the asset simple, as this is your first 3D polygon model.

### Poly modelling

Poly modelling, also known as edge modelling, gives you the most freedom and is highly effective at producing precise objects. You can create a mesh face by, in some cases starting the model with a single square face, or 'quad'. This method is slower than that of box modelling but will result in less manipulation and tweaking and allows you to ensure a good flow of polygons for animation early on. This method suits modelling organic assets better than hard surfaces and is ideal for the creation of organic meshes such as the human head.

To model a head, start with a primitive object called a **plane**, a single, four-sided face as seen in Figure 23.12. Ensure when you click and drag this plane into the viewport you have the width and length segments (highlighted by the yellow box) set to 1.

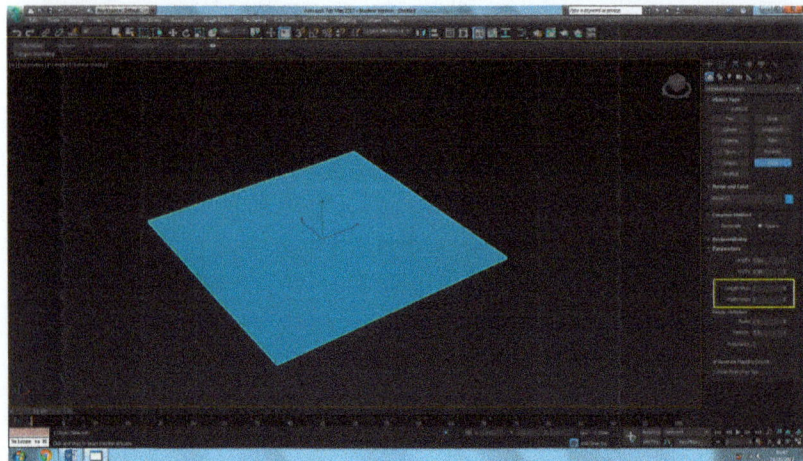

**Fig 23.12** To model a head, start with a primitive object called a plane

Now convert this plane to an editable poly by right-clicking it and selecting: Convert To > Convert to Editable Poly. Then activate the edges by pressing '2' on the keyboard or clicking the icon highlighted in green in Figure 23.13.

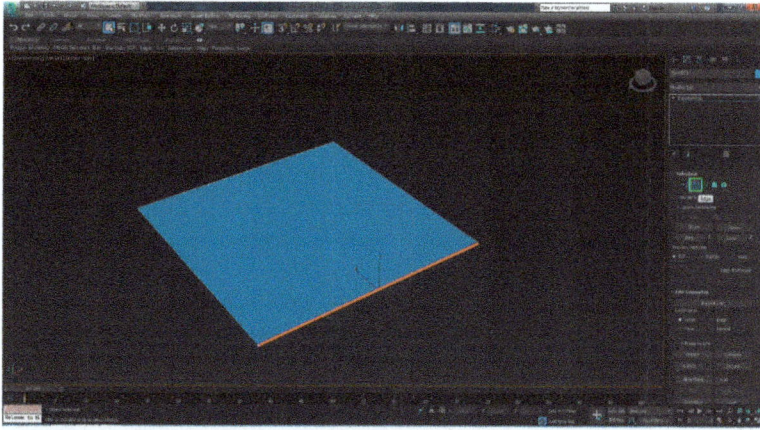

**Fig 23.13** Converting the plane to an editable poly

Select an edge you wish to extrude, which will turn red. Press 'w' on the keyboard to turn on the Move control and hold down the 'Shift' key to extend the edge, as in Figure 23.14.

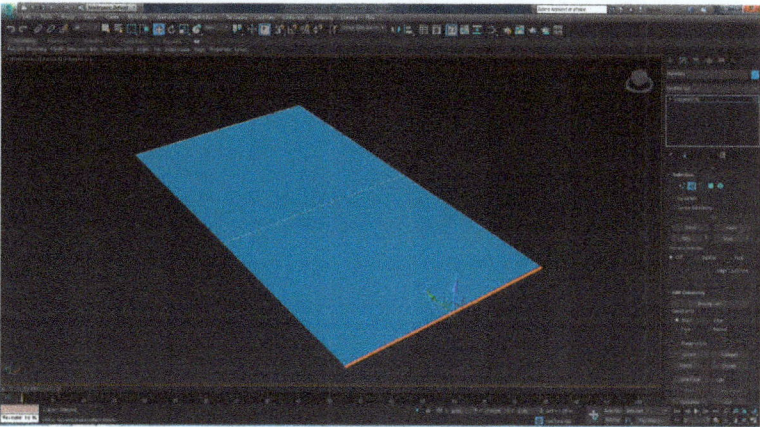

**Fig 23.14** Extending an edge of the plane

You can rotate or move the edge or each vertex in any direction. Select Vertices by pressing '1' on the keyboard and then use the Move control as above. A combination of poly modelling and manipulating the position of each vertex or edge can result in a highly detailed asset. The image in Figure 23.15 has been created using only those techniques, beginning as just two polygons/faces (highlighted in red).

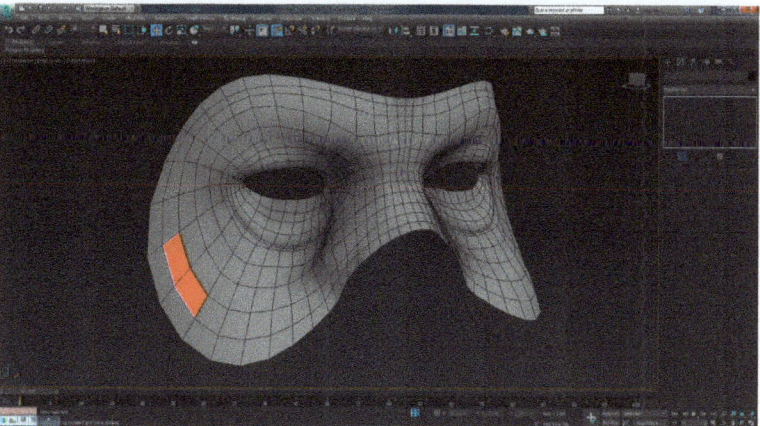

**Fig 23.15** Poly modelling and manipulating the position of each vertex or edge can result in a highly detailed asset such as this face

## Spline modelling

Spline modelling involves using 2D lines to mark out the initial shape of an object then allowing the computer software to fill in the rest. This requires you to draw lines, or splines, that mimic the outline or shape of the object. Splines enable you to draw shapes in two dimensions and turn them into 3D shapes. In this case the software converts these splines into polygons/faces, giving the object its 3D shape. Spline modelling is not used as much in contemporary 3D modelling because creating models with accurate details in this way can be a lengthy process.

To practise spline modelling, start by using the Shapes tab and selecting Line (highlighted in the green boxes in Figure 23.16). Then draw the outline of half a martini glass. You can do this in five clicks (see red dots).

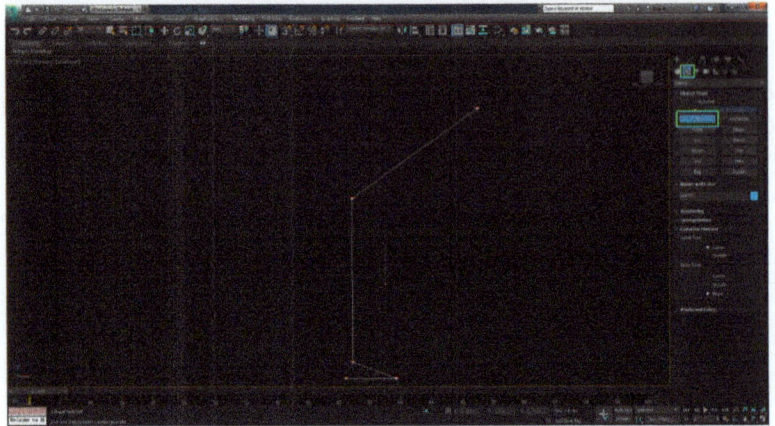

**Fig 23.16** Spline modelling: drawing the outline of half a martini glass

**Pivot** the point at which an object rotates
**Lathe** software tool that creates a 3D mesh using a profile drawn with splines

Then move the **pivot** of the object (the point around which it rotates) to the centre. To do this select the Hierarchy tab, click on Pivot and finally click Move pivot only (all highlighted by green boxes in Figure 23.17). Using the Move control ('w' on the keyboard), move the pivot horizontally so it is in line with the centre of the half martini glass, as shown by the red box. Click the 'Affect pivot only' button to deactivate it.

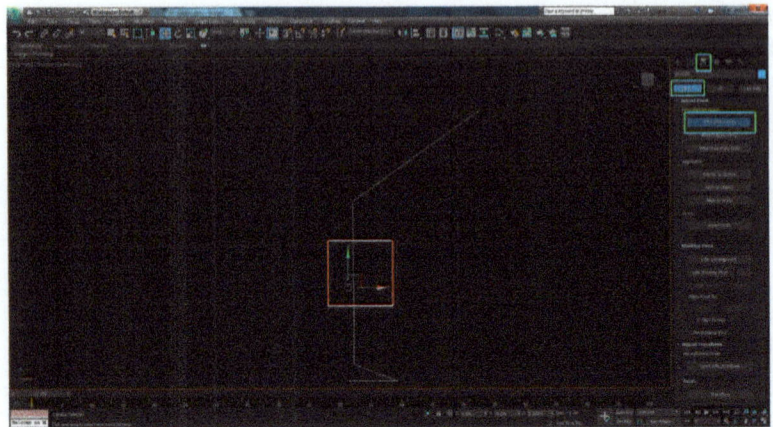

**Fig 23.17** Spline modelling: moving the pivot horizontally so it aligns with the centre of the half martini glass

Finally, select the Modify tab and select the **Lathe** tool (both highlighted using a green box in Figure 23.18). This will automatically create a 3D mesh from the splines you have drawn.

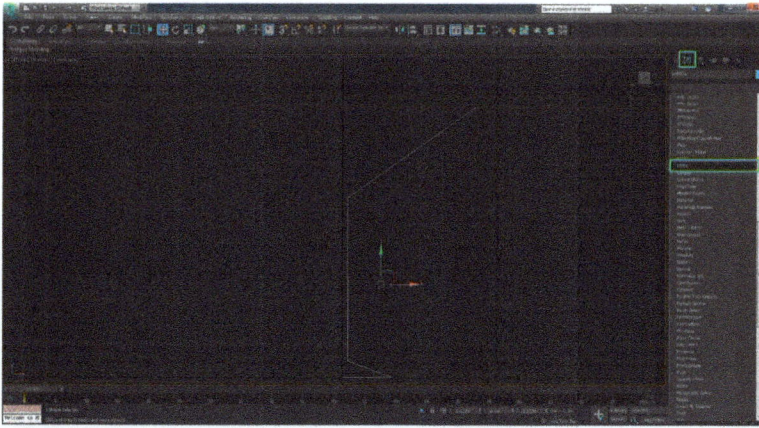

**Fig 23.18** Spline modelling: creating a 3D mesh from the splines

The result will be a fully formed 3D martini glass, as shown in Figure 23.19.

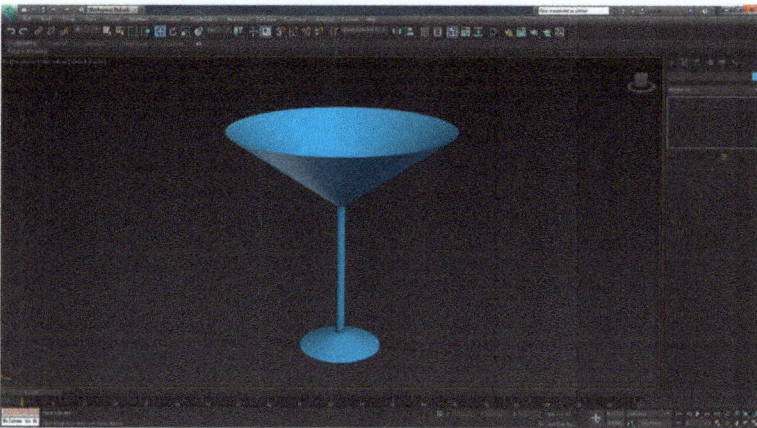

**Fig 23.19** Spline modelling: the finished 3D martini glass

> **Top Tip**
>
> When modelling, treat the software as you would a drawing. Sketch the object first with simple shapes before adding detail. For example, if you were drawing a character you would sketch their outline and clothing before detailing their facial features, buttons, pockets and zips. Creating a 3D asset is no different.

### Project work: **Create 3D models**

Download the 3ds Max software and practise each of the three modelling methods described above:

1. Create a 3D model using the box modelling method.
2. Create a 3D model using the poly modelling method.
3. Create a 3D model using the spline modelling method.

# 23.4 CREATING A 3D ANIMATION

## OBJECT HIERARCHIES

Once you have created your 3D models, you can then start animating them.
    When animating some complex objects, a hand for instance, you must create a hierarchy. This is necessary when you want to keep the model together but be able to move some parts of it independently.

The hand in Figure 23.20 is made from individual boxes. Ideally you would be able to move the hand and then the fingers and thumb would move as well. To do this, click the Link tool icon (top left), to link each finger section to the hand; in this case link Thumb3 > Thumb2 > Thumb1 > Hand. To check you have linked each section correctly, open the Schematic view (highlighted in red).

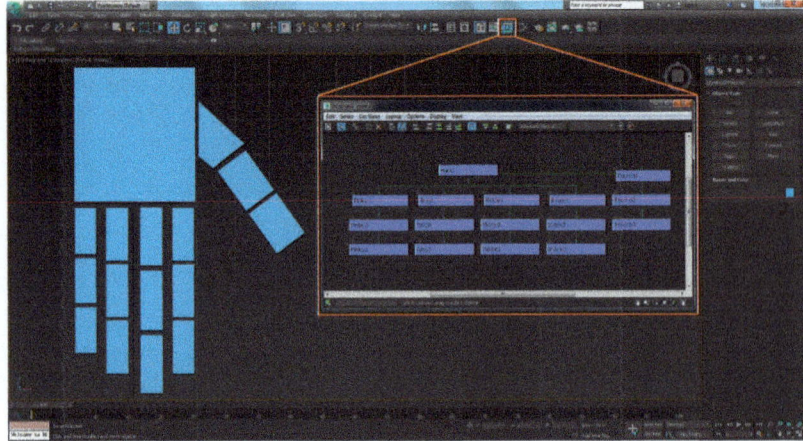

**Fig 23.20** 3ds Max software hand and finger boxes

## FORWARD KINEMATICS AND INVERSE KINEMATICS

Forward kinematics and inverse kinematics are two basic ways to calculate the movements of a model.

- Forward kinematics is where movement of a joint will only affect other joints lower down in the hierarchy of body movement. For example, in Figure 23.20, moving Index 1 will also move Index 2 and Index 3. This means the designer must work through the hierarchy joint by joint individually, until the desired pose is reached.
- Inverse kinematics is the reverse process. Here the terminating joint in the hierarchy can be directly placed and the software will automatically position all joints above it. So, in the example in Figure 23.20, moving the Index 3 would affect Index 2 and Index 1 automatically.

Skills Task: **Create and link primitives**

Draw two standard primitives into your viewport. Link one primitive to the other by using the Link tool. Open the Schematic view to check whether you have linked these two primitives together correctly.

## CREATING A BASIC ANIMATION

To animate a bouncing ball, for example, you would begin by drawing the primitive model 'sphere' in the front viewport and maximising the viewport (Alt + w). Move the sphere to the left-hand side, as in Figure 23.21. Change the animation length to 20 frames by clicking the 'Time configuration' button at bottom right.

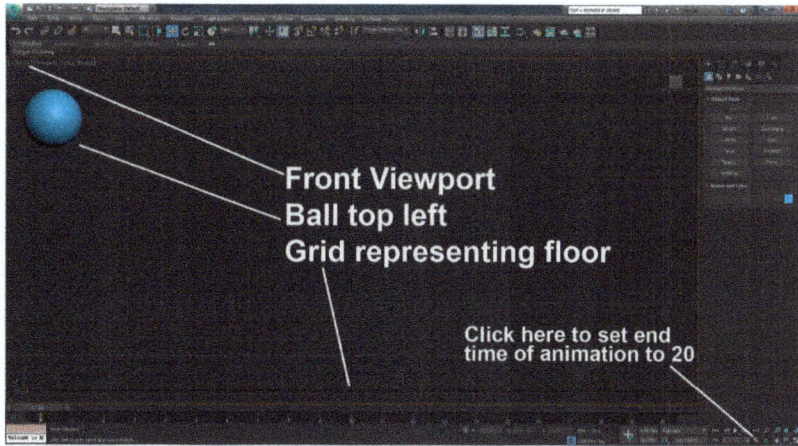

**Fig 23.21** The first steps in creating a bouncing ball animation

Next, right-click the sphere and select 'Object properties' (Figure 23.22). Tick the option for Trajectory (highlighted with a red box). This lets you see the path of the object when animated. Finally, ensure 'Auto key' is turned on. The viewport should now have a red border.

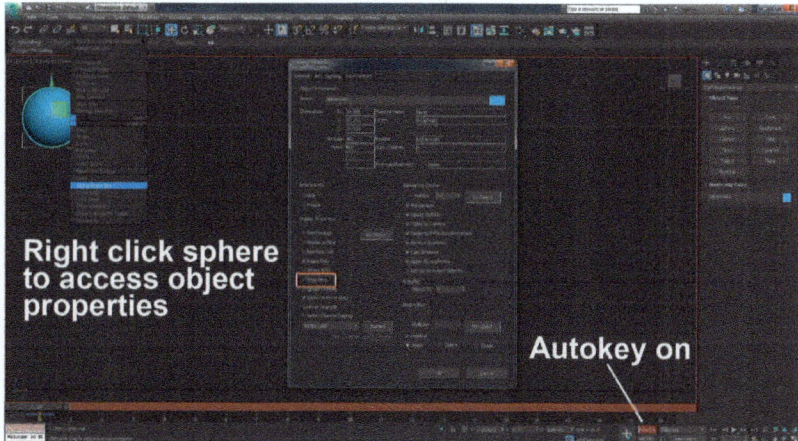

**Fig 23.22** Creating a bouncing ball animation: using Object properties and Auto key

Next, move your time slider to frame 10 (Figure 23.23) and then move the sphere to the bottom of the viewport position centrally.

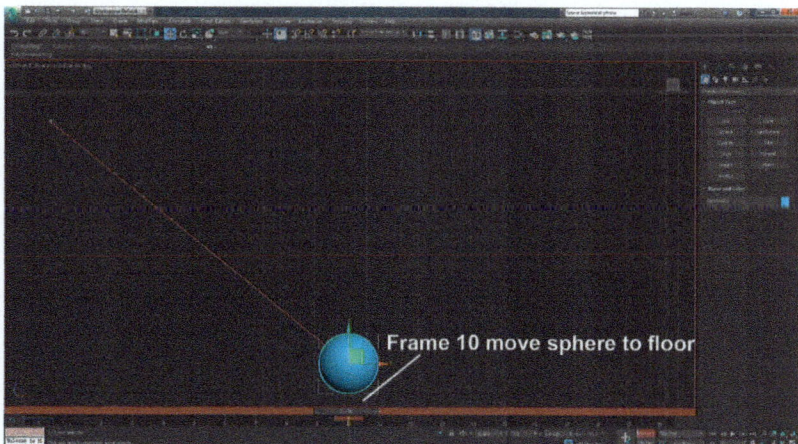

**Fig 23.23** Creating a bouncing ball animation: repositioning the sphere on frame 10

Next, on frame 20, move the sphere to the top right of the viewport (Figure 23.24).

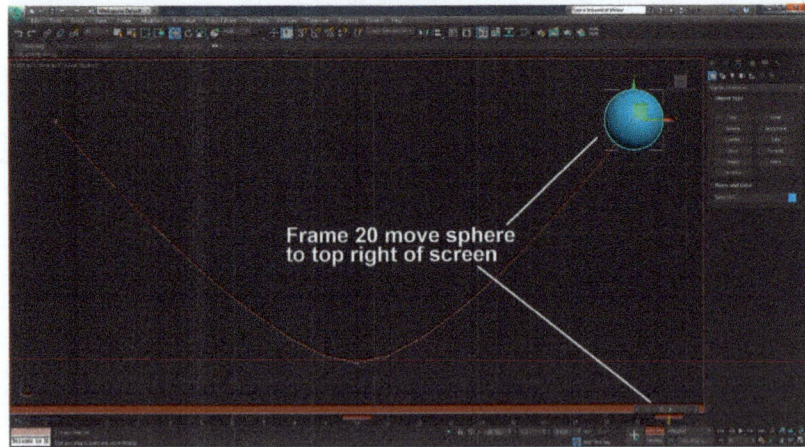

**Fig 23.24** Creating a bouncing ball animation: repositioning the sphere on frame 20

If you play the animation it will not look like a bouncing ball. This is because the spacing of frames is incorrect. To change the spacing you need to open the Curve editor, as in Figure 23.25.

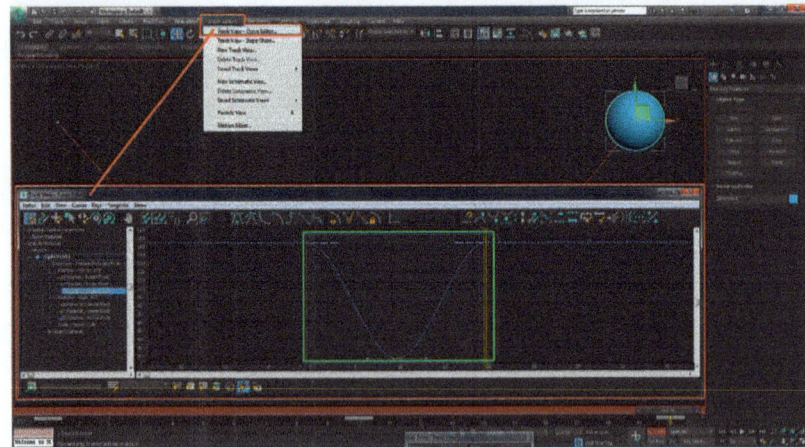

**Fig 23.25** Creating a bouncing ball animation: opening the Curve editor

First, select from the left of the Curve editor the Z position of the sphere (highlighted blue in Figure 23.26). You will now see one blue line in the

**Fig 23.26** Creating a bouncing ball animation: using the Curve editor to adjust the handles

curve editor. This line will have three key frames, at 0, 10 and 20. Click on frame 10 (the one at the bottom). The key frame will have two handles. Holding down Shift allows you to move each handle individually. Move the left handle to 140 height and set in between frames 5 and 10. Move the right handle to 140 height and set in between frames 10 and 20.

Playing the animation now should result in a much more natural and realistic bounce. As you can see in Figure 23.27, the spacing of the frames (white dots on red line) are no longer constant – there are more frames at the top of each arc, and less where the ball meets the floor. More frames = slower animation, fewer frames = faster animation.

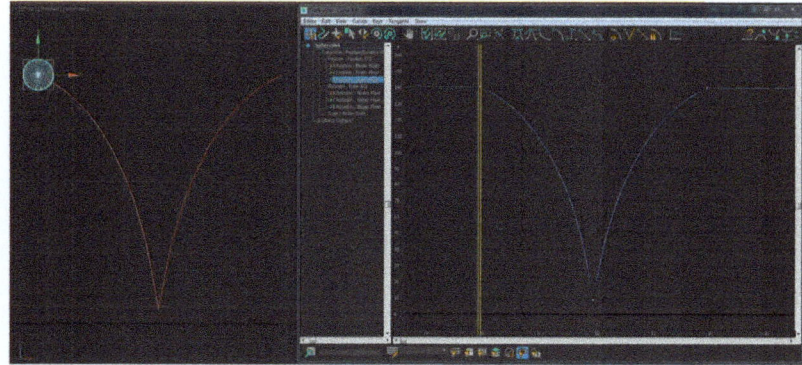

**Fig 23.27** Creating a bouncing ball animation: final animation trajectory

## Project work: **Animate a bouncing ball**

Using 3ds Max or equivalent animation software, animate a ball bouncing through an obstacle course, such as the one in Figure 23.28.

- Ensure you use reference, either online or filmed.
- Build an obstacle course using polygon or edge modelling.
- Start with key frames. In the example below there are 13 key frames

As with the previous task of bouncing a ball from left to right, use the graph/curve editor to manipulate the splines and affect the trajectory and motion of the ball.

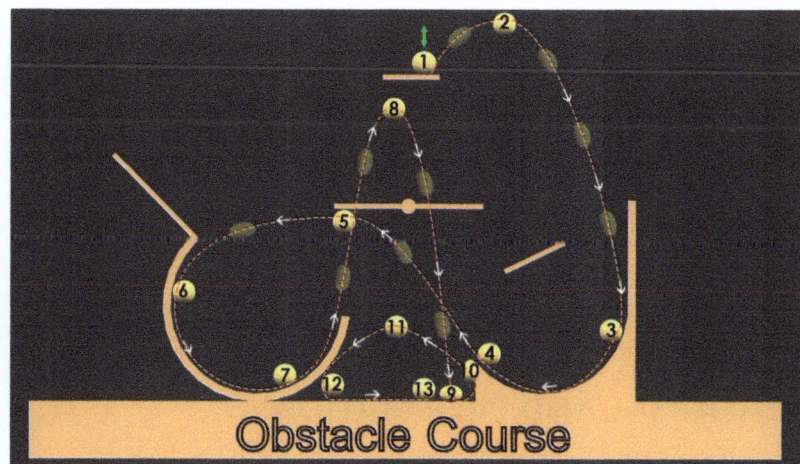

**Fig 23.28** The keyframe positions for a 3D animation of a bouncing ball around an obstacle course

### Further references

- *3ds Max Modeling for Games Volume 1* (A. Gahan, 2011)
- *3ds Max Projects* (Chandler and Podwojewski, 2013)
- *Poly-Modeling with 3ds Max* (T. Daniele, 2008)

# 24 Digital film-making

## Learning Aims

By the end of this chapter you will be able to:
* Understand how to prepare actors and contributors for filming
* Set up and shoot a dialogue scene
* Set up and shoot a documentary interview
* Research and prepare locations for a film

In this chapter you will look at how to work with actors and other contributors to your production. This is often overlooked by people designing moving image sequences and can cause problems if not done carefully. You will also work on creating camera set-ups for dialogue and documentary scenes and researching locations.

## 24.1 BRIEFING AND WORKING WITH TALENT

When making a digital film, one of the most important considerations is how you work with your **talent**. Talent in this chapter refers to any actors, musicians, presenters, interviewers or contributors to your digital film. Unless you are very lucky, it is highly unlikely that you will be working with professionals. This means that you will have to work hard to make your talent feel comfortable, as making films is probably something they are not used to. They are likely to be nervous and unsure about what to do, where to stand or even how long filming is going to take. Your job as a film-maker is to make the process as easy as possible for them (particularly if they are not being paid).

Planning is crucial. Even though you may have a clear idea of the structure of your film, shooting it in sequence is probably not the best use of your talent's time. For example, if you have a character that appears in the first two scenes and then not again until the end of the film, you should probably shoot all three scenes at once. This can be confusing but it can also avoid actors waiting on set for hours.

When planning, look at which actor or contributor is used in which location and for what shots. Then build a schedule for filming that minimises the time they need to wait around not being used. Professional production companies usually ensure the talent is on set for only the minimum time needed to record their footage. For example, if filming begins at 09:00, it might be necessary for the lighting technician to begin at 08:00 and the camera and sound crew to begin at 08:30. In this case you should avoid having an inexperienced actor or a nervous contributor for a documentary waiting around between 08:00 and 09:00 while people set up and test equipment. One solution is to use **stand-ins** – people of a similar build to the talent wearing similar clothes – when you are checking the camera framing, focus, white balance, exposure and audio levels, and so on.

### REHEARSAL AND PREPARATION

When you film a scene, you are bringing together a wide range of people and considerations including costume, hair, make-up, lighting, set, action scene choreography, camera angle, camera movement and sound. It is a good idea,

**Talent** performers, presenters, interviewees and other on-screen contributors to a moving image production

**Stand-ins** people of similar build and appearance to the main actors or contributors and who substitute for them while the film crew sets up a shot

therefore, to work with your cast or brief your talent before they enter this environment. You can do this by reading through a script together and giving advice and support about how you want them to play the part or deliver their lines. This is also a good time to discuss and if necessary adjust the script until the performers are comfortable delivering the lines naturally and more convincingly.

**Fig 24.1** Actor rehearsals are an important element to making a scene appear convincing

At this stage, some film-makers give their actors the outline of a script, have them improvise their lines, and develop the final script from what the actors say. The British film director Mike Leigh is renowned for using this approach to develop very realistic dialogue in films such as *Life is Sweet*, *Secrets and Lies* and *Vera Drake*. If you have a cast who are very inexperienced, allowing them to manipulate their lines to reflect their normal speech patterns may work well and prevent them from acting in a very self-conscious way.

In order to do this, you will need to conduct some workshops with your actors before filming, during which they **stay in character** all the time, even when not rehearsing the script. When Mike Leigh introduces his actors to one another, he has them stay in character and they often spend time together building relationships between themselves in character. The actors are first briefed about their character's backstory, personality and relationships with the other characters, and then they all go out for a meal while staying in character. This helps build the ability of the actors to react to one another naturally during scenes. Leigh also withholds information about the script from the actors, which means they react instinctively to events because they have established and practised their behaviour and interaction patterns.

**Stay in character** to behave (as an actor) when not filming as if you are still playing the character

## WORKING WITH CONTRIBUTORS TO DOCUMENTARIES

When making a documentary you will likely be filming people who have never experienced a film set or been surrounded by crew and equipment. They may be an expert in the field relating to your documentary or a witness to an event that you are discussing. It is your job to make them feel comfortable and help them to express themselves when they are talking on camera. As with actors, do not keep contributors waiting on set; it is preferable to use stand-ins when setting up the equipment.

Although you are unable to rehearse what a contributor will say in a documentary interview, you can prepare them so they can give the best possible interview. When discussing the interview before filming, it is a good idea to tell them the questions you want to ask and whom else you will be using in the documentary. As they are likely to be unsure about this process, give some directions. For example, you might ask them to mention something that you have found out about their experience from your research. On the other hand, be careful not to over-prepare an interviewee: you want them to appear natural and spontaneous. It is important to strike a good balance here.

## Skills Task: **Improvisation workshop**

Prepare a script outline for several scenes involving three or more characters but do not reveal all the events to your cast. Discuss with each cast member their character's history, personality and relationships with the other characters. Conduct a workshop in which your cast meet each other in several different situations: having a family meal, for example. Watch how they interact while in character and give feedback so they learn patterns of spontaneous interaction. Finally, try filming some of the events in your script, revealing new developments to the cast (a death in the family, for example) just before you start filming.

### Top Tip

If you find that actors are struggling to deliver their lines convincingly take a short section of your script (perhaps two pages) and translate the lines into a different language that the actors are not fluent in (for example, from English to French). Have the actors read the script in the new language and they should act more naturally because they have to concentrate on the new language rather than the script.

# 24.2 CAMERA SET-UPS FOR DIALOGUE

A typical dialogue scene would have two characters, perhaps sitting either side of a table in a café while they talk, as in the image below from the opening scene of Quentin Tarantino's 1994 film *Pulp Fiction*.

**Fig 24.2** Amanda Plummer (left) and Tim Roth (right) in a dialogue scene from Quentin Tarantino's *Pulp Fiction* (2004)

Normally this requires at least three separate camera set-ups to capture everything in the conversation. This means the two actors will have to perform the scene at least three times. As we will see later there are many different ways of directing the camera, but in most circumstances you would

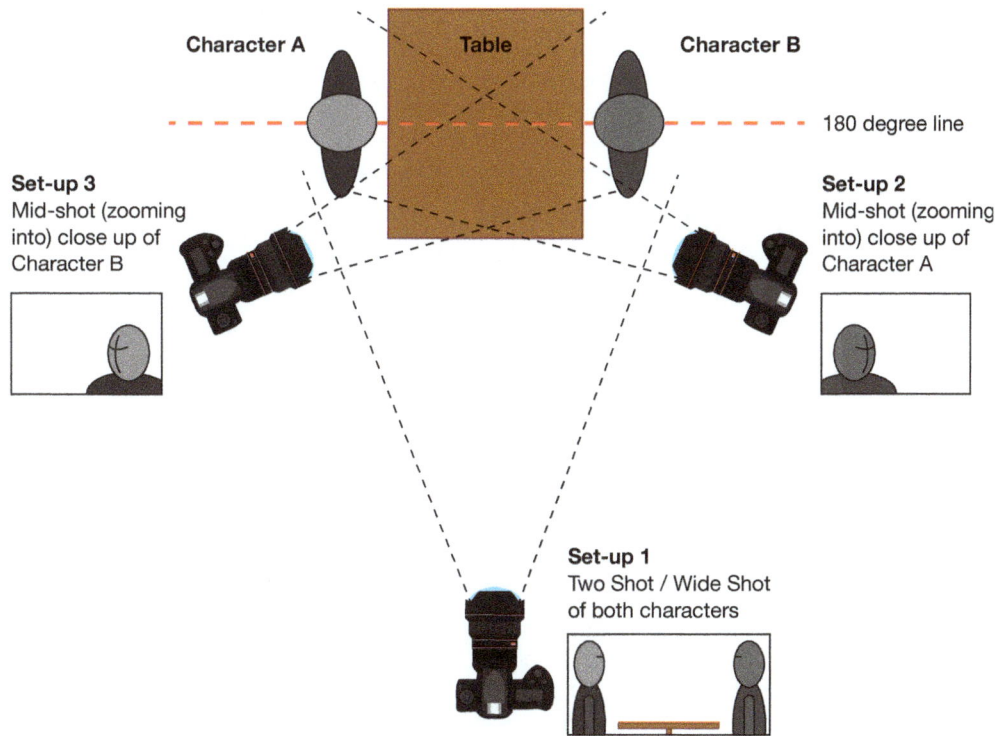

**Character A**    **Table**    **Character B**

180 degree line

**Set-up 3**
Mid-shot (zooming
into) close up of
Character B

**Set-up 2**
Mid-shot (zooming
into) close up of
Character A

**Set-up 1**
Two Shot / Wide Shot
of both characters

**Fig 24.3** A typical set-up for shooting a dialogue scene from three angles

use the three camera angles illustrated in Figure 24.3: a two shot/wide shot of both characters, a mid-shot of Character A and a mid-shot of Character B.

## SET-UP I – TWO SHOT/WIDE SHOT OF BOTH CHARACTERS

This will usually be a side-on view showing the audience where both characters are in relation to each other. This shot can also give the audience information about the location of the scene, for example, showing other customers in the café and the position of the table where the characters are sitting. Because this shot often establishes details of the setting, it can also be called the **establishing shot**. In order to get full coverage of the scene the actors would perform the entire script from this angle.

When filming this shot you must watch the actors closely. Any significant movements (for example, Character A picks up a glass of water with their left hand and drinks before delivering their first line) must be repeated at the same time for each subsequent camera set-up. If the film cuts from this wide shot to a close up shot with the glass of water in the character's right hand, the audience will notice the inconsistency and this will break the illusion that they are watching the action taking place in sequence.

## SET-UP 2 – MID-SHOT ZOOMING INTO CLOSE UP OF CHARACTER A

This shot will show one of the characters' faces from a slight angle, as if the camera is positioned behind the shoulder of Character B. The size or framing of the shot will depend upon the intensity of the dialogue. You may want to record the entire scene in a mid-shot (from the character's waist up) first, before zooming in to film additional takes in medium close up (shoulders and head) or close up (face only). When recording the scene from this angle it is important to have the second character deliver their lines exactly as they did

**Establishing shot** camera shot that tells the audience where the action is taking place and in what kind of environment

241

in Set-up 1, so that we can still see how Character A reacts. Filming from each side of the conversation allows you to focus on the performance of the actor. Think about when you want them to pause and how you want them to look when they are listening to what the other character is saying.

### SET-UP 3 – MID-SHOT ZOOMING INTO CLOSE UP OF CHARACTER B

This set-up will film Character B with a similar framing to Set-up 2. Because you are likely to be cutting a lot between these last two set-ups, the transitions between shots of the two characters will be less noticeable if they have similar framing. As with Set-up 2, the different sizes of framing (mid-shot, medium close-up and close-up) must be filmed with the second actor delivering and reacting to lines throughout the scene.

### THE 180-DEGREE RULE

When filming a series of shots with the intention of editing them together, it is important to remember the 180-degree rule. If you look from above and draw an imaginary line between the two characters in your scene (the red broken line in Figure 24.3), the camera should never cut to an angle that crosses this line. Crossing this line will make the two characters appear to have swapped places at the table.

If you use the three set-ups as described above when filming a dialogue scene, the entire scene will need to be performed by both actors at least seven times: once in Set-up 1 and at each framing size (mid-shot, medium close-up and close-up) in Set-ups 2 and 3. You must ensure that the action and performances in each of the seven takes is similar enough to edit together to create your final version of the scene. You will also need to take notes when there is a particularly good line delivered or a very good reaction, so that you know what to include in your final sequence.

Project work: **Film a dialogue scene**

Using two actors and one camera, film a dialogue scene using the three camera set-ups described above. You could use a detailed script or create an improvised scene, but you should ensure you film the following shots:

1. Two shot/Wide shot of both characters
2. Mid-shot of Character A
3. Medium close-up of Character A
4. Close-up of Character A
5. Mid-shot of Character B
6. Medium close-up of Character B
7. Close-up of Character B

# 24.3 CAMERA SET-UP FOR DOCUMENTARY

When filming a documentary interview, generally the set-up will be similar to Set-ups 2 and 3 in the dialogue scene previously discussed, although there is now far more emphasis on the set-up that shows the contributor speaking and reacting, as in the images below. Using two cameras to capture a wide-shot of both the interviewee and interviewer is rarely used, unless in live TV studio programmes, as the additional crew and equipment is both expensive and can be somewhat intimidating for the interviewee, which could lead to them not giving as revealing an interview.

As soon as the contributor is ready, it is a good idea to start filming in case they say anything interesting. You must ensure that you have enough memory card or hard drive capacity to film all of the time that your contributor is available. In this set-up, the camera would zoom in depending on the importance of the scene. If the contributor said something very important or perhaps became emotional, you could zoom in to a close-up. The best way to do this is when the contributor pauses or stops talking (often when the interviewer is asking questions) so that the camera moving during the shot does not disturb the audience.

A lot of film-makers start an interview by asking the contributor to give their name (asking them to spell it) and their official title or role if appropriate. This has three purposes: to check their details for potential use as subtitles; to relax the contributor by starting with an easy question; and to check the sound levels (people often talk at their normal volume when spelling something).

You can then start asking your questions. Remember that it is unusual for the final film to include many of the questions asked by the interviewer. In most cases the audience would be put off by continually seeing the interviewer asking questions. Because of this, ask your contributor to try to include the wording of the question in their answer.
Consider the two example interviews below.

Interviewer: Can you tell me how long you have worked as a
Police Officer?
Contributor: Ten years.

If you only focus on the contributor, the answer 'Ten years' could relate to anything thereby making the interview difficult to understand unless we also include the question.

Interviewer: Can you tell me how long you have been a Police Officer
and could you include the question in your answer?
Contributor: I have worked as a Police Officer for around ten years now.

In this second example, you can edit out the interviewer entirely and focus on the contributor.

Although most documentaries do not focus on the film-maker or presenter, there are some notable exceptions. If you do include the interviewer you should retain this style throughout, as this can be one approach to telling the story. Some documentary film-makers achieve this by using one camera to film the interviewer asking the questions and nodding to show them reacting to the interviewee. This creates a sense of the interview being a conversation (which audiences are used to watching through dramas) and also helps with the editing (you can cut to the interviewer reacting (or nodding) to cover the joining of two separate pieces of interview footage without the audience noticing.

## NON-TRADITIONAL DOCUMENTARIES

Many documentary makers (sometimes called guerrilla film-makers) adopt more agile practices that are suited to hostile, challenging and changeable locations. For example, they may use **fly-on-the-wall documentary** camera techniques that show both the interviewer and interviewee throughout, as if the audience is observing the action unknown to the film-maker and the contributors. This is a much less controlled environment than conventional documentary film-making and interviewing. The interviewee could decide to walk away from the

**Fig 24.4** Interviews normally begin with a mid-shot of the subject (top) before zooming in to a medium close-up (bottom)

**Link**

See Chapter 20, pages 198–199, for an explanation on using the cutaway technique when editing a documentary on gangs.

**Fly-on-the-wall documentary** shows the main protagonists (including interviewer) in action, as though the audience were watching in real time

interviewer if they are unhappy, or another contributor may appear uninvited and join in the conversation. This can be exciting to watch and gives the audience a sense that what they are seeing is the real record of what happened.

Film-makers, such as Nick Broomfield (see case study), Michael Moore and Morgan Spurlock, make sure they are seen throughout their documentaries. In Broomfield's films the audience sees the story of the documentary evolve through his struggle to meet the contributors and ask them questions, and he is almost always on screen (usually carrying a microphone and sound recording equipment, as in Figure 24.5). Typically, we might see footage of Broomfield's drive to an office building where he has arranged to meet a witness to interview. Then we would see Broomfield walking through the lobby of the building and taking the elevator to the office, only to be confronted by the witness's lawyer telling him that he cannot film the interview. Broomfield might also include a voiceover explaining this frustrating development.

**Fig 24.5** Nick Broomfield (right) conducts an interview through a gate in Los Angeles; from *Tales of the Grim Sleeper* (2014)

In this way the documentary not only focuses on the story but also how the story has been developing and the struggle to tell it. Documentaries such as this are said to be **self-reflexive documentaries**, because they focus as much on the process of creating the film itself as on the story it was trying to tell in the first place.

### Skills Activity: **Filming an interview**

Conduct an interview with a contributor using one of the techniques described above. Follow the steps below:

- Prepare the interview location before the contributor arrives, checking sound, equipment, lighting and camera shot.
- Once the interviewee arrives, begin recording and do not stop until they leave. Ask them to spell their name and give their title.
- Begin the interview in mid-shot then zoom into medium close-up and close-up when the interviewer is asking questions.
- Make sure that all questions asked are included in the answers. Do not worry about asking the interviewee to repeat their answers if it is an important point and you need it developed or expanded on.
- Film the interviewer asking the questions and reacting to the answers.

## 24.4 RESEARCHING LOCATIONS

Early film-making was confined to studio spaces that were relatively safe, controllable and easy to travel to, but as film-making equipment has become more portable there has been a move to filming on location. The number of locations you use can have a big impact on how difficult your project is likely to be. For each location, you must consider the following:

- How the cast and crew will travel there: if the location is remote, you will need to arrange transport or advise the cast and crew of their likely travel time. This should be included in communication with your talent and crew.
- The length of time (and time of day) you have access to the location: on some occasions you may wish to film in a location that has limited availability, for example, a restaurant that has to open for business. In addition, the natural light will be affected by the time of day. If it takes you all day and evening to film a scene that lasts a couple of minutes, you must ensure the lighting remains constant (for example, by using portable lighting rather than relying on natural light).
- The permissions you need to film: it is necessary to have the permission of the owner of any private location or a publicly owned building before you begin filming. In case you are challenged during filming (by a security guard, for example), make sure you have to hand evidence that the owner has permitted the filming and the owner's contact details.
- Whether you will have to deal with members of the public: people will become curious (and potentially even hostile) when they see filming. It is worth going to the location beforehand to check the likely levels of interruption you will experience. Figure 24.6 shows actors in the film *Once*, which included scenes in the busy streets of Dublin. The actors wore hidden radio microphones (notice the scarves) and were filmed from a distance so that the public were largely unaware of the filming.
- Whether you will have access to electricity: identify any available power sockets and check that you have permission to use them. If there are none and you need to use lights, you may have to use a generator. These can be both expensive and noisy, meaning their placement and use has to be carefully planned.
- How the weather may affect the location: when designing your filming schedule, remember to include contingency days to rearrange filming in the event of bad weather. Sensitive camera equipment does not work well in the rain and microphones perform poorly in windy conditions.
- What hazards are present: to film in any location, you must provide a risk or hazard assessment. Ask yourself what risks are present from the environment, from the equipment you will be using and from the activity itself. For each identified risk, outline a **control measure** – what you will do to reduce the risk, as in the example on the right.

**Fig 24.6** Glen Hansard (left) and Markéta Irglová in *Once* (2007)

**Control measure** action taken to reduce a risk identified in a risk assessment

**Identified risk**

Trailing power cables for portable lights posing a trip hazard, leading to potential injury and damage to equipment

**Control measure**

Crew to arrive one hour earlier than cast, tape down all cables with gaffer tape, check and carry out a set inspection in advance of cast arrival

## Project work: **Location research**

Choose three different types of location that could be used for your moving image production. Create a folder of information for each location, including:

- address and travel directions
- permission to film from the location owner and their contact details
- a risk assessment including risks from the environment, equipment and the activity
- a plan of the location detailing the camera set-ups, positioning of actors, props and power sockets
- photos of the location showing all the most important areas
- a call sheet explaining times for each member of the cast and crew to meet at the location.

## Case study: **Nick Broomfield – self-reflexive documentary maker**

**Fig 24.7** Aileen Wournos (centre) in court in *Aileen: Life and Death of a Serial Killer* (2003)

Nick Broomfield is a renowned British documentary film-maker born in 1948. Many of his subjects have been high profile and controversial. He made *Kurt & Courtney* about American rock singer Kurt Cobain's death and investigated the killings of rappers Christopher Wallace and Tupac Shakur in *Biggie & Tupac*. In 1992, Broomfield made a documentary *Aileen: The Selling of a Serial Killer* and in 2003 followed this up with *Aileen: Life and Death of a Serial Killer* (see Figure 24.7) that investigated the trials and procedures concerning death row inmate Wournos' crimes. (Charlize Theron later won an Oscar playing Wournos in the film *Monster*.)

Part of Broomfield's unusual approach is that he negotiates extensive access to his subjects, getting very close to people such as Aileen Wournos. This has two main impacts on his storytelling. First, it allows him to build trusted relationships with the people that he is interviewing. Second, it can lead to the films taking time to get to the heart of a story. We often see him being turned away from interviews or dwelling on the details of how interviews or meetings are arranged before seeing him actually meet people. Broomfield is a self-reflexive film-maker, meaning that much of the subject matter is about the process that he goes through to tell the story.

Broomfield says his style is about showing a completely honest view of his story. Most documentaries tell stories that make it easy for the audience to understand, including only the most 'important' elements. Broomfield by contrast shows the audience everything that happens and challenges them to decipher the story.

One example is his approach to editing interviews. Documentaries usually film an interview and use parts of it throughout the programme to comment on different elements of the story or different topics. A witness to a crime might appear multiple times to talk about different aspects of the crime. In a Broomfield documentary, however, the entire interview would be presented in one section. There may be some edits but these would be made obvious to the viewer with jump cuts showing that footage had been removed.

**Fig 24.8** Nick Broomfield photographed while editing *Ghosts* (2006)

This approach conflicts with the storyteller's requirement to cut the story into manageable, apparently seamless chunks. One way of looking at it is that Broomfield believes the audience has the ability to follow the imperfect and meandering storytelling in order to get a more honest version of the story.

## Further references

### Books
- *In the Blink of an Eye: A Perspective on Film Editing* (W. Murch, 2001)
- *Visual Pleasure and Narrative Cinema* (L. Mulvey, 2013)

# 25 Visualising a narrative

## Learning Aims

By the end of this chapter you will be able to:
- Generate an idea for a moving image project in pictures
- Create a visual narrative
- Produce a list of shots for a scene
- Understand and apply the five stages of a story
- Create a storyboard

Throughout history, people have told stories to one another. Storytelling was a necessary way for humans to form groups or tribes and establish cultures through language. We are pre-programmed to use language when we tell stories, and this is why generating moving image ideas is difficult. If you tell somebody a story you will most likely do this using words rather than pictures.

In this chapter you will explore how to generate ideas for your moving image sequences, whether literal stories or visual ones. You will also work to construct a scene from a concept or idea and explore typical features of a drama. You will investigate the different ways of using narrative in film and consider how this impacts character types, stereotypes and archetypes. Finally, you will learn how to express your ideas in the form of a storyboard.

## 25.1 GENERATING VISUAL IDEAS

Visualising your story requires you to consider how your audience uses its visual language(s) to interpret the story. You also need to define clearly how you will tell your story. For example, if you are making a film in which a man stands on a city street, you must think about the following:

- who the man is
- what he is wearing
- which street and city it is and how you tell the audience this (with landmarks, for instance)
- other people in the shot
- the weather and time of day
- what camera shots you are going to use to show all of these things.

### CONSTRUCTING A VISUAL NARRATIVE

Film-making began with silent films, when film-makers had to develop a strong visual language to communicate with the audience. That language still influences film-making today. For example, in silent films most close-up shots were **reaction shots** (Figure 25.1) that were explained in a following slide, which showed (in words) what had been said to provoke the reaction, as in Figure 25.2.

Today, film-makers still linger on reaction shots in dialogue scenes, to show the audience the impact of the words spoken by other characters. It is often more rewarding for an audience to be shown themes and ideas rather than to be told them. We have all watched poorly scripted films where the

**Reaction shot** a shot that shows the reaction of a character as they hear the lines or watch the actions of other characters

**Fig 25.1** Charlie Chaplin (left) and Jackie Coogan (right) in the silent movie *The Kid* (1921)

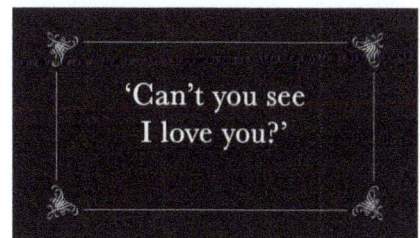

'Can't you see I love you?'

**Fig 25.2** In silent era cinema, title cards were used to explain what the actors were thinking or saying after reaction shots

characters have to explain the story to us through voiceovers. Director Ridley Scott's classic sci-fi film noir *Bladerunner* (1982) notoriously had a voiceover from the main character Deckard added by the studio after the film was finished. Many feel this made the storytelling too obvious and it led Scott to release his own 'Director's cut' version of the movie, without the scripted narration.

Because thinking visually is vital to storytelling in moving image media, you must practise this skill. Think about what you did when you first woke up today and imagine how that could be shown in a one-minute moving image sequence. The sequence might run as follows:

- black screen and the sound of an alarm clock becoming louder
- screen fades into a blurry close-up of the digital read-out of the alarm clock, showing 06:30, which slowly comes into focus
- extreme close-up of one of your eyes with your head on a pillow
- slightly wider shot showing the whole of the alarm clock on a table as a hand slams down onto the off button (the alarm goes silent).

## Top Tip

When reading a scene in a book or a news report, try to imagine a series of camera shots, movements and transitions that could present the scene as a moving image sequence.

## Skills Task: **Visual storytelling**

Develop the example of waking up described above by imagining the next 1–2 minutes of the sequence. Describe the camera angles you would use, the audio, the length of shot and the transitions between shots. Create a shot list then, using a mobile phone camera, take a still of each shot. Arrange the images into a presentation to tell the story of your morning.

## CONSTRUCTING A SCENE

When constructing a scene from a series of images, it is useful to think about how you might show the audience all the information they need to know. For example, scenes often start with a wide establishing shot that shows the general location of the scene. They then typically show the context of the characters' situation and the dynamics of any conversations (for example, how close they are, who is dominating the conversation).

The following might be a sequence in a crime drama:

### Shot 1: Establishing shot

Shot 1 is of the outside of a police station at night, with police cars parked outside and a shield emblem on the building or sign reading 'Police Department'. The shot explains that this scene will be set in this location, while a night scene suggests that the characters inside are coming to the end of their working day. After a few moments, the film cuts to an **interior shot**.

**Interior shot** a shot that is filmed indoors

### Shot 2: Interior shot

This shot is a wide shot of a dimly lit police office with lots of desks. The two main characters are seated in a desk near the middle of the office (with desk lamps providing light) and the rest of the room is empty. This tells the audience that the characters are in the office working late on this particular case. The shot also establishes where the two characters are in relation to one another, so that when the film moves to closer shots we can remember where each character is. We will also see the characters' general body language and so get an idea of their mood and their relationship.

### Shots 3 and 4: Mid-shots/close-ups

These shots show a conversation between the two characters. To begin you would probably use **mid-shots** (showing the characters' faces and bodies) so that the audience can see their body language. This conversation would normally take the form of the **shot-reverse shot** format that we explored in the previous chapter. As the conversation becomes more intense it would be normal to use Shots 3 and 4 to move closer to the characters (perhaps starting with a mid-shot and ending in a close-up). The closer the shot, the better we can see emotions and expressions.

### Shot 5: Action shot

Depending on what you want the characters to do in the scene, choose a camera angle that shows this action clearly. For example, if one character accuses the other character of protecting the killer they are trying to catch and angrily walks over to the other's desk, in this case Shot 5 could be a wide shot showing the whole office or an angle tracking the movement of the character making the accusation.

In some cases you will withhold information about the scene from the audience. If this was a horror movie, for instance, you might want to make the audience feel uneasy, perhaps to sense that the characters are somehow in danger; so, in Shot 2, for example, you would not show everything in the office. You might frame a shot around the characters and only light their desks, to emphasise that they are alone and vulnerable in a dark, empty room where anything could be lurking in the shadows. You could emphasise the sounds of the empty office (ticking clock, windows rattling) or use a **POV (point of view) shot**, as though looking through the eyes of a third character witnessing the conversation from a far corner of the room.

# 25.2 SETTING THE SCENE – ENVIRONMENTS AND LANDSCAPES

As in the example of Shot 1 above, it is often a requirement for a moving image sequence designer to use a shot at the beginning of a scene to establish the location and context of the scene that follows. In the example above, an easily recognisable location gives the audience a sense of location. Opening shots from cinema can also very quickly establish the context of the action that is about to take place.

In George Lucas's *Star Wars – Episode IV: A New Hope* (1977), the opening shot shows the audience that the action is set in space by tilting the shot upwards from the edge of a planet into space. Next, a large spacecraft flies past the camera; there follows a much larger spaceship, which appears to be pursuing it. This one shot gives the audience the understanding about the location of the film, but also sets up the relationship between the two sides of this battle (and the subsequent story) – the small rebel forces and the immensely powerful Empire.

Directors will often send a separate filming crew (the **B Unit**) to film large-scale establishing shots, as these can be logistically difficult to film. In this case Lucas would have instructed his special effects team to construct the scene. The director can then concentrate on telling the story to the audience through scenes involving the main cast.

> **Link**
>
> See Chapter 24, pages 240–242, for more on the use of the shot–reverse shot format.

**Mid-shot** a shot of a character showing their torso and head (used to begin most dialogue scenes)
**Shot-reverse shot** when a dialogue scene is filmed from at least two angles, each showing the opposing actor
**POV shot** point of view shot, where the camera is positioned and moved as though looking through the eyes of another character within the film
**B Unit** secondary camera team used to shoot large-scale establishing shots of environments or landscapes

**Fig 25.3** The opening of *Star Wars Episode IV: A New Hope* immediately establishes the setting as space and the relationship between the two spacecraft

Using a school classroom, family home or other space, create a scene similar to the one described above using Shot 1 through to Shot 5. Write a script and think about how you will direct your actors. Plan how you will use your location and what establishing shot will show the audience the location of your scene.

Project work: **Visualise a story opening**

Think about the following story: twins are separated at birth. They look identical but one grows up to be wealthy and successful and the other grows up poor and destitute.

In 26 words write a scenario that could be the premise for an engaging film. How would you visualise the opening of this film without words? Think about the many different things you would need to show to the audience to make them understand this premise. How many characters, what scenes and locations (for example, a maternity ward), visual and sound effects, would you use? Create a list of shots you could use for the film opening.

# 25.3 CHARACTER DEVELOPMENT

## CHARACTERS AND MOTIVATION

When creating a fictional film you will need to be clear about your characters and how they should be developed. If you are not using professional actors it may be a good idea to use people who are similar to the characters. This way they will be more natural delivering lines and feel more at ease. In the previous chapter we looked at how getting the actors to improvise their lines to develop the script can lead to more natural performances.

It is often useful to think about **character motivation**. The audience will usually only believe in the actions of a character if it makes sense for them to do these actions. For this reason you must continuously ask: 'What would the character's motivation be in this situation?'

Often the narrative of a film is about cause and effect. This scene happens and this causes the actions in a following scene and so on. When telling stories it is helpful to map out ideas on this basis. Think about how the events in one scene affect the characters' motivations. Actors should know where they are on their characters' motivational pathway throughout a story.

> **Character motivation** personality traits or personal history that drive a character to act in particular ways
> **Archetype** characters that embody good or evil (the archetypal hero/villain) and are easily recognisable by the audience

## CHARACTER TYPES, STEREOTYPES AND ARCHETYPES

Many film-makers use types, stereotypes or **archetypes** to convey elements of a character to the audience. This helps define characters using the audience's knowledge of similar characters in other films or stories.

For example, imagine an action film in which the hero encounters a large, muscled man, dressed in black with a scar across his face. The audience's knowledge of previous action films will tell them that this character is a villain and that the hero will need to defeat him. This is a character type.

Character types became prevalent in early cinema, particularly in Hollywood, where the same film studios would use the same costume designers, actors and similar sets, leading to similar characters being visible in many different films (especially Westerns). In Bollywood movies, actors have become famous for playing similar roles. Sanjay Dutt, for example, has played villains in many Indian films, acting in a similar way each time.

When these character types become more extreme, perhaps for comic effect or if the character development has become a little lazy, they are known as stereotypes. A stereotype is a character type with exaggerated characteristics and some film-makers are criticised for using too many stereotypical characters. Storytellers do use them, however, as they provide a convenient, quick way to explain the traits of a character.

An archetype is an escalation of this kind of thinking. Archetypal characters tap into people's unconscious perceptions of fundamental characteristics, such as good or evil, and provoke similar reactions in all viewers. Darth Vader from the *Star Wars* movies is a good archetypal villain, who instantly evokes the same negative, fearful reactions in all who see him. In Figure 25.4, he is seen on the right with two other character types – a rebel soldier (middle) and a Stormtrooper.

The archetypal hero in Western cinema usually comes from outside the conventional society or group. They then use their 'otherness' or what makes them different to save the group from attack or disaster. Once they have succeeded, they leave the group, as ultimately they are different to everyone else and do not belong there (the archetypal Western hero rides off into the sunset). In the 1985 Western *Pale Rider* (directed and starring Clint Eastwood), the final scenes depict some of the townsfolk pleading with Eastwood's hero to stay; he grimly ignores them and rides away.

**Fig 25.4** Darth Vader (right) the archetypal villain from *Star Wars Episode IV: A New Hope* (1977)

## SUBVERTING CHARACTER TYPES

Film-makers often subvert or challenge the typical portrayal of character types, stereotypes or archetypes. In Sergio Leone's Westerns, such as *A Fistful of Dollars* and *For a Few Dollars More*, Clint Eastwood's hero was more morally ambiguous than previous Western heroes – more scornful and cynical. This was reflected in the fact that we never learn his name. In the *Alien* science fiction films (beginning with Ridley Scott's *Alien* in 1979), Sigourney Weaver (right) portrays Ripley, a tough, brave and decisive action hero who subverts this character stereotype because she is a woman not a man.

Stories often have two categories of character: **protagonists** and **antagonists**. Both words come from the Greek *ago*, meaning to lead or bring. The protagonist is the main character who makes a quest or journey; the antagonists are the people who attempt to stop them and who must be overcome.

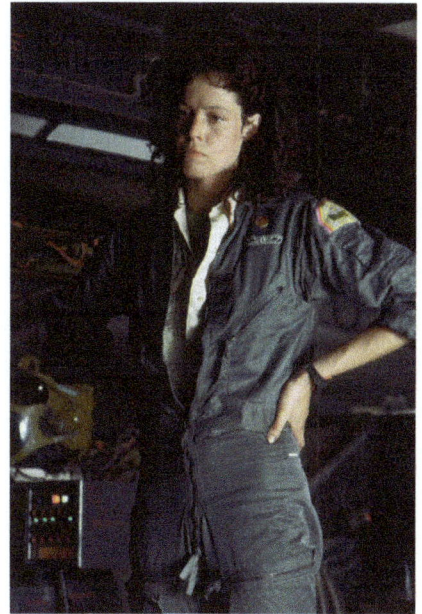

**Fig 25.5** Sigourney Weaver as the female hero Ripley in *Alien* (1979)

# 25.4 FIVE STORY STAGES

Stories often develop over a series of stages or acts. Philosopher Tzvetan Todorov described a typical story as consisting of five stages. Let's look at these stages using the example of Steven Spielberg's thriller about a killer shark, *Jaws*.

- EQUILIBRIUM: The story begins with the characters at peace during their everyday lives before the main drama. In *Jaws*, we see the beach resort, Amity Island, with young people partying around a campfire.
- DISRUPTION: There is a disruption to the equilibrium. A giant great white shark begins attacking swimmers in the waters around Amity Island.
- REALISATION: The characters realise there is a quest that needs to be

**Protagonist** character(s) in the story who goes on a quest or journey
**Antagonist** character(s) or forces who attempt to stop or frustrate the protagonist

**Fig 25.6** The crew of the fishing boat struggle to catch the shark in Steven Spielberg's *Jaws* (1975)

undertaken to resolve the disruption. In the town of Amity, to begin with only Police Chief Brodie and marine biologist Hooper really think there is a shark problem, and they try to persuade the town authorities to act.

- STRUGGLE/CONFLICT/QUEST: There is a conflict or struggle between protagonists and antagonists and a quest is undertaken. After several arguments with Brodie and Hooper, the town authorities realise there is a problem. Brodie and Hooper enlist shark hunter Quint to find and kill the shark. They battle the shark in the ocean (see Figure 25.8) but the shark kills Quint and destroys their boat.
- RESOLUTION: There is a resolution of the disruption and we return to equilibrium. Brodie destroys the shark, and he and Hooper return home.

# 25.5 WORKING WITH A SCRIPT: STORYBOARDING

Now that you have begun to think about your ideas visually, the best way to express them is through a storyboard. Combined with a script, a storyboard ensures that everyone on the cast and crew know exactly what to do.

There are eight elements in a complete storyboard, as detailed below.

### Image

This holds most of the information required for the storyboard. Images have to be clear and give the information about the shot, but they do not necessarily have to be great works of art. The point of a storyboard is that it communicates what the camera needs to do. Drawings with stick men will be sufficient, as long as the framing is correct. Alternatively, you could take photographs and create a storyboard by importing the images into a word processing or DTP programme.

### Cell number

The cell number explains the order of each shot and gives the number of the shot throughout film-making (including in editing and post production). Importantly, it also explains which new cells are results of a camera move or significant piece of action. For example, if you start Shot 3 with a wide shot then zoom into a medium close-up, this second part of the shot will be referred to as Shot 3a on the storyboard. If Shot 3a then pans around to show an empty chair, this will be Shot 3b. Only when the storyboard is showing a new camera shot will this be referred to as Shot 4.

### Transition

Transition information goes between each cell, to explain how one cell moves to another. At the beginning of the storyboard it might read 'fade from black to…', showing how the film will open with a fade. Using the example above, between Shots 3 and 3a it would read 'zoom in to', between Shots 3a and 3b it would read 'pan right to', and between Shots 3b and 4 it would read 'cut to.'

### Flow arrows

Flow arrows are usually black, solid arrows that show which cell comes next. Although this may be obvious because of the cell numbers, there are many different types of storyboard template, with some arranging cells vertically and others arranging them horizontally. Flow arrows make the storyboard easier to read.

## Duration

This should be expressed in seconds in the bottom corner of each cell. If you are unsure how long some shots are, use your script as a guide. People typically speak at a rate of three words per second, so if you intend two shots containing dialogue with 25 words, collectively these shots will need to last just over 8 seconds (25 divided by 3 = 8.333).

## Shot description

This box uses the abbreviations for shots that will be covered in the next chapter. The shot description should also include descriptions of action. For example, a shot description might say 'MS (mid-shot) of John running towards the camera.'

## Audio information

You can give music direction, for example, 'fast paced music gets louder towards the end of this shot', or link the shot with lines of dialogue, such as 'It was you, Jane. It was always only you' over a close-up reaction shot of Jane. It may be impossible to include all of the script in your storyboard, but some lines will help link up the script to the images.

## Camera movement arrows

Whenever the camera moves, you can express this on a storyboard by drawing white arrows showing the direction of the camera movement. This is also true of significant action from objects within the frame (for example, a character running into shot).

## Project work: **Create a storyboard**

Using storyboard templates similar to the description above, develop the 'waking up in the morning' sequence you developed earlier in this chapter. There are 10 or 12 frames or cells to show in this scene. Force yourself to draw them quickly (almost without thinking or worrying about making great drawings); give yourself just 10 seconds to draw each cell. After 2 minutes you will have an outline of your idea. Next, complete the other seven elements of the storyboard as described above. Finally, spend time refining your drawings to complete your storyboard.

## Further references

### Books
- *The Cinema Book*, 3rd ed. (P. Cook, 2008)
- *Contemporary Cultures of Display* (E. Barker, 1999)
- *Film Art: An Introduction* (Bordwell and Thompson, 2012)
- *Film Studies: The Essentials* (W. Buckland, 2010)
- *The Oxford Guide to Film Studies* (J. Hill and P. Gibson, 1998)
- *Screen Media: Analysing Film and Television* (J. Stadler and K. McWilliam, 2009)
- *The Skin of the Film: Intercultural, Cinema, Embodiment, and the Senses* (L.U. Marks, 2000)
- *Video Production: Putting Theory into Practice* (S. Dawkins, 2010)

# 26 Composing image sequences

Many of the skills you learned in terms of using scale, composition and formal elements to construct images in digital photography are relevant to the medium of moving image, too. It may be helpful to look back at Chapter 19 and consider how the features outlined there could apply to creating image sequences here. In this chapter you will explore how to combine what you have learned about digital film-making and visualising a narrative in order to start filming your moving image sequence. You will learn about the different shots you might choose, as well as how to use each of the functions of the camera to shoot like a professional and how to edit your shots into a final sequence.

## 26.1 TYPES OF CAMERA SHOT

How you use a camera has perhaps the greatest impact on how well your moving image production will be understood and appreciated by the audience. In general, unless you want to convey a specific message with your technique, you should make the camera work and editing as unobtrusive as possible. The audience should be focused on what your subjects and your images are saying rather than on how your content is presented.

At the most basic level, if the audience notices that there is a microphone suspended above one of the actors, their focus will be drawn to this and the 'suspension of disbelief' that underpins all film-making will be lost. Similarly, if you overexpose one scene compared to others, or if you set up one camera shot on a slant when all other shots are level, the audience will notice and the illusion you are trying to create will collapse. To be fully engaged, the audience must forget they are watching a collection of camera shots.

### COMMON CAMERA SHOTS

To communicate effectively it is important that everyone uses the correct terminology when describing camera work. Here are the most common camera shots you will use.

### Extreme close-up (ECU)

This is a shot that shows only part of the subject, for example, a tear on a character's cheek or the trigger of a gun about to be fired. This is often used in dramatic situations to show intense emotion or fine detail. Director Sergio Leone uses extreme close-ups in his Western films such as *A Fistful of Dollars* or *The Good, The Bad and The Ugly* (see Figure 26.1) to show the extreme tension on the faces of gunfighters just before they shoot their guns. You might also use an ECU to show a detail that the audience would not normally be able to see from their distant vantage point, a classic example being the very first frames of Orson Welles' 1958 film *Touch of Evil*, which shows someone's hand activating the timer on a bomb.

**Fig 26.1** An extreme close up of Clint Eastwood in *A Fistful of Dollars* (1964)

## Close-up (CU)

This is a standard shot used in dialogue scenes and interviews as well as to show emotion on an individual's face as they talk or react. When used for people, a close-up shows most of the subject's head, with perhaps the top of the head cropped. It is often used once the character's body language has been established by a long shot or medium shot. Using a close-up for a long time can be challenging for viewers and demands their attention. Music video director John Maybury used an extended close-up of the singer Sinead O'Connor very effectively to convey the intense emotional impact as she sang the song 'Nothing Compares 2 U' (1990).

**Fig 26.2** An example of a medium close-up in *Moonlight* (2016)

## Medium close-up (MCU)

This shot reveals the shoulders and hair (or headwear) of the subject, as in Figure 26.2. It is often used in interviews and dialogue scenes, and is a more relaxed shot than a close-up – something that viewers often feel more comfortable with. Television interviews usually begin with the subject being framed with a mid-shot before moving to a medium close-up.

## Mid-shot/medium shot (MS)

This shot shows the subject from the waistline upwards and can reveal their body language. This shot is also less intense to watch than close-ups, as the audience is slightly removed from the subject. Interviews with people usually begin in mid-shot before moving to closer shots.

**Fig 26.3** A long shot of the priest arriving at the house in *The Exorcist* (1973)

## Long shot (LS)

This is a shot showing the whole of the subject's figure. It is often used to establish the subject in their surroundings, so that the audience can see where they are and what is around them. It is also used for action shots, so that the camera can capture the figure's movement. In the shot from William Friedkin's horror film *The Exorcist,* (Figure 26.3) the viewer can see the full length of the figure in shadow pausing before entering the house.

**Fig 26.4** A two shot shows both characters in a conversation scene in *Gong Li* (1991)

## Two shot (2S)

The shot in Figure 26.4 shows two characters. It is useful in a dialogue scene to show how far two characters are apart from one another, as well as how they are interacting.

## Wide shot (WS)

Wide shots are used to show an entire scene. There may be multiple people in shot as well as buildings and vehicles. Wide shots also give the moving image sequence a sense of scale. Wide shots of open areas can make a sequence more cinematic than focusing on narrower spaces.

**Fig 26.5** A wide shot shows a large area of the city behind the characters in this still

## Very wide shot (VWS)

These shots show even greater scale and background scenery than wide shots, presenting the subjects of the film as very small components of a much larger environment. Director Terrence Malick made the film *Badlands* (1973) using very wide shots to depict the vast expanse of the countryside in which the story unfolds and suggest the relative smallness of the humans that inhabit it.

## Point of view shot (POV)

These are taken from the perspective of a character watching the subject of the shot. They are often used in horror or thriller films, so the audience sees that the subject is being watched by someone but doesn't know who (or what) is watching. Typically, this shot would use a hand-held camera that moves behind and around objects, such as trees or walls, to demonstrate that

**Fig 26.6** Very wide shots show off the scenery in *Badlands* (1973)

**Fig 26.7** A point of view shot, as viewed by a prisoner, of Jodie Foster in *The Silence of the Lambs* (1991)

it is the viewpoint of another character. Directors often add sound effects, such as a heartbeat, breathing or footsteps.

The thriller *Silence of the Lambs* made particularly effective use of POV shots when the main villains – Hannibal Lecter and Buffalo Bill – were watching or hunting FBI agent Clarice Starling (see Figure 26.7).

### Over-the-shoulder shot

Shots from over the shoulder are typically used in dialogue scenes where the camera is literally over the shoulder of one of the characters, so showing the other person in the conversation. This technique allows for the shots to remain close (as in mid-shot or medium close-up) but also tells the viewer about the physical distance between the two characters.

> **Project work: Create a library of camera shots**
>
> Work in small groups to devise and film examples of each of the shot types described in the previous section. Save these together in a 'library' of shot types you can refer to for future projects. If possible, create shots using similar subjects and themes. In each case, try to ensure that you use the shot for a particular purpose (for example, mid-shot for the beginning of an interview).

# 26.2 FRAMING CAMERA SHOTS

When film-makers worked with physical film, the film stock itself was a significant cost – every minute of filming required over 20 metres of film. The camera operator would therefore have to be absolutely sure that they had set the shot up perfectly before filming began. Today's digital technologies make filming much less expensive; however, it is still important to be disciplined when framing your camera shots.

## FILMING PEOPLE

Generally, when you are filming a conversation, you should not have the actors looking directly at the camera because this breaks the convention that characters do not talk directly to the audience. In most cases you should arrange your actor and the camera so that the audience can see most of the actor's face but the camera appears to be to one side of the actor (as if being filmed from over the shoulder of the person they are talking to). There should be space between the actor and the side of the frame so that they are not talking into the edge of the frame. Only if you had a very good reason for a character to engage the audience would you have them talk directly to camera.

One common mistake when framing people is leaving too much **headroom** in the shot. Unless it is important to see what is above the character's head, aim to put the upper part of the frame just above the head of the subject.

Applying the rule of thirds can be a good starting point when framing your shot. If you divide the screen into thirds, the eye line would fit on the line that represents two-thirds of the height of the shot and the closest eye on the camera would be one third of the way across the frame. If you start with this framing you can then adjust the camera until you are happy with the shot.

In Figure 26.8, from *Bladerunner 2049* (2017), we can see a number of these framing rules being applied. Firstly, the character is positioned so there is

> **Headroom** the distance between the top of a subject's head in a shot and the top of the frame

> **Link**
>
> See Chapter 16, page 153, and Chapter 19, pages 180–181, for more information on the rule of thirds.

a lot of space between her head and the left-hand side of the frame. There is only a very small gap between the top of her head and the top of the frame, limiting the headroom in the shot. This shot has also been composed using the rule of thirds. Her head is two-thirds of the way across the frame, the black arm rest stops a third of the way across the frame, her arm (and the shadow along the floor in the background) draw a line two-thirds of the way from the bottom of the frame to the top, and the edge of the desk and her legs are one-third of the way from the bottom of the frame.

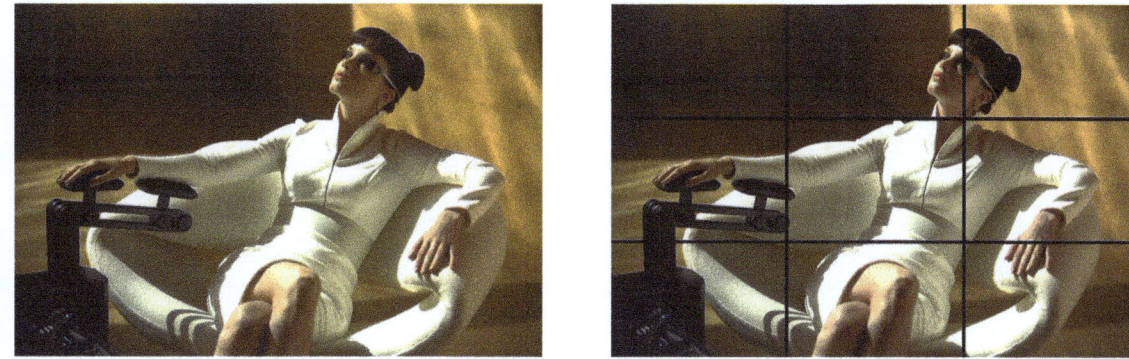

**Fig 26.8** This mid-shot of Sylvia Hoeks in *Blade Runner 2049* (2017) has been composed using the rule of thirds

# 26.3 SETTING UP SHOTS

## EXPOSURE

To make the audience believe in your production, you must ensure that your shots are correctly exposed, so that your scenes look as bright as they would in real life. A shot is over-exposed if the scene appears too bright, and under-exposed if the scene appears too dark. Cameras have automatic metering (light measurement) functions that can adjust the exposure to fit in with the light conditions in your scene, but sometimes this exposure change can appear unnatural (particularly with moving shots). Consequently, professionals set their exposure manually using three functions on the camera:

- Gain (on video cameras)/ISO (on DSLRs)
- Shutter speed
- Iris (on video cameras)/Aperture (on DSLRs).

## GAIN/ISO

Professional and many consumer video cameras use a Gain setting to amplify the video signal in low light conditions. The Gain value here refers to the brightness of the image and is expressed in decibels (dB) (unrelated to decibels measuring audio signals) or as L, M or H (low, medium or high). A setting of 9 db (or M) or 18 db (or H) means that the brightness of the image has been artificially amplified. This reduces the image quality because high Gain images have more picture noise and appear more 'grainy' than low Gain images.

If you are using a DSLR camera that can capture high quality video, the Gain function is usually expressed as an ISO value. ISO stands for the International Standards Organisation and refers to the sensitivity of different photographic films. An ISO speed of 1600, for example, would give a grainy image but be able to capture shots in low light (or with very fast shutter speeds). An ISO rating of 100 would give a much better quality image but would need more light to expose the shot correctly.

**Top Tip**

Whenever possible you should set a low Gain setting and add light using portable lights, rather than relying on the Gain value.

## SHUTTER SPEED

Shutter speed refers to the number of times the camera takes an image of whatever it is filming or allows the image sensor to receive the light coming in through the lens. A slow shutter speed (for example, 1/12 sec – meaning that the camera switches the light sensor on and off twelve times each second) will provide a very bright image, whereas a fast shutter speed (such as 1/3200 sec – meaning the camera switches the image sensor on and off 3200 times each second) will provide a very dark image, because the image sensor spends an increased amount of time switched off. The drawback of a slow shutter speed is that the human eye can detect the individual frames once the speed drops below around 1/25 sec. Moreover, if there is to be significant action in the shot you would need to increase the speed further to capture movement thereby sacrificing image brightness. As a starting point it is a good idea to set the shutter speed at 1/25 or 1/50 sec and the Gain setting at 0db (or L) / the ISO setting at 200. This will then allow you to adjust the Iris/Aperture to expose your shot correctly.

In Europe, Asia, South America and most of Africa, videos are broadcast using the PAL standard, which uses 25 frames per second. In the USA (and subsequently on YouTube, Vevo and other streaming sites) videos are published using the NTSC standard of 30 frames per second. Setting your camera to a higher shutter speed than the intended broadcast standard will avoid a **strobe effect** (the image seeming to intermittently go still) in the final moving image product.

## IRIS/APERTURE

The camera's Iris control (referred to as Aperture on DSLRs), changes the size of the hole at the rear of the lens that allows light to hit the camera sensor. The Iris/Aperture setting is expressed in numbers preceded by the letter F, known as **F-stops**. Each ascending F-stop lets in half the amount of light as the previous one; a setting of f/5.6 has half as large an aperture for the light to come through the lens as a setting of f/2.8. Consequently the shot becomes darker. Changing the Aperture has no real impact on the quality of the shot (influenced by gain/ISO) or its smoothness (influenced by shutter speed), but it does affect how the shot can be focused.

A wide-open aperture (f/2.8) leads to the shot having a very shallow **depth of field**. This means that you can focus the image either on the foreground or on the background but not on both. Parts of the image will therefore be out of focus. This tends to work well for focusing on subjects you wish to highlight. David Lean famously used this technique in his film

**Strobe effect** effect whereby the viewer sees moving images as a series of stills, usually created when using slow shutter speeds

**F-stop** measurement of the ratio of the focal length of a lens and the size of the aperture; the larger the number the less light is let in and vice versa

**Depth of field** the range of distance in front of and behind an object which is in focus

**Fig 26.9** Omar Sharif appearing from the desert in *Lawrence of Arabia* (1962)

*Lawrence of Arabia*, with Omar Sharif's character Sherif Ali slowly emerging from the desert, first as a blurry unfocused figure then coming into focus only at the last minute as he approached the camera/other characters.

If you will need to show both the background and foreground in focus you will need to close the aperture to a value of around f11. To compensate for the resulting loss of light, add brightness by increasing the ISO value, reducing the shutter speed or by adding artificial light to the scene. When making *Citizen Kane* (1941, directed by Orson Welles) cinematographer Gregg Toland experimented with high speed film stock (having the same effect as an increased ISO) and bright lighting to achieve shots with a very large or 'deep' depth of field. In the shot in Figure 26.10 both Welles in the foreground as well as the characters along the long table are all in focus.

**Fig 26.10** A very long depth of field has been used to keep everyone in focus in this shot in *Citizen Kane* (1941)

## FOCUSING ON THE SUBJECT

Depth of field is important in moving image production because to replicate the human experience not all elements of a shot should be in focus at the same time. Our eyes are constantly adjusting their focus on different elements of the scene, and automatic focus systems on cameras cannot replicate this ability of the human eye. Consequently, if you want to avoid parts of your image moving in and out of focus (particularly in action shots) and disturbing the viewer, use manual focus when filming.

Sometimes you may want to shift the viewer's attention between objects or characters in the foreground and the background. This can be an effective way of introducing a character, for example, entering the scene at the back of a room and diverting attention from a character in the foreground. To do this you need to perform a **focus pull**, which means adjusting the focus during the shot to change from one subject to another. You usually do this by rotating the ring on the lens closest to the front of the camera. Professional lenses have distance markers on the focus ring to show how far away a subject needs to be from the lens in order for it to be in sharp focus.

**Focus pull** changing the focus of the camera during a shot in order to bring an object in or out of focus

## WHITE BALANCE

Every environment we enter has a slightly different brightness. Daylight, for example, is significantly brighter than the light from an electric tungsten bulb. Different light sources also have a different colour or hue (daylight glows blue while tungsten bulbs glow orange, for example). Humans can automatically correct this, as our brains can work out what colours certain objects should be, whereas cameras cannot unless they have an automatic white balance setting. We correct this by programming the camera to respond correctly to the colour white – a process known as 'white balance'.

With digital video cameras you can set the white balance manually to respond to the light in a particular location, for example, an exterior scene (blue daylight) or an interior scene (orange tungsten light). This involves filling the screen with a piece of white card or paper (where the subject of the shot is likely to be) then telling the camera (usually by pushing and holding the white balance button) that this is what white is supposed to look like. The camera will then use this as a reference point to ensure that white appears as white in the footage (and not as light orange under tungsten light, for example). Consequently all of the other colours in the shot will be balanced with the white and will look natural.

> ### Skills Task: **Combining aperture, ISO and shutter speed settings**
>
> Set up a camera and two objects, placing one object in the background and one in the foreground. Set the camera to ISO 200 with shutter speed 1/50. Now vary the aperture settings as you film; note which settings allow one of the objects to be in focus and the other to be blurred. Attempt a focus pull to switch the focus from one object to the other. Now change the ISO, shutter speed and aperture settings so that both objects are in focus.

# 26.4 CAMERA MOVEMENTS AND MOUNTS

**Link**

See Chapter 20, pages 197 and 200, for more information on the frenetic, 'shaky-cam' technique used in Paul Greengrass's Jason Bourne films.

**Camera mount** method of holding, placing or fixing the camera in position

In the early days of cinema it was difficult to move cameras because they were incredibly heavy and fragile. Today we have ultra-portable, lightweight cameras that are weatherproof. This evolution has had a huge impact on the way films are made. For example, compare the camera work in a silent movie from the 1920s – composed mainly of static wide shots with the characters carefully directed to move around and interact – with the Jason Bourne films in which the hand-held camera rarely stops moving.

Below is a list of camera movements and different **camera mounts** (ways to place or hold the camera) you can use. When designing a moving image sequence, only use camera movements if they add something to the meaning of your production – otherwise they can disrupt the audience's suspension of disbelief.

## CAMERA MOVEMENTS

### Zoom

Zooming is when the camera operator adjusts the length of the lens (the distance between the different pieces of glass within the lens) to make the subject appear larger or smaller without moving the camera. When zooming in, the camera makes the subject appear larger; when zooming out the subject appears smaller. Zooming can have the disadvantage of increasing **camera shake** (the amount the camera moves when being held) so it is preferable to move the camera towards the subject rather than relying on zooming in, although this is not always possible (for example, when dealing with an emotional interviewee).

**Camera shake** involuntary camera movement; often occurs with hand-held shots
**Fluid head tripod** camera tripod with a mount that allows for flexible camera movement in different directions

### Pan

Panning is turning the camera to the left or right while it remains still. This can be done to show more of the location (panning across a bookshelf to reveal all of the book titles, for example) or to follow action (such as panning as someone runs across the frame). Panning is easy to achieve with a **fluid head tripod** (see below).

### Tilt

Like panning, tilting means the camera stays in one place but the direction it points in is moved, in this case vertically up or down. You might tilt up to reveal the top of a tall building or to show something thrown in the air. Tilting is easy to achieve with a fluid head tripod (see below).

### Crane

A crane shot is when the camera and therefore the audience's perspective is lifted into the air to show the location below. Crane shots are expensive, as they require specialist equipment, although today many film-makers use drones to achieve these shots much more cheaply.

### Track

Tracking is when the camera moves alongside moving characters or moving objects in a shot. Car chase scenes typically have tracking shots, with a camera mounted on a separate car being driven alongside the car being filmed.

## CAMERA MOUNTS

### Tripod

Tripods create a solid platform for still shots and should also be used if the intention is to zoom into a closer shot (to avoid camera shake). Fluid head tripods usually allow you to move the camera up and down as well as left and right, allowing for tilting and panning shots.

### Hand-held

Hand-held shots allow the director to move the camera around the scene with a lot of freedom and tend to add a sense of realism (as though the viewer is witnessing the scene first-hand). Many documentaries use hand-held camera techniques, as events may unfold in an unpredictable way and require the camera operator to react instinctively to the action as it unfolds. Some action films now use hand-held techniques to give a sense of realism to the story.

### Steadicam

Steadicams are mountings for a camera that allow the camera operator to move with the same freedom as they would when using the camera hand-held but with less camera shake (the mounting keeps the camera 'steady'). One of the first uses of steadicam was in Stanley Kubrick's horror film *The Shining* (where the camera follows a child riding his tricycle along the corridors of a hotel.

**Fig 26.11** A still from the extended steadicam shot from Joe Wright's *Atonement* (2007)

**Fig 26.12** The original use of a steadicam from Stanely Kubrick's *The Shining* (1980)

More recently, in his film *Atonement* (2007), British director Joe Wright included a five and a half minute tracking shot of the British Forces awaiting rescue from the beaches of Dunkirk, filmed in Redcar.

Wright and cinematographer Seamus McGarvey elected to capture the entire scene in one shot due to limited time with the hundreds of extras and the fact that the tide was advancing up the beach. Reportedly, only three takes of the shot were filmed as steadicam operator Peter Robertson collapsed during the fourth.

### Dolly and track

A dolly is a tripod that has wheels that allow it to be pulled to create moving tracking shots. Large budget productions lay tracks down for the dolly to move along in a precise and smooth movement.

### Jib

A jib is a large camera mount that uses a large pole pivoted on top of a tripod; it allows the camera to make large movements up and down or in an arc. Jibs are very large and require some specialist set-up but can provide some very dramatic shots.

### Rostrum

A rostrum is a camera mount that points the camera down onto a surface that can be then used to film shots of text within books or of photographs. 2D animators use rostra for their cameras if working on a flat surface.

# 26.5 EDITING, TIMING AND PACE

Once you have completed filming, you will likely spend as much time again in post-production editing. Editing is a series of questions and choices about which frames you cut. For example:

- How long do you hold a shot on an interviewee who is becoming upset?
- When cutting between two actors in a dialogue scene, how often will you cut from the person speaking to the person listening to see their reactions?

Experienced editors are able to make decisions such as this and intuitively decide the correct frame to edit two shots together using their sense of 'timing'. This is a skill that is developed with practice and, like drawing, the more you do the better you will become. The timing of the cut is often debated between the editor and the director. When you have a dialogue scene and want to cut between two characters, experiment with leaving longer pauses between the characters' lines (leaving the viewer watching the non-speaking character) and choosing when to cut from the speaking character to the reacting character. Through this exercise you will get a sense of timing and pace for your scene. The shorter the pauses you leave between lines and reactions, the faster the 'pacing' is and vice versa.

There are two main types of editing that you will have seen in moving image products: continuity editing and montage editing.

## CONTINUITY EDITING

Continuity editing is used in almost every narrative moving image product. It assembles the shots in the order that they show events in a scene, without the viewer becoming aware that this is happening. Continuity editing should be invisible or unobtrusive, so that the audience can watch the story unfold without noticing how the different elements of the film-making process have been used to create the scene. When cutting together a dialogue scene, for example, you should make the size of shot consistent and only change it slowly over the course of the scene. For example, it would be jarring to cut directly from a wide shot of one character to a close-up of another character and back again.

You should also match action shots to make the audience believe that the action only happened in the story once (rather than being filmed twice from different angles). If a character picks up a coffee cup, we need to make the audience feel this happened only once, even though we might have filmed it in a wide shot and again in medium close-up. When cutting these shots together, you would need to match the timing in both shots of the character's hand reaching for and touching the cup and lifting it up, so that the audience sees just one movement. For example, the wide shot could end the moment that the character's hand touches the cup and the medium close-up could start at the same moment.

## MONTAGE EDITING

The word *montage* actually means 'editing' in French, but it is widely used to describe a form of editing where shots are brought together not to tell a story but to convey an idea. Early Soviet film-maker Lev Kuleshov demonstrated the power of montage by cutting the same shot of an actor (he had been asked to give a neutral expression) with a series of different shots and then asking viewers to describe how the actor was feeling. When the viewer saw the neutral expression next to a bowl of soup, for example, they said that the actor looked hungry; when they saw the same shot of the actor cut together with a shot of a coffin, they said he looked upset. Kuleshov demonstrated here the effect of putting two shots together to create meaning. This approach was adopted by notable Soviet film-makers, including Sergei Eisenstein and Vsevolod Pudovkin, and became the dominant form of editing in Soviet cinema.

When creating a montage, identify and focus on the key ideas that you want to convey to the audience. Imagine the scene of you waking up and getting ready in the morning that you developed in the previous chapter on visualising a narrative. To convey that you were tired, you could repeat throughout the scenes a close-up shot of your actor yawning. To convey that your alarm clock is loud and annoying, you could repeat an extreme close-up of the clock rhythmically throughout the shot sequence, to demonstrate your feelings of annoyance.

With a montage sequence the edit itself becomes the important element in the sequence, so unlike continuity editing the edit should be visible. Montage allows you to express ideas with perhaps more freedom than continuity editing, but it does disrupt the audience's suspension of disbelief by demonstrating that they are watching a creative production.

It is also possible to use elements of montage in largely continuity-based work, to add meaning to scenes. Nicolas Roeg's *Don't Look Now* is an excellent example of a movie that tells a story through an artful combination of montage and continuity scenes. The film opens with a scene where Donald Sutherland's character is inspecting photographs on slides and keeps seeing a red stain in the images. This is intercut with shots of his daughter in her bright

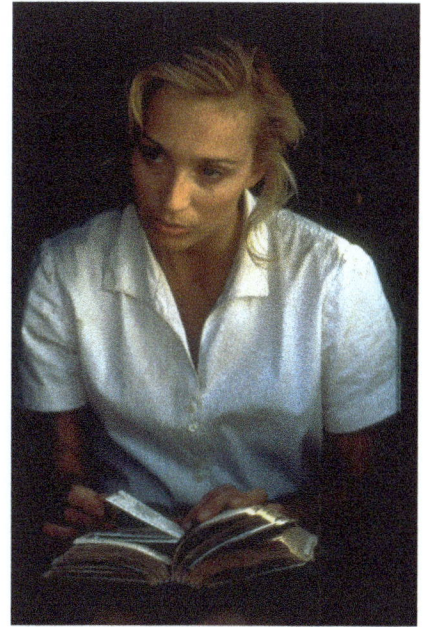

**Fig 26.13** If cutting to a close-up of the book when continuity editing, the pages and the actress's hands would need to be in the same position

**Fig 26.14** Nicolas Roeg used a combination of montage and continuity editing for the opening sequence of *Don't Look Now* (1973)

red coat playing near water outside. The stain matches the shape and colour of her coat, linking the two scenes.

Individual edits can be categorised into four main types:

### Temporal edits

A temporal edit brings together two shots that are linked by time. It might be that the two shots are cut together to demonstrate the passage of time, for example, a character gets into a car and it drives away in Shot 1, and we see the car arrive at its destination in Shot 2. Alternatively, the two shots may be linked to show that they are happening at the same time, as in the coffee cup example described above.

### Spatial edits

A spatial edit is a cut that links two shots to convey the spatial relationship between things. If you cut from one shot showing Character A to another shot showing Character B across the table, you are showing the audience where the characters are in relation to one another. Spatial and temporal editing is very important when creating continuity sequences. You must always consider what each edit is telling the audience about the time between different shots and the spatial relationship between subjects in your film.

### Graphical edits

Graphical edits cut together two shots that have a relationship in terms of the shapes and colours in each frame. Directors of music videos often cut together shots that have very different graphic properties, to keep the audience engaged. Some film-makers repeat shapes and colours across shots, to link elements or ideas. Perhaps the most famous example is in Stanley Kubrick's *2001: A Space Odyssey*, which cuts together a bone thrown into the air by a prehistoric human with the next shot of a similarly shaped spacecraft. In one edit this **graphic match** linked the ideas of early human discovery of tools to our ability to explore space.

> **Graphic match** different objects that are similar looking (in shape or colour), which are used in successive shots to link ideas

### Rhythmic editing

Sometimes edits are made in order to create rhythm and keep time with the action or music. This is particularly true of music videos where the rhythm of the music is very important to the overall experience. Similarly, in action films, rhythmic cutting across action scenes can convey a pace to the scene and generate excitement within the audience. Edgar Wright's recent action film *Baby Driver* contains many action scenes that are rhythmically cut together to the soundtrack used in the film. This can be achieved by marking the timeline where the beats or points of emphasis are in the soundtrack (they appear as markers on the timeline) and then making sure the cuts happen at exactly those moments.

### Skills Task: **Cutting and editing techniques**

Take a 30-second sequence from two narrative and two non-narrative moving image products. Identify all of the cuts/edits in each sequence. Categorise each cut/edit (temporal, spatial, and so on). Identify which products use montage editing (rhythmic and graphic edits) and which use continuity editing (spatial and temporal edits). Discuss the effects these techniques have on the meaning conveyed by each product.

## Project work: **Editing pace and timing**

Working in small groups, write a dialogue between two characters. Film the scene with at least two cameras (one for each character's lines and reactions) or, if you have only one camera, film the scene repeatedly using different shots and framing to capture both characters' lines and reactions. Then combine your footage, cutting between both characters. Experiment with leaving longer or shorter pauses between the characters' lines and reactions, as described above. Show the results to the class and discuss.

## Further references

### Books

- *Cinematography: Theory and Practice: Image Making for Cinematographers and Directors*, 2nd ed. (B. Brown, 2011)
- *Film Directing Shot by Shot* (S.D. Katz, 1991)
- *Pulling Focus* (J. Stadler, 2012)

# Games design and mobile and multimedia applications

# 27 Communicating ideas and meaning through interactivity

Interactivity supports communication in two directions. A good way to understand this is to use McLuhan's hot and cool media definition. McLuhan defines hot media as something that requires very little input from the user; watching a film at the cinema, for example. Cool media on the other hand, is anything that requires input from the user; a website the user navigates, for example. The user's input drives the two-way communication that makes something interactive. Interactivity therefore contains three elements:

- the user's intention
- an interface that interprets the intention
- a device or system action that satisfies the user's intention.

A good interactive system is therefore directed by the user's activity. For example, the user presses a button and the system reacts by indicating that the button has been pressed, but also presents the user with the next logical step. If the system lags behind the user or reacts incorrectly then the system is not interactive enough, or is 'unresponsive'.

# 27.1 TYPES OF INTERACTIVITY

### Human-to-human interactivity
When people communicate they interact, but in a digital media context the digital application, for example, mobile telephony, internet messaging or email, facilitates the human-to-human interaction.

### Human-to-device interactivity
Human-to-device interaction happens via an interface. This could be the touchscreen on a smartphone, the navigation system on a website, or the physical controls on a games console. The interface is the primary method for communicating with the system.

### Human-to-content interactivity
People also interact with digital content. For example, educational content online and in museums uses interactive animations, copy and images to engage and inform users and guide their activity. Likewise, digital video is used to inform people but also encourages them to make purchases. In each

case the user interacts with the digital content through the interface but the content is the enabler of interactivity and the medium through which the interactivity takes place.

### Device to device interactivity

Device to device interaction relates to the communication that enables human interaction to take place. Multiplayer gaming, social media and instant messaging all involve complex communication between different devices that enable users to interact.

# 27.2 PURPOSES OF INTERACTIVITY

Designers use the different types of interaction to convey meaning in various ways, but the main ones are:

- communication
- navigation
- feedback and additional information
- user generated content
- advertising.

## COMMUNICATION

When people use a platform such as Skype or FaceTime, they interact with the digital interface as well as with the person they are communicating with. The interface needs to be as simple and intuitive as possible to enable the communication. Other communication products, such as social media or interactive television, combine different functions, enabling users to consume content and interact at the same time, for example, by posting messages that appear alongside the television broadcast.

## NAVIGATION

Enabling the user to navigate a digital space is fundamental to interactive media. From a simple website drop-down menu to an immersive 3D game environment, the three stage process of user intention, interface interpretation and device or system response forms the basis of many digital products and services.

For example, a travel website might guide the user through the interface using layout, images and icons to **signpost** areas of the screen that relate to processes, such as search, flight booking or certain types of holiday. Travel websites often use a grid system to divide the screen in a balanced and visually appealing way. They have critical interactive elements such as buttons relating to holiday type and text input boxes. Photographs are often an important feature and are large on the page, saturated with colour to increase the visual appeal and draw attention to promotions and advertising copy.

> **Signposting** a way of directing user interaction using relevant language
> **Interactive banner** an image on a website that prompts the user to click, launching another website

## INTERACTIVE ADVERTISING

Online and digital advertisers often use **interactive banners** that link to other websites to promote brands and drive sales. Interactive banners also enable the advertiser to track the online activity of the user who clicked on the banner. There are some basic guidelines for creating banners:

- Use attention-grabbing images and copy. Banners are usually displayed on a page with a lot of other content so they need to stand out.

**Tooltip** a small box showing text that helps to guide the user through a process
**Supporting copy** copy shown on a screen that helps the user progress through a process on-screen

- Include a clear 'call to action' that encourages users to interact with the banner, for example, 'click here'. It must be clear that the banner is not just another image on the website.
- Apply the size and format standards that websites allow for advertising banners.

## FEEDBACK AND INFORMATION

Many digital applications incorporate feedback and additional information into their structure, in order to guide the user through complex processes. For example, **tooltips** are small explanatory textboxes that pop up when users scroll over or point to a particular button or icon on an interface. Figure 27.1 shows an Adobe Photoshop tooltip that tells the user what the tool is, as well as the keyboard shortcut to access it.

Websites use **supporting copy** in the same way. Figure 27.2 shows an online business card creation tool that uses supporting copy boxes to guide users along a process.

More complex feedback examples include immersive games, where the user is presented with information relating to the gameplay environment. For example, game interfaces that use a first person perspective sometimes include a feedback element as part of the interface, such as motion tracker on the player's 'wrist'. Data is presented to the player within the game world through the interface, so helping them to decide on their next move and enhancing the gameplay experience.

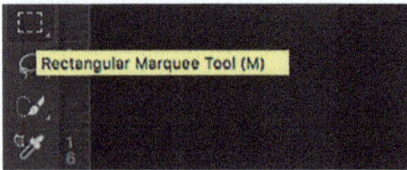

**Fig 27.1** Adobe Photoshop tooltip

**Fig 27.2** A business card

## SOUND AS FEEDBACK DEVICE

Sound is also often used to support a user through a process. For example, smartphones and tablets use the camera shutter sound to confirm to the user they have successfully taken a photograph. When choosing sound, try to match your sound with the interaction (like the camera shutter) or the tone of your message, for example, applause for positive feedback. While sound is an effective way to apply meaning to interactivity, take care neither to overwhelm the user with sounds nor rely solely on sounds to indicate interactivity. People often use devices in silent mode, so when a user clicks a button the interaction should be apparent without sound.

## USER-GENERATED CONTENT

The internet began as a one-way communication medium where users just consumed content; the introduction of Web 2.0 websites that enable two-way communication and interaction with content has led to an explosion of interaction with content, content sharing and user-generated content. Now users can post comments, images and video to websites and start conversations around pre-existing or new content. This user-generated content covers everything from Twitter conversations and Facebook video streaming to posting a comment on a blog.

Before you enable this two-way communication, think about the best way to proceed. For example, good practice for website reader comments is:

1. Comments should be moderated before they appear on a live website. This way anything abusive can be deleted.
2. Limitations should be placed on word/character count. This way, overly long comments can be avoided.
3. Choose carefully where on a website you enable commenting, for example, on every page or just selected areas, at the bottom of each page of content or elsewhere.

---

### Skills Task: **Identifying interaction types**

Work in groups. Choose an item you buy online and consider the process of buying it.

- Step 1: Identify the different types of interaction that take place.
- Step 2: Write each type of interaction on a sticky note.
- Step 3: Arrange the sticky notes as a timeline on a wall.
- Step 4: Explain the process to the rest of the class, invite feedback and discuss possible improvements.

---

# 27.3 INTERACTIVE APPLICATIONS AND FORMATS

Digital interactivity has many types and purposes. In this section we explore the most common interactive formats and applications:

- Websites
- Mobile applications
- Interactive TV
- Multiplayer online games
- Immersive role-player games
- Augmented reality
- Virtual reality
- Immersive installations and events

## WEBSITES

Today's websites can involve anything from simple read-only pages to complex multimedia interactive platforms, such as Facebook and Twitter. This rapid expansion in web technology has also led to online software applications becoming readily available. Creative Cloud®, for example, provides a full suite of website design products such as Dreamweaver. Similarly, G Suite enables you to create, share and store ideas and sketches.

Websites need to be both visually engaging and usable if they are going to stand out from the crowd. Organisations such as the Good Web Guide

**Link**

See Chapter 28, for a more detailed explanation of how to design websites.

help designers keep up with developments in web design. Here are some guidelines for designing websites:

- Design for your user (your target audience) first – establish who this is during the research phase.
- Plan your website navigation structure using diagrams.
- Arrange your content with a clear, consistent purpose using sitemaps and wireframes.
- Plan your layout carefully, for example, by using a grid system.
- Design for all devices and screen sizes.
- Strong visuals are often simple rather than complex.
- Effective design is also about good usability and functionality, such as how quickly a website loads.

## MOBILE APPLICATIONS

Mobile applications now include social media, content streaming and location-based services, as well as apps that help with banking, travel and many other aspects of work and life. For digital designers, this means that being aware of the latest trends and advances in mobile technology is an essential part of good interactive design. Manufacturers, such as Android™ and Apple, publish their design guidelines online and update them regularly, but here are some principles you should consider when designing for mobile:

- focus on what the end user needs to achieve
- keep navigation and the user interface simple
- minimise copy content
- use sound and animation to guide users
- understand the device functionality and limitations as much as possible
- plan user interactions with sketches and wireframes
- keep any animation or video short and informative.

**Link**

See Chapter 29, for more detailed guidance on designing for mobile.

## INTERACTIVE TV

Television used to be a one-way medium. Today, interactive TV users can create their own TV schedules by accessing on-demand services and connect with the

**Fig 27.3** Netflix interactive storytelling

broadcaster in many different ways. For example, Netflix now offers 'Interactive Storytelling', which combines the '**branching narrative**' aspect of video gaming – where the user chooses where they go next in the story – with the linear narrative of film and TV. Figure 27.3 shows the user touching the tablet screen in the Netflx app. This then triggers the next part of the video story.

<aside>**Branching narrative** a story that does not go in a straight line but branches out in different directions</aside>

## MULTIPLAYER ONLINE GAMES

Online gaming platforms use a combination of gameplay functionality with social connectivity. This means that players can connect with each other in real time within the same game environment via an internet connection. For example, the fantasy game Elvenar and the construction game Minecraft enable players to join communities of players. For digital designers this means focusing on interface ideas that work with a keyboard and a mouse rather than complex console controllers, as this is the most commonly used gameplay method within the user community.

<aside>**Link**

See Chapter 31, for more information on immersive games design.</aside>

## IMMERSIVE ROLE-PLAYER GAMES

Fully immersive gaming uses interactivity to create environments that respond to the user to create compelling gameplay scenarios. For example, in Figure 27.4, the player is presented with a first-person viewpoint showing an interface that displays relevant data, such as acceleration, race position and the number of laps left to race. These create the sense that the player is part of the gameplay world by using emotional and sensory triggers.

## AUGMENTED REALITY

Augmented reality is digital technology that superimposes or adds computer graphics, sound effects, video or location data to our view of the world through digital devices such as smartphones. Designers use this method to create simulations of the world that can be interactive or just show information.

**Fig 27.4** An example of an immersive role-player experience

## VIRTUAL REALITY (VR)

VR uses headsets that provide visual and sometimes audio inputs to generate realistic sensations that make the user feel as though they are in an actual physical environment. A person using virtual reality equipment is able to 'look around' the artificial world, and in some cases move about in and interact with it. Due to the recent launch of META's Oculus and Apple's Vision Pro headsets, virtual reality games and media content are now a much bigger part of the digital landscape. Both platforms enable users to interact with each other and with applications in a computer-generated environment.

## IMMERSIVE INSTALLATIONS AND EVENTS

Digital technology can be used to create fully immersive experiences. For example, interactive art exhibitions and installations often encourage the viewer to interact with the exhibits, blurring the lines between viewer and content.

Figure 27.5 shows the artwork *Worlds Unleashed and then Connecting* by teamLab®. Triggered by the dish, the artwork uses projections to create an interactive experience inside the restaurant that changes with the seasons, using the restaurant walls and tables as a canvas. When a dish is placed on the table, the world contained within the dish is unleashed, and gets connected with other worlds unleashed from others' dishes, creating a unified artwork. The work constantly changes from moment to moment and no two moments are alike.

<aside>**Link**

See later in this chapter, and Chapter 31, for more information on immersive installations.</aside>

**Fig 27.5** An immersive installation by teamLab: *Worlds Unleashed and then Connecting* (2015) Interactive Digital Installation, Endless, Sound: Hideaki Takahashi

# 27.4 METHODS OF INTERACTIVITY

Designers use three main methods of interactivity:

- Key-modal
- Direct manipulation
- Linguistic

## KEY-MODAL INTERACTIVITY

Here the user interacts with the interface using function keys or a keyboard of some sort, corresponding to different 'modes' or user behaviours. There are four common key-modal interaction styles:

### 1: Menu-based interaction

The interface presents the user with a display of options; if the user selects an option then more options may be presented.

### 2: Question-and-answer

The interface presents the user with a series of questions in text form and the user is required to respond using a keyboard or a touchscreen equivalent.

### 3: Function-key interaction

The user makes a series of selections by selecting function keys or using some other special-purpose hardware. The user is guided or prompted by displayed information.

### 4: Voice-based interaction

This is often used with voice-operated systems such as games that use narration to communicate with the user. For example, a character in a game may issue instructions and then ask that the user press a button to continue.

Key-modal interaction is associated with systems that require a user to carry out a series of steps within a process. For example, interactive exhibitions sometimes ask users for specific information that relates to them personally; once this process is complete, further interaction is possible.

Figure 27.6 shows the SkyPad™ interactive guestbook that was installed at the Space Needle building in Seattle. Visitors selected their country of origin from a list on a touchscreen display showing an interactive 3D map of the world.

**Fig 27.6** Space Needle SkyPad™ Interactive Wall, designed by Belle & Wissell, Co.

The display then showed the number of visitors to the Space Needle since it first opened in 1962 and connected the country of origin to Seattle on the map.

Visitors could also explore the history of the Space Needle through an interactive photographic exhibit that showed early tower designs and memorabilia. In this image visitors are scrolling through images on the exhibit using the touchscreen. They could also enlarge selected images and view more information.

## DIRECT MANIPULATION

Otherwise known as 'point and click', this mode is used when a user is required to apply actions to an object contained within the interface such as a digital photograph. The main type of direct manipulation style is **graphical direct manipulation**. This is when a user selects a graphical element, for example, a tool icon in Adobe Photoshop, to perform an action such as editing an image.

> **Graphical direct manipulation**
> a software process that involves moving and manipulating elements directly

## LINGUISTIC

Linguistic interaction involves the system responding using the same language as the user. For example, if a user types a question into Google such as 'What is the capital of Japan?', Google will respond in English.

Many digital media products use a combination of all three interaction styles. The key to using interaction styles is understanding which style is suited

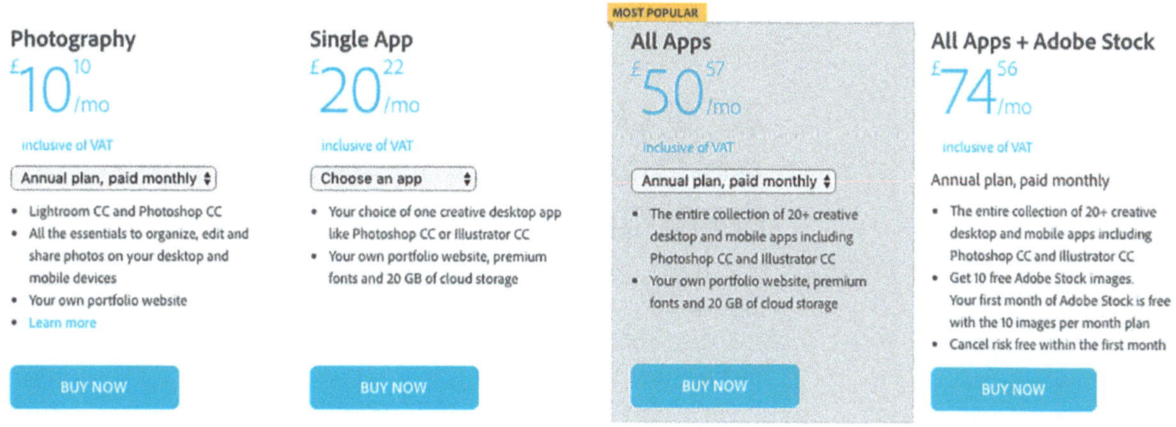

| **Photography** | **Single App** | MOST POPULAR  **All Apps** | **All Apps + Adobe Stock** |
|---|---|---|---|
| £10.10/mo | £20.22/mo | £50.57/mo | £74.56/mo |
| inclusive of VAT | inclusive of VAT | inclusive of VAT | inclusive of VAT |
| Annual plan, paid monthly ⬍ | Choose an app ⬍ | Annual plan, paid monthly ⬍ | Annual plan, paid monthly |
| • Lightroom CC and Photoshop CC | • Your choice of one creative desktop app like Photoshop CC or Illustrator CC | • The entire collection of 20+ creative desktop and mobile apps including Photoshop CC and Illustrator CC | • The entire collection of 20+ creative desktop and mobile apps including Photoshop CC and Illustrator CC |
| • All the essentials to organize, edit and share photos on your desktop and mobile devices | • Your own portfolio website, premium fonts and 20 GB of cloud storage | • Your own portfolio website, premium fonts and 20 GB of cloud storage | • Get 10 free Adobe Stock images. Your first month of Adobe Stock is free with the 10 images per month plan |
| • Your own portfolio website | | | • Cancel risk free within the first month |
| • Learn more | | | |
| BUY NOW | BUY NOW | BUY NOW | BUY NOW |

**Fig 27.7** Interaction styles: buying and using the Adobe Illustrator application

to which part of a process; for example, the process of buying and using the Adobe Illustrator application. The sign-up and purchase process would involve some key-modal elements, such as selecting the product type and payment plan as in Figure 27.7, and linguistics such as entering purchase details and user information.

Using the software application would involve direct manipulation, such as moving graphic elements around the workspace and some key-modal interaction when selecting tools and menus. In Figure 27.8, you can see the Adobe Illustrator interface with several tool menus opened through key modal interaction and a stack of letters created and edited in the main work area using direct manipulation. The Help section would use linguistics so people can search for and find answers to written questions.

**Fig 27.8** Direct manipulation in Adobe Illustrator

---

Skills Task: **Identifying interaction methods**

Using a simple software product, such as Microsoft Word or Google Docs, identify the different methods of interaction that have been used to construct the interface and, if relevant, how they have been combined. Then try a more complex application, such as Adobe Photoshop or a game that you are familiar with. Demonstrate your findings to the class and discuss the methods of interactivity and how they are used in the application.

---

# 27.5 USER EXPERIENCE (UX) AND USER INTERFACE (UI) DESIGN

In addition to defining how a user interacts with digital media, designers also shape the emotional or sensory experience resulting from the interaction. This aspect of the design process is called User Experience (UX) or User Interface (UI) design. For example, if a creative brief calls for a businesslike, efficient experience for the user, such as a banking website, then the type of interaction should reflect this. The HSBC website in Figure 27.9 uses a combination of strong colours, simple language, regular shapes and a clear navigation system to create a sense of professionalism and trustworthiness.

Websites and applications with a more playful focus would use different interactive elements, layouts, colour choices and visual styles. The Quarked!™ website, for example, uses a subtle but strong rollover effect on the main navigation buttons, which change shape to inform the user that they can click. When combined with the quirky typography, irregular shapes and layout, and vibrant, clashing colours, the effect reinforces the fun aspect of the website without compromising the usability.

Many designers now use animated sequences with voiceovers to explain content ideas, for example, products or services being offered. This approach means that complex ideas can be explained as linear animations. To ensure that such an animation works, some points to consider are:

- Limit animations to 90 seconds maximum – anything more is unlikely to hold the viewer's attention.
- Use a voiceover that does not need to synchronise exactly with the animation – it will be much easier to create.
- Try to match the character and tone of your voiceover with your content.
- Make sure your animation works without sound as well as with sound.

**Fig 27.9** An example of the HSBC website interface

# 27.6 COMBINING DIGITAL MEDIA

Digital interactions can be simple or complex, from reading an email to playing an immersive game in virtual reality, but they all combine media and design elements to achieve the desired results. Simply reading an email involves interacting with a device, accessing software, understanding content and then deciding to respond, delete or archive. When you consider that an email may include links, images and other media, the list of elements and potential interactions becomes even longer. How you combine different digital elements (often called multimedia) is a significant part of your design process.

## COMPOSITION AND VIEWPOINT

Advances in connectivity and internet speed now mean that multimedia can form a part of any digital experience. The challenge for the designer is how to make the best use of what is available without overwhelming the user with too much information. To achieve this you need to understand how designers successfully combine digital media using composition and viewpoint.

### Structural and visual composition

In the case of digital media, the term composition refers to both visual composition and structural composition, which refers to how key elements are arranged on-screen. Early website design was often an imitation of printed pages, with rigid structures such as columns and rows. Combining media, however, enables designers to engage viewers and convey meaning in new ways. For example, scrolling header areas on new websites enable viewers to choose from multiple stories while being on the same 'page' of the website, while embedded video players enable full-screen viewing in pop-up windows that overlay text.

**Link**

See Chapter 16, pages 152–156, for more information on visual composition.

### Layout grids

**Functional grids** are the structures that support visual designs by providing a screen with a formal shape, structure, stability and consistency. This means that the user will understand the interface on a subconscious level, making the site easier to explore. In this way, a grid system can reduce user errors and allow users to navigate content with confidence and achieve their goals.

A grid can support numerous layout ideas and concepts. An area containing a video player, for example, can expand to fill either the whole screen or just a specified area. As discussed earlier, many websites now incorporate banner advertising. Applying a grid system means that advertising units can be integrated into a complex screen layout.

The example shown in Figure 27.10 is a grid system for a website that guides the user around the screen, starting at the top left where the box marked 'Logo' sits. In a traditional European reading mode, the eye scans from left to right and then back again to the start of the next line. The point at the very bottom right of the screen is called the **terminal anchor**, and this is where the reader's eye will come to rest having scanned the page. Grids enable the designer to

**Functional grid** a grid-based model for arranging content on-screen
**Terminal anchor** the bottom right part of a screen

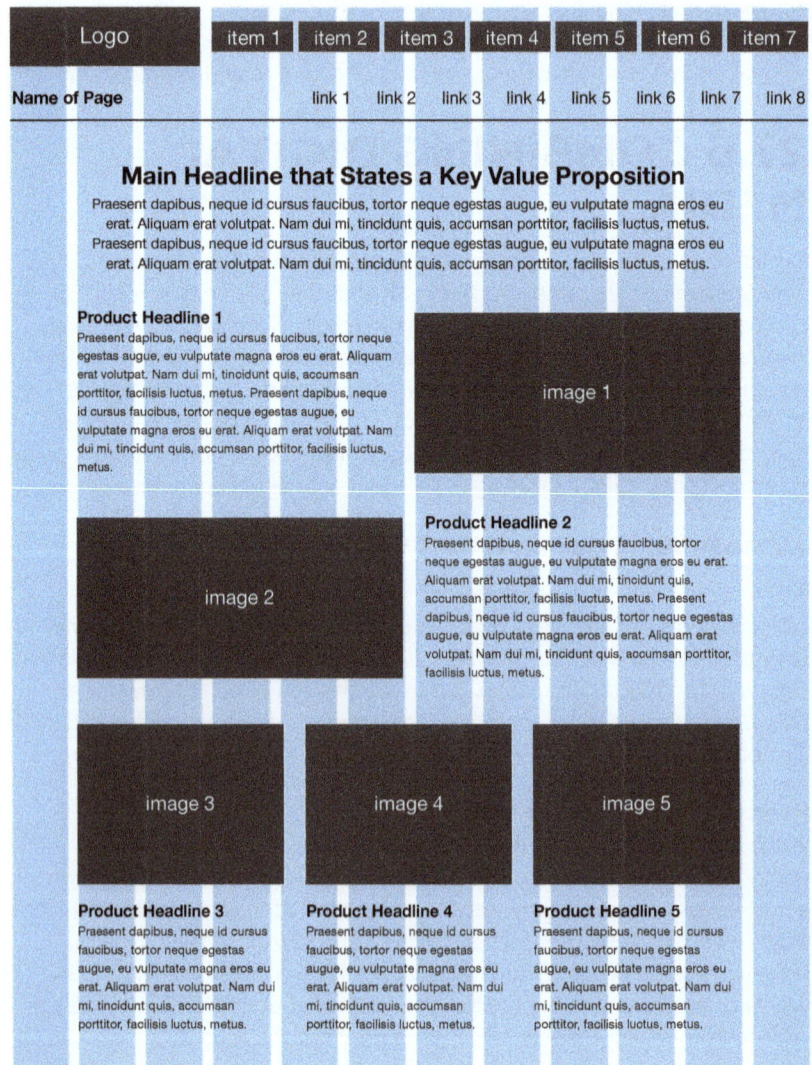

**Fig 27.10** A screen layout grid example

create a '**content hierarchy**', the most important content being placed in the main box on the top right of the layout (marked 'Image 1'), with content of less importance shown in the areas further down the page.

Many news and information-rich websites present multiple streams of content within a grid system. This is partly because digital storytelling and news no longer needs to be linear. The reader can read a chapter or section then watch a short video, listen to part of the story as dialogue, watch a live video feed of breaking news or an animation that explains an aspect of the story, and then move onto the next chapter. This '**fluid experience**' enables the writer and designer to present viewers with multiple options and to choose their own experience.

For example, the website of the UK newspaper *The Times* (Figure 27.11) shows a combination of interactive text and visual content along with these interactive features:

- headlines in black, bold text that link to more content and underline when the reader scrolls over them
- recently updated content in the light grey section below the main image titled 'In the news'
- a large advertising banner placed before the main content showing 'Subscribe Now' options
- a 'Show More' navigation button at the bottom of the screen that reveals more content.

So how would you create such a website without it becoming a confusing mess? Here are some simple rules:

- Arrange your content on a grid system to maintain a consistent look.
- Combine horizontal and vertical copy sections that prevent the reading experience from becoming too repetitive.
- Place the user in control; notice how in Figure 27.11 the user has the option to expand sections in the advertising content – it does not launch automatically.

> **Content hierarchy** the way that content is arranged according to its importance
>
> **Fluid experience** a non-linear way of consuming a story using multiple media types

**Fig 27.11** Home page of the UK newspaper, *The Times*

**Fig 27.12** Miguel Chevalier, *Sur-Natures* (2012) interactive installation produced by Digitalarti at Charles de Gaulle Airport

### Top Tip

You can download functional grid templates from websites such as 960.gs, either in digital formats to be used in applications such as Adobe Photoshop or as PDF files that you can print and use for sketching.

- Use signposting whenever possible; notice how the copy on the smaller sections at the bottom of the screen give the reader a very brief overview, or 'teaser', about what the articles contain.

## VIEWPOINT AND SPACE

The **viewpoint** is what the user sees when they interact with a screen, and the space is the actual screen itself. For example, in a desktop computer experience, the viewpoint and space are 'fixed' by the viewer and the screen. Immersive digital experiences, however, enable the user to 'break out' of the screen and create new viewpoints, depending on where the user chooses to be. Many VR experiences allow the users to explore environments in different ways: the user may be able to 'fly' through a digitally created space, for example, or trigger content by looking in a particular direction. Fully immersive installation designers such as Digitalarti make use of physical spaces, turning walls into interfaces and enabling users to control the environment around them using hand movements or simply by walking through the installation. In the installation shown in Figure 27.12, the digital flowers respond to the visitor's movement by moving as if blown by the wind.

In a similar way, augmented reality and virtual reality can enable users to become part of the interactive environment. Microsoft's Kinect gaming console, for example, has been adapted to read and translate sign language. The Kinect interface records the user's hand gestures and then translates them digitally, effectively creating a new way of communicating.

The VEO Group has developed a tablet application that uses a combination of real-time video recording and a graphical interface (superimposed on top of the video display). This enables observers to video-record lessons and simultaneously or retrospectively tag certain teacher and student actions by pressing the graphical icons on the VEO interface. They can then view and reflect on the lessons and identify areas of possible improvement.

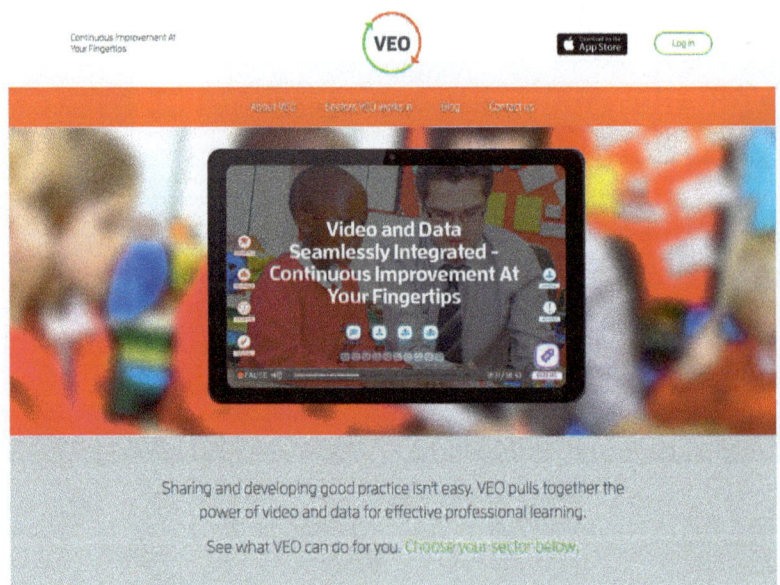

**Fig 27.13** VEO Group tablet application, showing graphical interface over video image

## Skills Task: **Create a grid layout**

1. Create a screenshot of a website or other design that you feel works well.
2. Import the image into Photoshop.
3. Place Photoshop Guides over the image in the main page elements and identify the underlying grid system that the design uses. Guides are used to align objects in your image and do not show up in your final image file. To use guides go to: View > Show rulers > Show guides. You can now create a guide by dragging from the top or bottom ruler in the image viewer.
4. Subdivide the grid into smaller sections.
5. Add blocks of colour to the subdivided areas on separate image layers, to create a new layout. Pay attention to how the dynamics of your subdivisions affect the overall impression.
6. Turn off the background Photoshop layer and work with the new layers you have added. Once you have a new grid system, try using it for a new design.

## Project work: **Scope out a virtual reality experience**

Working in small groups, design a themed virtual reality experience; it could be something from the real world or something imaginary. Think about the following questions:

- What will your user/viewer journey look like?
- What interactivity will you incorporate into your design?
- Will you need an actor? If so, how will you use them?
- Will you need to re-create an environment or create a new one?
- What images, sounds, video and other media will you use?
- What viewpoint will you use?

Research and record all the file and media types you will need to create the experience.

# 27.7 ACCESSIBILITY, USABILITY AND ENJOYMENT

In this section you will explore factors to consider in order to ensure that your digital designs are fit for purpose and deliver the right experience.

Accessibility refers to the practice of removing barriers that prevent users with disabilities from interacting with digital experiences such as websites and applications. If digital experiences are designed inclusively and correctly, it means that all users have equal access to them. Disabilities come in many forms and there are numerous guidelines around what needs to be incorporated into a digital design project; the following examples provide an overview.

When designing for a user with impaired vision you would consider guidelines including:

- use good colour contrasts and a larger font size where possible
- use combinations of colour, shapes and text to clearly express ideas rather than just copy

**Top Tip**

Guidelines for accessibility are available to view online via the W3C website.

- place buttons and notifications in context; so, for example, a button should show near to the written content it relates to.

Similarly, when designing for users with browser screen readers you would describe any images used, provide transcripts for any video content, and write descriptive links and headings.

## PROCESSING POWER

High specification computers with advanced processing power are now much more widely available. This should not mean, however, that you only create digital products for high specification hardware. Any restrictions on hardware processing power will form part of the initial client brief.

## RESPONSIVE DESIGN

Many users now access web content from mobile devices such as phones and tablets. As a result, websites must 'respond' to the viewer's chosen device so that they are still able to access the content. For example, a website that has been designed for a full screen monitor with a lot of text will not show on a small screen, as the text size will be too small. In order to address this, the website structure senses that it is being viewed on a smaller device and restructures the pages and navigation to fit.

## BANDWIDTH

Bandwidth is the maximum data transfer rate of an internet connection. A complex video streaming website that delivers high resolution content to a desktop computer will need a high level of bandwidth, while a mobile web application that enables instant messaging will need very little bandwidth. Designers must consider these factors when creating web experiences, and so bandwidth must form part of a functional design brief and testing plan that answers these questions:

- What is the minimum bandwidth and connection speed your application needs to operate?
- What will the user see if there is insufficient bandwidth for your application to work properly – an error message or further guidance?

## BACKWARDS COMPATIBILITY

Implementing backwards compatibility means incorporating older versions of hardware or software into the project plan. When creating new games, for example, designers must consider older consoles. Mobile app designers must think about the fact that many users still have older devices that may not have all the latest functionality. Website designers must test their designs on older versions of the major browsers.

### Skills Task: **Designing for visual impairment**

Imagine you are developing a retail website for the visually impaired. List the issues you would have to consider when creating your design. Then separate the factors into technical considerations that will form part of the website build and visual considerations that are more aesthetic. Once you have done this, think about where these factors would fit into a client brief and how they could be expressed.

### Top Tip

To check whether a website is responsive, open the website on a standard desktop browser, then make the browser window smaller by resizing from the bottom right-hand corner. Do you see the 'responsive' design taking over when the viewing window becomes too small for the original design?

# 27.8 AESTHETICS AND EMOTIONAL RESPONSES IN MULTIMEDIA AND MOBILE APPS

There are various elements of multimedia design where consideration of the user and viewer's aesthetic experience is obvious. When designing an immersive photography experience, you should always be considering the importance of the emotions you are trying to evoke from your audience. The creators of the Seattle Space Needle photography exhibit have created an unique aesthetic experience for their visitors – evoking emotions such as awe and excitement. Similar emotions that the viewers of the Digitalarti interactive flower exhibition will have felt in Paris.

This power to evoke emotions is also true of less obvious multimedia applications. For example, banking applications will include simple to use menus, clean lines and clear text. This appearance is designed to inspire confidence and denote security. The designers of this application would not have used, for example, a cartoon animal on their main screen. This is unlikely to inspire confidence in the professionalism of the bank. Conversely, an application designed for children learning to read is going to use bright colours, a bold font and potentially audio to engage and encourage children to feel happy while using it.

This section discusses the various elements that make up the design of multimedia and mobile applications, all of these elements can be used to create an aesthetic experience for the user or the viewer. It is up to you as a designer to make judgements as to what is appropriate and suitable for your work. If working from a client brief, you may be asked to elicit a specific response from your audience. If creating your own ideas, you will have to consider what is the appropriate response and plan from there, researching as appropriate. With these types of digital products, however, there is often the opportunity to test and review responses. This will help you to ensure the aesthetic experience you are creating is having its intended effect.

# 27.9 FILE FORMATS AND ASSET SIZES

Combining digital media involves using many different file formats in different ways. So how do you decide which to use? The following table shows the standard media types and the associated file types.

| File formats | File types | File uses |
|---|---|---|
| Text | MS Word, rich text, Font files, Hypertext | Copy in the form of characters and sometimes typographic elements, such as fonts and spacing |
| Moving image | .AVI, .MP4, .WMV, .MOV, .MPEG | Images that can be played in sequence, for example, video and animation |
| Static image | .Gif, .JPG, .PSD, .TIFF, .PDF | Images that do not move, for example, photographs, illustrations or drawings |

| File formats | File types | File uses |
|---|---|---|
| Audio | .MP3, .WAV, .AIFF | Sound files that play with no visual element, for example, MP3 files |
| 3D | .max, .blend, .lwo, .skp | Used to create three-dimensional environments for either gaming or VR |

## Link

See Chapter 4, pages 37–39, for a fuller explanation of native file types.

## NATIVE AND OUTPUT FORMATS

Many software products have a native file type. This is a type of file that can only be opened or used by that particular software. For example, Adobe Photoshop uses the .PSD file extension, which defines it as a Photoshop file – so when you create a new Photoshop document this is the default file type. Output files are file types that can be used by other applications. For example, you can create different files for different purposes from a single Photoshop document, either by exporting or simply saving as a different option. These output options include file types, such as: GIF, PNG, JPEG, TIFF, RAW, PDF.

Understanding these options for all software products is essential when creating and combining digital assets, as it forms part of the development process. For example, when creating graphics for the web, images need to be compressed in order to take up less memory, so they should be in a

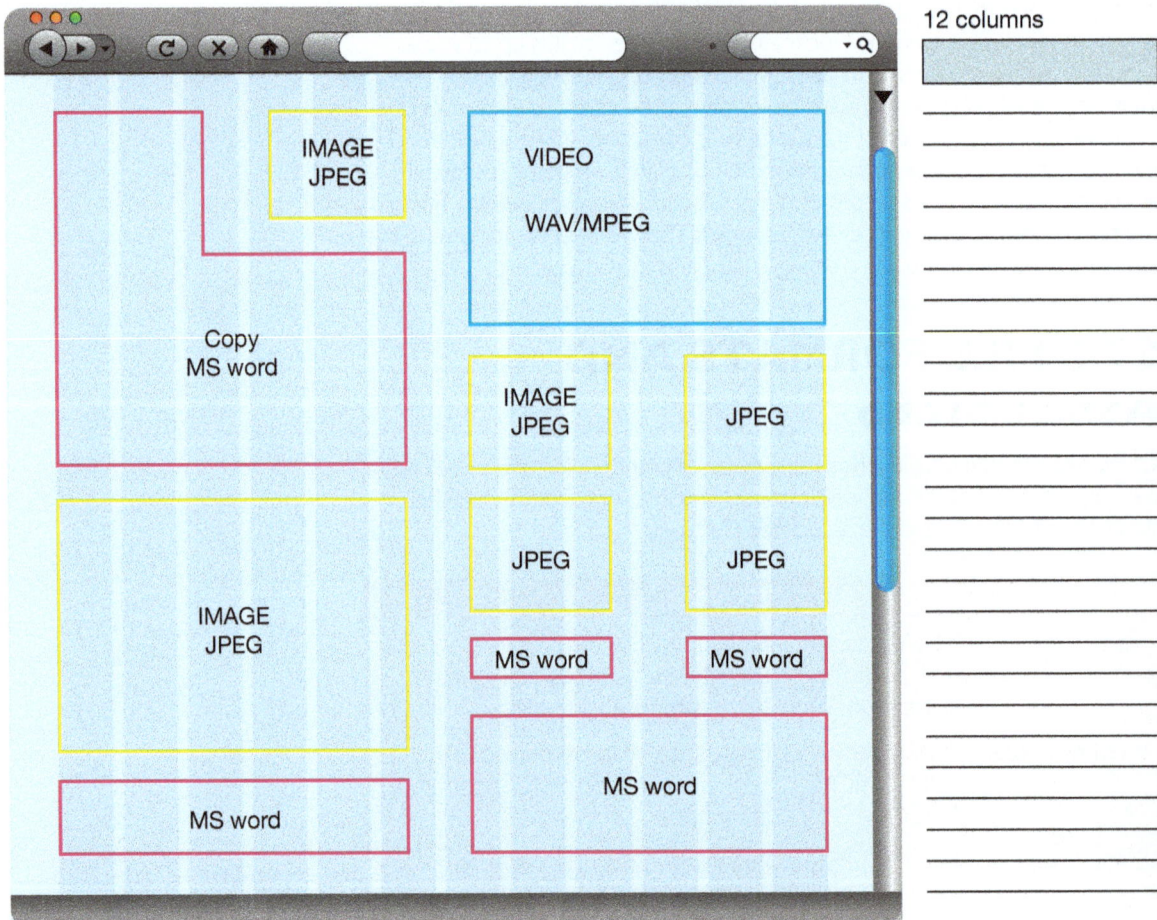

**Fig 27.14** A grid example showing file types

web-friendly format (.gif, .png and .jpeg). If images are for print use, however, then the .TIFF format is more commonly used, as it integrates well with graphic and print design applications.

---

**Skills Task: Organising media file types**

Select a grid template from the website 960.gs and organise where you would use the different media and corresponding file types when creating a complex website. This will help you to understand how different media types fit together. You should end up with something like the image shown in Figure 27.14; note how the colours define content areas: blue for video, yellow for images and purple for copy. You can then decide the exact file types and sizes.

---

## ASSET SIZE

A common question when creating digital assets is 'How big should it be?' The size is defined using a number of methods, all of which are relevant, as they can have a significant impact on how a digital design functions, for instance, overly large asset sizes can cause applications to run slowly or in some cases not run at all. Images to use on a standard website should comply to the following restrictions:

- Resolution: 72 dpi
- Pixel size: As described in the visual mockups
- Memory size: Max 45kb.

Resolution refers specifically to images and how an image is displayed on-screen. Website images, for example, all have to be set at a resolution of 72 dpi to work correctly in a browser, while print images usually need to be 300 dpi.

Pixel size refers to the size of an image asset in pixels and refers to the actual physical size of the asset as it appears on-screen, so 250px is equal to 250 pixels in length. Memory size refers to the size in terms of how much memory it takes up on a hard drive. Memory size is measured in bytes, kilobytes and megabytes. By sticking to these parameters the final website should load quickly and give the user a good experience. All asset sizes should be clearly defined in the client brief.

# 27.10 STORING AND ADMINISTERING ASSETS

To ensure that everyone in your team has access to all the digital media assets they need, you should create a central storage space online. **Cloud storage** enables users to buy space on servers that are accessible through an internet connection. You can then share folders and files with other users. Cloud storage uses synchronisation rather than duplication, meaning that it can be accessed and edited by different people and everyone is always looking at the same file and not a copy. This contrasts with email, when the file is duplicated and so it is possible to end up with multiple versions of the same file in different locations! Many software companies, such as Dropbox, Google and Apple, now offer cloud storage.

If you have content that needs to be used in different ways across different platforms, it is important to set up a process for using the same content in

---

**Link**

See Chapter Chapter 17, pages 165–167, for a fuller explanation of resolution.

---

**Top Tip**

For all the assets you need for a digital project, create a checklist showing the output file type, pixel size, resolution and memory size. This will allow you to check that each asset you develop meets the specific requirements of your project.

---

**Cloud storage** virtual file storage space accessed online via a browser

**Fig 27.15** You can turn 3D models into still images for print or online use

> **Central asset repository** a central storage area where all assets are kept
> **Non-destructive editing** a way of editing a digital file or asset without altering or degrading the original

## Top Tip

Many web image software products incorporate non-destructive editing as part of their functionality. Fireworks®, for example, automatically creates new files when exporting for web use.

different formats to ensure consistency. To do this, create a **central asset repository** and call it something specific, such as 'master content'. It should also show the date that the content was created. This folder will contain the source content for the project, such as images, copy, 3D models or sound files. You can then use this content to create different project assets. For example, you can use copy to create graphical elements.

In Figure 27.15, the letter S has been used to create a 3D illustration. Starting with just the font character 'S', further levels of detail have been added using a graphics package such as Photoshop, to give the impression of a 3D object that can be used in an animation or title sequence.

Similarly, you can turn 3D models into still images for print or online use. This involves exporting the 3D image as a 2D format such as a JPEG, as happens with the 3D models used in animated films when production companies want to decorate posters or packaging with printed images of the characters.

The production team must define asset size, resolution and format. It is vital that this core content is not changed in any way. This is ensured by implementing **non-destructive editing**, so that the source file remains unchanged and accurate versions can be created. By using this approach you maintain the quality of your image, as editing can sometimes lead to loss of quality. By keeping a source file you also ensure that you can edit the image again and again in different ways. This is done by using the 'Save as' function, which is part of all software products. For example, imagine you have a high resolution image that needs to be used in different ways on a project:

- first, open the image file
- use 'Save as' to save under another name that shows what the file will be used for
- carry out any edits and amends.

This process preserves the original file and makes a copy that can then be exported and compressed. The same approach could be used when creating a 2D image from a 3D model – in this case the model would be positioned and then an 'Export as' option selected from the file menu. As previously, this process creates a 'version' of the original file while maintaining the original source format.

## Skills Task: **Non destructive editing**

Starting with a photographic image, create three new images that fit the following asset descriptions:

- JPEG format at 300 × 200 pixels, 72 ppi, no bigger than 10 KB
- JPEG format at 350 × 100 pixels, 72 ppi, no bigger than 20 KB
- JPEG format at 500 × 300 pixels, 72 ppi, no bigger than 35 KB

Once you have done this, carry out the same exercise but this time export as PNG files.

Keep track of your original file, always use it as the starting point and always end up with new versions of your file.

# RECORD-KEEPING

When a project has so much content and so many variations that it becomes confusing, **version control** comes into play. Version control enables the production team to track which version of the project they are currently working on and what came before. A simple way to do this is to number the stages of the project. You can do this using a spreadsheet and the following columns:

- Version number: This starts at 1.0 and continues to 1.9 before moving on to 2.0. You define any smaller increments by adding an extra digit, for example, version 1.1.1.
- Date: this states when the version was completed.
- Notes: This states what the main changes were and who carried out the changes.

This system allows the production team to easily determine what the most recent version of the content is and to access older versions. Software development companies often use similar processes when creating products. These versions are known as **product releases** and form part of the production process.

> **Version control** a way of recording edits to an asset or group of assets
> **Product release** a way of defining a specific version of a software product

## Case study: **CluedUpp Games**

CluedUpp Games creates innovative experiences using specific locations and mobile technology known as 'geolocation'. Users participate in escape-room style challenges to unlock game levels, crack clues and complete challenges to solve a themed mystery against the clock. In each case, the experience is based in a specific location so the cityscape itself becomes part of the story narrative, and users become active participants in the mystery-solving using their mobile phones.

To achieve this, the CluedUpp app makes use of phone functions such as location-based services, the microphone and gestural controls to create a unique user experience. For example, in the 'Alice in Wonderland' experience, users are asked to blow out a candle on a birthday cake. This is achieved by using the microphone in the mobile device in combination with an animation of a candle flame. By blowing into the microphone, the flame animation reduces in size, giving the impression that the user is actually 'blowing out' the candle. By adding a time restriction, the user experience and game narrative are further enhanced. Other examples include augmented reality, which allows users to join their favourite characters and take a selfie, and the use of interactive maps to guide users to different parts of the location to find clues.

**Figure 27.16** This example is from the Beauty and the Beast themed game, where users have to pick a lock against the clock in a time challenge.

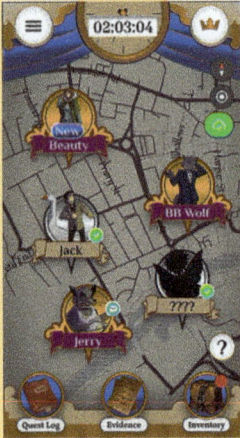

**Figure 27.17** This example is also from the Beauty and the Beast game, and shows the interactive map.

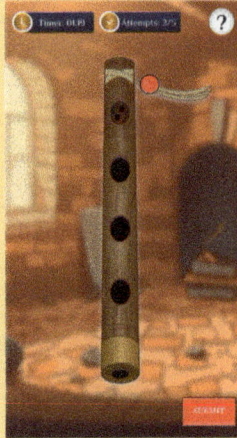

**Figure 27.18** In this mini game, users blow gently into their phone's microphone to play the flute to calm the Beast.

## Further references

**Books**
- *Digital Design Theory (Design Briefs)* (Helen Armstrong, 2016)
- *Interdisciplinary Interaction Design: A Visual Guide to Basic Theories, Models and Ideas for Thinking and Designing for Interactive Web Design and Digital Device Experiences* (James Pannafino, 2012)
- *Multimedia Storytelling for Digital Communicators in a Multiplatform World* (Seth Gitner, 2015)
- *Practical Approaches For Designing Accessible Websites* (Smashing Magazine, 2015; ebook)
- *Practical Augmented Reality: A Guide to the Technologies, Applications and Human Factors for Ar and Vr* (Steve Aukstakalnis, 2017)

# 28 Website design

## 28.1 WHAT IS A WEBSITE?

Websites are now a fundamental part of how we work and live. The first website was published in 1991 and now there are at least 300 million websites, with more being added every day. So, what exactly is a website? In simple terms, a website is some documents (called **web pages**) arranged under a specific name (or **domain**) that is accessible using a device connected to the internet. You access a website using a piece of software on the device, called a **browser**, which connects to the website name via a specific format called the Uniform Resource Locator (or **URL**). The most important aspect of any website design, however, is the end user and how they use the website.

Think of a website as a box of paper documents (web pages) with its unique name written on the outside (the URL). To find the box you just need the name and to open the box you need a special tool (the browser). The browser interprets website elements such as copy, images and hyperlinks as well as files that contain other information that control layout and interactivity. The browser presents the website content so that it makes sense to the user. The challenge for the designer is to create appealing designs that also work within the restrictions of the browser. Figure 28.1 shows a typical company website with logos, images, hyperlinks and **hypertext** (text that contains links to other text) all highlighted in green. It contains the following key elements common to most websites:

- **Header**: area at the top containing critical information that generally appears on every page of a website, for example, the company logo.
- **Navigation bar**: a row of navigation buttons at the top of the screen, often within the header, that guide the user to key content.
- Main content areas: areas of the page that hold the text and visual content, frequently updated or changed.
- **Footer**: area at the bottom of the screen that generally appears on every page of a website, often containing company contact details and links to social media.

**Web pages** digital documents (written in HTML) that display website content

**Domain** the actual name that forms the website address

**Browser** software for viewing website pages

**URL** Uniform Resource Locator, the website's address on the internet

**Hypertext** copy or text used on a web page, often linking to other information, such as text or graphics

**Header** section of a website that appears at the top of each web page

**Navigation bar** a series of navigation buttons that guide the user to content

**Footer** section of a website that appears at the bottom of each web page

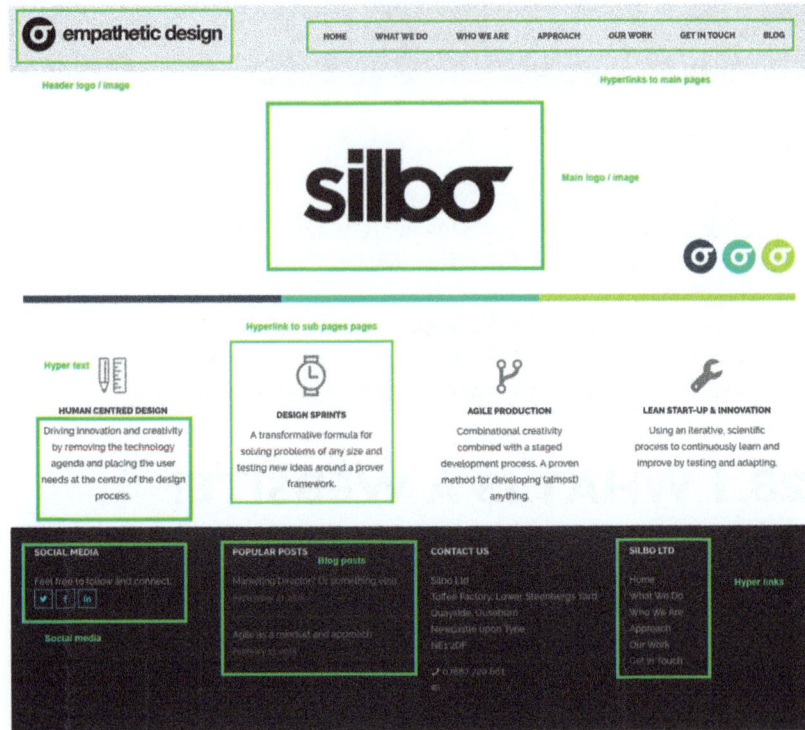

**Fig 28.1** The Silbo website showing the main areas highlighted

# 28.2 PRINCIPLES AND DESIGN OF WEBSITE NAVIGATION

In many cases the most important part of a website is its navigation. How a user finds what they need and how quickly they are able to do this, is essential to the user experience. A good way to start thinking about this is to split the navigation into three stages: primary, secondary and tertiary navigation.

## PRIMARY NAVIGATION

This is the most important element and shows what the user absolutely needs to access. In Figure 28.2 the primary navigation is shown in a navigation bar at the top of the page and outlined in red. This presents the user with the key areas of the website.

## SECONDARY NAVIGATION

This is less critical than the primary navigation but still important. It often takes the form of a sub-navigation or a menu that appears when a primary navigation option has been selected. In Figure 28.2, the secondary navigation 'Design Sprints' (highlighted with the red box in the centre) presents content related to the primary navigation option 'What we do'.

## TERTIARY NAVIGATION

This option usually refers to other navigation elements that do not relate to the website aims or content but have to be included, such as Terms and conditions. In this case the tertiary navigation (highlighted in yellow) replicates the primary navigation in the website footer.

# SIGNPOSTING

In addition to the navigation elements, you should consider signposting. This refers to the style of language used when creating a navigation system. For example, a website for a design company will need a section that shows examples of their previous work and so, as in this case, you might use 'Our Work' (or 'Portfolio') to signpost that work.

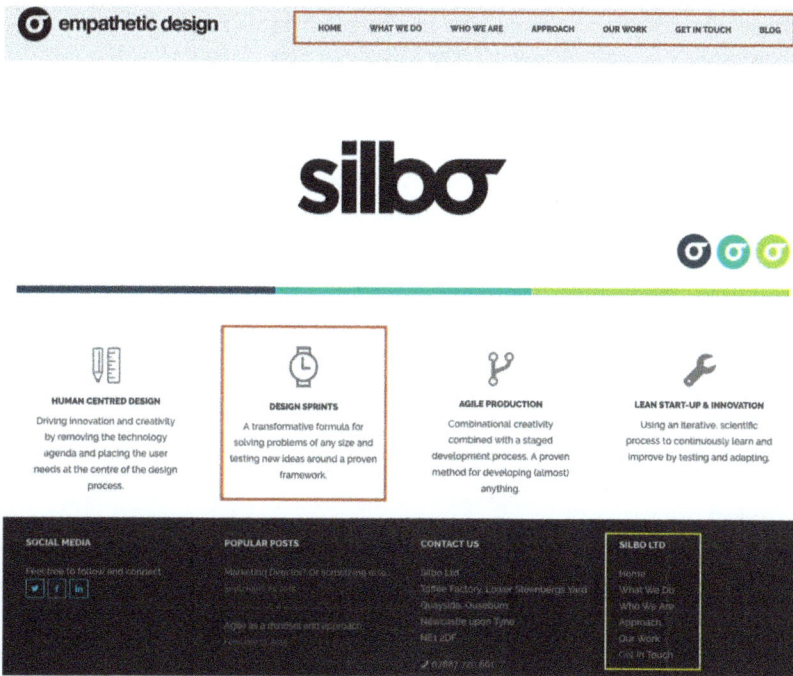

**Fig 28.2** The Silbo website showing signposting

# 28.3 INFORMATION ARCHITECTURE

One of the most common problems faced by designers of complex websites is how to arrange the content in a meaningful and intuitive way. Information architecture design deals with this issue by creating systems that guide the users through the website content, so they can find what they need.

While all websites are different and have varying levels of content, there are some basic ground rules that should be followed.

## RESEARCH YOUR USERS

As discussed in Part 2, understanding your users' needs is essential to any design process. Research what your users will want to see and when. Use personas to understand your users in as much detail as possible. For example, where will they be when they access the website – at home, in the office or on the move? This will enable you to create information architecture that will enhance their experience.

### Have a clear purpose

Every website should have a clearly defined purpose, whether to sell a product, to entertain or to inform. Without a clear purpose, it can be difficult to create any kind of meaningful information architecture.

### Be consistent

Consistency will help users to learn the information structure and be able to find what they need as quickly and efficiently as possible.

## SITEMAPS

To create your information architecture, first sketch out the information flow using sitemaps and wireframes. Sitemaps are ways of visualising the information contained in a website as a series of pages and page titles. There are many different types of sitemaps but here are some of the most common:

### Ladder or sequential diagrams

A **ladder diagram** is used to represent a website's information architecture in a linear fashion. This approach works well when users need to perform a specific set of actions in a process. Many banking applications or websites that use complex security are mapped out using a ladder diagram. A banking website might require users to follow a procedure, such as:

- launch a home page
- enter login details
- enter secondary login details
- access accounts
- select main account.

This process would be mapped as a series of vertical (ladder) or horizontal (sequential) steps, as in Figure 28.3.

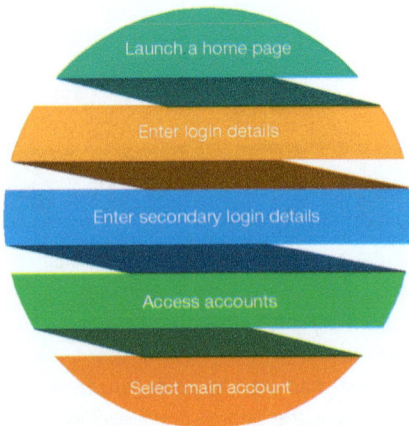

**Fig 28.3** A ladder diagram represents a website's information architecture in a linear fashion

**Ladder diagram** method for visually organising web pages in a sequence
**Tree diagram** method for visually organising web pages by section or title

### Tree diagrams

This approach is used when more complex levels of information are involved and when the user may need to navigate to different parts of a site that are not immediately visible. The content is often arranged according to the primary, secondary and tertiary navigation structure discussed earlier. The example in Figure 28.4 shows a **tree diagram** for a web design company.

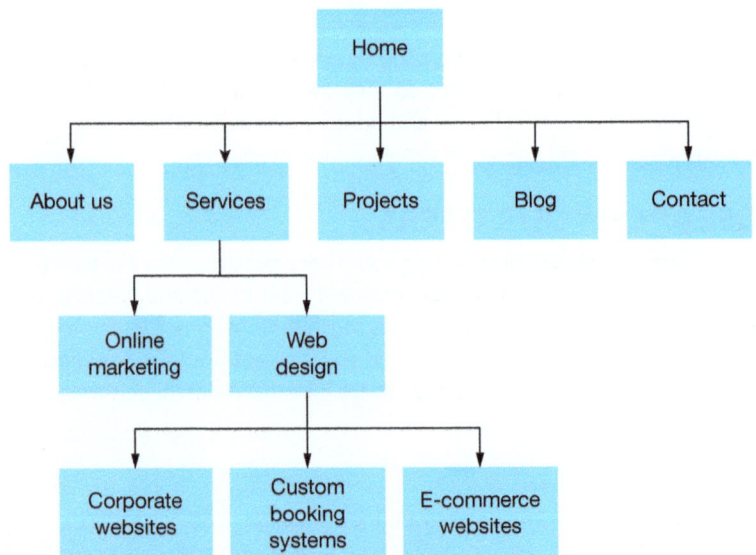

**Fig 28.4** A tree diagram for a web design company

## Full sitemaps

A complex website will require a full **sitemap** that shows all sections of the site. In this case you would colour code specific areas of the website, to define types of interaction or different user groups; see the example shown in Figure 28.5 which shows a full sitemap for a large technology company's website. Creating a full sitemap with each area defined will enable you to create a website that helps users find what they need as quickly as possible.

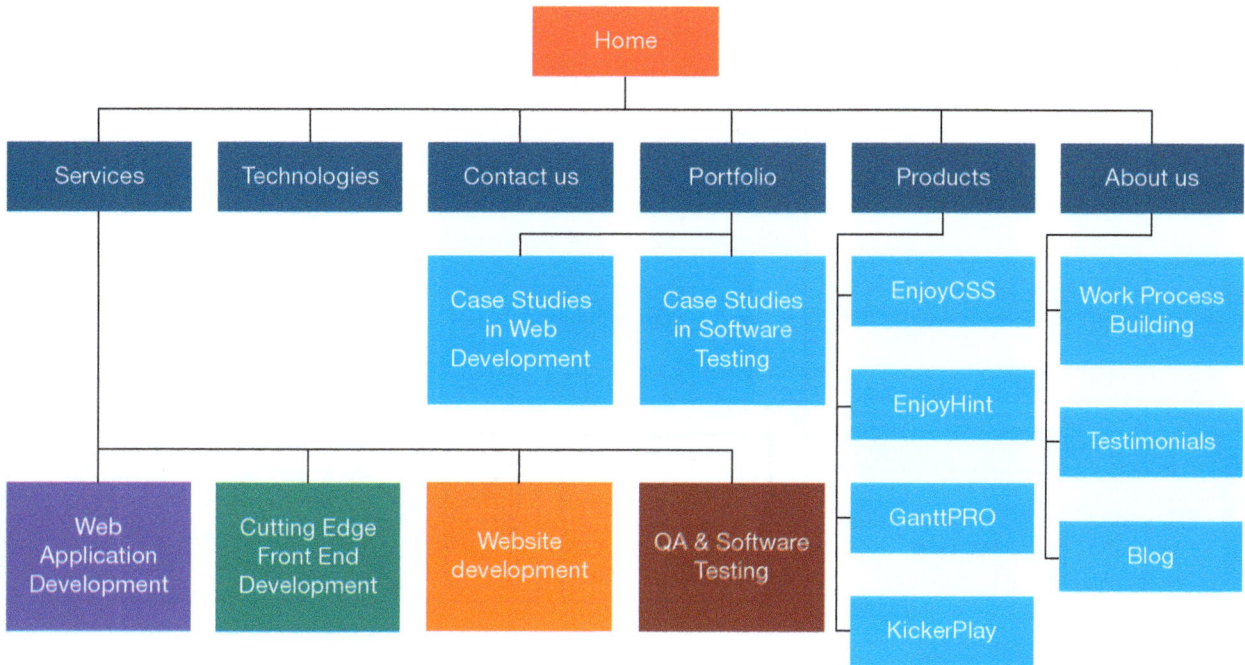

**Fig 28.5** A complex website requires a full sitemap

## Wireframes

Wireframes are versions of the pages that show what the user needs to see at each stage and what each page contains. Wireframes also include basic layout elements and indicate how a page will look when it has been created. You can do **wireframing** by hand-drawing the pages or using wireframing software, such as Balsamiq and InVision. By creating wireframes you can add more detail to your designs. Once completed, wireframe designs can be shared with a client for feedback and then used to create screen designs.

Figure 28.6 shows a wireframe created using the Balsamiq application and demonstrates where key elements, such as company name, images, copy and the video player, will sit on this web page.

---

### Project work: **Create a sitemap and wireframes**

Imagine you are creating a website for a small company that sells a product or service. Create a sitemap of the website using whichever method suits the information architecture best. Then create wireframes of at least five of the pages. Share these with your class. Discuss why you chose to create the sitemap the way you did and what the wireframes show.

**Sitemap** diagram or model of a website's content that shows how the content is organised and how different content elements relate to one another
**Wireframing** method for creating simple diagrams of individual web pages

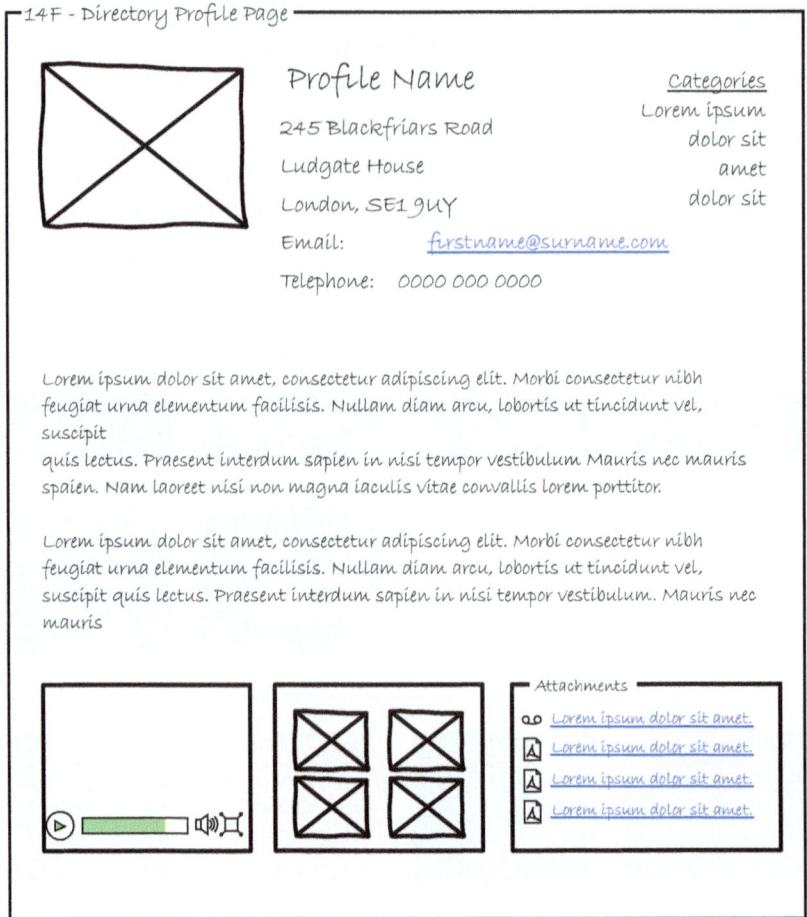

14F - Directory Profile Page

**Profile Name**

245 Blackfriars Road

Ludgate House

London, SE1 9UY

Email:          firstname@surname.com

Telephone:    0000 000 0000

Categories
Lorem ipsum
dolor sit
amet
dolor sit

Lorem ipsum dolor sit amet, consectetur adipiscing elit. Morbi consectetur nibh feugiat urna elementum facilisis. Nullam diam arcu, lobortis ut tincidunt vel, suscipit
quis lectus. Praesent interdum sapien in nisi tempor vestibulum Mauris nec mauris spaien. Nam laoreet nisi non magna iaculis vitae convallis lorem porttitor.

Lorem ipsum dolor sit amet, consectetur adipiscing elit. Morbi consectetur nibh feugiat urna elementum facilisis. Nullam diam arcu, lobortis ut tincidunt vel, suscipit quis lectus. Praesent interdum sapien in nisi tempor vestibulum. Mauris nec mauris

Attachments
Lorem ipsum dolor sit amet.
Lorem ipsum dolor sit amet.
Lorem ipsum dolor sit amet.
Lorem ipsum dolor sit amet.

**Fig 28.6** An example of a wireframe

# 28.4 USING GRIDS AND LAYOUT DESIGNS

The visual design of a website is defined by a range of factors. For example, a client may have clear branding guidelines relating to colour usage and a logo. A website that uses a lot of video will require a different visual design to a text-heavy magazine. There are, however, some basic principles that you should apply when creating page designs.

## GRID SYSTEMS

A grid system provides a visual structure for a website that enables content elements to be organised so that information is presented clearly and consistently. A grid system also enables a designer to create multiple layout options quickly without having to start afresh each time while helping the user 'learn' how to use interfaces that always present certain elements in the same places.

### The 960 grid system

One of the most commonly used grid systems is the 960 grid, which has a width of 960 pixels that fits into a 1024 x 768 pixel display without the need for horizontal scrolling. There are two variants: 12 and 16 columns. The 12-column grid is divided into sections that are 60 pixels wide. The 16-column grid consists of 40 pixel sections. Each column has 10 pixels of margin on the left and right, which create 20-pixel-wide borders between the columns.

Each variation of the grid allows the designer to create different layouts and use the space in different ways. The examples in Figures 28.7 and 28.8 from the grid templates website 960.gs show the 12-column grid on the left and the 16-column grid on the right. Notice how the 12-column grid is used to position the visual elements so they are balanced. The 16-column grid example is usually used when a design needs to contain more visual elements. If you look closely at the 16-column grid example, it includes more screen content; also, the grid system supports the visual structure of the main image and the content box to the left-hand side that is superimposed over the main image. In both cases the grid is used to support the main navigation by placing it in a prominent place at the top of the screen.

You can use grid systems to create **mock-up images** of your website pages in a graphics package such as Adobe Photoshop and add them to website templates.

> **Mock-up images** digital designs used to show how a website will look
> **Transform tool** Photoshop tool for transforming things, such as scale, size and rotation
> **Shape tool** Photoshop tool for creating simple shapes
> **Photoshop guides** grid lines used to help designers layout content
> **Slice tool** Photoshop tool for slicing a larger image into smaller images

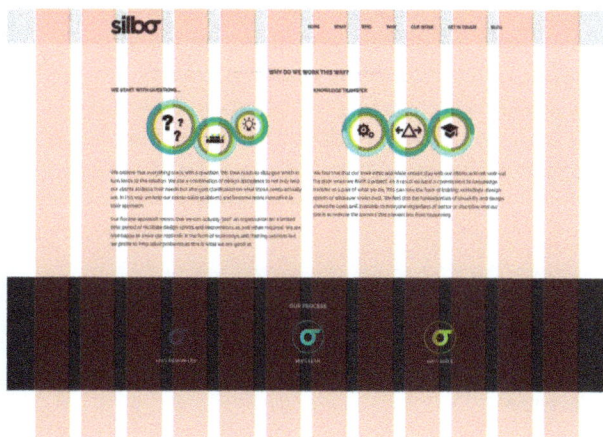

**Fig 28.7** A 12-column 960 grid system

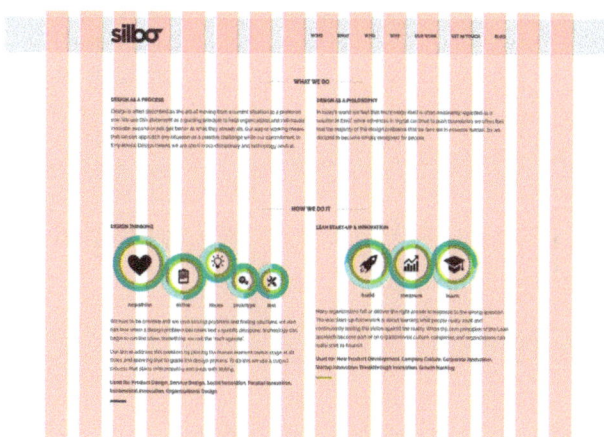

**Fig 28.8** A 16-column 960 grid system

- Download a grid system Photoshop file from the 960.gs website.
- Save the file as a new file on your desktop called 'layout_01.psd'.
- Create a folder on your desktop called 'content'.
- Create 'text' and 'images' sub-folders and add text and images to them.
- Add images to 'layout_01.psd' and resize using the **Transform tool**.
- Add text to 'layout_01.psd' by drawing a text box and inserting text.
- Add shapes to 'layout_01.psd' by using the **Shape tool**.
- Make sure you align everything to the **Photoshop guides** that make up the grid.

You should then have an image with some layout elements, similar to Figure 28.9, which you can export as a JPEG file to show to clients and to be coded into a web page.

You will also need to export the images you used. Use the **Slice tool** to draw a box around the images and use the 'Save for Web' option to export the images in the correct format and resolution. The Slice tool allows you to divide your design into areas and to save the images separately, making the web development workflow a lot smoother.

**Fig 28.9** A screen showing the Photoshop guides

## LAYOUT DESIGNS AND READING DIRECTION

As well as creating consistency, layout designs also enable you to take advantage of how users generally read through a design. The most common examples of layout designs are the Gutenberg layout, the Z-pattern layout and the F-pattern layout.

> **Top Tip**
>
> To view your design without the Photoshop Guides, go to View > Show > Guides and untick the Guides option.

## The Gutenberg layout

The Gutenberg layout shown below in Figure 28.10 is often applied to text-heavy content such as in newspapers or magazine websites. It divides the layout into four areas:

- The **primary optical area** is located in the top/left. This is where the eye 'starts' when looking at the page.
- The strong **fallow area** is located in the top/right. Fallow areas are where the eye is less active.
- The weak fallow area is located in the bottom/left.
- The **terminal area** is located in the bottom/right. The terminal area is where the eye comes to rest or 'finishes' reading.

The pattern helps the eye move across and down the page in a series of horizontal movements called **axes of orientation**. Each eye movement starts slightly further from the left edge and moves slightly closer to the right edge. The eye travels from the primary optical area to the terminal optical area, and the path is referred to as the **reading gravity**. This applies to left-to-right reading languages such as English and would be reversed for right-to-left reading languages such as Arabic. In the Gutenberg layout you should place important page elements, such as logos, headlines or key images, either in the primary optical area or somewhere along the reading gravity path.

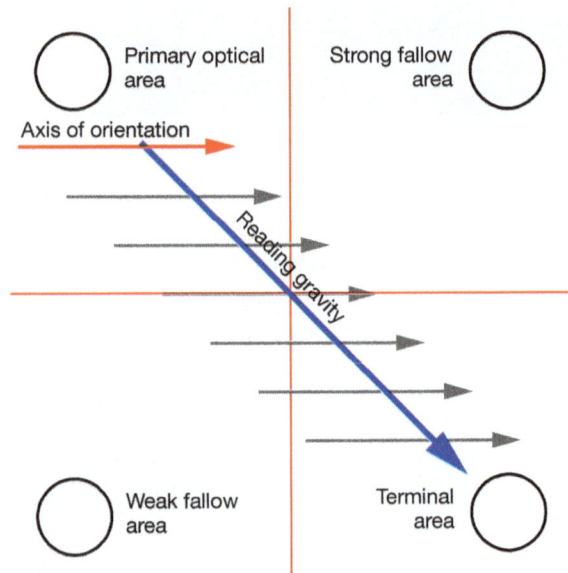

**Fig 28.10** The Gutenberg layout: logos, headlines or key images are placed in the primary optical area or along the reading gravity path

## Z-pattern layout

This follows the shape of the letter z, as shown in Figure 28.11:

- starts top left
- moves across the page to top right
- then moves diagonally down the page to the bottom left
- finishes with another horizontal movement to the bottom right.

You would use a Z-pattern layout when your page contains fewer elements. As with the Gutenberg layout, it is best to place important elements either at the starting point in the top left or somewhere along the reading gravity path.

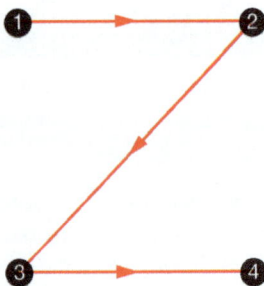

**Fig 28.11** The Z-pattern layout

### F-pattern layout

This pattern follows the shape of a letter F, as shown in Figure 28.12:

- starts top left
- moves across the page to top right
- moves back to the left edge before moving horizontally to the right, but not as far as before
- the eye moves less and less to the right as the reader progresses down the page.

In an F-pattern layout it is best to position important information across the top of the page because the viewer reads the whole line length. Place less important information along the left edge of the layout, ideally using bullet points, because this is where minimal horizontal eye movement is required to read the content.

## WHITE/NEGATIVE SPACE

Each of the layout designs shown demonstrate how to arrange elements on a page. Another important aspect of web design is how to use the space in between, sometimes called white space or negative space. Designers can use the white space to draw attention to imagery and create a feeling of clarity, spaciousness and balance.

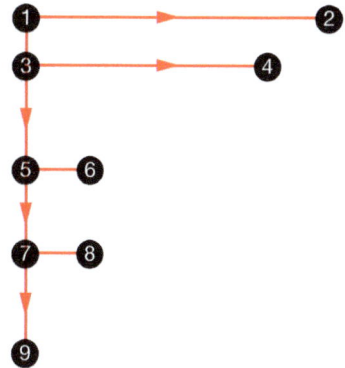

**Fig 28.12** The F-pattern layout

---

### Skills Task: **Layout designs**

Search the web for examples of each layout type discussed in this chapter. Then in small groups decide how you would redesign each website using different layout designs. For example, if website A originally used a Z-pattern layout, think about how you would change it into an F-pattern layout, a Gutenberg or a 960 grid pattern. Also consider how white space is used. Present your ideas to the class and discuss.

---

# 28.5 RESPONSIVE AND ADAPTIVE DESIGN

Web designers have no control over how the end user will view the website. If a designer creates a layout for a large monitor, what happens if the user only has a small laptop or mobile phone screen? Designers solve this problem by creating responsive and adaptive designs that change to match the screen size (Figure 28.13).

## RESPONSIVE DESIGN

This adapts to the size of the screen no matter what the target device, as seen in the image below. Notice how the main content on the mobile version has been rearranged to display vertically. Responsive design uses **cascading style sheets (CSS)** to change website dimensions and style based on the target device specifications, such as display type, width or height. Many new websites use responsive design, which has been made easier by software systems, such as WordPress, Joomla!® and Drupal, that have responsive design capabilities. To ensure that a responsive design works, designers often create visual mock-ups of all screen sizes, to ensure that everything has the right visual appeal.

> **Cascading style sheets (CSS)** files that control the styles used on all the pages of a website

**Fig 28.13** A website shown on different screen sizes

## ADAPTIVE DESIGN

This detects the screen size being used and then chooses the appropriate design from a selection. While this approach works it can be time consuming to create up to six versions of a website or interface to ensure that a user can access the content. Adaptive design is useful for making an existing website more mobile friendly. This allows the designer to create designs for different devices, enabling control that is not possible using responsive design.

### Skills Task: **Prepare responsive/adaptive mock-ups**

Do a web search using the terms: responsive, design, psd, template, free. This should provide a responsive design template that you can download for free and use in Photoshop. Open a new Photoshop document and create a basic web page layout using a grid and blocks of colour. Then open your responsive design template and copy and paste your layout into the desktop PC part of the template. Try to replicate the layout in the other devices in the template. Can you make the design work in all the devices?

### Project work: **Produce a web page layout**

Using the 960 grid and the skills practised in this section, produce a basic 12-column layout of a new website with text, images, shapes and any other elements that you have collected. Remember: the grid system will automatically provide the consistency and structure, so experiment with layout design and think about white space. Print out an example of the 960 grid and then use highlighters to define your layout areas. Do not worry too much about your design looking finished, as this exercise is about understanding layout.

## 28.6 WEBSITE USABILITY PRINCIPLES

Usability describes how easy user interfaces are to use. The word 'usability' also describes methods for improving ease-of-use during the design process. For example, usability testing for an interface would revolve around things such as how long a user took to make a decision and whether they remembered how to do the same thing at a later stage. A good example is a TV remote control. A user will rarely stop to appreciate the aesthetics of a remote control but they will react to how easy it is to use.

Many of the core principles of website usability were defined by usability expert Jakob Nielsen in his book *Designing Web Usability* (1999). Nielson identifies five elements of usability:

- Learnability: How easy is it for users to accomplish basic tasks the first time they encounter the design? Can they find the elements they need and is everything presented in a user-friendly way?
- Efficiency: Once users have learned the design, how quickly can they perform new tasks? Do they already know how to achieve a task or do they need to learn it again each time?
- Memorability: When users return to the design after a period of not using it, how easily can they reorient themselves? Do they need to ask questions or is the interface easy to remember?
- Errors: How many errors do users make, how severe are these errors, and how easily can they recover from the errors? Is the interface design frustrating to use? Do users become angry or stressed when using the interface?
- Satisfaction: How pleasant is the design? Does it have a good visual appeal and do the interactions flow naturally? If not, how could this be addressed?

Another important aspect to usability is utility, which refers to the design's functionality: Does it do what users need it to do and does it help or hinder the user? To study an interface's design utility or usability, you can follow a simple three-stage process.

1. Utility: whether it provides the features the user needs.
2. Usability: how easy and pleasant these features are to use.
3. Usefulness: usability + utility.

This process can help in the initial design of an interface and also when testing an interface to determine whether it is working correctly and meeting the users' needs. For example, a website's utility would incorporate the key aims of the website as presented by the information architecture and layout design. Questions such as: 'Can my users complete key tasks?' and 'Are the elements clearly signposted?' should form part of this stage. A website's usability would relate to how those aims were supported and fulfilled. Questions such as 'Did I get lost when I clicked the navigation?' and 'Did I have to search for anything?' should form part of this stage.

## Skills Task: **Exploring website usability**

In pairs or small groups, use the three-stage process described above to examine and analyse the interface of a website that you are familiar with, thinking about Nielsen's five elements of usability. Present your findings to the class and then discuss each group's findings.

## Case study: **No Strings website**

No Strings is an International NGO (non-governmental organisation) that uses a combination of puppets and film-making to teach life-saving messages to children. No Strings' first project focused on landmine awareness in Afghanistan and used a well-known children's story to illustrate how to recognise and avoid landmines. The website was designed and constructed by Offstone Publishing in the UK.

Offstone and No Strings started by identifying the purpose of the website and user personas and motivations. They identified two main user types: fundraiser/activist/follower and partner/associate. Offstone then created a simple tree diagram showing all the relevant pages and content areas and tested it for usability against a series of scenarios, focusing on the number of mouse clicks potential users needed to access different areas of the site.

The second stage was to create a visual look and feel inspired by the hand-made puppets and the children's responses to them. The site uses a lot of photographs of the work that No Strings does to reinforce the visual impact. In addition the site uses video content streamed from the Vimeo platform using embedded code. The colour palette uses vibrant orange and black for the dominant elements such as the header image, a more muted yellow and green for sub-navigation, and bright blue for the News and call to action 'Take Part'. The primary navigation uses dark red in conjunction with the orange to create a clear navigation bar at the top of the page. Testimonials and quotes from patrons and associates are incorporated into the design, balancing the area to the right of the news section.

The website is laid out on a basic grid system that uses a combination of Z- and F-patterns to guide the user through the content. The Z-pattern leads the reader across the screen until the 'News' section and the F-pattern 'finishes' the screen by presenting the user with the 'Take Part' button at the bottom of the screen. The site uses simple but effective signposting such as 'About Us' and 'Programmes', while the additional links stating 'view' tell the user that there is more to see if they click.

Offstone used a WordPress template for the website, enabling them to create a visually striking, functional website without the need for extensive coding. WordPress plug-ins enabled the image gallery shown on the home page and the social media feeds in the footer. Some HTML and CSS development was needed, but only to make small changes to the underlying structure and colour usage. This meant that the development time was reduced considerably and as a result costs were kept relatively low.

**Fig 28.17** The No Strings homepage

### Further references

#### Books
- *Balanced Website Design: Optimising Aesthetics, Usability and Purpose* (Dave Lawrence and Soheyla Tavakol, 2010)
- *Designing Web Usability: The Practice of Simplicity* (Jakob Nielsen, 1999)
- *Web Design Start Here: A no-nonsense, jargon-free guide to the fundamentals of web design* (Stefan Mischook, 2015)
- *Wordpress for Beginners 2017: A Visual Step-by-Step Guide to Mastering Wordpress* (Andy Williams, 2016)

# 29  Mobile applications

## Learning Aims

By the end of this chapter you will be able to:
- Understand design for mobile devices and incorporate images, animation and audio content
- Explain the visual design process
- Understand the elements of UX and UI
- Understand contemporary practice in developing mobile apps, and for multiple devices

## 29.1 DESIGNING FOR MOBILE

When designing user interfaces (UI) and user experiences (UX) for **games design and mobile and multimedia applications**, professional designers must consider elements such as icon design and layout. For example, Apple has an **software development kit** (SDK) called UIkit. This is a programming framework that uses graphical interface elements that fit into three main categories:

- **Mobile app bars**: these horizontal elements stretching across the app display tell people where they are in the app, provide navigation, and may contain buttons or other elements for initiating actions and communicating information, as shown in Figure 29.1.

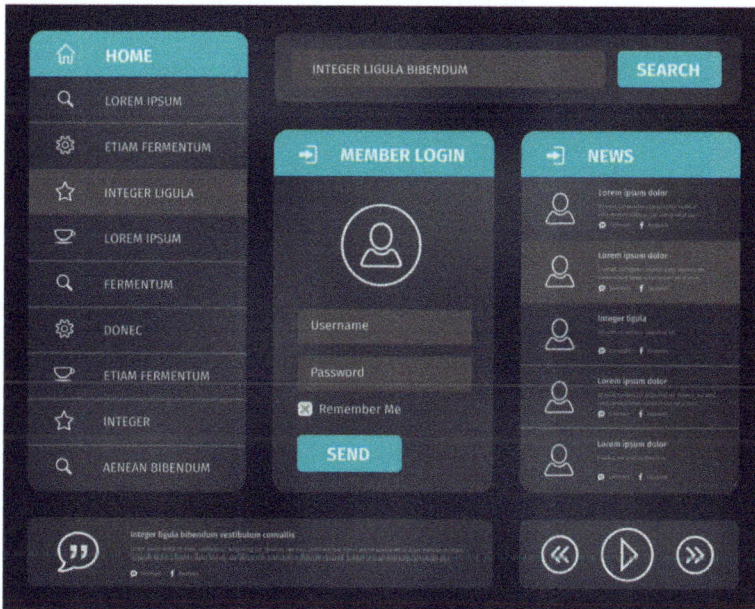

**Fig 29.1** A mobile interface view

- **Mobile app views**: these contain the primary content people see in the app, such as text, graphics, animations and interactive elements. Views can enable behaviours, such as scrolling, insertion, deletion and arrangement.

**Mobile app bars**  horizontal UI elements that tell users where they are in an app

**Mobile app views**  UI elements that contain the primary content, such as text graphics or images

**Games design and mobile and multimedia applications**  digital applications which combine media, are accessed through mobile devices, or are designed for entertainment or educational purposes.

**Software development kit (SDK)**  used to create apps for a specific device

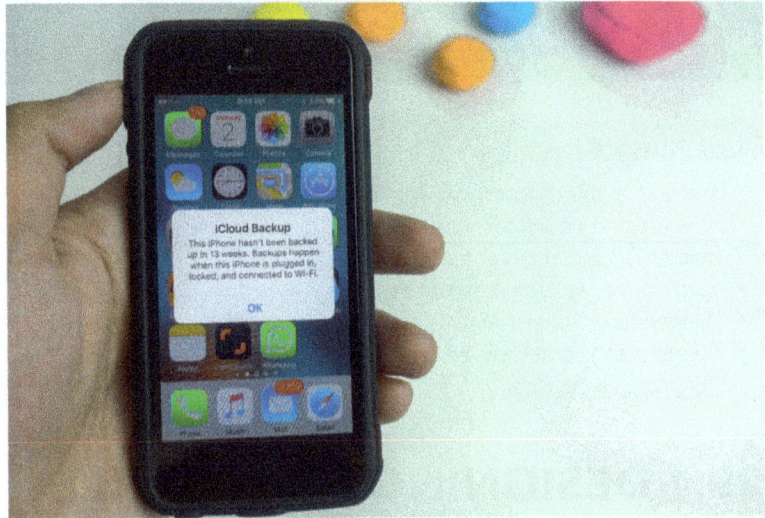

**Fig 29.2** Mobile interface controls

**Mobile app controls**  UI elements used to initiate actions, for example, buttons

**Fig 29.3** Buttons (left) and text fields (right) are examples of mobile app controls

- **Mobile app controls**: these initiate actions and convey information. Buttons, switches, text fields and progress indicators are examples of controls.

These elements are adaptable, so developers can create a single app for multiple Apple devices while maintaining a consistent appearance. They also automatically update when the IOS system introduces appearance changes. When designing an app you incorporate these elements into your screen designs and Apple provides a library of graphical assets for this purpose. If you do not have access to a developer account, interface elements are also available as Photoshop image files from websites such as Medialoot.

In addition to defining the interface, UIKit defines the functionality your app can use. For example, UIKit enables apps to respond to gestures on the touchscreen and supports features such as drawing and printing. Apple also provides guidance and restrictions around other elements, such as animation, branding, colour usage, layout and typography. These guidelines instruct designers how to make the best possible use of the SDK and device specifications. As system software changes and devices are upgraded, it is essential that designers stay up to date with the latest guidelines and UI elements; otherwise Apple will reject their apps and they will never appear in App Store.

Android devices have similar UI and UX guidelines for app creation, called Material Design. This is a guide for graphics, animation, video and interaction design across all Android devices. The guidelines for using Material Design are freely available online and incorporate elements, such as motion, style, layout, components and usability. As with Apple apps, it is essential for any designer developing Android apps to fully understand the relevant SDKs, device specifications and guidelines.

When designing mobile applications, as well as the guidelines and SDKs published by manufacturers, there are also some basic design principles to consider.

## SCREEN DESIGN FOR MOBILE

Mobile devices by their very nature usually have quite a limited screen size. Fortunately, both the Apple iOS and Android platforms have published extensive guidelines so that designers have a ready-to-use set of resources to hand. Apple iOS guidelines are available at the Apple website under 'Human Interface Guidelines'. Similarly, Android guidelines are shown under the Google search term m3.Material.io.

# MAKE NAVIGATION SIMPLE

Touchscreens can make navigation difficult because they are so sensitive and because people have varying finger sizes. To address this prioritise your navigation around key functionality – make sure the most commonly used elements go at the top of the screen, and minimise the levels of navigation involved. Keep things simple and ensure your navigation signposting is clear and concise.

# MINIMISE COPY CONTENT

Do not overwhelm your users with too much copy, or require them to scroll down too much. The small screen works well for animation and video but is less well suited to large chunks of text.

# INTEGRATING AUDIO

Mobile devices are used in a wide variety of environments. In order that users of your app can hear your audio content clearly in a noisy environment, ensure that your audio is distinctive and clearly audible as soon as it starts to play. You should also provide a quick and easy way to turn the audio down or off when users are in quiet environments, as well as incorporating subtitles or transcripts for any film content or voiceovers, so that users can access the content in silent mode or when it is too noisy to hear anything.

# INTEGRATING ANIMATION

Animations attract attention and can make apps more user-friendly by explaining how they work and guiding users through tasks. However, they must neither distract from the main purpose of your app nor use up too much processing power or memory.

When thinking about animation, consider the following three types: visual feedback, visual prompt and orientation in space.

## Visual feedback

You can use animation to tell your user that they have completed a task or reached a goal, for example, by a 'check' or tick symbol appearing from the right of the screen. Visual feedback also indicates to the user that the app is working properly and they are in control.

## Visual prompt

You can also use animation to tell the user what to do next, for example, elements such as arrows and pointers can appear on-screen to indicate to the user that they need to swipe or press to proceed. This approach is employed when users need to complete a process in order to sign up or use an application.

## Orientation in space

A screen that contains a lot of elements can appear cluttered. You can use animation to show users where elements such as sub-navigation buttons are by moving other elements off the screen; for example, when the Home button is pressed, animated icons may 'rearrange' themselves on the display, or a sub-navigation may only appear when an element is pressed. Apple's iPhone uses animation to make the app icons enlarge and reduce in size when selected.

## INTEGRATING IMAGES, VIDEO AND ILLUSTRATIONS

Clear, bold and relevant imagery helps to engage users and keep them focused. The following principles and practices can help you effectively incorporate images and video into your mobile application experience.

- Make sure your images are context-specific, and relate directly to where the user is within the app.
- Use simple images with a strong focal point; due to the small screen size images need to be bold and vibrant, so do not use anything too abstract and try to avoid stock photography.
- Remember that your app users may be outside – looking at a screen in bright sunshine, or at night-time, or in pouring rain – so make images clear and bold.

Combine photography and illustration in the same experience if you feel this combination can communicate more.

## THINK ABOUT USER INTERACTIONS

When a user holds a device they may accidentally click buttons or get lost in the user flow when their hand covers part of the screen. They may also have a short attention span and become lost when they are trying to complete a task. To address this, try to consider as many user scenarios (and types of users) as possible when you start to design your app and make sure you explore them fully in the sketching stage. Also make sure you fully understand your user.

# 29.2 THE VISUAL DESIGN PROCESS

In many ways, designing for mobile is no different from designing for the web and is usually a four-stage process involving sketching, wireframing, **visual production** and prototyping. At each stage the user journey is the critical priority.

## STAGE 1: SKETCHING

Sketch the user interactions for your app on separate pieces of paper. A good way to approach this is to use a basic screen template and write the user actions along with any other UI elements that you feel need to be included such as buttons. The basic elements that make up these screens can come from user stories or they can be your own ideas. Figure 29.4 shows a sketch for the process of launching an app, logging in, editing and saving a profile.

Place the sketches in sequence on a large wall. Then map the interactions and corresponding transitions between the pages by identifying the type of interaction that triggers the transition, for example, a swipe left or 'next' button. Continue until you have completed the user journey. It may not be possible to complete the whole journey on one wall, in which case divide the user journey into smaller sections. Make sure your UI elements correspond with the SDKs and device specifications discussed earlier. Then get feedback on your user journey and user interactions from your client and, ideally, your target audience.

**Visual production** using detailed mock-ups to visually represent an app process

### Link

See Chapter 6, pages 66–68, for more on user stories.

### Top Tip

When thinking about UI and UX, creatively mapping the visual design process will help you to identify any problems as you work, and allow you to create solutions more easily.

| Launch app | Login | Open Profile | Edit and Save |
|---|---|---|---|

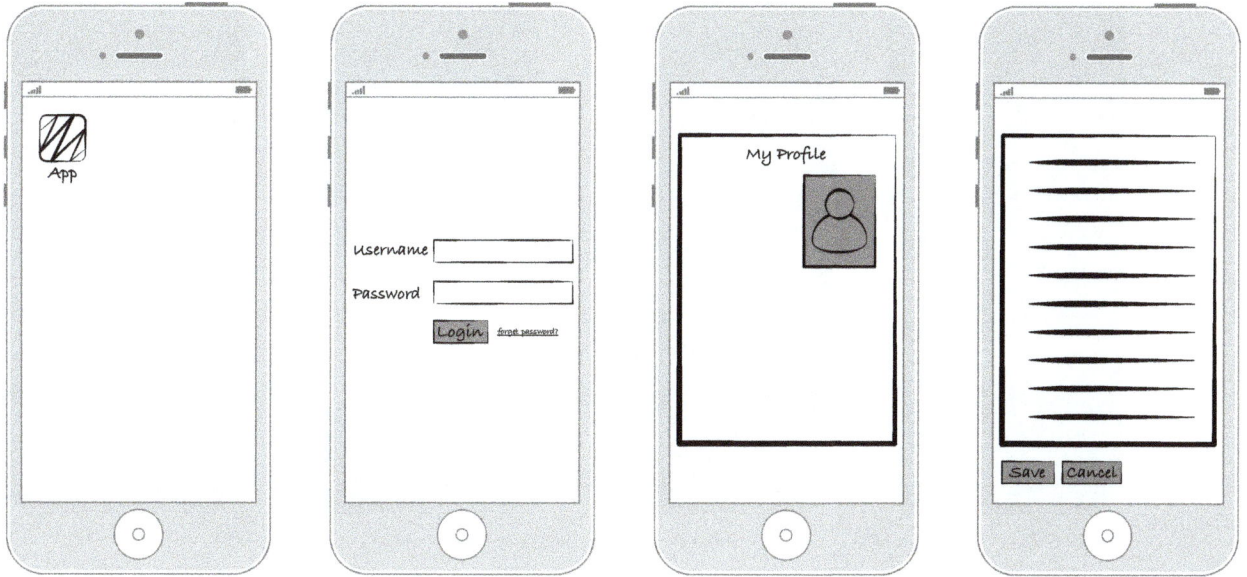

**Fig 29.4** Sketching elements on a device template

| Launch app | Login | Open Profile | Edit and Save |
|---|---|---|---|

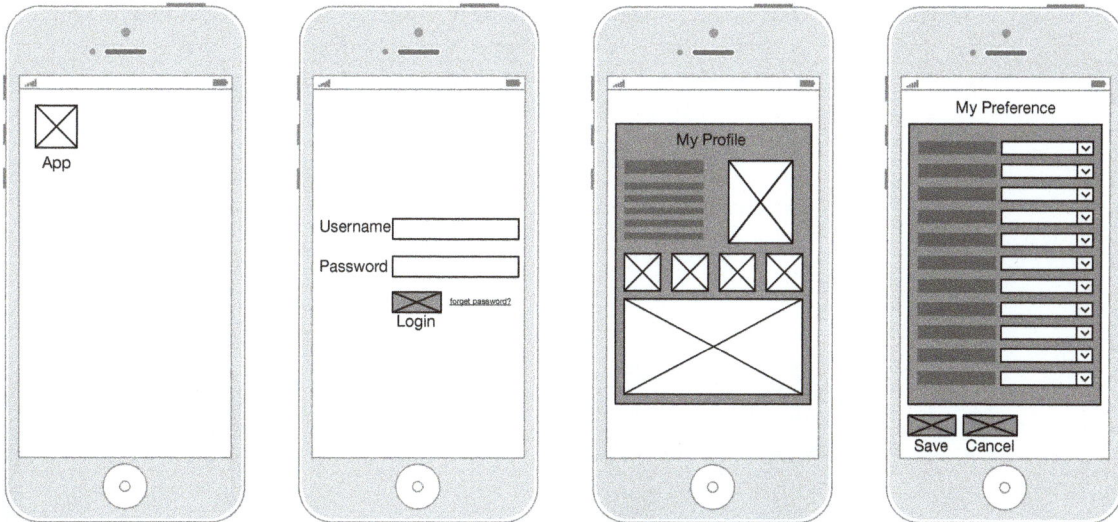

**Fig 29.5** Sketching a user process

## STAGE 2: WIREFRAMING AND INTERACTION DESIGN

Now that you have sketched your app screens and interactive elements, you need to create wireframes. Wireframes are simplified screens that tell both the designer and the developer exactly what each screen will show. Figure 29.5 shows wireframes for the same device as the sketch in Figure 29.4 – launching an app, logging in, editing and saving a profile.

The main reason for wireframing is to clarify the exact elements that will be used in the application. While the sketching phase is all about flow and user intention, the wireframe phase clarifies the details by visualising the screens and allowing for finer adjustments. The wireframe also provides the development team with a definitive blueprint for the final application.

| Launch app | Login | Open Profile | Edit and Save |
|---|---|---|---|

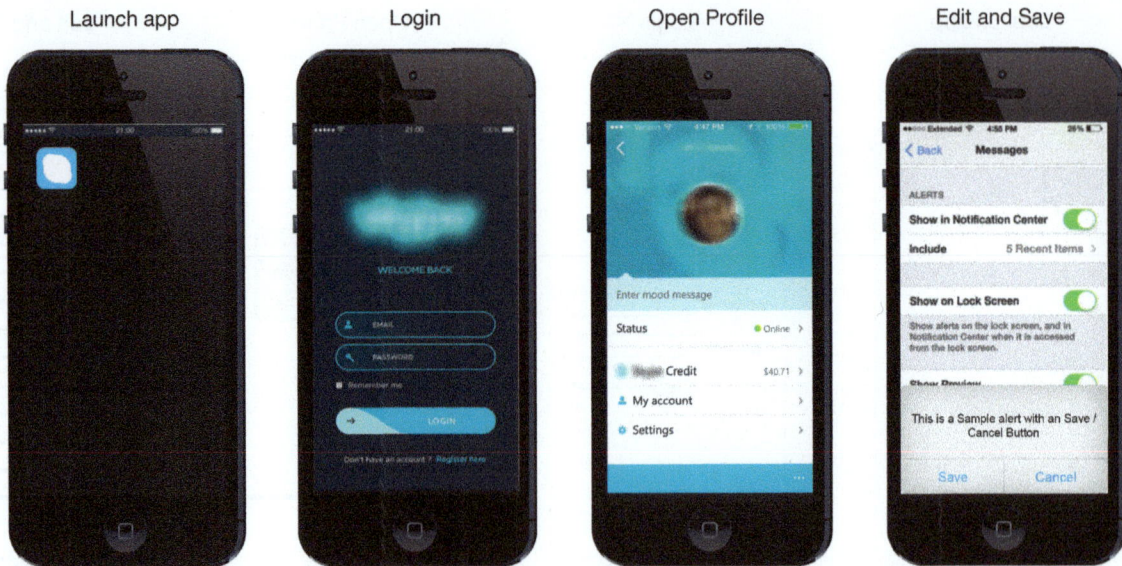

**Fig 29.6** Visual productions of the wireframes above for launching an app, logging in, editing and saving a profile

## STAGE 3: VISUAL PRODUCTION

The next stage is to create visual representations of the screens. This involves creating static images in a graphics application such as Adobe Photoshop. You can use mock-up templates of the actual device to show how the final application will look when it is working. Due to the small size of mobile devices you can create these mock-ups at full size and at full screen resolution by using a Photoshop template and by just adding in the screen elements when needed. All the IOS elements such as buttons are available to download from the Apple website as Photoshop files. Figure 29.6 shows visual productions of the wireframes in Figure 29.5 for launching an app, logging in, editing and saving a profile.

| Login | Edit and Save |
|---|---|

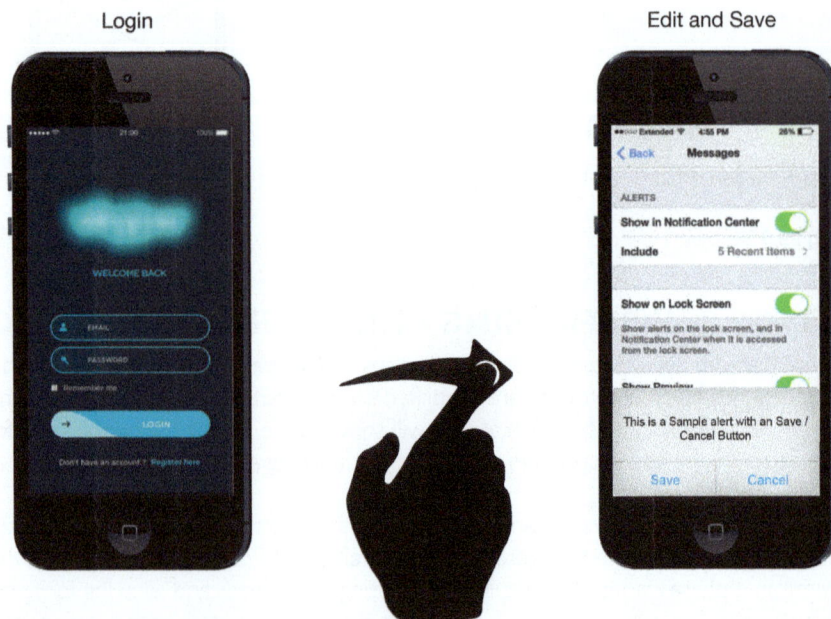

**Fig 29.7** Visual production showing interaction between screens

This enables you to create all the screens that make up the application as they will appear on the device. You can then present the application to the client as a series of static images showing exactly what the user will see. In addition, your visuals can also show how the user navigates between screens, for example, by showing a swipe symbol as in Figure 29.7, which shows the transition between logging in and editing a profile.

You can use the Photoshop visuals as a basis for the actual application development. To do this, isolate areas of the screens (such as the background) and then export them as images and bring them into the app development platform. When doing this, ensure that your Photoshop document has everything on separate layers and then turn off the layers that contain anything apart from the background image. Then export your image in a relevant format such as PNG.

## STAGE 4: PROTOTYPING AND TESTING

The final stage involves creating an actual version (working prototype) of the application that can be viewed and tested on a device. There are a number of ways to do this. One is to show people the screens as static images on the device, to re-create the user experience. A more comprehensive way is to use some testing software to deploy your app to a device without releasing it to the public. For instance, TestFlight® enables designers to do this.

Once your application is installed on a phone, the final stage of testing can begin. This involves asking users to use the application as they would in a real world situation and getting their feedback. You will need to address any issues that users raise before releasing the app. To do this you can either go back to the wireframe stage to make changes, or you can change the visual production screens. Next, make the changes to the prototype application and carry out further testing.

> **Top Tip**
>
> Some interactive wireframe applications such as Balsamiq enable a user to test the application screens on a desktop computer and click through the screens. Therefore it is worth using wireframe applications to save time.

---

Skills Task: **Sketching an app**

Choose a simple mobile application that you use frequently, something with a straightforward user journey. Now imagine you are designing the application for the first time. Go through the sketching process and map the screens and corresponding user interactions.

---

Project work: **Planning a mobile app**

Your client wants you to develop a mobile app for an online store that sells fitness trackers. Working in small groups, create sketches and visual productions.

- Identify some graphical assets you could use from Apple or Android and which wireframing application/tool you will use.
- Break down the work into specific processes, for example, 'logging in' or 'browsing products',
- Develop sketches of the processes.
- Develop wireframes from your sketches.
- Develop visual productions using Photoshop or a similar application.
- Present your ideas and work to the class.

This process is all about collaboration and listening to each other. When you have finished, reflect on how well everyone in your team contributed and encouraged others to contribute.

## Case study: REALRIDER®

REALRIDER® is a mobile app created by UK public safety technology company Realsafe Technologies Ltd. It detects when a motorcyclist has had an accident and notifies the emergency services so they can send an ambulance to the motorcyclist's last known location.

The application uses the accelerometer, motion sensors and location functions of a smartphone to create accurate journey data. To activate the application, the motorcyclist launches the app and hits a start button. Throughout the journey the app uses GPS to record location data that can be accessed and tracked using a browser.

The really innovative part of the REALRIDER® app is the way that it recognises a crash situation. It uses the accelerometer function to record rapid changes in speed or orientation. If a motorcyclist is travelling normally, slowing down or even braking suddenly, the orientation of the phone will not change and so the app will not react. But if the accelerometer records a sudden drop in speed, combined with rapid changes in orientation, the app goes into 'potential crash' mode and listens for further activity from the accelerometer and motion sensors. If it detects motion, that suggests that the rider is standing and able to walk, and the app comes out of potential crash mode.

If no movement is detected after a set amount of time, the app will try to alert the rider with an on-screen and voice alert, phone vibration and app notification every second. If there is still no response, the app enters crash-reporting mode and alerts the emergency services. Because the app has been continuously recording journey data, the emergency services have the exact location of the crash, as well as details for the rider including their name, phone number, bike type, as well as their blood group and medical history. The user has to input this information before they start using the app.

Figure 29.8 shows the REALRIDER® app in crash detection mode. The central circular element visually represents the software 'counting down' in order to move onto the next stage of the crash-detection process. The button at the bottom of the screen enables the rider to cancel the crash detection by pressing 'I'm OK'.

The REALRIDER® team started the app development by simulating motorcycle crashes by throwing various different smartphones out of car windows on test tracks at various speeds. This enabled them to identify the exact conditions that constitute a crash and the corresponding accelerometer data that would trigger the emergency alert.

Another key challenge was working out how to accommodate unpredictable user behaviour. To avoid the app generating a false accident alert if a motorcyclist drops their phone when starting a journey, the app includes special 'auto-pause' technology. This automatically turns accelerometer sensor monitoring on once the rider reaches a particular speed, and automatically deactivates sensor monitoring when a rider drops below that threshold.

REALRIDER® incorporates a route mapping and recording function. This enables motorcyclists to record and share their routes, creating a community of users, sharing their riding adventures and inspiring other riders. A Group Riding feature uses location services to help up to 12 bikers stay together and see where each other is.

REALRIDER® uses a simple interface with minimal copy to enable a lot of functionality. The app also uses strong contrasting colours to ensure that the interface is always understandable. 'The screen designs had to be

**Figure 29.8** This example shows the screen when a crash has been detected. The user has the option to cancel if there are unhurt otherwise the app will alert the emergency services.

clear and intuitive but also fluid enough to accommodate new elements,' explains UX designer Paul Bingham.'The team used a lot of sketching and wireframing but also worked extensively with motorcyclists to test the product, for example, by recording user interactions with the app on video. So we got great feedback!'

**Figure 29.9** This example shows the screens that relate to crash detection and also the ride recording functionality. Note the use of colours to denote which part of the application is being used.

### Further references

- *Beginning Adobe Experience Design: Quickly Design and Prototype Websites and Mobile Apps* (Rob Huddleston, 2017)
- *Designing Mobile Apps* (Javier E. Cuello and José Vittone, 2014)
- *Essential Mobile Interaction Design: Perfecting Interface Design in Mobile Apps* (Cameron Banga and Josh Weinhold, 2014)

# 29.3 MOBILE APP DEVELOPMENT (beyond the syllabus requirements)

Mobile devices are now an essential part of everyday life and our interactions with the world around us. Mobile phones and tablets are phones, cameras, music players and diaries. They provide users with a dazzling array of communications and data management services in the form of mobile applications or apps, covering everything from instant messaging to personal finance to fitness training. Mobile technology also includes wearable technology such as fitness trackers that users synchronise with other devices and platforms.

A mobile app is a piece of software created for use on a mobile device. Any application starts with a user need, or function, such as checking social media, reading the news or finding directions. Mobile application designers respond to user needs and create solutions based on the capabilities of mobile devices and their operating systems.

To create apps, designers need two tools: mobile device specifications provided by the manufacturer, such as Apple or Samsung, and a software development kit (SDK), which is also provided by the device manufacturers.

> ### Skills Task: **Mobile phone applications**
>
> Think of one of your favourite mobile applications and try to list all the functionalities of the device that the application uses and how they are used.

## DEVICE SPECIFICATIONS

Unlike other digital media designers, mobile app designers must have a complete understanding of the device they are designing for. For example, the Apple iPhone 7 device specifications include:

- Display size and resolution: **display resolution** refers to the clarity of the screen, expressed by the number of horizontal and vertical pixels
- Memory capacity
- Sensors, including: touch ID for fingerprint login; **three-axis gyroscope** to sense which way up the device is held (device orientation) and whether it is moving; **accelerometer** to sense more complex motion such as shaking
- Notifications: alerts used to communicate with the user via the screen
- Location tracking
- Mobile and wireless connections
- Camera specifications
- Physical device controls: for example, volume control or touchscreen controls.

These specifications are published on the Apple website and updated upon each new version release. Understanding these capabilities and limitations helps designers avoid creating an app that cannot work or only partially works.

## SOFTWARE DEVELOPMENT KIT (SDK)

The second tool that designers need is the software development kit (SDK). An SDK is a set of software development tools that allow the creation of applications specific to an operating system such as Apple IOS or Android. It provides clear guidelines for developers about what is technically possible and what will provide the optimum user experience.

For example, imagine you want to create a mobile app game that makes sounds when you move the device through the air; if you hold the device perfectly still for two seconds it makes a different sound. Players take turns with the device to see who can hold it still the most often and record their turn by saying their name into the microphone. You want to sell the game worldwide. You must check whether the device supports this type of interactivity. Will the accelerometer or gyroscope detect this type of motion and is the sound alert fully supported? It must have a microphone record option and the device must be able to set time frames. The operating system must also fully support all major languages. If the answer to any of these questions is no, you must revisit your idea and either change some of the features or start again. However, if your application passes this **scoping exercise** then you can use the SDK to create the user interactions you want.

Once you understand both the device specifications and the SDK you can start to be creative. For example, some fitness apps enable music files to be played directly in the application as a motivational aid. Likewise, some apps enable 'in-app purchases', so that users can buy products directly without using a browser. Designers are constantly seeking new ways to combine what a device can do with what users want.

**Display resolution** measure of display clarity, expressed in pixels
**Three-axis gyroscope** motion sensors in a mobile device that detect device orientation
**Accelerometer** motion sensors in a mobile device that detect different levels of motion

**Scoping exercise** process for deciding what an application will do and how

### Top Tip

You can create apps based around a particular device function or capability. The Hipstamatic app, for example, uses the mobile phone or tablet accelerometer to randomise image filters that users apply to their photos. The user shakes the phone to select a random filter option. This makes the accelerometer an interactive element and not just a sensor.

## Skills Task: **Device scoping**

Research what is required to create the motion-based game discussed above.

1. Select a range of mobile devices.
2. Identify what specifications and SDKs you need.
3. Research what you need to do/what you must pay to get them.
4. Report back to class, compare your findings for different devices, and consider:
   - Would the game idea work on all of your chosen devices?
   - If not, could you amend the game idea to work on all devices? What would you need to do?

# 29.4 DEVELOPING APPS FOR MULTIPLE DEVICES (beyond the syllabus requirements)

You have explored the options for creating apps using SDKs for specific devices. This is called **native development**. However, what if you wanted to create an app that would work on all devices and operating systems? You could create two separate applications but that would double your development time and you would have to make any updates to your app twice. One way to avoid this is to use a cross-platform application development tool. This software product enables designers and developers to create a single application and then export it in different formats for different devices and operating systems. This means that there is only ever one version of the application and any changes are made only once. Adobe PhoneGap™ and Xamarin are examples of cross-platform development tools.

Another way to address the problem of designing for multiple devices is to create a web version of your application and use an adaptive design approach. This would enable you to create an accurate 'mobile version' of your app – technically it would not be an app, so it would not need to be sold via an app store. This approach is often used when testing the viability of an app before any complex development takes place. In other cases, existing web applications can be optimised to work on mobile devices, to ensure that they deliver the right experience for the user.

> **Native development** term to describe app development for one platform only

## Project work: **Beginning app production**

Using the sketches, visual production and other assets you created in the previous Project work, begin the production process by identifying what software you need. This may include the following Adobe products: Experience design, Preview CC, PhoneGap Build™, Animate, Spark and Scout. Then plan out your application development and create a visual timeline showing the production process. Make sure you follow the four-stage process outlined in this chapter and include any wireframing applications. Practice using the software you need and then start building your app.

# 30 Games design and development

## Learning Aims

By the end of this chapter you will be able to:
- Understand the elements that make up a game and game genres
- Explain how game concept art works and how characters are developed
- Explain how game storyboarding works

# 30.1 USE YOUR CREATIVITY

Games design is about creating a whole experience for the player, rather than simply asking them to carry out a series of tasks to unlock levels. Try to place yourself in your player's shoes and create something that will resonate with them on a personal level. In this way, the gaming experience becomes a lot more immersive and enjoyable.

When considering ideas for your game project, try looking outside the usual places for inspiration. For example, is there something about a character from a book that you have read that you could incorporate into your work in some way? Perhaps you saw something in a film or TV programme that you thought was really creative and original? Inspiration can come from unlikely places, so try to keep your options open and note down ideas whenever they strike.

# 30.2 THE ELEMENTS OF A GAME

Games now form a significant part of the digital landscape, from simple mobile games to the latest multiplayer console games. All games include six key elements: objectives and themes, rules, boundaries, artefacts, interfaces, and feedback.

## OBJECTIVES AND THEMES

The fundamental element common to all digital games is the game's primary objective: what a player is actually trying to achieve, from stacking blocks in a mobile phone game to defeating an army in an online multiplayer game. In more complex games, designers also create secondary objectives that support the primary objective, in order to make the gameplay enjoyable and engaging.

Many games also include a dominant theme. This is the environment the player experiences in the game world. For example, the game Silent Hill uses the theme of a monster-filled town to define the gameplay experience.

## RULES

Game rules define what the player can or cannot do. For example, in Silent Hill the rules dictate that the main character the player controls is an ordinary man and so he gets tired after any exertion, which then shows in his behaviour.

## BOUNDARIES

**Game boundaries** set limitations on the game world – the virtual space where the play happens and where certain rules apply. In Silent Hill, various rooms and environments represent the boundaries that the main character has to navigate in order to achieve the game objectives.

# GAME ARTEFACTS

**Game artefacts** are objects that the player uses or interacts with, such as vehicles and other characters. In Silent Hill, key artefacts include a flashlight, a portable transistor radio and weapons.

**Game props** also appear in many games; however, unlike artefacts, the player does not interact with them. Instead, props support the visual appeal of a game, adding context, atmosphere and emotion. In Silent Hill the gameplay environment, such as the rooms, are stylised to create a feeling of suspense and horror through the use of certain textures and colours.

# INTERFACES

All games have an interface – the method by which a player interacts with a game. In a digital gaming environment a **graphical user interface (GUI)** is needed along with an input device, such as a computer keyboard or joystick. Silent Hill was initially created for the Sony PlayStation but now includes other formats.

# GAME FEEDBACK

This communicates with the player as they are playing. When a player does something using the interface or control mechanism, such as moving a character through a room or steering a car, the game informs the player they are successfully engaging with the game world. Feedback takes many audio and visual forms, from a simple noise or animation when a character moves to bangs, flashes and explosions when guns are fired. Without feedback the gaming experience would be quite dull. Feedback differs from interaction in that it relates directly to the game world and supports the gameplay. It is the result of an interaction.

There are two categories of feedback:

* **Explicit feedback** is activated when a player performs an action.
* **Implicit feedback** presents players with information, such as a signpost that guides them in a specific direction.

In Silent Hill, explicit sound is used to signify the health of the main character, as he can often be heard gasping for breath after running. In earlier versions of the game implicit sound was used: the sound of radio static on the transistor radio alerted the player to the presence of nearby enemies.

## Skills Task: **Digital games review**

In groups, consider your favourite digital games.

* Identify the primary and any secondary objectives.
* Identify and list the fundamental rules, boundaries and artefacts. (This may get very complex, so start with something simple!)
* Finally, identify the visual and audio feedback elements and categorise them as explicit or implicit feedback.

Present your lists to the class and discuss with the other groups. Is there anything you would have done differently? Why? Refine your list to improve it after your discussions.

---

**Game boundaries** the limitations on the game world, such as where the user can and cannot go

**Game artefact** a key object in a game that the player interacts with

**Game prop** a supporting element in a game used to create emotion or atmosphere

**Graphical user interface (GUI)** the method the player uses to control the gameplay

**Explicit feedback** visual or audio signals triggered when the player performs an action

**Implicit feedback** visual or audio signals used to guide or inform the player

# 30.3 GAME GENRES

You should now have a firm grasp of the six fundamental building blocks of any game. So how can you apply and combine these basic elements to create compelling gameplay experiences? Game genres provide a starting point.

## ROLE-PLAYING GAMES

These games are based on the development of the central characters. Many incorporate other game genres, such as adventure and combat.

Dungeon Siege® is a role-playing game set in a fantasy world that the player views through a virtual camera, which follows the main character that they control. This establishes the boundaries of the game by presenting the environment through the eyes of someone behind the central character. This set-up is known as a **third person view** and contrasts with first person views in many role-playing games (where the player is looking through the eyes of the main character). Dungeon Siege makes particularly good use of game artefacts by enabling the players to customise how they appear in the game.

> **Third person view** style of game where the player's view is from behind the character they are controlling

## REAL-TIME STRATEGY GAMES

The objective of these games is to create and/or manage resources using planning, strategy and tactics. War is a common theme, as is building communities.

Command and Conquer is a good example of this type of game. The game rules demand that the player constructs a military base and acquires resources in order to play. Boundaries are enforced in the early part of the game through the establishment of a construction yard; here the player must construct game artefacts, such as vehicles and buildings. Having completed these tasks, the player can move beyond the construction yard boundary and extend their base.

## SPORTS

This type of game involves a character that either appears in the game or is another player. The objective of the game is to win within defined rules. Sports games include racing and fighting and can include fantasy settings.

Tony Hawks® Pro Skater™ is a sports game in which the primary objective is to perform stunts on a skateboard to score points. The principal game artefacts are the skateboard and the skating environment; rules are enforced by a scoring method that tracks each player's performance. Feedback is also provided by the sound of the skating and a musical sound track.

## ADVENTURE

Adventure games often require the user to take a journey and can involve complex interactive stories that unfold along with the gameplay.

Walking Dead establishes the objective of the game (staying alive after a zombie apocalypse) by using a narrative from a well-known comic book series. Artefacts are used in the form of other characters that the player must interact with in order to progress. The game has been praised for its use of 'player choices' that make up the game experience. For example, dialogue choices made by the player may impact how other characters respond later in the game.

## ACTION

These games involve little thought, challenge gamers' reactions and manual dexterity, and provide instant entertainment.

Mutant Mudds™ is a good example of this genre. The game interface is simple but intuitive, using basic commands to carry out actions, such as jump and shoot. The game feedback is consistent and supports the gameplay experience without being intrusive. This is achieved by using a combination of sound track and explicit sound feedback when the character jumps or achieves a goal.

## SIMULATIONS

These games simulate an actual activity such as piloting a plane and often seek to re-create the experience in detail.

Blazing Angels® Squadrons of WWII is a simulation game that replicates the experience of flying World War II aircraft by replicating the actual aircraft controls using the platform controllers. For example, the Nunchuck as a joystick. The game artefacts in the form of the aircraft are accurately and realistically drawn. The boundaries and rules depend upon which plane the player is flying and the chosen scenario.

## MANAGEMENT

Similar to real-time strategy games, these games often involve creating teams or communities. The difference is that in a management game, the objective is to make the community thrive and so economics and planning take precedence over battles and conquest.

Football Manager™ utilises this approach well by turning the many pitfalls associated with being a football manager into the rules and boundaries of a compelling game experience. For example, in 'Career Mode' the player is able to control every management decision relating to players, teams and strategy. Artefacts, such as stadiums and crowds, along with feedback, such as realistic match play, also feature prominently in the game and help to support a clear objective.

## ONLINE GAMES

These games involve mass social interaction online. Players access the game through an online portal and connect with other players as part of the gameplay experience.

Bin Weevils uses artefacts, such as characters and environments, from an existing television show as the basis for an online game whose objective is to build and maintain a nest. Boundaries are established through the 'Bin' where the game takes place; rules restrict what the players can add to their 'nest' within the bin environment. Players can also upgrade their experience in numerous ways by paying a premium. The player controls the experience using a simple keyboard and mouse.

## MOBILE GAMES

Mobile games are video games that are typically played on a mobile phone or tablet. Advances in mobile technology and device design, mobile gaming has become a huge part of the digital and gaming landscape.

Mobile games have been developed on a wide range of platforms in the past, but today the majority are developed and released to work on either Apple's iOS or Google's Android operating systems.

While mobile games have limitations, including screen size and memory, many designers have incorporated innovative ideas into their games. For example, location-based technology such as GPS means that a player's physical position can become part of the game play. Similarly, by using GPS and Bluetooth, games designers are able to create innovative 'treasure hunt' style experiences using geocaching.

## GAME ENVIRONMENTS

The game environment is the graphical representation of the game world that the player interacts with. There are two types of game environment: two-dimensional (2D) and three-dimensional (3D).

### 2D environments

2D environments operate in a linear way, where the gameplay moves along a horizontal and vertical axis. This often involves the game's characters moving along a scene and interacting with objects along the way, such as in the game Super Meat Boy, in which the characters progress from left to right on-screen through various scenes while avoiding deadly obstacles and fighting their enemies.

While 2D games only use 2D space, some of them make use of a parallax approach, to give the impression that the player is in 3D space. **Parallax design** layers different parts of the scene, such as foreground and background. These different scene elements then move at different speeds across the screen as the player moves to give the illusion of three-dimensional space or depth, as in the image below.

### 3D environments

3D environments enable the player to move around a three-dimensional space. Many console games use 3D game mechanics to create complex environments and characters that react realistically to commands and inputs from the player.

The image below shows an example of a 3D ancient Egyptian environment that creates a greater sense of depth and atmosphere compared to 2D environments.

Fig 30.3 A 3D rendering of an immersive natural environment

> **Parallax design** 2D design method that uses different background layers to give the impression of perspective and depth

Fig 30.1 An example of a 2D game environment

Fig 30.2 An example of a 3D game environment

> **Concept artwork** a rendering of an element or elements in a creative project, as part of the visual development of characters, costumes, environments, etc.
> **Game Design Document (GDD)** document that defines game development, including game objectives, elements, interactions and processes

# 30.4 THE GAME DESIGN PROCESS

Prior to production, designing a game generally involves four main stages: creating **concept artwork**, developing characters, creating game assets and storyboarding. The starting point in the whole design process is the **Game Design Document (GDD)**.

# GAME DESIGN DOCUMENT (GDD)

This defines some core objectives and elements of the game. Your GDD would initially include:

- target audience
- gaming platform or device
- game genre and theme (includes the game's 'high concept' or key ideas)
- player motivations (Why will the player want to play?).

Once you have these elements, you can start to incorporate the other key elements discussed at the start of this chapter. Many GDDs are adaptive documents that evolve over time as new aspects of the proposed game are introduced. Once aspects such as rules are decided GDDs can become quite complex, so starting with the basic elements is important.

> **Top Tip**
>
> You can find a detailed example of a GDD on the Iron Belly Studios website.

# CREATING CONCEPT ARTWORK

Once you have decided on the target audience, platform, theme and genre, the next stage is to start creating **concept artwork**. The purpose of concept artwork is to convey themes, ideas and moods that can then be interpreted by designers and developers in the later production stages. Concept artwork is used to convey a representation of a game design but not the design itself. Concept artwork can involve anything from complex scenes and plans for game props, to mood boards and hand-drawn backgrounds. An important aspect of concept artwork is that it should be an iterative process (one that evolves gradually over time) before you create the final versions of your game.

In the early stages this may simply involve doing some internet research to find images that have the right visual appeal. Do not worry too much about details but more about the overall feel. For example, if your game involves a car, explore what type you want and how you want to display it, for example, as a cartoon or a realistic image. You could also develop a colour palette or a mood board that contains visual elements that will form part of the player's experience. This can be anything that you think has the right kind of visual feel, from photographs and illustrations to interface designs. Once this stage is complete you can move on to character development.

> **Top Tip**
>
> Creating concept artwork and drawings of your characters and imagery will help you to generate further ideas, as well as documenting the creative process.

# DEVELOPING CHARACTERS

Game characters can fulfil many different roles and purposes. They can take the form of figures but they can also be **functional characters** that take the form of machines or objects (a car in a racing game, for example). Some games also use **non-visual characters** as narrators who do not appear in the game world but still have to be designed. You must also understand what your characters will be doing in the game environment. For example, if a character needs to run and jump, make sure their clothes are easy to animate and do not get in the way of the action.

Character design follows a three-stage process.

### Stage 1: Research

Research other similar characters in order to add more detail to your initial description. It is important to consider how other designers have approached character creation, so this phase may involve researching not just game characters but also comics, films and animation. In the example in Figure 30.4 from digital design studio Atomhawk, you can see from the notes how the character designers have considered typical horror and fantasy characters.

> **Functional character** physical character that appears in the game world
> **Non-visual character** character that features in the game world but not visually, for example, a narrator

**Fig 30.4** Game character designs

### Stage 2: Technical constraints

Decide what platform you are using and understand its capabilities and limitations. If you are creating a simple online game then your character will need to be in a 2D format that is suitable for web delivery, for example, at a screen resolution of 72 dpi and as an image format, such as .JPEG or .PNG. You need to create something that works in the development phase and not just the concept stage.

### Stage 3: Visual design

Typically, you will hand-draw characters at this stage before creating them digitally, as in the image from Atomhawk. It is best to draw the character in a number of poses or situations at this stage, to try and ensure that the character works in as many different game scenarios as possible.

---

### Skills Task: **Develop a GDD**

In groups, develop a Game Design Document (GDD) for an existing game that everyone in your group is familiar with. Start with something simple and web-based that works in a browser rather than a console game. Concentrate on the core game elements discussed in this chapter. Then research the main character's backstory:

- Where did they come from?
- How did they become part of the game world?
- Why do they wear the clothes that they wear?

---

## CREATING GAME ASSETS

Once you have developed your concept art and characters, you can start to create specific game assets. Game assets are the graphic elements that make up the game environment. This includes backgrounds against which the game is played, props used to add interest to a scene, gameplay artefacts that the player interacts with, and the main characters. Everything is informed by the previous phases. Your concept art will show how everything will look. Any technical constraints on your game assets will be defined by the platform your game is to be played on, and will define things such as the file size and resolution. This is why the planning and concept stage is so important.

Figure 30.5 shows a background asset developed by Atomhawk. The software you use to create game assets will also be dictated by the visual style you define with your concept art. For example, if you want a flat

**Fig 30.5** A game background asset developed by Atomhawk

2D background, use a vector graphic package, such as Adobe Illustrator. Vector graphics are fully scalable and will not become pixelated and lose clarity when enlarged, so they can be used in a variety of different scenarios. If you want complex 3D game assets, however, it is better to use a combination of 3D modelling software and textures created in Adobe Photoshop.

You should create all the game assets as individual images and files, name them and arrange them into folders. This makes the developer's job much easier when they start to use your assets to create the game.

## STORYBOARDING

Storyboarding for games maps out specific sections of gameplay or animation using the specific assets you have created. The advantage of storyboarding games is that all aspects of the gameplay can be planned in advance. Storyboarding also enables you to test on paper the six fundamental elements of games, such as rules, boundaries and feedback mechanisms, before turning them into digital versions. For example, a storyboard for a simple 2D racing game would show:

- the game boundaries in the form of the screen
- game rules, such as the maximum speed of the car on a graphical speedometer
- how audio feedback mechanisms would work.

Once you have storyboarded the game you can then go into game production.

### Project work: **Create a GDD**

Working in groups, create a Game Design Document (GDD). Follow the processes discussed above and include the following:

- High concept: a short overview of your game that sets the scene and explains key ideas (for example, 'Planet X is under attack, your mission is...').
- Character design: include characters' backstory, visual descriptions and sketches or ideas from existing games.
- Game environment: describe the 2D or 3D world in which your game exists. Where is it and what does it look and feel like? Include concept art, such as sketches, mood boards and existing game ideas.

Present your ideas to your class, get feedback and refine your GDD.

# 30.5 AUDIO AND MUSIC FOR GAMING

The primary function of sound is to make an image feel more real. Sound provides information to the player in terms of what is around them and also delivers feedback about their actions and status. Sound not only reinforces the image to make it more convincing but also describes it, lending substance, character and in some cases personality. Sound is incredibly important to any gaming experience and it is worth remembering that bad sound will have a far greater negative impact than bad visuals. To illustrate this try playing your favourite game with the sound turned off and see how the experience is diminished and altered.

### Project work: **Storyboarding games**

Create a storyboard of a game you know. Map out the interactions and the feedback the player receives. Start with a very simple game and then try something more complex. Then storyboard a simple game process of your own.

### Top Tip

When you create game assets, start thinking about the sound elements early on. If you are creating a weapon for an action game, think about what sound it will make and try to describe it in some way. If this is too difficult, research some existing examples and use them as a basis.

The three main areas of sound use are:

- reality and characterisation
- immersion and emotion
- information and feedback.

## HOW TO INCORPORATE REALITY AND CHARACTERISATION

Sound gives us information about the nature of an object or character. When game reviewers talk about the 'power' and 'weight' of game objects, most of this data is created by the use of sound to make game assets feel real.

## HOW TO CREATE IMMERSION AND EMOTION

**Symbolic sounds** sounds used to create an emotional response or atmosphere

Immersion is when the player loses sense of the outside world and is 'lost in the flow' of the game. You can enhance the mood or atmosphere of an environment by using sound; for example, some ambient or distant sounds are called **symbolic sounds** and are used to create tension. Barking dogs and breaking glass, for example, can be used to create a sense of danger; likewise, the sound of dripping water in a dark room can create the feeling of cold. When thinking about your game environment, consider the sounds it makes, such as the wind blowing or the sounds made on hard or soft surfaces, such as floors. Try to record some sounds that relate to your game environment using a smartphone or microphone and save them to match with your design later.

## HOW TO USE INFORMATION AND FEEDBACK

Feedback is one of the core game elements, so it is vital to consider how sound could be used to provide feedback. Action games often use spoken dialogue, which can provide extra information for the player as they progress through the game environment. Think about the type of feedback you want to guide the player with. Imagine a scene in a game project that you would like to work on then list all the potential feedback elements you could use and identify the three main feedback types you will use.

## AMBIENT SOUND

It is often said that there is no such thing as complete silence; we can always hear something, even if it is just our heartbeat. Similarly, every scene that you create in the game world will have its own feel and ambience. For example, take an outdoor scene in a game where it is raining: the scene appears to be running a soundtrack of rain created from a looped sound file. In reality, however, the rain sound is comprised of six different rain sounds overlaid in different areas of the scene: general rain, rain on trees, rain on water, rain on a metal roof, rain on hollow metal barrels, rain on plants. This method enables the game designer to create environments that feel realistic. While this is a very complex process, you can start to incorporate ambient sound into your game project by thinking about what kind of environment you are attempting to create. Then research some existing ambient sounds from the web and try recording your own.

> ## Skills Task: **Classifying sounds within gameplay**
>
> Working in groups and using a game that you are familiar with, identify how sound has been used within the gameplay. It could be a very simple soundtrack or feedback sound, or it may involve highly complex feedback, music and ambient sounds. Classify the sounds under the three headings of:
>
> * Reality and characterisation
> * Immersion and emotion
> * Feedback.

## AUDIO CONCEPTING

**Audio concepting** is the process of exploring how sounds work with visuals at the concept art stage. When developing characters it is advisable to start incorporating some audio concepting. Defining how a character sounds will have an impact on how the character is received by game players. For example, if a car asset needs a revving engine sound, the quality of that sound will depend on whether you want it to be an old car or something new and powerful.

To audio concept a car with a revving engine you would do the following:

* Find an image of a car that could be used in a game environment, preferably an animated 3D model.
* Find car revving sounds from a website, such as Freesounds, 99sounds or soundjay, or record the sounds yourself.
* With your car image open, play the sound files and note what you feel when the sound and image are combined. Do they fit or do they conflict?

> **Audio concepting** method of testing how sound and images work together
> **Diegetic sound** sounds that come from within the virtual game world

## MUSIC IN GAMES

Music in gaming environments falls into two main categories: diegetic and non-diegetic sound.

### Diagetic sound

Music that appears to come from inside the reality of the game world, and which is played by or through objects or characters in the game, is called **diegetic sound**, as it exists inside the 'diegesis' or narrative space. For example, think of a driving game where the player can hear music coming through the car music system; this is music that relates directly to the environment. Diegetic sound is often used to reinforce cultural aspects of the environment or to help define the lead character in some way.

### Non-diagetic sound

**Non-diegetic sound**, on the other hand, sits outside the diegesis and is used to accompany the action, such as an orchestral score in the background that is not heard by the characters in the game world. Now think of a driving game where a fast-paced soundtrack accompanies the gameplay to reinforce the idea of speed and motion; this is non-diegetic music.

Certain musical styles are closely associated with game genres. For example, racing games are likely to include a soundtrack of upbeat pop or dance music. When creating a music soundtrack it is important to acknowledge that game players will often expect certain musical styles when playing certain types of game.

> **Non-diegetic sound** sounds that come from outside of the virtual game world

### Puzzle games

This type of game is often associated with hand-held devices such as smartphones. If you are creating a game for a device with limited power and memory, you would ideally use simple repetitive music that takes up less memory and reinforces the hypnotic feel of the gaming activity.

### Arcade

This is what people commonly associate with the term 'game music'. This is often synthesised and can be made to sound like older arcade games. If you are creating a game in this genre, first research the music style that fits with your game in order to reinforce its appeal.

### Driving/simulation/sports

In these games, you might use music as a supporting theme rather than as an interactive element. Driving and other simulated activities are associated with playing music or listening to the radio. In sporting games music is often used to represent location, so if your game moves around different countries you would ideally choose different music styles to accompany each country.

### Strategy – real time/role playing/multiplayer online

In these games you might use music to define the location or culture of the surroundings. Although music often responds to gameplay activity, other factors come into consideration, such as number of characters, length of gameplay and complexity of gaming environment. For example, many multiplayer games incorporate on-going gameplay with no specific start or end point, making narrative sound such as voiceovers almost impossible. Likewise, the complex gaming environments associated with strategy games can make anything but very simple background music impossible, because it would be an unwelcome distraction.

### Adventure/action/shooter

This is often the most cinematic of game genres; the music in these games often aims to support the emotional impacts of the game narrative, such as exciting, fast-paced music in a car chase. This presents a huge challenge in that many gamers expect a movie-standard music score but in a game environment.

**Game balancing** testing method used to establish whether a gameplay experience is at the appropriate level for players

# 30.6 PREPARING AND TESTING PROTOTYPES

The next stage of the creative process is the prototype phase. A prototype is a version of the game that is used to prove the concepts and ideas from the earlier stages. At this stage, you will want to ask yourself:

- Do the concept ideas work?
- Do the characters come across well?
- Do the gameplay ideas work?
- Is the interface intuitive and easy to use?
- Does the art and visual style work in the right way?
- Does the music style fit with the visual style?
- Do the sound assets work with the visuals and animation?

To answer these questions, create a section of the final game as a testing environment using your choice of game development software. For example, for a driving game the prototype would be a short race with one of the best cars. This gives an overview of the gameplay without having to commit to the entire production process. This also provides insight into **game balancing**. This is a testing process that helps to define whether a game delivers a balanced experience, for example, whether the gameplay is at the right skill level and feels fair to the players. Asking questions such as these can help you ensure that the game delivers the right experience. In many cases you would show a prototype to focus groups and game testers in order to gain as much player feedback as possible. Once the prototyping has been completed, the game can go into production.

Artwork 30.6 shows a prototype of a game environment developed by Atomhawk design studio.

**Fig 30.6** A prototype of a game environment developed by Atomhawk design studio

> ### Top Tip
>
> A prototype should always represent a section of gameplay with a beginning, middle and end. It should also be aimed at the middle level of difficulty. This means you can make the game either harder or easier if you feel it is necessary.

# 30.7 SOFTWARE TOOLS FOR GAMES DEVELOPMENT

You have explored the processes and concepts behind games design and development, but what are the tools that designers use and what exactly are they used for? Games design software is classified into three main areas: graphics, audio, and game development.

## GRAPHICS SOFTWARE

This is used to create the visual assets that are used in the game. 2D graphics software includes Adobe products Photoshop, Illustrator and Animate. You can use Photoshop and Illustrator to create 2D graphics but not animation. Adobe Animate enables you to create graphics and animations and then import them into game production software, such as Adobe SDK and Unity.

Adobe Photoshop and Adobe Illustrator can also be used to create textures and surfaces that can then be applied to 3D models. For example, if you want to create a 3D wooden box to be used in your game you would:

- create the box shape as a 3D model of a cube
- create a 2D image that resembles wood
- 'wrap' the 3D model with the wood using texture mapping, as shown in Figure 30.7.

**Fig 30.7** Creating textures and surfaces to be applied to 3D models

3D graphics applications include AutoDesk 3ds Max, AutoDesk Maya and Blender. You can use 3D applications to create models and assets from complex characters to simple shapes, such as cubes and polygons, which you then incorporate into game production engines such as Unity. Figure 30.8 shows the application window of the AutoDesk 3D Studio Max software.

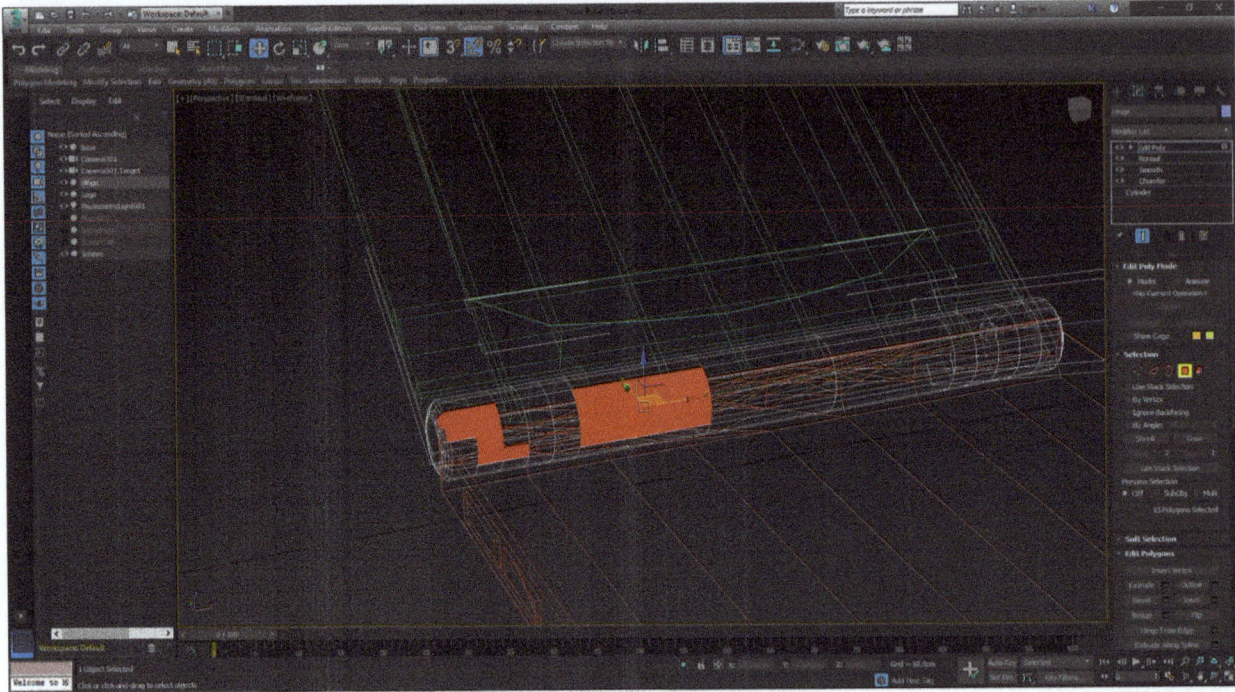

**Fig 30.8** The application window of the AutoDesk 3D Studio Max software

## AUDIO SOFTWARE

Packages such as Audacity and Adobe Audition are used to edit the sound and audio assets used in game production. This would include any music, ambient or feedback sounds that your game will use. You can download or record sound and then import it into the audio software, then edit and export it as MP3 or WAV files that can then be imported into game development software.

## GAME DEVELOPMENT SOFTWARE

Unity and Adobe Gaming SDK software create the actual game world and all the interactions that the player experiences. You can use game development software to bring all your assets together and publish the game as a single entity that can be played by the end user.

To get started with Unity:

1. Create a Unity account at the unity3d website to access the software. Select the 'Personal' option to access a free version of the software for students.
2. Explore the video tutorials and asset libraries that contain visual elements needed to create games.
3. Explore the community of developers and designers.
4. Start creating your game.

## Project work: **Game creation using Unity**

Follow the steps described above and start designing a simple game that is:

- based around a tutorial example from the Unity website
- a single player game.

First create a basic Game Design Document (GDD). Start with something very simple, as game development can be extremely complex. Then start creating the game in Unity. Try to import sounds or music. Present your game to your class, explain how it works in simple terms and then let your peers play it and provide feedback.

## Further references

### Books
- *3D Game Textures* (Luke Ahearn, 2016)
- *The Game Maker's Apprentice: Game Development for Beginners* (Jacob Habgood and Mark Overmars, 2006)
- *Modeling Game Assets in Blender for Absolute Beginners* (Kamil Pakula, 2017; ebook)
- *Unity 3D Game Development by Example Beginner's Guide* (Ryan Henson Creighton, 2010)

# 31 Immersive experiences and interactive designs

## Learning Aims

By the end of this chapter you will be able to:
- Understand how immersive design differs from interactive design
- Understand the principles of and contemporary practice in immersive design
- Explain how immersive experiences are created and how to plan your own
- Create a spatial plan for an immersive experience

In the preceding chapters, which explored aspects of digital media and design, you learned about creative skills, work practices and design examples that revolve around using screens. In this chapter we will explore how you can move beyond the screen and create experiences that enable users to view, move around in and interact with digital environments. These techniques and digital designs are known as 'immersive experiences' and you can find them in physical spaces, such as interactive museum exhibitions, art galleries and nightclubs, as well as in imaginary spaces created using augmented or virtual reality technologies. The term 'immersive' describes how the user feels part of the design because:

- they are able to move around or within it
- they are able to interact with it
- combinations of different sensory media, such as sound and touch, make the viewer feel part of their surroundings in a **multi-sensory design**.

**Multi-sensory design** design that stimulates multiple senses, not just sight and hearing

**Surround sound** sound played through speakers that surround the listener

**Fig 31.1** Visitors to the DX17 Centenary Sound Sculpture – a sensory art installation created by multi-disciplinary artist Nick Ryan to mark 100 years of the Imperial War Museums (IWM) and RAF Duxford

# 31.1 TYPES OF IMMERSIVE DESIGN

Immersive design often incorporates elements of narrative and storytelling as part of the user experience. Designers use immersive design in:

- interactive museum exhibits
- art installations
- large-scale digital projections
- immersive and interactive music events.

## INTERACTIVE MUSEUM EXHIBITS

Many museums and cultural spaces use immersive and interactive digital technology to enhance the visitors' experience. This can include things such as: interactive screens that play video and audio content; motion sensors that detect when a user is near an exhibit; 360-degree video projection and **surround sound** that enable viewers to feel that they are part of the exhibit.

## ART INSTALLATIONS

Immersive art integrates technology, art and design to create new experiences and is often created by groups including programmers, animators and mathematicians. The work shown in Figure 31.2 by the art collective teamLab, for example, projects flowers onto the bodies of visitors to the installation and uses sensors to direct the development of the experience: if visitors move the flowers die but if they stay still more flowers grow and without visitors nothing will be present in the space. When the flowers bloomed on a visitor coming close to another person they spread in that direction and connect. By making the visitor central to the installation via real-time rendering, teamLab creates an intimate, interactive journey.

**Fig 31.2** *Flowers Bloom on People* (2017) by teamLab, Digitized Nature, Endless

## LARGE-SCALE DIGITAL PROJECTIONS

Designers can now project high quality video and animated content onto any surface including buildings and rock faces, effectively turning them into giant screens. This is called **projection mapping** and uses specialist software, such as MapMap or Sparck, to mathematically map physical spaces so they can be projected onto. Designers then use media servers such as Smode to manage, edit and display video and images.

## IMMERSIVE MUSIC EVENTS

Music events have a long history of combining visuals with sound. Recent developments in technology, such as multiscreen video, now mean that visual artists can perform alongside musicians in real time. For example, Video DJs (or **VJs**) use combinations of projection mapping and image/video manipulation software to accompany DJs and live concerts.

**Projection mapping** technique for projecting digital designs onto large surfaces
**VJ** artist who creates dynamic digital imagery, usually to accompany music

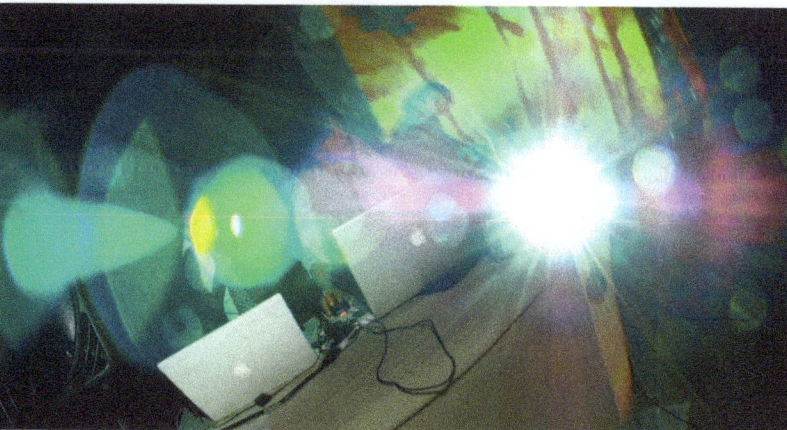

**Fig 31.3** VJing at an art performance and dance party in Tucson, Arizona, USA

# 31.2 IMMERSIVE AND INTERACTIVE DESIGN GUIDELINES

As immersive design is a relatively new discipline, there are few clearly defined theoretical rules. There are, however, some guiding principles that you should be aware of and apply.

## IMMERSIVE DESIGN IS STILL DESIGN

While immersive design focuses more on experience, it is still a design practice and the core principles still apply. For example, if your installation uses video, animation and interaction then consider and adapt the basic principles of each discipline.

## DESIGN FOR DIFFERENT SCENARIOS

Installations and immersive experiences rarely follow a simple linear path. Different viewers may walk around the space and see things in a different sequence or from a different perspective or angle. For example, the interactive experience WHIST created by AΦE uses interactive virtual reality (VR) and augmented reality (AR) to guide the participant through 76 possible pathways depending on where they look. Participants focus their VR headsets on physical objects in an art installation, see Figure 31.4. This triggers a pre-recorded video inspired by the work of psychoanalyst Sigmund Freud, which the participant watches through the VR headset. Depending on where they look during the video, the headset directs the participant to approach the next physical object in the installation and they continue their journey. At the end the participant gets a psychoanalytical profile based on their journey.

## TELL A STORY AND TELL IT WELL

Immersive design often involves a narrative of some sort. Museum exhibits, for example, often try to tell a story from history while art exhibits such

**Fig 31.4** Participants at the WHIST exhibition – an immersive experience that is part theatrical piece, part art installation and part video game

as the WHIST experience often have more complex themes. When designing your experience, be clear about what you are trying to achieve and decide what you want your viewers to feel or know at the end of the experience.

## USE PERSPECTIVE TO YOUR ADVANTAGE

Designers create visual impact using size, contrast and colour, and these design elements may be magnified in immersive design. Size is based on the distance between the user and a piece of content, while colours may vary depending upon the lighting conditions you choose. Be aware of these variables when creating your design.

## ENCOURAGE YOUR USERS TO LOOK AROUND

Immersive experiences are all about using a full field of vision. People are also used to turning their heads or bodies to view things, so make sure you incorporate this into your design and do not just design for a single viewpoint.

## CREATE CLEAR BOUNDARIES

Immersive design is about creating compelling experiences. However, ensuring that your viewer knows when the experience starts and ends is an important part of how they engage with your project. Just as a film or video starts with the titles and finishes with a screen that says 'The End', so your installation should have clear boundaries so your viewers know where they are.

## VIEWER CONSENT IS OFTEN NECESSARY

Some immersive installations take place in dark environments and use light sources, including strobe lighting. This may be uncomfortable or even frightening for some viewers and so you must inform them and may need to confirm they are happy to take part. This could be something as simple as a notice at the start of the experience to explain what will happen, or a consent form that needs to be completed before people can enter.

# 31.3 IMMERSIVE AND INTERACTIVE DESIGN TOOLS

To achieve immersive and interactive effects, designers use a range of hardware and software tools.

## VOICE RECOGNITION AND SOUND SENSORS

Voice recognition software enables a digital device to detect the human voice as an input or trigger. Some voice recognition software can detect specific words while other less complex examples just recognise sounds. In immersive design you might use voice recognition to lead the viewer into new areas of the experience or to launch an animation or video sequence.

**Fig 31.5** Casa Magica, *Lux Eucharistica* (2013) Cologne Cathedral, Germany

## STREAMING TECHNOLOGY

This involves using cameras to record either video or still images that are shown in real time, either as projections or on video screens. For example, the Fly Open Air electronic music event in Edinburgh streamed images of the crowd onto screens that surrounded the DJ booth onstage.

## SOCIAL MEDIA

Some interactive experiences enable visitors to generate content via social media that then forms part of the design. For example, photographs taken by attendees at an event can be uploaded using Facebook and edited into a photomontage using a media server application. Similarly, Twitter hashtags can also be used to show user-generated copy that is then animated onto a screen.

## LAPTOPS AND TABLETS

Laptops and tablets can be used as the central controlling device for a complex installation. In addition, they are light and portable. They can also be adapted either to form part of an exhibition when used as a display unit or as a way of creating content.

## MOTION SENSORS AND PRESSURE PADS

Motion sensors and pressure pads detect where users are within a particular space or if they are close to an exhibit or installation. A museum exhibit may start displaying information when the motion sensor detects that someone has entered the space around it. Similarly, pressure pads may be used to detect when users enter a space and trigger sound, video or other media.

## PROJECTORS

Projectors can create cinema-like experiences in large and small spaces. This can be anything from small-scale installations that just show simple video content to a multi-screen 360-degree experience. When used in conjunction with projection mapping technology, projectors can be used to turn anything into a screen.

## INTERACTIVE SCREENS

Interactive screens enable users to interact with content as they would on a tablet or phone but in a much larger format.

## USER-OWNED TECHNOLOGY

You can use people's smartphones or tablets as part of an installation. For example, the *Wander through the Crystal Universe* exhibition (Figure 31.6) at the National Museum of Singapore by teamLab consists of a seemingly infinite number of LEDs within a three-dimensional space, creating a real-time, interactive light sculpture which can be controlled digitally. Visitors can interact with the work through their smartphones by choosing a desired element and swiping toward the installation to add their selection to the space. While Crystal Universe is created by elements selected by the viewers, each element affects one another. The viewer's position within the artwork also influences how the work unfolds; thus, the artwork is continuously changing.

**Fig 31.6** teamLab's *Wander through the Crystal Universe* (2016) Interactive Installation of Light Sculpture, LED, Endless, Sound: teamLab

## Project work: **Designing for different scenarios**

In groups, imagine you are designing an experience for a very simple scenario. Your immersive/interactive space is a corridor with:

- an entry and exit door
- one other door that is not open
- a painting on each side wall
- a video screen on one wall near the exit door
- one light switch near the entry door.

Identify and list all possible interactions (for example, turning the light on or off) and user journeys through the space and define the boundaries of the experience. Then research, discuss and document all the content and tools that you would need to design this experience. Then make the scenario more complex by adding new content or sensory experiences to each interaction (as in the WHIST experience).

## Skills Task: **Scoping immersive designs**

In small groups, choose an example of one of the following types of immersive or interactive design: a museum installation, an interactive music event or an immersive art exhibition. Research, document and discuss the following:

- the story or theme of the design
- the types of content and/or interactions
- the software and hardware tools used
- any other useful or notable information.

# 31.4 THE IMMERSIVE DESIGN PROCESS

Designing an immersive or interactive experience generally follows a five-stage process:

1. Defining the story
2. Choosing the physical space
3. Manipulating the space
4. Interaction and user journey design
5. Technology review.

## 1. DEFINING THE STORY

Good immersive design takes the user on a journey and tells a story. You should clearly define what you want to express and why. This could be an episode from history for a museum piece, a VJ projection or an art installation. Your definition should ideally be no longer than a sentence. This provides the basis for the interactions and emotional responses that make up the experience.

## 2. CHOOSING THE PHYSICAL SPACE

Immersive design extends outside the screen and into physical space. Therefore you need to decide where your installation or design will be displayed. Define a space for your installation, take measurements and make a plan of the space, including floors, walls and other surfaces and objects that may be useful. Consider the light, acoustics, textures and other sensory characteristics of the space and measure anything that you feel is relevant.

In some cases, the physical space may have historical or cultural associations that add special meaning. For example, the *Deep Time* projection mapping event created by 59 Productions that opened the Edinburgh International Festival in 2016 used the iconic Edinburgh Castle and the volcanic cliffs upon which it sits as a canvas for images of geological and human history (see Figure 31.8); this was accompanied by a live soundtrack by the Scottish rock band Mogwai. You can watch the event on YouTube.

**Fig 31.7** Fujiko Nakaya, London Fog (2017) on the South Terrace of Tate Modern's Switch House, London

**Fig 31.8** *Deep Time* projection mapping event on Edinburgh Castle at the Edinburgh International Festival, 2016

# 3. MANIPULATING THE SPACE

What aspects of the physical space can you use creatively? You should ask the following questions:

- Do you want to alter the space or add to it?
- Are you working in sympathy with the space or against it?
- Do you want to re-create another space inside the space?
- Will your installation involve placing objects in the space and if so why?

## Dimensions

This doesn't just mean how big something is but whether it is an open space or an enclosed area containing smaller areas. How does this impact on your story and the user journey? Does the space contain interesting shapes that could be used in some way?

## Light qualities

What type of lighting does the space have? Is there much natural light and does it change markedly throughout the day or vary within the space? – if so, this could form part of the experience. To assess the light, visit the space at different times. Take photographs or video using the same camera settings and compare the images. If there is a marked difference, for example, lighter and darker sections of the space, consider how you will work with the light or alter it artificially and where you will place your displays. The *Deep Time* designers would have considered the natural and artificial light levels in Edinburgh in early August to calibrate the brightness and timing of the projections.

## Textures and colours

Consider the dominant textures and colours within the space. Are they in harmony or in conflict with your story or the atmosphere you are trying to create? For example, *Deep Time* made dramatic use of jagged, rough cliff faces to show the power of volcanic eruptions and lava flows. If you want to tell an emotional story, take care that the textures and colours in the space do not appear too cold and clinical. If there are any dominant colours in the space could you use them to enhance the experience by illuminating them or projecting onto them?

## Acoustics

How does the space project sounds or music? Does it echo or muffle sound? Are the floors hard or soft? If your installation incorporates sound you must consider acoustics and the background noise your installation may create. *Deep Time* incorporated Mogwai's distorted guitar music, so creating 'walls of sound' that echoed off the cliffs and around the monumental setting as well as complementing the sometimes violent visual content. To assess the acoustics, play any sounds or music you intend to use beforehand. Ideally have as many people in the space when you test as you would expect to be viewing or visiting your project, in order to replicate real-life acoustic conditions as closely as possible.

## Atmosphere

Does the space have an overriding atmosphere? Light, acoustics, textures and colour combine to generate emotional responses. For example, people may describe spaces as open and fresh or gloomy and claustrophobic. As with the *Deep Time* project, the history of a space can be used to generate atmosphere around an installation or event.

### Lines of sight

Does the space have clear areas where users will walk or look and are there obvious lines of sight or obstructions that prevent viewing of certain areas of the space? If so, can you use this to your advantage to place certain elements in specific places? The *Deep Time* audience were placed in an area below the castle with a largely unrestricted view upward, a viewpoint that increased the drama of the spectacle. To identify optimum lines of sight spend some time walking around the space, looking at it from many different angles and, if possible, observing people's natural behaviour in the space prior to your project. Use a floor plan and sketch onto it where people walk and look, and identify key lines of sight. This simple exercise will help you to identify whether there is an intuitive route that people will follow or if you need to provide guidance.

## 4. INTERACTION AND USER JOURNEY DESIGN

Once you have your story and the space, you can start to think about how users will move within it or through it and interact with your content. Are you trying to create a sense of calm or tension, exhilaration or surprise? What types of interaction will you use to create these responses? Start with the plan of your space, what your story or user journey will be, and add the basic emotional responses you want to generate, for example, using sticky notes as follows:

- Emotional: the user feels…
- Sensory: the user sees…; the user hears…; the user touches…
- Outcomes: the user learns/moves/reacts…

You can then add potential interactions to generate these responses, such as:

- Video screen showing…
- Interactive screen showing…
- Projection showing…
- Motion sensor that triggers…

To make a simple interaction in your space you would need:

- a passive infra red (PIR) motion sensor to act as a trigger (USB motion sensors are easy to find and use with a USB connector cable)
- PIR software (usually supplied with the sensor)
- some video content that will play when triggered by the motion sensor, for example, when someone walks in front of the sensor
- a computer to store and play the content and control the motion sensor via the PIR software
- screens or projectors connected to the computer that display the content.

You would set up the PIR sensor to detect any motion in the space and connect it to the laptop using the USB cable. Using the PIR software, you would set the parameters for the sensor to trigger the video content, for example:

- What happens if there is more motion? Does the video start again?
- Does the video play in its entirety?
- Does the system reset if there is no motion?

## 5. TECHNOLOGY REVIEW

What technology do you need and what is available? Many of these considerations will be defined by your budget, but it is important to gain a thorough understanding of what you have to work with, from screens to connecting cables. A good way to carry out a technology review is to use a spreadsheet to list everything you need. The important thing is to collect as much information as you can in a single document.

By defining the story you establish what you intend to say, by defining and manipulating the space you define the physical boundaries of your experience, and the technology review defines what tools you have to tell the story with. The final stage of designing the user journey brings everything together and tells your story in a meaningful and relevant way. Effective immersive design is a balance between technology, story and physical space where no one aspect dominates the user experience.

### Skills Task: **Creating a spatial plan**

Working in small groups, choose a space either at your school or at home and create a spatial plan incorporating all the surfaces and objects that could be used as part of an interactive or immersive experience. Measure and document the following:

- the dimensions of the space and possible audience capacity
- the light (natural or artificial) in your space and lines of sight you can use
- the acoustics in your space – does it echo or feel quiet?
- the textures, wall shapes or objects you could project onto
- power access – can you connect all the devices you need?
- user access and safety – can people move around safely?

Present your plan to the class. Discuss the possible interactions and immersive experiences you could develop in this space.

# 31.5 DISPLAYING IMMERSIVE DESIGNS

When displaying digital designs visually, there are generally two options: projected images and screen-based images. There are advantages and disadvantages to each approach.

## PROJECTIONS

Projected images can be much larger, as in the *Deep Time* event, but they also need more space to work effectively and they require clear uninterrupted lines of sight between the projector and the surface being projected onto. In order to accurately map a projection space, you need to define the width and the height of the surface you are projecting onto as well as the distance from your projector(s) to the surface. This will help you to define where and at what size your images can be projected and to determine whether projection is a suitable method for your space. You will need to align and adjust your projectors (usually by adjusting the lens or moving the projector) to ensure the image appears clearly on your chosen surface.

## SCREENS

Screen-based media use standard display screens and monitors to show images and content. While these types of screens tend to be smaller than projection screens or surfaces, they can easily be set up to become interactive touchscreens by using a screen overlay. An overlay converts a standard screen into a touchscreen. Standard screens are self-contained and do not need the same clear lines of sight as a projector.

This table summarises the advantages and disadvantages of each method.

| | Advantages | Disadvantages |
|---|---|---|
| Projections | ✓ Larger images possible<br>✓ 'Cinematic' experience<br>✓ Multiple projection surfaces possible<br>✓ Anything can be used as a surface | ✗ Interaction is possible but problematic if screens are very large<br>✗ Requires clear line of sight between projector and surface<br>✗ More expensive as more equipment required<br>✗ Restricted to a darker environment |
| Screens | ✓ Touchscreen interaction possible<br>✓ Short set-up time and reduced cost<br>✓ Simpler to use<br>✓ Works better in a lighter environment | ✗ Restricted by screen size<br>✗ Not possible to incorporate other objects<br>✗ Content restricted to screen space |

Some designers will combine display types with various media, a good example being video DJs or VJs who mix moving visual art (usually video) with music on large displays, screens or other surfaces, such as walls and ceilings. VJs use libraries of images, animation clips and video footage that complement the music and in some cases even echo the peaks and troughs of the musical structure. Part of the skill of the VJ is creating interesting combinations. To start VJing you would need a projector linked to a computer, VJing software, such as VDMX, ProVideoPlayer 2 or Resolume, and of course a sound system.

## Top Tip

Not all projections use flat screens (or buildings) as the medium; objects or natural landscapes can sometimes be used and the combination can be very effective.

## Skills Task: **Practice VJing**

Using the VJing approach outlined above, choose some music and research some visual ideas that complement the music. The key to finding VJ content is to follow your creative instincts. Then use the VJ software of your choice to create live visuals along with the music, and connect your computer to a projector so you can display your work to a larger audience.

## Project work: **Develop an immersive experience**

Working in groups and using the spatial plan you developed earlier, develop an immersive and interactive exhibit or experience concept to present to your class. Your project presentation should include your story, the responses you want from your audience, sketches, details of all interactions, sensory inputs and outputs such as audio, and all the considerations discussed in the five stages of the design process (described above).

## Case study: **THE WORD**

The Word, National Centre for the Written Word, was created as a cultural venue in South Tyneside, UK, that celebrates writing and storytelling. When it was set up, the building incorporated numerous interactive and immersive digital experiences, including a children's media wall with touchscreen displays, interactive touch-tables and an immersive storytelling experience, StoryWorld. UK-based digital hardware and software company LamasaTech designed and installed several of these interactive experiences, as well as training The Word staff in how to use them.

The StoryWorld exhibit combined projections and sound effects that supported the human presenter to create an immersive storytelling experience. For the experience to work for children, the storyteller had to almost become part of the projected backdrop when they stood between the audience and the images. This had an impact on the types of screens used: projection was used, as it enabled four large screens to be incorporated into the experience so the audience could listen to the storyteller and watch the images simultaneously.

LamasaTech carefully measured the room in which the StoryWorld was created, mapping the walls onto which the media content would be projected to ensure that the projections would not be obscured when the room was full of children. They also had to consider the acoustics, light quality and ambience of the room, to ensure that the experience did not become overwhelming or overly hot when the projectors were running. To help The Word staff control the content, LamasaTech developed bespoke app-based software that enabled The Word to load the projection content and control the speed and motion of the animated backdrop using a mobile device.

**Fig 31.9** StoryWorld, a previous exhibit at The National Centre for the Written Word, South Tyneside, UK

# Glossary

**3D filter** software tool that adds 3D properties, such as tone and texture to 2D drawings

## A

**Accelerometer** motion sensors in a mobile device that detect different levels of motion

**Action** the job or task the user needs to perform

**Action points** actions to be implemented, often agreed in a meeting

**Additive colour model** colour model where adding colour makes the colour lighter

**Aesthetics** the look of an object; principles relating to beauty

**Agile** project management term to describe a repetitive approach to planning and guiding project processes

**Agile board** visual representation of the Agile process shown in a studio

**A href** HTML code used when creating links

**Amplitude** the strength of a sound wave; high amplitude equals loud sound

**Analogue** something created or built using non-computer methods

**Animatic** a preliminary version of a moving image production, produced by filming or animating successive sections of a storyboard and adding sound and/ or effects

**Animatics** method of showing a process as a series of images using animation

**Antagonist** character(s) or forces who attempt to stop or frustrate the protagonist

**Archetype** characters that embody good or evil (the archetypal hero/ villain) and are easily recognisable by the audience

**Architecture** where an application is used in physical space, for example, an interactive kiosk in a railway station

**Art boards** screen format based on a sheet of paper on a physical desk, shown to clients to express ideas; visuals shown to a client to express ideas

**Artefacts** objects and artworks

**Asset library** storage area for assets used to build websites

**Association** a way of interpreting a sign through making links with other known objects or information

**Atmospheres** sounds of long duration, that indicate where and when the action takes place

**Audience** the group of people who read or watch your work

**Audio concepting** method of testing how sound and images work together

**Axes of orientation** horizontal eye movements a reader makes across a page

## B

**Backdrop** screen behind model/subject

**Backdrop photo** photographic image showing the background environment or scene

**Background** the distant space far from the viewer in a visual image

**Balance** the way that elements appear in a visual design

**Banners** coloured strips running across the top of a page

**Bass frequencies** low frequency sounds

**Bevel** software tool that enables a designer to extrude a face/polygon and scale it simultaneously

**Bitmap image** a digital image comprised of dots

**Blades** components of the aperture cover

**Bootstrap framework** free software for creating visual elements for #

**Branching narrative** a story that does not go in a straight line but branches out in different directions

**Brand values** what an organisation represents and how it wishes to be seen

**Brainstorm** technique for generating multiple ideas and making sense of ideas generated

**Broadcast media** the distribution of audio or video content

**B-roll footage** footage shot in secondary filming sessions (without the cast or main contributors), used for cutaways and establishing shots

**Browser** software for viewing website pages

**Brush strokes** visible lines created on the surface of a painting by the artist's brush

**Built-in obsolescence** artificially limiting the lifespan to a certain length of time

**B Unit** secondary camera team used to shoot large-scale establishing shots of environments or landscapes

**Burndown chart** a progress chart showing how a project is progressing

## C

**Camera mount** method of holding, placing or fixing the camera in position

**Camera roll** all the photos stored on a digital camera

**Camera shake** involuntary camera movement; often occurs with hand-held shots

**Carbon footprint** the total amount of carbon emissions a person generates through their use of fossil fuels each year (for example, by using airplanes to travel)

**Cascading style sheets (CSS)** files that control the styles used on all the pages of a website

**Catch-up services** various services that allow viewers the opportunity to watch television shows and sport events after their initial airdate

**Censorship** to remove certain types of offensive contents

**Central asset repository** a central storage area where all assets are kept

**Character motivation** personality traits or personal history that drive a character to act in particular ways

**Characters** symbols that make up an alphabet or have particular meaning within a certain language

**Character turnaround** series of drawings that show the proportions of a character or object from many angles

**Chroma** the purity of a hue in relation to grey

**Chunking** a method of organising a lot of written content

**Client brief** document that describes a project in detail

**Clone stamp tool** option for cloning and moving pixels in a digital photograph

**Closed questions** used to elicit research data; they limit the possible responses and include yes/ no or male/ female questions

**Cloud storage** virtual file storage space accessed online via a browser

**Cluster analysis** way of organising data into groups based on their similarities

**CMYK** colour model used for printing based on mixing cyan (blue), magenta, yellow and key (black); a subtractive colour model

**Code of ethics** a company's official practice on ethical issues

**Colour look-up table (CLUT)** digital store of all colours used in an image used by the indexed colour model to match to one of 256 basic colours

**Colour palette** a combination of colours adopted by a client

**Colour strike** a combination of strong colours that creates an optical illusion

**Colour swatch** a combination of colours to be used in a design project

**Colour wheel** a diagram showing the primary, secondary and tertiary colours and their relations to each other

**Competitive advantage** something a company's product has that makes it more attractive than its competitors' products

**Composite** the final completed image sequence made from a series of layers

**Compressed** file type used to store images at low resolution

**Computer net work** a group of computer systems and other computing hardware systems that are linked together

**Concept artwork** a rendering of an element or elements in a creative project, as part of the visual development of characters, costumes, environments, etc.

**Cones** nerve cells in the eyeball that perceive red, blue and green

**Content** a piece of information or a message; what is shown as part of the application, for example, website content

**Content hierarchy** the way that content is arranged according to its importance

**Control measure** action taken to reduce a risk identified in a risk assessment

**Cookies** small bits of information generated by a website and saved by your web browser that enables a website to remember your preferences, for example, your login username and password, web pages visited

**Copyright** official ownership of intellectual property

**Copyright holder** the person or agency who owns the image

**Creative Commons licence** copyright licence that allows authors, artists and designers to give people the right to share, use, and build upon work they have created

**Creative direction** the overall approach to be taken in terms of visuals

**Creative exploration** exploring different ideas and concepts within a design context

**Creative jolt** a way of looking at things differently in order to generate ideas

**Creatives** people whose work involves being creative

**Critical understanding** active engagement in analytical and independent thought. An ability to express an informed response

**Critique** analyse critically

**Cutaway** a shot used to show the audience some information about what is being talked about (also used to cover edits in spoken sequences)

# D

**Daguerreotype** early type of black and white photographic image

**Daily stand-up** a daily meeting to discuss what the team is working on; team members are not allowed to sit down during the meeting, to keep it brief

**Darkroom** the room used to develop photographic film in analogue photography (it must be closed to any light)

**Data mining** analysing databases to generate profiles on users' habits

**Data protection** procedures to keep users' data safe online

**Decibels (dB)** the unit of measurement of amplitude

**Democratisation** opening up to everyone regardless of ability

**Demographic** the social or age group that a persona belongs to

**Depth of field** the range of distance in front of and behind an object which is in focus

**Diagrammatic** a graphical icon that shows a diagram or representation of something

**Diegetic sound** sounds that come from within the virtual game world

**Diffuser** box that makes the light appear softer

**Digital** data expressed as a series of 0s and 1s; also relating to the use of computer technology

**Digital audio workstation (DAW)** any computer and software combination that allows you to edit, arrange and output audio

**Digital drawing** using digital technology to draw or paint digital designs

**Digital footprint** the total amount of data stored about a person online

**Digital image file** the method used for storing digital photos

**Digital landscape** all the types of technology, applications and processes in the world around us influenced by digital technology

**Digital outcome** a work or product which is hosted in a digital environment

**Digital photography** photography where images are captured, digitised and stored as a computer file

**Digital Revolution** advances in technology that started in the 1980s, with the move from analogue electronic and mechanical devices to digital technology used today

**Direct communication** where an audience understands a message directly, for example, we hear gunfire meaning someone has shot a gun

**Disclaimer** written declaration that someone is not legally responsible for something

**Display resolution** measure of display clarity, expressed in pixels

**Domain** the actual name that forms the website address

**Domain name server (DNS)** registry where a domain name is kept

**Dope sheet** document that describes the key details of an animated sequence

**Drop-down menus** menus that appear in full on-screen when you click on an icon

**Dynamic range** the range of the amplitude of the sound in your piece, from very quiet to very loud; (in digital photography) the range of light and shade a camera can capture

**Dynamic tension** a method of leading the viewer around a visual design

# E

**Edge** a line that joins vertices

**Electrical charges** the light signals that create a digital photograph

**Electronic image sensor** light sensitive plate that captures photos in a digital camera

**Electronic viewfinder** large viewfinder in body of a digital camera

**Embed code** code used to enable video/audio content from other websites to be played on a web page

**Entrepreneur** someone who starts their own business, especially when this involves identifying a new opportunity

**Equal opportunities** giving everyone the same employment possibilities and legal rights in the workplace

**Equilibrium** balance

**Establishing shot** camera shot that tells the audience where the action is taking place and in what kind of environment

**Etching** a technique where a design is created by using strong acid to cut into the unprotected parts of a metal surface

**Ethics of manufacturing** producing goods/services without damaging the environment or exploiting workers

**Explicit feedback** visual or audio signals triggered when the player performs an action

**Export file types** file types used to transfer files from one programme to another where they can be worked on

**Exposure** the amount of time the aperture remains open for

**External factors** outside influences (for example, social, cultural, political) that impact the work of artists and designers

**Extreme poses** the most important frames/poses of the scene

**Extreme telephoto lens** a lens for focusing on small details from far away

# F

**Face** a 2D shape, for example, triangle or square, formed by three or more edges

**Failure point** part of a user story that describes when a feature is not satisfactory

**Fallow area** place on a web page where the reader is naturally less focused

**File transfer protocol (FTP)** method used to transfer files from a developer's computer to the website hosting space

**Final pose** the pose or frame that ends a scene

**Fish-eye lens** a lens that gives a curved, distorted view of a wide scene

**Flash heads** controls for flashlights

**Flattened** process of file conversion to make layered fi les usable

**Flow chart** a method for showing how a user progresses through a process

**Fluid experience** a non-linear way of consuming a story using multiple media types

**Fluid head tripod** camera tripod with a mount that allows for flexible camera movement in different directions

**Fly-on-the-wall documentary** shows the main protagonists (including interviewer) in action, as though the audience were watching in real time

**Focal length** distance from which the camera can focus on an object

**Focus group** gathering of a group of people to participate in a discussion about a product/service

**Focus pull** changing the focus of the camera during a shot in order to bring an object in or out of focus

**Foley** the process of creating and recording sounds (for example, footsteps) that match actions and images onscreen

**Font** a subset of a typeface, for example, Bodini 10 pt Bold

**Footer** section of a website that appears at the bottom of each web page

**Foreground** the front space near the viewer in a visual image

**Form** the shape and feel of an object; how a digital product looks and feels to the user

**Formats without borders** animated images, light and music projected onto points in the space around the viewer to create a 3D experience

**Fps** frames per second presented to the viewer, between 12 fps and 24 fps for animations

**Frame** border of the photograph

**Frames** single still images used in sequence to create an animation

**Frame within a frame** use of elements within the subject itself to contain the central subject

**Fresco** a watercolour painting done quickly on wet plaster on a wall or ceiling, so that the colours penetrate the plaster and remain after it dries

**Frequency** (of sound) the rate at which a sound wave vibrates; high frequency equals high pitched sounds

**From life** working directly from a real scene or object without sketching first

**F-stop** measurement of the ratio of the focal length of a lens and the size of the aperture; the larger the number the less light is let in and vice versa

**Full frequency sound** when a speaker system is capable of playing sound throughout the range of normal human hearing, from 20 Hz to 20 kHz

**Function** the job that something is designed to do; what a digital product does for the user

**Functional character** physical character that appears in the game world

**Functional grid** a grid-based model for arranging content on-screen

**Functionality** how something works; the exact functions a digital project needs to deliver

# G

**Game artefact** a key object in a game that the player interacts with

**Game assets** different types of content used to create a game, for example, audio, animation, text, photos

**Game balancing** testing method used to establish whether a gameplay experience is at the appropriate level for players

**Game boundaries** the limitations on the game world, such as where the user can and cannot go

**Game Design Document (GDD)** document that defines game development, including game objectives, elements, interactions and processes

**Games design and mobile and multimedia applications** digital applications which combine media, are accessed through mobile devices, or are designed for entertainment or educational purposes

**Game prop** a supporting element in a game used to create emotion or atmosphere

**Game world** the virtual environment created for a particular game

**Gaming engine** software programme used to build a game framework

**Gantt chart** visual calendar to planning a project

**Genre sound** sounds and music associated with a particular genre of media

**Glare** the shine of a harsh uncomfortably brilliant light

**Golden ratio** a visual method for dividing space

**Grading layer** a layer that sits on top of the animation and live action layers that gives a moving image sequence a particular look

**Graphical direct manipulation** a software process that involves moving and manipulating elements directly

**Graphical user interface (GUI)** the method the player uses to control the gameplay

**Graphic match** different objects that are similar looking (in shape or colour), which are used in successive shots to link ideas

**Graphics tablet** computing device for hand-drawing images, graphics and animations that uses a pen-like stylus; computer input device for hand-drawing images, graphics and animations that uses a pen-like stylus

**Grid system** the format used by graphic designers to compose pages

# H

**Harmony** how a visual design appears to 'work'

**Header** section of a website that appears at the top of each web page

**Headroom** the distance between the top of a subject's head in a shot and the top of the frame

**Healing brush tool** option for brushing in more pixels in a digital photograph

**Heightened contrast** increasing the intensity of the light and dark areas

**Hertz (Hz)** unit of measurement of sound frequency

**High concept approach** method of explaining complex ideas simply by using existing examples

**Highlights** lighter areas of an object that show tone and texture

**Hue** the technical term for a colour

**Human–computer interaction** the way that users actually make use of a digital device

**Human factors** the user and what they are able to do

**Hypertext** text that links to other information, such as text or graphics; copy or text used on a web page, often linking to other information, such as text or graphics

**Hyper Text Mark-up Language (HTML)** code used to create websites

# I

**Icon** a religious image, generally of a holy figure, normally created on wood; graphical sign that resembles the thing it represents

**Ideas** thoughts or concepts; plans or creative intentions; imagined images, experiences or memories

**Ideogram** a character showing the idea of something, without using the sounds you would use to say it

**Image layers** different images arranged together to create a single image

**Image resolution** the number of pixels that form an image; sharpness and clarity of a digital image

**Immersion** placing yourself within the real world environment that directly relates to or reflects your idea, concept or design process

**Immersive art** images and sounds that are projected or displayed in the space all around the viewer

**Immersive experience** the perception of being physically present in a virtual world

**Implicit feedback** visual or audio signals used to guide or inform the player

**In-between frames** frames are single still images used in sequence to create an animation; in-between frames link or transition between the key frames

**Index** a sign that has a direct link to the object it represents and often has a sensory aspect

**Indexed colour** colour model of just 256 colours used to convert RGB or CMYK into smaller digital files while maintaining visual quality

**Indirect communication** where a message is decoded by an audience, for example, we see a gun, we deduce the person with the gun is a criminal or police officer

**Industrial design** the physical from that something takes, for example, a hand-held device

**Information Age** period starting in the 1970s characterised by growth in use of personal computers and changes in how quickly and widely information is shared

**Information architecture** how information is presented to the user, for example, menus and screens

**Initial pose** starting pose or beginning of a scene

**Intensity** the brightness or dullness of a hue

**Intensity value** number (between 0 and 255) showing the amount of colour used in a single pixel on a screen-based display

**Intention** the user's aim in using a product/service

**Interactive banner** an image on a website that prompts the user to click, launching another website

**Interior shot** a shot that is filmed indoors

**Interview schedule** a set of prepared questions designed to be asked as worded

**Intuitive** easy to use for non-specialists

**Isolation** working alone, away from outside influences

**Iterations** versions of a digital product

**Iterative design** making many different prototypes of the same concept in order to develop it further

**Iterative design process** practice of constantly updating and improving versions of a digital product

# J

**Jump cut** a visible cut in a sequence of footage that tells the viewer the sequence has been edited

**Justified** type that is aligned right and left in a block

**Juxtapositioning** contrasting different subjects by placing them next to each other

# K

**Key frames** frames are single still images used in sequence to create an animation; key frames are the most important poses, actions or expressions

**Kilohertz (kHz)** unit of measurement of sound frequency

# L

**Ladder diagram** method for visually organising web pages in a sequence

**Lathe** software tool that creates a 3D mesh using a profile drawn with splines

**Layered** file type used to separate different elements of an image

**Leading lines** elements of visual composition that lead the eye into a visual image

**Leading lines rule** the rule dictating the direction that the eye travels when viewing a visual image

**Left-to-right rule** the direction that people in the West 'read' a visual image

**Licensing fee** money paid to image libraries to reuse their images

**Lifespan** the length of time a product is considered useful

**Light stands** supports for lights

**Line engraving** a technique in which a metal plate is engraved with lines of varying thickness

**Lithography** a technique where an image is created by treating material with a greasy substance so that ink will stain some areas but not others

**Live view** feature on many DSLR cameras that enables video playback of a sequence of still images

**Looped sound** sounds that are repeated seamlessly

**Lossless audio** digital audio formats that are uncompressed, usually used in professional contexts

**Lossy audio** digital audio formats that are compressed for ease of distribution, usually used in consumer contexts

**Low-energy building** buildings constructed to save energy through better insulation, use of renewable energy sources, and so on

**Luminance** the amount of light; the amount of light each hue reflects

# M

**Macro typography** the way that blocks of type are displayed on a page or screen

**Mass communication** the imparting or exchanging of information on a large scale to a wide range of people

**Meeting agenda** document showing the key topics for discussion and desired outcomes of a meeting

**Meeting minutes** a formal written record of what occurred in a meeting and the outcomes, decisions or action points

**Mesh** a collection of vertices, edges and faces that defines the shape of a 3D object

**Micro typography** the way that letters are adjusted individually to create an effect

**Mid-shot** a shot of a character showing their torso and head (used to begin most dialogue scenes)

**Mixing console** electronic device for combining and changing volume level, timbre and/or dynamics of many different audio signals, for example, microphones being used by singers, acoustic instruments

**Mobile app bars** horizontal UI elements that tell users where they are in an app

**Mobile app controls** UI elements used to initiate actions, for example, buttons

**Mobile app views** UI elements that contain the primary content, such as text graphics or images

**Mock-up images** digital designs used to show how a website will look

**Moderate content** to check and censor content published online

**Modes** types of photography (for example, portrait)

**Mosaic** a picture or pattern produced by arranging together small pieces of stone, tile, glass or other material

**Motif** design used to create a pattern, often through duplication

**Motion graphics** pieces of digital footage or animation that create the illusion of motion or rotation on screen

**Motivation** reason for doing something

**Moving image** an area of creative practice which includes video, animation and documentary filmmaking

**Moving poses** small movements such as blinks or hair moving in the wind that give life to animated characters who are not moving

**Multi-sensory design** design that stimulates multiple senses, not just sight and hearing

# N

**Native development** term to describe app development for one platform only

**Native file types** file types used to create and store files within a programme

**Navigation bar** the bar across a screen with the menus and commands on it; a series of navigation buttons that guide the user to content

**Negative** the reverse image produced on photographic film

**Negative space** empty areas surrounding drawings, which can be used to create particular visual effects

**N-gon** a polygon/face with more than four sides

**Non-destructive editing** a way of editing a digital fi le or asset without altering or degrading the original

**Non-diegetic sound** sounds that come from outside of the virtual game world

**Non-visual character** character that features in the game world but not visually, for example, a narrator

# O

**Onion skinning** technique whereby frames are made translucent, enabling the animator to see several frames at once and draw the next frame in the sequence more easily

**Online streaming** websites that allow users to watch content on the internet

**Open questions** used to elicit research data; they allow the respondent to give longer, more complex answers

**Optic nerve** nerve that transmits light signals from the eyeball to the brain

**Original source** the person who created the image

**Overlapping** elements placed partially on top of one another

# P

**Page layout** term often used to describe digital design compositions

**Painterly** with the characteristics of an oil painting; stylised

**Painting tools** software features used for drawing, shading and colouring

**Parallax design** 2D design method that uses different background layers to give the impression of perspective and depth

**Parallax effect** technique that uses layered backgrounds moving at different speeds to create the illusion of perspective and movement

**Patch tool** option for cloning and moving pixels in a digital photograph

**Patent** a licence to protect the use and applications of someone's invention

**Permission** approval for someone to use content from the copyright holder

**Persistence of vision** the illusion of continuous motion created when we see a rapid sequence of still images

**Persona** a method used to define a user

**Perspective** sense of depth created in an image by representing elements far from the viewer as smaller

**Photo collage** image made from cut photographic images reassembled

**Photographic film** light sensitive film that captures photos in an analogue camera

**Photojournalism** news stories told through photographs

**Photo libraries** online archives of visual images with permission for reuse

**Photomontage** image made from various photographs superimposed on one another

**Photoshoot** collection of shots of one subject

**Photoshop guides** grid lines used to help designers layout content

**Pictograph** a pictorial symbol for a word or phrase

**Pinhole camera** very simple camera made from a box

**Pitch/presentation** conveys information from a speaker to an audience; they are typically demonstrations of an idea or product

**Pivot** the point at which an object rotates

**Pixels** dots of colour that form a digital image on-screen

**Plagiarism** copying someone else's ideas or work and using them as though they were your own

**Plane** a flat four-sided polygon/face

**Plasticine** synthetic modelling clay used to make figures and objects for animation

**Platforms** different types of digital delivery format, for example, mobile devices, desktop computers, DVDs

**Point-and-shoot camera** an automatic camera

**Polygon** a 2D shape, for example, triangle or square, formed by three or more edges

**Positive space** the subject of an image, or focus

**POV shot** point of view shot, where the camera is positioned and moved as though looking through the eyes of another character within the film

**Pre-production** project research carried out before production starts

**Presence** the sensations whereby a games user feels connected to the virtual world via digital technology

**Primary optical area** place on a web page where the reader naturally starts

**Primitive objects** standard 2D and 3D points, lines and shapes used to create 3D animation

**Principal identifier** the main part of a website domain name

**Printing press** a machine for printing text or pictures from types or plates

**Print media** content that is still produced in a hard copy, such as in newspapers, journals or books

**Product backlog** a list of outstanding features not yet developed

**Product owner** Agile team member who represents the client

**Product release** a way of defining a specific version of a software product

**Product website** the manufacturer's website that explains the software's features and how to use them

**Pro forma brief** brief template

**Project assets** the fundamental building blocks to be used in the project

**Projection mapping** technique for projecting digital designs onto large surfaces

**Project management** the act of managing the project to ensure it is completed on time and to standard

**Project plan** plan to show how a project will be completed

**Proposal** an act of putting forward or stating something for consideration; design ideas of what a final outcome might look like

**Protagonist** character(s) in the story who goes on a quest or journey

**Prototype** an early sample, model, or release of a product built to test a concept or process

**Prototyping** method of creating a working model

**Purpose** the message, emotion or atmosphere an image is trying to convey

**Put out to tender** invite proposals and quotes for a job

# Q

**Quad** a four-sided polygon/face

**Qualitative research** complex or nuanced information that requires interpretation and often comes from primary sources such as focus groups

**Quantitative research** information that can easily be mathematically analysed or 'quantified' and often comes from secondary sources such as large data sets

# R

**Radial line** line that passes through the centre of a circle, cylinder or sphere

**Raster graphics** a digital image comprised of pixels

**Reaction shot** a shot that shows the reaction of a character as they hear the lines or watch the actions of other characters

**Reading gravity** direction the reader follows when scanning down a page

**Realise** produce work that successfully communicates or demonstrates ideas and intentions

**Recruitment** the process of advertising jobs and finding new employees

**Reference** an author that is mentioned in a piece of research

**Refined search** making a search more precise by using key words or definitions

**Reflector** attachment that intensifies the light

**Remote testing** testing a product when the participant and the tester are in different locations

**Render** to draw, make or represent artistically

**Rendered animation** a sequence of frames played back at 12–24 frames per second (fps)

**Resolution independent** when the quality of the image doesn't change when it is enlarged

**RGB** standard colour model for screen-based colour based on mixing red, green and blue; an additive colour model

**Rods** nerve cells in the eyeball that perceive black and white

**Rostrum camera** camera used to shoot animation, which is placed above multiple panes of glass displaying the image layers

**Royalty** money paid to the copyright holder each time their content is used

**Rule of odds** rule that says an odd number of subjects in the foreground of an image is more pleasing than an even number

**Rule of thirds** proportional rule used to position subjects within an image

# S

**Safeguards** security measures

**Saturation** the amount of pure colour in a specific hue

**Scoping exercise** process for deciding what an application will do and how

**Score** music that is specifically composed for a particular project

**Screen capture software** software that enables remote testing through recording (capturing) what the participant does on their computer

**Screenprinting** a printing technique where a mesh is used to transfer ink onto a substrate, except in areas made impermeable to the ink by a blocking stencil

**Screenshot** a digital image that shows the contents of a computer display.

**SCRUM** Agile process for problem solving

**SCRUM master** Agile team member who organises and manages the team

**Selection/de-selection** the process of choosing what to include and leave out of your research or feedback findings

**Self-reflexive documentary** includes the story of how the documentary was made, presenting the interviewer's own reflections or emotions

**Semantics** a subset of semiotics that refers to language

**Semiotics** the study of signs and symbols and their use and interpretation

**Semiotic system** a system of sign and symbols that work together

**Semi-structured interview** interview that contains a set of open questions that will prompt discussion and allow for follow-up questions to explore particular responses further

**Sepia** brownish colour sometimes used to print old monotone photographs

**Serif** the lines at the top and bottom of a letter

**Shade** a hue produced by adding black

**Shadows** darker areas of an object that show tone and texture

**Shaky-cam** filming technique where the camera movement (shaking) alerts the audience to the fact that someone is holding a camera

**Shape tool** Photoshop tool for creating simple shapes

**Sharpened focus** increasing the resolution and quality

**Shooting on twos** showing each frame on-screen for double the amount of time

**Shot** photograph

**Shot–reverse shot** when a dialogue scene is filmed from at least two angles, each showing the opposing actor

**Showcase** to display to the public

**Shutter speed** the speed at which the shutter opens to expose the electronic sensor to light

**Signified** the concept that the sign seeks to represent

**Signifier** the form that the sign takes

**Sign-off** the final part of a project

**Signposting** a way of directing user interaction using relevant language

**Sitemap** a diagram or model of a website's content that shows how the content is organised and how different content elements relate to one another

**Skills** abilities or accomplishments

**Slice tool** Photoshop tool for slicing a larger image into smaller images

**Snoot** attachment that focuses light on one particular area

**Software development kit (SDK)** used to create apps for a specific device

**Solid drawing** drawing in three-dimensional space that gives characters and objects volume and weight

**Sound design** how sound is used to communicate to the user, for example, a mobile phone alert; the process of acquiring and generating audio for a project

**Sound palette** collection of sounds related to the narrative or setting

**Soundtrack** all sounds included in a digital media product

**Sound waves** pressure waves of acoustic energy generated by something vibrating

**Sources** places to collect data, such as the internet, books or research participants

**Splice** to join together two clips of footage, such as two separate sentences in a documentary interview

**Spline** a flexible curve that can also be manipulated to create straight lines and corners; they allow artists to draw shapes in two dimensions that can later be turned into three dimensions

**Splining** method of instructing software to fill in the animation between key frames with in-between frames

**Stand-ins** people of similar build and appearance to the main actors or contributors and who substitute for them while the film crew sets up a shot

**Stay in character** to behave (as an actor) when not filming as if you are still playing the character

**Stepped animation** software setting that keeps a character's pose the same from one key frame to the next

**Stills** individual photographs, or individual frames of a moving image product

**Stock art** images available from paying image libraries

**Story arc** the emotional journey a character takes in a story

**Storyboard** a graphic organiser that consists of illustrations or images displayed in sequence for the purpose of pre-visualising a motion picture, animation, motion graphic or interactive media sequence

**Storyboarding** method of showing a process as a series of images

**Strobe effect** effect whereby the viewer sees

moving images as a series of stills, usually created when using slow shutter speeds

**Structured interview** clearly defined questions in a set order that are asked in exactly the same way to each interviewee

**Stylised** having a clearly non-naturalistic style; conforming to a particular style

**Subtractive colour model** colour model where adding colour makes the colour darker

**Supporting copy** copy shown on a screen that helps the user progress through a process on-screen

**Surround sound** format that outputs sound from speakers on all sides of the audience; sound played through speakers that surround the listener

**Survey sample** selected people who are a representative of the target audience or society as a whole

**Sustainability** the careful use of resources at a rate that ensures they will not run out but will be available for future generations to use

**SWOT analysis** method of evaluating a design or product by focusing on its Strengths (S), Weaknesses (W), Opportunities (O) and Threats (T)

**Symbol** a sign that does not resemble anything but conveys an idea

**Symbolic sounds** sounds used to create an emotional response or atmosphere

**Symmetrical balance** the way symmetry is used in a visual design; also known as static balance

**Symmetry** where different parts of an object/image are balanced in shape and the same size

# T

**Tags** pieces of HTML code that define specific sections of the web page

**Talent** performers, presenters, interviewees and other on-screen contributors to a moving image production

**Target audience** the audience at which a product/service is aimed

**Target session** method of recording ideas using a target model

**Temp sound** sound that you include temporarily, which might come from a variety of sources, that you will replace with sound you create yourself

**Terminal area** the final place on a web page the reader naturally reads

**Text boxes** item of text set inside square frames on the page

**Texture** materials the subjects are made of

**Thangkas** a Buddhist painting, usually on cotton or silk, of a deity

**Third party photos** photographs taken and published by others

**Third person view** style of game where the player's view is from behind the character they are controlling

**Three-axis gyroscope** motion sensors in a mobile device that detect device orientation

**Three-ring target approach** method for brainstorming ideas

**Thumbnails** reduced-size versions of pictures or videos, used to help in recognising and organising them

**Tiled images** images that can be seamlessly repeated horizontally or vertically

**Tint** a hue produced by adding white

**Tone** intensity of light and shade

**Tooltip** a small box showing text that helps to guide the user through a process

**Trademark** a visual sign that distinguishes goods/services of one company from others so they cannot be copied

**Transform tool** Photoshop tool for transforming things, such as scale, size and rotation

**Treble frequencies** high frequency sounds

**Tree diagram** method for visually organising web pages by section or title

**Tri** a three-sided polygon/face

**Tweening** process whereby in-between frames are automatically completed and inserted by software

**Typeface** everything in a typeface family, for example, Bodini

# U

**Ultraviolet (UV) light** an electromagnetic radiation wave

**Ultra-wide angle lens** lens for taking big landscape shots

**URL** Uniform Resource Locator, the website's address on the internet

**Usability** how easy or complicated the process of using something is

**User behaviour** what a user does when they interact

**User experience** the user's feeling about interacting with a product/service; the experience of the user when using an application or product

**User interaction** how a user uses a product/service; the way that a user interacts with an application or product

**User response** the emotions or sensations a user feels when using a product

**User story** describes the type of user, what they want and why

# V

**Vector graphics** a digital image comprised of vectors

**Vector image** digital image comprised of vectors

**Vectors** lines forming 3D geometric shapes that are used to form digital images on-screen

**Version control** a way of recording edits to an asset or group of assets

**Vertex** a single point of a 3D model

**Video call** visual communication via computers that allows the people participating in the call to see each other as they talk

**Video conferencing** a telecommunication technique that allows people in different locations to speak to and see each other using software

**Video sharing platforms** services that are able to host multimedia content

**Video streaming** multimedia that is constantly received by and presented to the end user

**Viewpoint** the point from where the user views the screen

**Virtual reality** an artificially created environment that seems real to the senses

**Visible spectrum** the range of light that humans can see

**Visual communication** communicating through images, symbols or signals, for example, via an advertising billboard

**Visual design** how something looks and its visual appeal

**Visual language** visual elements used to communicate ideas. For example, line, colour, shape, form, texture, scale, etc.

**Visual production** using detailed mock-ups to visually represent an app process

**VJ** artist who creates dynamic digital imagery, usually to accompany music

# W

**Wavelength** the distance between waves of light that determines colour

**Web pages** digital documents (written in HTML) that display website content

**Website code** computer language used to build websites

**Website host** browser where a website is located on the internet

**Wireframe** an image or collection of images developed from the sitemap which show elements of a website or web page

**Wireframing** method for creating simple diagrams of individual web pages; also for planning an interactive app process

**Woodblock printing** a technique using wooden blocks to print text, images or patterns

**Workflow** the sequence of processes through which a piece of work passes from initiation to completion

**WYSIWYG editor** HTML editor that displays how a web page will look online

# Index

# Index

# Index

# Acknowledgements

The publishers gratefully acknowledge the permission granted to reproduce the copyright material in this book. Every effort has been made to trace copyright holders and to obtain their permission for the use of copyright material. The publishers will gladly receive any information enabling them to rectify any error or omission at the first opportunity.

The publishers would like to thank the following for permission to reproduce copyright material:

Key: (l = left, r = right, t = top, b = bottom)

## TEXT ACKNOWLEDGMENTS

An extract on p.13 from "Teens, Social Media & Technology Overview 2015", 09/04/2015. Source: Pew Research Center, http://www.pewresearch.org; A Cisco marketing phrase on p.50 as published in *Network World*, 30/01/1989, p.31. Reproduced by permission of Cisco; The Case Study 'Landscape photography planning' on p.168. Reproduced courtesy of Paul Heaton, www.fotocraftimages.co.uk and www.fotocraftimages.co.uk/blog; The Case Study 'No Strings' on p.306. Reproduced with permission of No Strings International, http://www.nostrings.org.uk; and The Case Study 'REALRIDER®' on pp.316–317. Reproduced with permission of Realsafe Technologies Ltd, http://www.realrider.com.

## PHOTOGRAPH ACKNOWLEDGEMENTS

pp2–3 Everett Historical/Shutterstock.com, p5 Robert Kneschke/EyeEm/Getty Images, p6 thipjang/Shutterstock.com, p7r Dragana Eric/Shutterstock.com, p8 Library of Congress, Washington, D.C., p9t photogolfer/Shutterstock.com, p9c imageBROKER/Alamy Stock Photo, p9b julius fekete/Shutterstock.com, p10 Moviestore collection Ltd/Alamy Stock Photo, p11 Austrian National Library/Interfoto/Alamy Stock Photo, p12 tanuha2001/Shutterstock.com, p143t Patrick de Grijs/Alamy Stock Photo, p143b Africa Studio/Shutterstock.com, p15 ELIJAH NOUVELAGE/AFP/Getty Images, p16l Apic/Getty Images, p16r © 2018 The Andy Warhol Foundation for the Visual Arts, Inc./Licensed by DACS, London. Dimensions each 20 × 16' (50.8 × 40.6 cm). Gift of Irving Blum; Nelson A. Rockefeller Bequest, gift of Mr. and Mrs. William A.M. Burden, Abby Aldrich Rockefeller Fund, gift of Nina and Gordon Bunshaft in honor of Henry Moore, Lillie P. Bliss Bequest, Philip Johnson Fund, Frances Keech Bequest. Acc. n.: 476.1996.1-32, digital image © 2018 The Museum of Modern Art, New York/Scala, Florence, p18r Chronicle of World History/Alamy Stock Photo, p20 Ttstudio/Shutterstock.com, p21 Jeffrey Coolidge/Getty Images, p22t Chris Willson/Alamy Stock Photo, p22b Elizabeth Whiting & Associates/Alamy Stock Photo, p23l Matthew Corrigan/Alamy Stock Photo, p23r urbanbuzz/Shutterstock.com, p27 Courtesy Getty Images, p28 © Amy Wright, p29 MARKA/Alamy Stock Photo, p30t ymgerman/Shutterstock.com, p30bl Lois GoBe/Shutterstock.com, p30br Jonny Browne/Shutterstock.com, p31t garagestock/Shutterstock.com, p31b courtesy

WFTO, p32 www.hollandfoto.net/Shutterstock.com, p35t cm studio/Alamy Stock Photo, p35b Carolyn Jenkins/Alamy Stock Photo, p36 Bloomicon/Shutterstock.com, p38t Christian Mueller/Shutterstock.com, p38b Iulian Valentin/Shutterstock.com, p39 Iconic Bestiary/Shutterstock.com, p40 © Adobe Systems Incorporated. All rights reserved. Adobe, Dreamweaver, Illustrator, InDesign and Photoshop are registered trademarks of Adobe Systems Incorporated in the United States and/or other countries, photo: HarperCollins, p41 Autodesk screen shots reprinted courtesy of Autodesk, Inc., p42t Autodesk screen shots reprinted courtesy of Autodesk, Inc., p42b courtesy SketchUp, p44 © Adobe Systems Incorporated. All rights reserved. Adobe, Dreamweaver, Illustrator, InDesign and Photoshop are registered trademarks of Adobe Systems Incorporated in the United States and/or other countries, Silbo webpage courtesy Phil Veal, p45l courtesy WordPress, p45c Drupal is a registered trademark of Dries Buytaert, p45r courtesy Joomla, pp46–47 blackliz/Shutterstock.com, p52 Aila Images/Shutterstock.com, p53 Iryna Sunrise/Shutterstock.com, p57 Petr Vaclavek/Shutterstock.com, p59 Rawpixel.com/Shutterstock.com, p66 Monkey Business Images/Shutterstock.com, p71t Jacob Lund/Shutterstock.com, p71b Twin Design/Shutterstock.com, p74t karen roach/Shutterstock.com, p74b Kaspars Grinvalds/Shutterstock.com, p75 REDPIXEL.PL/Shutterstock.com, p76 Mihai Surdu/Shutterstock.com, p79 mavo/Shutterstock.com, p80 guruXOX/Shutterstock.com, p82 Trinet Uzun/Shutterstock.com, p84 Martina Vaculikova/Shutterstock.com, p86 Rawpixel.com/Shutterstock.com, p90 Gabriele Maltinti/Shutterstock.com, p92tl Aha-Soft/Shutterstock.com, p92tr Irina Adamovich/Shutterstock.com, p92b Art work/Shutterstock.com, p93l James Mattil/Shutterstock.com, p93r designmaestro/Shutterstock.com, p95 Anton_Ivanov/Shutterstock.com, p99t © Succession Picasso/DACS, London 2018, photo: The Art Institute of Chicago/Helen Birch Bartlett Memorial Collection/Bridgeman Images, p99b © Succession Picasso/DACS, London 2018, photo © Christie's Images/Bridgeman Images, p102 Pixabay, p105 © Adobe Systems Incorporated. All rights reserved. Adobe, Dreamweaver, Illustrator, InDesign and Photoshop are registered trademarks of Adobe Systems Incorporated in the United States and/or other countries, p108 REDPIXEL.PL/Shutterstock.com, p109 oatawa/Shutterstock.com, p110t Gianni Dagli

Orti/REX/Shutterstock, p111b Cultura Creative (RF)/Alamy Stock Photo, p111t attaphong/Shutterstock.com, p110b Oana_Unciuleanu/Shutterstock.com, p112b PaulPaladin/Alamy Stock Photo, p113tl Photo by © Historical Picture Archive/Corbis/Getty Images, p113tc jmeyersforeman/Alamy Stock Photo, p113tr blickwinkel/Alamy Stock Photo, p112t opicobello/Shutterstock.com, p114t Claudio Divizia/Shutterstock.com, p114b Iain Masterton/Alamy Stock Photo, p115r AF archive/Alamy Stock Photo, p115l medesulda/Shutterstock.com, p121 passion artist/Shutterstock.com, p122t passion artist/Shutterstock.com, p123 Alila Medical Media/Shutterstock.com, p124 Fouad A. Saad/Shutterstock.com, p125 Designua/Shutterstock.com, p126 The Secret World of Foley', stills reproduced courtesy of Foley artist Sue Harding, p127 United Archives GmbH/Alamy Stock Photo, p130 urbanbuzz/Shutterstock.com, p133 Avid® Pro Tools® | HD screen image used with permission of Avid Technology, Inc. Avid Pro Tools | HD screen image © 2018 Avid Technology, Inc. All rights reserved.   AVID, the Avid logo, and Pro Tools are either registered trademarks or trademarks of Avid Technology, Inc. in the United States, Canada, European Union and/or other countries., p134 Photo 12/Alamy Stock Photo, p136 Zern Liew/Shutterstock.com, p137 Jacob Lund/Shutterstock.com, pp138–139 National Geographic Creative/Alamy Stock Photo, p140l Mike P Shepherd/Alamy Stock Photo, p140r FRANCOIS-XAVIER MARIT/AFP/Getty Images, p141 Granger Historical Picture Archive/Alamy Stock Photo, p142 Everett Historical/Shutterstock.com, p143 Universal History Archive/UIG/Getty Images, p144l National Gallery of Art, Washington, D.C., Chester Dale Collection, p144r The Metropolitan Museum of Art, New York, Bequest of Julia W. Emmons, 1956, p145l © Man Ray Trust/ADAGP, Paris and DACS, London 2018, photo: Telimage, p145r © DACS 2018, photo courtesy Germanisches Nationalmuseum (credit TBC by museum), p146 © David Hockney, photo: Richard Schmidt, p147t Oxford Science Archive/Print Collector/Getty Images, p147bl © Steve McCurry/Magnum Photos, p147br The Metropolitan Museum of Art, New York, Alfred Stieglitz Collection, 1949, p148 © The Dorothea Lange Collection, the Oakland Museum of California, Gift of Paul S. Taylor, photo: Private Collection/Granger/Bridgeman Images, p149tl Kay Roxby/Alamy Stock Photo, p149tr Image courtesy of The Advertising Archives, p149bl Vladyslav Bashutskyy/Alamy Stock

# Acknowledgements

Photo, p149br Dserov/Shutterstock.com, p150t IanDagnall Computing/Alamy Stock Photo, p150b FocusDzign/Shutterstock.com, p153 Library of Congress, Washington, D.C., p153 Library of Congress, Washington, D.C., p154t CrowdSpark/Alamy Stock Photo, "p154b Courtesy CAAC - The Pigozzi Collection, © Seydou Keïta/SKPEAC", p155 Collection Center for Creative Photography, University of Arizona, © The Ansel Adams Publishing Rights Trust, p155 Collection Center for Creative Photography, University of Arizona, © The Ansel Adams Publishing Rights Trust, p155 Collection Center for Creative Photography, University of Arizona, © The Ansel Adams Publishing Rights Trust, p156 Marie Tsyganova/Shutterstock.com, p157l Irina Mosina/Shutterstock.com, p157c iravgustin/Shutterstock.com, p157r PRO Stock Professional/Shutterstock.com, p158 Iris & B. Gerald Cantor Center for Visual Arts at Stanford University; Gift of Raymond B. Gary, © Robert Frank; courtesy Pace/MacGill Gallery, New York, p161 Micheko Productions, Inh. Michele Vitucci/Alamy Stock Photo, p162tl Logan Brown/Shutterstock.com, p162tr Adrian Pluskota/Shutterstock.com, p162bl Kraft_Stoff/Shutterstock.com, p162br VanderWolf Images/Shutterstock.com, p163 ymgerman/Shutterstock.com, p166t&b aldorado/Shutterstock.com, p168t © Paul Heaton/Fotocraft Images, p168ct © Paul Heaton/Fotocraft Images, p168cb © Paul Heaton/Fotocraft Images, p168b © Paul Heaton/Fotocraft Images, p170 iunewind/Shutterstock.com, p173 Pakhnyushchy/Shutterstock.com, p174 Milles Vector Studio/Shutterstock.com, p175 David Alexander Stein/Shutterstock.com, p176t © Man Ray Trust/ADAGP, Paris and DACS, London 2018, photo: Telimage, p176b Michael R Ross/Shutterstock.com, p177 Enchanted Studios/Shutterstock.com, p178 Hero Images Inc./Alamy Stock Photo, p180 Stuart Monk/Shutterstock.com, p181t PaeJar/Shutterstock.com, p181b Bill45/Shutterstock.com, p182 Corbis/VCG/Getty Images, p183t Kumar Sriskandan/Alamy Stock Photo, p183b logoboom/Shutterstock.com, p184t Ondra Vacek/Shutterstock.com, p184b Galyna Andrushko/Shutterstock.com, p185tl Helder Geraldo Ribeiro/Shutterstock.com, p185tr pr_camera/Shutterstock.com, p185b Paolya/Shutterstock.com, p186 © Adobe Systems Incorporated. All rights reserved. Adobe, Dreamweaver, Illustrator, InDesign and Photoshop are registered trademarks of Adobe Systems Incorporated in the United States and/or other countries, photo: chaoss/Shutterstock.com, p188t&b © Adobe Systems Incorporated. All rights reserved. Adobe, Dreamweaver, Illustrator, InDesign and Photoshop are registered trademarks of Adobe Systems Incorporated in the United States and/or other countries, pp190–191 Serge Ka/Shutterstock.com, p193 AF archive/Alamy Stock Photo, p194t Prana-Film/Kobal/REX/Shutterstock, p194c Hammer/Kobal/REX/Shutterstock, p194b Zoetrope/Columbia Tri-Star/Kobal/REX/Shutterstock, p195 Danjaq/EON Productions/

Kobal/REX/Shutterstock, p197 Moviestore/REX/Shutterstock, p198 & 199 SpeedKingz/Shutterstock.com, p200t Jasin Boland/Universal/Kobal/REX/Shutterstock, ", "p200c Jasin Boland/Universal/Kobal/REX/Shutterstock, p200b Jasin Boland/Universal/Kobal/REX/Shutterstock, p202 © Catherine Sabine, p205 © Mike Acosta, p206 © Mike Acosta, p207 Bika Ambon/Shutterstock.com, p208 canbedone/Shutterstock.com, p209 Macrovector/Shutterstock.com, p210, 211, 212 © Adobe Systems Incorporated. All rights reserved. Adobe, Dreamweaver, Illustrator, InDesign and Photoshop are registered trademarks of Adobe Systems Incorporated in the United States and/or other countries, photo: Phil Veal, p211 © Adobe Systems Incorporated. All rights reserved. Adobe, Dreamweaver, Illustrator, InDesign and Photoshop is/are either [a] registered trademark[s] or a p213 REX/Shutterstock, p214 redsnapper/Alamy Stock Photo, p215 Snap Stills/REX/Shutterstock, p216 Bob Caddick/Alamy Stock Photo, p217t Katrina Brown/Alamy Stock Photo, p217b Jeff Morgan 04/Alamy Stock Photo, p218t Jeff Morgan 05/Alamy Stock Photo, p218b Glasshouse Images/Alamy Stock Photo, p219t age fotostock/Alamy Stock Photo, p219b WENN UK/Alamy Stock Photo, p220 221 & 222 © Adobe Systems Incorporated. All rights reserved. Adobe, Dreamweaver, Illustrator, InDesign and Photoshop are registered trademarks of Adobe Systems Incorporated in the United States and/or other countries, photo: Lesley Davies, p223 Mila Basenko/Shutterstock.com, p225 © Mike Acosta, p226 Autodesk screen shots reprinted courtesy of Autodesk, Inc., p227t&b, 228t&b, 299t, c&b, 230, 231t,c&b, 232t&b, 233t&b, 234, 235t,c&b, 236t,c&b, 237t&b, Autodesk screen shots reprinted courtesy of Autodesk, Inc., artwork created by Mike Acosta, p239 keith morris/Alamy Stock Photo, p240 Miramax/Buena Vista/Kobal/REX/Shutterstock, p243t Brittaápedersen/Epa/REX/Shutterstock, p243b Brittaápedersen/Epa/REX/Shutterstock, p244 Barney Broomfield/South Central/Hbo/Sky Vision/Kobal/REX/Shutterstock, p245 Snap Stills/REX/Shutterstock, p246t Lafayette/Kobal/REX/Shutterstock, p246b Roger Bamber/REX/Shutterstock, p247t World History Archive/Alamy, p247b © Richard Brennan, p249t Lucasfilm/Fox/Kobal/REX/Shutterstock, p249b Lucasfilm/Fox/Kobal/REX/Shutterstock, p251t Lucasfilm/Fox/Kobal/REX/Shutterstock, p151b 20th Century Fox/Kobal/REX/Shutterstock, p252 Universal/Kobal/REX/Shutterstock, p254 PE.A/Kobal/REX/Shutterstock, p255t REX/Shutterstock, p255ct Warner Bros/Hoya Prods./Kobal/REX/Shutterstock, p255c Era International/Kobal/REX/Shutterstock, p255cb Moviestore Collection/REX/Shutterstock, p255b Moviestore Collection/REX/Shutterstock, p256 SNAP/REX/Shutterstock, p257 REX/Shutterstock, p257 REX/Shutterstock, p258 Columbia/Kobal/REX/Shutterstock, p259 Alex Kahle/RKO/Kobal/REX/Shutterstock, p262t Greg Williams/Focus Features/Kobal/REX/Shutterstock, p262b Warner Bros/Hawk Films/Kobal/REX/

Shutterstock, p263t Moviestore Collection/REX/Shutterstock, p263c Snap Stills/REX/Shutterstock, p263b Snap Stills/REX/Shutterstock, pp266–267 Lenka Horavova/Shutterstock.com, p270 © Adobe Systems Incorporated. All rights reserved. Adobe, Dreamweaver, Illustrator, InDesign and Photoshop are registered trademarks of Adobe Systems Incorporated in the United States and/or other countries, p272 courtesy Netflix, p273 Cigdem Simsek/Alamy Stock Photo, p274 Worlds Unleashed and then Connecting, teamLab, 2015, Interactive Digital Installation, Endless, Sound: Hideaki Takahashi, p275t photo courtesy Belle & Wissell, Co., p275b © Adobe Systems Incorporated. All rights reserved. Adobe, Dreamweaver, Illustrator, InDesign and Photoshop are registered trademarks of Adobe Systems Incorporated in the United States and/or other countries, p276 © Adobe Systems Incorporated. All rights reserved. Adobe, Dreamweaver, Illustrator, InDesign and Photoshop are registered trademarks of Adobe Systems Incorporated in the United States and/or other countries, artwork created by Phil Veal, p277 chrisdorney/Shutterstock.com, p279 The Times/News Licensing, p280t Producer: Digitalarti, artist: Miguel Chevalier, reproduced with permission, p280b courtesy VEO Group, p286 SAHAS2015/Shutterstock.com, p287 CluedUpp Games Limited, reproduced with permission, p288l CluedUpp Games Limited, reproduced with permission, p288r CluedUpp Games Limited, reproduced with permission, p290 Courtesy Phil Veal, p291 Courtesy Phil Veal, p295tl & tr Courtesy Phil Veal, p295b Courtesy Phil Veal, p298 Georgejmclittle/Shutterstock.com, p300 courtesy No Strings International, p301 mileswork/Shutterstock.com, p302t Soundaholic studio/Shutterstock.com, p302b Fleur_de_papier/Shutterstock.com, p308 Realsafe Technologies, the producers of the REALRIDER® app., p309 Realsafe Technologies, the producers of the REALRIDER® app., p316t Super Meat Boy Forever by Team Meat, p316l andik76/Shutterstock.com, p316br Henry Sy John/Shutterstock.com, p317 Courtesy Atomhawk and various Atomhawk artists, p318 Courtesy Atomhawk and Charlie Bowater, p323 Courtesy Atomhawk, Charlie Bowater and Roberto F. Castro, p324 Autodesk screen shots reprinted courtesy of Autodesk, Inc., artwork created by Phil Veal, p326 Malcolm Haines/Alamy Stock Photo, p327t Flowers Bloom on People, teamLab, 2017, Digitized Nature, Endless, p327b A.T. Willett/Alamy Stock Photo, p328 'WHIST', courtesy AO|E, photo by Paul Plews, p329 Sabine Weissinger/Alamy Stock Photo, p331 Wander through the Crystal Universe, teamLab, 2016, Interactive Installation of Light Sculpture, LED, Endless, Sound: teamLab, p332l Simon Balson/Alamy Stock Photo, p332r Guillem Lopez/Alamy Stock Photo, p337 courtesy South Tyneside Council.